ALSO BY JAMES PECK

*Washington's China: The National Security World,
the Cold War, and the Origins of Globalism*

IDEAL ILLUSIONS

IDEAL
ILLUSIONS

HOW THE U.S. GOVERNMENT
CO-OPTED HUMAN RIGHTS

JAMES PECK

METROPOLITAN BOOKS   HENRY HOLT AND COMPANY   NEW YORK

Metropolitan Books
Henry Holt and Company, LLC
Publishers since 1866
175 Fifth Avenue
New York, New York 10010
www.henryholt.com

Metropolitan Books® and ® are registered trademarks of
Henry Holt and Company, LLC.

Library of Congress Cataloging-in-Publication Data

Peck, James, 1944–
  Ideal illusions : how the U.S. government co-opted human rights /
James Peck.—1st ed.
      p. cm.—(American empire project)
  Includes bibliographical references and index.
  ISBN 978-0-8050-8328-6
  1. Human rights—Government policy—United States.   2. United States—Foreign
relations—1945–1989.   3. United States—Foreign relations—1989–   I. Title.
  JC599.U5P373 2010
  323.0973—dc22   2010034799

First Edition 2010

Designed by Kelly S. Too

Printed in the United States of America
1   3   5   7   9   10   8   6   4   2

In Memory of
Hao, Helen, and Sol
and for
Laurie

CONTENTS

Introduction   1

1. Washington's World Before the Rise of Human Rights   11

2. The Carter Years: American Foreign Policy Finds a Soul   45

3. The Reagan Administration: Democratization and
   Proxy Wars   85

4. Human Rights and China   130

5. Post-Reagan: Humanitarianism Amid the Ruins   177

6. Terrorism and the Pathology of American Power   230

Notes   287

Acknowledgments   355

Index   357

IDEAL ILLUSIONS

INTRODUCTION

"Follow an idea through from its birth to its triumph," Bertrand de Jouvenel observed in his 1948 volume *On Power,* "and it becomes clear that it came to power only at the price of an astounding degradation of itself. The result is not reason which has found a guide but passion which has found a flag."[1] The widely heralded rise of human rights is not free of such complications. For the history of human rights in the United States—as a movement, as an impassioned language of good intentions, and as an invocation of American idealism—owes far more to the inner ideological needs of Washington's national security establishment than to any deepening of conscience effected by the human rights movement. Thousands of national security documents (from the CIA, the National Security Council, the Pentagon, think tanks, and U.S. government development agencies) reveal how Washington set out after the Vietnam War to craft human rights into a new language of power designed to promote American foreign policy. They shed light on the way Washington has shaped this soaring idealism into a potent ideological weapon for ends having little to do with human rights—and everything to do with extending America's global reach.

This obviously isn't the way human rights leaders have understood the movement's history. For years they extolled its rise as the triumph of a compelling new moral vision that began with the United Nations' Universal Declaration on Human Rights in 1948. Out of the reaction to Nazi atrocities, goes the popular narrative, came human rights. Never again would the world stand by in the face of wholesale torture and murder. As human rights became the vocabulary of a vibrant new conception of public good, it promised a sense of solidarity beyond borders, a voice raised on behalf of victims everywhere. By the late 1970s, these early hopes and aspirations had come to flourish in a vigorous movement developing in think tanks, foundations, law schools, UN forums, congressional committees, professional associations, and international nongovernmental organizations (NGOs).

The United States, with its longstanding ideals and its traditional respect for civil liberties, was a natural ally, a powerful force for global human rights, according to Amnesty International USA.[2] The greatest advantage of Human Rights Watch, wrote its longtime director, Aryeh Neier, was its "identification with a country with a reputation for respecting rights."[3] Of course, the movement's leaders note, Washington itself has committed some terrible human rights violations—CIA-fomented coups, renditions, Guantánamo. But these and similar "mistakes" or "shortsighted strategic calculations" could not permanently tarnish Washington's moral authority. When mistakes or crimes occurred, those committed to opposing such egregious acts saw their task as shaming Washington into changing its ways.

At the same time, the willingness of American citizens to expose their own government's brutalities offered further evidence of freedom at work. For the movement's leaders and for many ordinary citizens, the ability to criticize was inextricably paired with the nation's deeper virtue. No other country enjoyed such immunity. Indeed, where the countless human rights abuses committed by the Soviet Union, China, and other nations exposed who they really were, our own were aberrant— a reflection of who we really weren't. Whatever moral equivalence there was among atrocities did not extend to the parties committing them. American policies were fundamentally progressive. With all these views Washington's foreign policy leaders heartily concurred.

Of course, when a government and its critics share the same language, they are not necessarily saying the same thing. But adept leaders, as Harold Lasswell noted in his classic 1927 study *Propaganda Technique in the World War*, know that "more can be won by illusion than coercion."[4] And no ideological formulation has been more astutely propagated by Washington for the past four decades than the notion that a "rights-based" United States is the natural proponent of human rights throughout the world. In part, the rise of human rights recapitulates the old tale of popular idealism seeking to affect power, and power, in turn, shrewdly subverting that idealism to its own ends. Even as the human rights community has methodically focused on Washington's— and others'—many violations, it has largely recoiled from analyzing the fundamental structures of American power. As a result, it has unwittingly served some of Washington's deepest ideological needs.

Not enough attention has been paid to the interweaving of idealism and national security concerns, yet it is here that the real history of human rights can be found. Human rights erupted into the mainstream of public debate only because two quite distinct needs came together. On one side, a profound revulsion over the Vietnam War led to the weakening of the anticommunist consensus. Appalled by Cold War rationales and tactics (overthrowing regimes, assassinating leaders, training torturers, supporting dictatorships), human rights advocates mobilized against both American "excesses" and Soviet "crimes," documenting in particular the atrocities of American-backed military regimes throughout Latin America, from Guatemala to Chile. On the other side, Washington was desperate for new ideological weapons to justify—both at home and abroad—its global strategies. Human rights advocates sought to infuse Washington's policies with their high-minded ethos just as Washington was fashioning a rights-based vision of America to support its resurgent global aims.

A central question is: who influenced whom? Human rights leaders are convinced they pressured Washington into taking up their cause. Yet in truth their movement gained much of its momentum from Washington's subtle promotion of what they think of as their own agenda. Before the major American rights groups were created, Washington's national security managers had been discussing the desirability of a national organization to offset the "foreign" influence of the London-based Amnesty International. Before human rights leaders began advocating for extending the laws of war to outlaw abuses by antigovernment guerrilla forces, Washington pursued the same goal as a way of discrediting almost all insurgency movements. And a new humanitarian ethos legitimizing massive interventions—including war—emerged in the 1990s only after Washington had been pushing such an approach for some time. In short, the vocabulary and the arguments of the human rights movement almost all have significant precursors in Washington's national security concerns.

From Washington's perspective, the fierce Cold War ideological battles between the "Free World" and its adversaries necessitated lumping together a wide array of radical movements, dissident ideas, and nationalist struggles—all perceived to be inimical to the demands of an America-centered world—in order to dismiss them. But Washington knew all too well that the Free World could hardly restrict its constituents to free countries; it had to align itself with various dictators and brutally repressive regimes. Still, the great "war of ideas" demanded a line be drawn between democratic societies—with free institutions, representative government, and free elections—and those that denied freedom and individual rights.

From the earliest years of the Cold War, Washington predicated its war of ideas on a set of deep divisions: between freedom and equality, reform and revolution, self-interest and collective interests, the free market and state planning, and pluralistic democracy and mass mobilization. American human rights leaders largely, if unknowingly, built on this divide. They usually felt more at ease associating human rights with civil rights and political freedoms, the individual, the market, and pluralistic openness, while seeing the perils in revolution and concentrations of state power. They preferred not to dwell on what might compel populations, as the Universal Declaration of Human Rights warned, "to rebellion against tyranny and oppression"; nor did they acknowledge that it often takes militant mass movements, both violent and nonviolent, to pressure states and powerful interests into acquiescing to programs promoting greater social justice. They considered the struggle for human rights largely apart from peace movements and efforts toward disarmament and the banning of nuclear weaponry, and they took no stand on issues of war and aggression. They mostly viewed resistance movements through the prism of individual rights rather than considering the role of resistance and mass mobilizations in the creation and nourishment of rights.

That Washington has sought to fashion both the conceptual basis and the direction of the human rights movement is hardly surprising—which is not to say that Washington controls the agenda, or that the national security establishment is not constantly competing with Congress, the media, and highly contentious interests abroad. Washington continually has to scramble, searching for ways to refine its strategies and bend ways of thinking to its own ideological ends. Still, it has remained as adept as it was during the Cold War at molding concepts, ideas, and code words. Understanding this process is key to understanding why the human rights movement has developed as it has.

The popular view of a rights-based, democratic American power not only obfuscates the way Washington operates but also advances a rather one-dimensional and parochial vision of human rights. We might more usefully look at human rights as two currents—sometimes contending, sometimes complementary. The first current largely embodies the popular American view, which emphasizes civil and political rights and embraces a moderate, democratic, step-by-step incorporation of human needs into a kind of rights-based legalism. Perhaps such rights are easier to understand in terms of individual freedom: they do more to liberate individuals from the deprivations of caste than of class, freeing them from archaic restraints and traditions but not from economic subjugation. And the outcome is paradoxical. Violations of women's rights, gay rights, and civil rights of all kinds are increasingly attacked while inequality grows. Diversity and multiculturalism are lauded even as the concentration of wealth and power reaches historic levels. The "laws of war" are applauded and efforts to protect the rights of noncombatants flourish even as wars rage and the larger issues of aggression and occupation are ignored.

The second current has less to do with individual freedom and more to do with basic needs. It is associated with popular mass movements, revolution by populations in desperate straits, and resistance. From this perspective, the human rights movement emerged not only as a response to the savagery of World War II and the Holocaust but, more significantly, out of the movements for independence that broke the grip of European colonialism. Central to the second current are challenges to corporate power, state repression, foreign occupation, and global economic inequality, as well as the protection of collective means of struggle, from labor unions to revolution. Historically, this current affirms the mass-based challenges that allowed human rights to emerge in the first place. It is the drive for both freedom *and* equality, so deeply embedded in diverse revolutionary traditions and popular struggles for emancipation and justice, that galvanizes this vision of human rights. Today, this current is far more prevalent outside the dominant Western spheres of power.

The first current tends to speak in terms of victims and perpetrators. The second judges a society by how well it treats the poor and the weak. It challenges power by asking why, in large areas of the world where civil liberties and the "rule of law" do hold sway, so little is done to meet the most basic economic, medical, and educational needs of the populace. The second current, then, is less about infusing rights into preexisting structures of power than about fundamentally altering how power works; it is more about transforming the institutional apparatus and the military basis of political power than about invoking rights to control it.

There have been laudable, if infrequent, efforts to honor both currents together. Martin Luther King Jr., for example, fiercely opposed the Vietnam War, insisting that the civil rights and peace movements needed each other to bring about a better world. But there has been little subsequent support for such a merger either in Washington or in the human rights movement. Instead, the prevailing individual-freedom view of human rights has repeatedly been invoked to condemn the "dark underside" of revolution, the corruptions of unchecked state power, the lip service to equality paid by hypocritical leaders busily suppressing freedom—but not to condemn aggression or crimes against peace.

For most human rights leaders today, the long travails of decolonialization and revolution and the search for alternatives to market-driven economic development represent little more than the backwaters of old Cold War battles that were hardly about rights at all. One looks almost in vain for accounts that show how Western power long subordinated the development of the Southern Hemisphere to its own needs and desires, how challenges in the non-Western world propelled the development of human rights laws and ideas, and how mass mobilizations broke the Gordian knot of colonialism and liberalism. Nor do human rights textbooks devote many pages to the great mass movements—not even the civil rights movement in the United States or the anti-apartheid struggle in South Africa.[5] The major studies of human rights law spend their time instead debating how to enforce UN pronouncements and covenants. The language of law dominates the discussion. But law is the language of institutions, courts, and politicians. The teachings of Mohandas Gandhi and King and the language of impassioned justice are notably absent.

The movement's deep uneasiness with all forms of radical and revolutionary social change was already evident in 1961, when the newly founded Amnesty International pronounced that no prisoners who advocated violence could be considered prisoners of conscience: thus no revolutionaries—not Nelson Mandela in South Africa, nor even the Berrigan brothers (who had destroyed draft-board records) in the United States. The movement has generally criticized revolutions and decolonializing rebellions as human rights travesties. No insurgency, including those in Vietnam and El Salvador, has escaped its censure for the killing of innocent civilians and the use of terror. No state redistributions of wealth and power have failed to rack up human rights violations; the Chinese Revolution is regarded as one huge atrocity. The Iranian Revolution is attacked as little more than a precursor to further repression. The upheavals of decolonialization are blamed for having opened the way to repressive authoritarian states.

Meanwhile, the virulent hostility of the United States in all these situations is either ignored in human rights reports or else dismissed as irrelevant to judging the violations. The black book of Communism is long and richly illustrated, and the crimes of the new human rights abusers are quickly added in the appendices. But where, we might ask, is the corresponding black book of anticommunism, of United States–backed "nation building" and "counterinsurgency," with their countless human rights violations, of invocations of the "rule of law" used to legitimize such systemic injustices as wars, occupations, and the economic violence of the marketplace?

None of the movement's uneasiness with violence and radical struggle translates into a commitment to nonviolence or pacifism. The conventional conception of human rights accepts certain kinds of controlled violence, "justified violence,"[6] "proportionality" in warfare, and the legalization of some forms of violence against others. It seeks to moderate war by protecting civilian noncombatants, regulating occupations and counterinsurgency campaigns, and controlling the excesses of governments and resistance movements alike. In other words, the idea is to impose the laws of war, not to outlaw war. Worthwhile as this undertaking may be, it tends to deflect attention from the larger truth that wars, occupations, and aggressive interventions are responsible for much of the violence in the world today. For there is only a thin line between advocating for the laws an occupying power should follow and tacitly legitimizing an occupation by lauding the rights-based methods that sustain it. It is bad enough to legalize some forms of violence with the "laws of war" while ignoring the larger underlying issue of aggression. It is still worse to accept some forms of state violence while outlawing almost all forms of nonstate violence that arise in reaction to it.

Today we look with perplexity at how slavery could coexist with the belief that all men are created equal, how liberalism could rise hand in hand with colonialism and brutal forms of exploitation, how calls for freedom could ignore women's rights, how the antislavery movement in England could coincide with the Opium Wars against China, and how democracies could fight colonial wars. We like to think these contradictions reflected incomplete developments. Indeed they did. But in various ways such blindness remains with us, a reminder of how tightly interwoven the competing and sometimes conflicting claims of human rights always are.

If we really begin to contend with the *contradictions* posed by these two currents, we will understand why later generations may look back on our present vision of human rights with the same perplexity. For the rise of the American human rights movement since the 1970s has coincided with an unprecedented increase in inequality, with brutal wars of occupation, and with a determination to establish American preeminence via the greatest concentration of military power in history. In the future, the downplaying of the issues of aggression and crimes against peace may not go unnoticed, for it fits with the character of Washington's power and its half-century-long war of ideas.

The world is changing profoundly. Yet the tectonic shifts in global power now under way have barely registered on either the Obama administration or human rights leaders. But as the old world gives way, it is urgent that we rethink the meaning of human rights. And nothing presents a greater hurdle to this task than the human rights community's close if often unwitting links to Washington. Without such a reexamination, the human rights movement may well continue to serve Washington's ideological needs. In the end, the movement must decide: Can it find a way to truly confront the abusive operations of wealth and power in all their many forms? Or will it consent to being a weapon of privileged power seeking to protect its interests—and its conscience?

1

WASHINGTON'S WORLD BEFORE THE RISE OF HUMAN RIGHTS

There is an oft-told, much cherished story of how in the early Cold War years Washington's wise and talented national security leaders, confronted with a war-ravaged world, put together a sweeping and magnanimous program to transform Europe and much of the rest of the globe. World War II had created an unmatched opportunity. The old colonial empires were crumbling. Britain, previously the center of the world's largest trading bloc, was bankrupt. Germany and Japan were defeated and occupied, their economies in ruins. The Soviet Union was economically weak and faced the immense task of rebuilding. Alert to the possibilities at hand and drawing on the reforming ethos of the New Deal, Dean Acheson, Averell Harriman, Robert Lovett, John McCloy, and other colleagues dedicated themselves to a dynamic internationalism, advocating the United Nations, the Marshall Plan, the World Bank, and the International Monetary Fund. Having emerged largely from the financial and business elite, these moderate, practical men, the story continues, rallied themselves to this near-Herculean task, steeling their nerves to wage Cold War against a Communist foe that sought to stymie their every effort, an enemy so relentless and so ideologically adept at stoking the widespread embers of hatred and conflict that it took utmost vigilance and dedication just to "contain" it.

Not since the Founding Fathers, the tale goes on, had America been so providentially blessed with such a surplus of political talent. With

greatness thrust upon them, they brilliantly seized the moment, bringing together the best wisdom of their era to create a new, progressive
international order.[1] They treated the Germans and the Japanese with
unstinting evenhandedness, reforming their societies and leading them
toward democracy. They recognized the cost of America's isolationist
retreat after World War I and vowed that the nation would never again
abdicate its global responsibilities. Having witnessed the devastating
economic protectionism of the Great Depression and the discrediting
of capitalism—disasters that had spawned the virulent nationalisms of
Nazism and Japanese Fascism—they were determined to prevent such
calamities from happening again. Whatever criticisms their policies
garnered later on, "at the creation" (as Acheson liked to say) these leaders skillfully laid the foundation for America's globe-spanning power
and provided the ideas and the vision to fight for it.

Of late, a somewhat mournful series of questions has been added as
a coda: Where are the comparable wise men today? Where are the leaders innovative enough to guide an America-centered world in ways that
would make us truly respected, if not always loved? Where, in short, is
that saving touch of moderation untainted by hubris and the arrogance
of power that would enable leaders to wage fierce struggles against
frightening foes while upholding the Constitution and building a world
order in which freedom, democracy, and human rights might flourish?[2]

Augustus Caesar, Edward Gibbon wrote in the opening pages of *The
Decline and Fall of the Roman Empire*, was wise because he "relinquished
the ambitious design of subduing the whole earth," introduced "a spirit
of moderation into the public councils" of Rome, and limited the size
of the empire.[3] Such was not the case with the "wise men," as Acheson
and his colleagues were called by later generations. Notwithstanding
the popular myth, they introduced policies that constituted one of history's most audacious and astonishing imperial undertakings. At the
center of U.S. foreign policy making, enshrouded in the often obfuscating ethos of national security, labored men whom Dean Acheson described
without embarrassment in biblical language: in the beginning was chaos,

out of which the Americans would create a global order unlike any ever seen before.

In reality, the wise men were anything but the moderates they saw themselves as. Nor did their views reflect an emerging consensus in America about the nation's post–World War II international role. They well knew that there were strong opposing conceptions of the national interest, and they saw their situation as precarious—a minority undertaking widely popular neither at home nor abroad. Yet they triumphed by claiming that they embodied the national interest for the presidents they served. What they sought and, to a remarkable extent, managed to do was capture the pinnacle of the American state for their own distinct vision of the world—one that has evolved but still holds sway.

Their approach was fervently visionary, using anticipation and prediction as a way of guiding forces and bureaucracies toward their objectives. Though sometimes inchoate as a source of policy, their intensely felt and intuited globalism—*visionary globalism*, in short—nevertheless offered a coherent faith that has provided the context for international policy discussions ever since.

Toward the end of his life, George Kennan, looking back on this emerging Cold War globalism, commented: "Do you know what Acheson's problem was? He didn't understand power."[4] In Kennan's eyes, Acheson and the other wise men's mistake—and their extraordinary hubris—lay in their conviction that Washington could actually fashion and coordinate a global system that would leave it as capable of controlling its allies as of confronting its enemies. Instead, Kennan said, they would find in the end that Washington was no more able to prevent the emergence of independent centers of power than the Russians were in Eastern Europe. Refusing to understand the limits of power, as Augustus perceived several millennia ago, was not to understand power at all.

What made the wise men extremists was what made their visionary globalism so total: they anticipated a complete reorganization of the globe from the top down, as opposed to the traditional American expansionism that moved from the bottom up. The notion George Washington laid out in his Farewell Address of "extending our commercial relations" with other countries while having "as little political connection as possible" was turned upside down: commercial relations were to become dependent on a new global politics centered on American power. America's long tradition of expansionism also came in for serious revision. For expansionism proceeds incrementally, as the state adds on pieces of territory and military bases; there is no direct path from this process to a doctrine of organizing the globe from the top down. Visionary globalism came about when American elites utilized the highly centralized system of presidential power that emerged out of World War II to order the world around the needs and interests of the United States. As President Harry Truman put it in a talk to the CIA: "You may not know it, but the Presidential Office is the most powerful office that has ever existed in the history of this great world of ours. Genghis Khan, Augustus Caesar, great Napoleon Bonaparte, or Louis XIV—or any other of the great leaders and executives of the world— can't even compare with what the President of the United States himself is responsible for when he makes a decision."[5] Or as Secretary of State John Foster Dulles told the Senate in 1955: "One man, and one man alone is so situated as to have the complete, overall picture. He is the President of the United States. He comprehends both the domestic and the international aspects of the problem."[6]

The national security establishment rapidly grew under this presidential aegis, its authority expanding into a wide network that came to include the National Security Council (NSC), the CIA, the Joint Chiefs of Staff, and the State and Defense departments, among other groups. The new national security managers fervently believed that only presidents and their advisors really had enough information to consider the national interest as a whole, and their task, as they saw it, was to rise above bureaucratic and parochial battles in order to formulate the *real* national interest for the president. Their mission was to help the president stand above special interests and limited ways of thinking, to bear in mind the big picture, the global perspective. And presidents, of course, came and went. In emphasizing the president's centrality, the managers reinforced their own, for their power flowed directly from his.

The globalism the national security managers embraced did have its ideological precursors—in Wilsonian rhetoric about the League of

Nations, in the one-world vision of Wendell Willkie, in Henry Luce's American Century, in the financial "internationalism" of corporate circles in the 1920s[7]—but never before had there been an opportunity to transform them into a comprehensive mission for the American state. This globalism did not develop "in a fit of absence of mind," as the British sometimes viewed the rise of their own empire.[8] Wartime planning was meticulous and ongoing. Franklin Roosevelt's vision of the postwar world has often been interpreted as an extension of his New Deal to the world at large, but more accurately it was a response to the New Deal's weaknesses at home: the way to go about countering the Depression and possible economic and social turmoil was to restructure the world capitalist system via the international institutions that were designed to reinforce American interests. Dean Acheson exhorted conservative businessmen during the war that they had it all wrong when they denounced the coming postwar globalism he advocated. Such "global responsibility," he told them, was precisely the way to undercut the statist economic tendencies of the New Deal and protect their corporate power in the coming world.

Yet the gap between their fervent aspirations to build a new America-centered global order and the ideological means to justify it was enormous. At home, the national security managers confronted the withering criticism of numerous opponents—from conservatives such as Senator Robert Taft of Ohio and former President Herbert Hoover to ardent New Deal advocates still fighting for major social and economic changes—whom they regarded as isolationists at heart, preoccupied with their own problems. The country "was being flooded with isolationist propaganda," Truman wrote in his memoirs;[9] it was "going back to bed at a frightening rate," lamented Secretary of the Navy James Forrestal in October 1945.[10]

The idea of using American power to impose order on a chaotic world also confronted frightful obstacles abroad. The burgeoning decolonialization movement and revolutionary upheavals were largely hostile to Washington's global agenda. Even in Europe, the United States confronted nationalist resentment from leaders who criticized the "assertion of U.S. world hegemony" that would make them "protectorates of the United States, deprived of some of the traditional attributes of sovereignty and equality."[11] The disintegrating British Empire was torn between its need for American financial assistance and opposition to American plans to destroy its system of preferential trade. Most critically, the Soviets, though war-weary and devastated, offered a military and ideological alternative in a tumultuous world, their developmental strategies increasingly resonant with the desperate needs of emerging new nations.

The ethos of World War II (the era of the "common man," the four freedoms, the four policemen of the world) provided no ideological weapons potent enough to promote American globalism against these obstacles. Such slogans had been fine for waging a world war in alliance with the Russians, but for the new tasks at hand they were hopelessly inadequate. Nor was there any equivalent of the French *mission civilatrice* or the British Imperial ethos available to Americans searching for a vision to draw on—as one CIA memo later put it—to "steady the nerves" and provide "the hardness and decisiveness" their mission required.[12] "Political warfare is foreign to our tradition. We have never done it before. We are not skilled in this. Many of our people don't understand it,"[13] George Kennan told the National War College.

To the wise men the task was clear: A great power needed "a persuasive ideological ethos" of worldwide significance, a "global psychological strategy" to rally support at home and win the "war of ideas" abroad.[14] The country required a "firm, well defined ideology which must be messianic and scientific at the same time—not purely nationalistic."[15] Communists were "providing the people of all parts of the world with a fighting faith."[16] The United States might stand for freedom, but how could we present our political philosophy in a way that could compete favorably with Communism's appeal?[17]

Not easily. "Take a look at our propaganda apparatus—and our ideological message. It is pitiful. It is really appalling,"[18] said Kennan, then head of the Policy Planning Board of the State Department, in 1947. In particular, he added, "we should cease to talk about vague and—for the Far East—unreal objectives such as human rights, the raising of the living standards, and democratization. The day is not far off when we are going to have to deal in straight power concepts. The less we are then hampered by idealistics slogans, the better."[19]

Kennan need not have worried. In State Department deliberations during World War II, the term "human rights" played only a modest role, usually appearing in discussions of the rule of law, a new internationalism, and the United Nations. FDR's New Deal, with its concern for social and economic problems, was occasionally evoked as contributing to human rights, but rights remained largely cast in the language of the individual—and rarely placed in the world of revolution or the desperation of the have-nots. One notable exception came from Gandhi, who wrote to Roosevelt in July 1942 that "the Allied Declaration that the Allies are fighting to make the world safe for freedom of the individual and for democracy sounds hollow, so long as India, and for that matter, Africa are exploited by Great Britain, and America has the Negro problem in her own home."[20]

Though historians often focus on the importance of the 1948 United Nations Universal Declaration of Human Rights, in reality human rights played virtually no role in American strategic policy in the early Cold War years. When the concept did appear, it was usually in the context of relatively secondary discussions over how to handle the internationally embarrassing problem of Southern segregation. So, for example, Truman administration leaders told Eleanor Roosevelt, who was chairing the UN Commission on Human Rights, that it was all well and good to produce a list of rights to inspire Americans so long as she made sure they could not be invoked on behalf of African-Americans. Truman feared that if the UN Declaration of Human Rights were to be used to challenge Jim Crow laws (as W. E. B. Du Bois, in fact, tried to do), he would be faced with a rebellion by Southern senators over a host of his other policies.

For a brief moment the Eisenhower administration looked for a way to charge the Soviets with human rights violations without appealing to the United Nations Declaration. UN Ambassador Henry Cabot Lodge Jr. asked the Psychological Strategy Board (PSB), a group that had been set up to devise psychological warfare strategies against the Soviets, for "hot journalistic items," "sensationalistic individual compelling stories of human rights violations" in which "factual certainty is desired, but should not be made a fetish."[21] But like Truman, Eisenhower and Dulles became alarmed at the domestic risk of having foreigners "prying around in human rights conditions in the United States"[22] and quickly put an end to any ideological warfare involving the UN human rights protocols.

Even setting aside the civil rights problem, there is little to indicate that human rights were ever intended to be a central weapon in the American ideological arsenal. They smacked too much of a "flabby, defenseless idealism." Speaking of political morality and "fuzzy minded rights," Senator J. William Fulbright remarked, was seen as "a sure sign that you didn't have the hard edged ferocity to fight communism" or to deal with other sources of global disorder.[23] The language might be fine for Eleanor Roosevelt, but not for the battle against the Soviets. Something fiercer, more aggressive was required to build the new global order. That was anticommunism.

ANTICOMMUNISM AND THE ORIGINS OF
THE NATIONAL SECURITY ESTABLISHMENT

What anticommunism offered was a nearly instantaneous rationale for globalism. The connection is clear in a top-secret 1950 National Security Council document that bluntly summed up the ensuing Cold War outlook: "In a shrinking world, which now faces the threat of atomic warfare, it is not an adequate objective merely to seek to check the Kremlin design, for the absence of order among nations is becoming less and less tolerable. This fact imposes on us, in our own interests, the responsibility of world leadership." While anticommunism focused on the immediate confrontation with the Soviets, the globalist commitment emphasized the "absence of order" that imposed the task of "world leadership."[24] The national security managers understood the difference between the two. "Since the Free World does not yet exist as a political or even a psychological community," went a typical 1952 pronouncement, one of our major objectives "should be to create it, and then give it the leadership it needs to survive."[25]

Washington's grand strategy was to create an integrated, cooperative global capitalism under U.S. leadership. About this there is no ambiguity; the goal was never far from the calculations of policy makers, and it remains a remarkably fundamental and consistent objective. However bitter the policy controversies at the highest levels of the American government, there was always agreement on the need for defending such a globalist esprit.[26] Not surprisingly, the formulators of this strategy never saw themselves as anything but realists dealing with brutal necessities and the specific interests of American power—hard-headed, cold-blooded men who made their decisions unencumbered by ideology.

National security managers became the custodians and exponents of the globalist faith, fervent proselytizers of its tenets at home and abroad. In studies of the managers, this fervor, with its obsessive anticommunism, has usually been dismissed as an embarrassing eruption of purple prose rather than as the authentic expression of an underlying ethos. "Who were the authors preaching to?" one researcher puzzles after examining early Cold War National Security Council documents,[27] and another observes, "This is not what one would expect in a top secret document destined not to be made public for a quarter of a century."[28]

Instead of attempting to understand the hortatory calls in policy documents, historians have too often viewed them as marginal. They have seen American leaders using ideology to manipulate others without acknowledging how deeply the tenets of the faith gripped these leaders themselves. Yet from the earliest days of the Cold War, the documents demonstrate a dynamic of elite self-persuasion whereby the making of policy and the propagation of a globalist faith became inseparable in the formulation of American foreign relations. In reality, the national security establishment was a center of both analysis and ideological warfare. Globalism's true believers stood at the apex of the American state, where their unrelenting effort to persuade (or "educate" or sometimes, frankly, "indoctrinate")[29] Congress and their fellow citizens as to the virtues of an America-centered world paralleled their own ardent self-indoctrination. They internalized the code words, the analogies, the ways of thinking that they would then insist were their utterly nonideological means of strategizing.

Because anticommunism insisted upon a close connection among events in vastly different regions of the world, it perfectly meshed with the aspirations of globalism. Onto the flesh-and-blood Stalin, anticommunism projected a Genghis Khan–like world conqueror (which he never was) instead of the mass murderer of his own people that he really was, carving out a defensive zone by occupying countries around him. "Today Stalin has come close to achieving what Hitler attempted in vain," an early NSC report averred.[30] Communism was a fanatical, messianic creed—a "20th century Islam," a godless faith in modern guise that fought to annihilate the "foundations of Western civilization."[31] Its "spiritual appeal" became a near obsession with the national security managers. "To me the fundamental question" in respect to our relations with Russia, Secretary of the Navy Forrestal stated in 1945, "is whether we are dealing with a nation or a religion."[32] Communism's claim to be "scientific and infallible" and its invocation of the "predetermined pattern of world history" made it a mighty ideological force. Moreover, the Soviets were highly organized—"unified in thought, unified in command, unified in action and unified in the goal they are seeking." Their tactics shrewdly subordinated diverging objectives to the imperatives of global strategizing, "joining together a "world plan of operations" with an "international crusading ideology."[33]

Only a counter-globalism, an equally "integrating ethos," could hope to defeat such an opponent. Each American action thus had to be considered "in the light of overall Soviet objectives." Contrary to the "time honored custom" of regarding " 'European policy,' 'Near Eastern Policy,' 'Indian Policy,' and 'Chinese Policy' " as "separate problems to be handled by experts in each field,"[34] it was understood that every localized political, economic, ideological, sociological, and military event "affects what happens in every other" area. "In the world we are living in, there are no 'things in themselves.' It is all tied together."[35] ("To ignore the inter-connection of events was to undermine the coherency of all policy," Henry Kissinger wrote in his memoirs.)[36]

"We should not be too proud to learn from the enemy where profitable," one memo admonished.[37] Mastering Soviet brilliance at creating "global strategy" and a "world plan of operations"[38] was at the top of the list. But Fulbright was closer to the heart of the matter when he asked, "Isn't it true that we very often tend to accuse someone with whom we are a rival of the very thing that we have in mind ourselves?"[39] The managers often portrayed themselves as rather reactive latecomers, but their view of the "enemy," as Fulbright shrewdly came to see, reflected the agenda they had set for themselves more than it did any objective perception of their Soviet opponent.[40]

Their depiction of an omnipresent, spiritually alluring Communist enemy thus led to a search for strategies to wage the "battle for men's minds." One was Truman's creation, in April 1951, of the Psychological Strategy Board, comprising the undersecretary of state, the director of central intelligence, and the deputy secretary of defense. Gordon Gray, later Eisenhower's national security advisor, was its first director. Its task was to coordinate and plan psychological warfare programs and to shape the American message for the ideological Cold War. Managers had to learn—as C. D. Jackson, special assistant to President Eisenhower, put it in 1953—that "psychological warfare . . . does not exist apart from the policies and above all the acts of governments." Policies and propaganda had to be tightly bound, the former shaping the latter.

Initially the very term "psychological warfare" was "intentionally dreamed-up to conceal" its covert aspects.[41] The overtones were unpleasant, but as Eisenhower's psychological warfare expert put it, "just because Dr. Goebbels and the Kremlin have debased it, that is no reason why we cannot elevate it."[42] Cold Warriors had to counter the Communist talent for offering both ideals that had a "certain universality of appeal" and "deceptively simple solutions."[43] Unlike the Nazis, who embraced no such attractive Enlightenment ideals, the Communists had shrewdly "perverted" Western values to their own ends. The "Soviets appropriate, degrade, and bastardize the words . . . liberty, equality, fraternity, independence, justice, freedom, democracy,"[44] one official complained. They used the "words of the West" as "bullets aimed at the brains of their targets to nourish confusion, doubt, suspicion, fear and incite hate, greed, venom and thereby appeal to the lowest instincts of man,"[45] another added. The Soviets had "succeeded, through clever and systematic propaganda, in establishing throughout large sections of the world certain concepts, highly favorable to their own purposes,"[46] agreed a third. And they were armed with categories of analysis that appealed to the discontented everywhere: class, imperialism, colonialism, revolution, capitalism, as well as a model for rapid industrial development.

In response, the national security managers created alternative theories to interpret global processes. They, too, had to learn to "present their conclusions in broad settings and historical perspectives," to engage in a "historical-philosophical dialogue about the current state of the world," as Zbigniew Brzezinski later summed up the challenge.[47] They, too, needed to evolve categories of analysis: neutralism, fifth columnists, dominos, credibility, containment, and so on. Such apparent mirroring was both conscious and unconscious. Kennan, for example, puzzled over the contradiction between the Soviets' realism and their fanaticism. "I must say I admire" the Communist leaders, he said in his lectures to the National War College in 1947, "for the realism with which they look to the essential features of power and do not allow themselves to be carried away by the more petty sorts of human vanity."[48] And yet, inexplicably, the Kremlin held fast to an ideological prism, distorting reality to suit its own needs (the class struggle, capitalism's decline, the certainty of revolution and of the economic development of Communist society). How could these men be at once so objective and yet so ideological? This was "*the* key question to understanding the whole system," Kennan concluded, "and I am frank to say I don't know what the answer is."[49] Greater self-awareness might have suggested a place to start.

Tellingly, Truman spoke of similarities between the two sides, although he kept his views private. "You know Americans are funny kids," he wrote in his diary. "They are always sticking their noses into somebody's business which isn't any of theirs. We send missionaries and political propagandists to China, Turkey, India, and everywhere to tell those people how to live. . . . Russia won't let 'em in. But when Russia puts out propaganda to help our parlor pinks—well that's bad—so we think. There is not any difference between the two approaches except one is 'my approach' and the other is 'yours.' Just a 'moat and beam' affair."[50]

The resemblance between the working world the Cold War managers were building for themselves and the way they depicted the Kremlin is striking. In 1946 Clark Clifford wrote admiringly to Truman about the "small group of able men" at the Kremlin's center, men endowed "with a remarkable ability for long-range forethought." To survive, America needed the same thing.[51] The United States was the one "source of power capable of mobilizing successful opposition to the communist goal of world communism"[52]—but only because the trained eye of the national security manager could see the underlying global conflict playing out in every part of the world.

These officials became archgeneralists in the hard, lean thinking of power. They exercised their skill in finding mobilizing code words, reductive phrases, and analogies that reduced the world to viable policy alternatives. "Credibility" was a favorite word, shorthand for the primacy of Washington's global commitments. Anticommunism nourished the language of credibility, of keeping our word, of defending the world order and civilization, of linking developments within any country to U.S. interests. Seeing the dangers of Communism everywhere was a way of seeing American global interests everywhere; obscure events and countries assumed their places in a familiar ideological landscape. A conflict in a faraway state was a test of Washington's credibility. Cuba, Korea, and Berlin were all, as Acheson so often warned, tests of the American will. Like their Communist opponents, the national security managers understood what power required, how to control it, how to manage it in endless crises. Power was about filtering out the welter of conflicting information and molding what remained into actionable choices that made sense of the world. They could spot a power vacuum, a domino, a failing state, or aggression and instantly link it with America's credibility, intuitively sensing the dangers of being "soft" or negotiating too quickly.

If the fate of greatness is to be misunderstood and feared, this was a burden willingly borne by these managers. The resentment of the weak and less well off needed to be understood: "Gratitude is a heavy burden to bear, and good deeds are hard to forgive," concluded one psychological warfare study.[53] As John Foster Dulles said to Charles DeGaulle, "In every society a minority always dominated. The question was how to do it. If the minority affronted the majority, it lost influence. If discretely exercised . . . the minority influence could be effective and desirable."[54]

Acheson was more acerbic: "you all start with the premise that democracy is some good. I don't think it's worth a damn. . . . People say, 'If the Congress were more representative of the people it would be better.' I say the Congress is too damn representative. It's just as stupid as the people are; just as uneducated, just as dumb, just as selfish."[55] Dealing with endless Congressional criticism, the attacks of Senator McCarthy, and frequent election cycles were challenging nuisances for these men but ones they felt ready to handle with almost any means at hand.

The national security managers were thus not hesitant to violate the spirit of America's ideals in waging the Cold War through covert operations. They believed it took brutal methods to deal with recalcitrant opponents and unhappy allies, as even a partial list of U.S. activities from a 1951 account makes clear:

> propaganda, political action; economic warfare; preventive direct action, including sabotage, anti-sabotage, demolition; escape and evasion and evacuation measures; subversion against hostile states or groups, including assistance to underground resistance movements; guerrillas and refugee liberation groups; support of indigenous anticommunist elements . . . deception plans and operations. . . . [56]

But these were years of deniability: America did not operate as an imperial power; it didn't interfere in the internal affairs of other nations; it didn't act unilaterally to fashion a global order; its actions were "defensive." Washington thus issued bold denials at home that America was engaging in nasty tactics, while secret NSC documents insisted that the integrity of the United States was not "jeopardized by any measures, covert, overt, violent or non-violent, which serve the purposes of frustrating the Kremlin Design."[57]

But if the Communist threat was so demonic, and if America's integrity remained intact, why was deniability of covert warfare so important for Washington? Why did American leaders find it impossible to publicly acknowledge the need to fight fire with fire? Why did their methods demand more secrecy than the renditions and torture that are public knowledge today? After all, the Soviets, not to mention the various nations on the receiving end, were often aware of U.S. covert programs.

Deniability was important because covert warfare was not only about achieving the specific objectives of anticommunism but also about reinforcing and augmenting the globalist policies that lacked support in the United States. Washington's reasons were often duplicitous. Covert warfare, for example, was significantly about discrediting opponents of American foreign policy at home. Some American critics of an emerging globalism were willing to acquiesce in the creation of NATO; but "the reconstruction of the political, economic, and social fabric in the friendly countries of Western Europe and Asia" was something else again. The United States, they charged, was utilizing a well-orchestrated effort to "bring about revolutionary changes in friendly countries without the knowledge or the consent of the peoples of the majority elements in the governments concerned." This was a policy of "forced internationalization," charged an in-house CIA critic, part of a "crusade to remake the world"[58] about which there was hardly consensus in the United States.

Promoting capitalist reorganization was not easy even in Western Europe. National security leaders knew that the notion of development on an American scale was neither popular nor inevitable there.[59] That "economic expansion is the driving force upon which US strength is based" remained uncontested in Washington,[60] but, as Dulles put it, "All the Western powers, except the U.S., are acting like shattered 'old people' who just want to spend their remaining days in peace.... Their hope is that the Soviets, like Genghis Khan, will get on their little Tartar ponies and ride back whence they came...."[61] The idea of a "concept of Europe" offered Washington a way to recruit a like-minded European elite: friendly European leaders and intellectuals could invoke it to overcome the "nationalistic parochialism" and "socialist inclinations" of their domestic adversaries. The national security managers' aim was to propagate a European capitalism that would break down state control over trade and make the United States the ultimate arbiter of economic integration; but they recognized that this was neither a popular goal nor an inevitable outcome.[62]

By the early 1950s, Washington could report considerable progress. As a CIA report to the Psychological Strategy Board concluded, "Major accomplishment of political action and propaganda operations in Western Europe have been in the area of European unification along the lines of the Atlantic unity concept."[63]

DEVISING A CONVINCING NARRATIVE
AT HOME AND ABROAD

A global power, the national security managers reasoned, must have not just a creed but a satisfying historical narrative as well. The "cunning of history" requires the cunning of historiography, and a new historical narrative was sorely needed in America. Charles and Mary Beard's epochal *Rise of American Civilization* (1927) had focused on America's revolutionary ferment, its social conflicts, and its deep-rooted struggles for equality and democracy. The Beards and others like them in the 1930s warned against the false prophets of internationalism, whose ideas, if adopted, would "redound more to the advantage of one nation than another, owing to differences in industrial advance and natural resources . . . in cruel truth, internationalism may be a covering ideology for the aggressive nationalism of one or more countries."[64] By 1945, views such as this were under attack as defeatist, isolationist, and un-American.

As the Director of Truman's Psychological Strategy Board phrased it, after World War I "America preferred to slough off its responsibilities." The widespread acceptance of the economic interpretation of history and life together with a revisionist approach to World War I led the average American to view all wars as "profit and persuasion: bankers and munitions makers reaped the profit and plied their fellow citizens and world opinion with appealing propaganda to increase their gains."[65] In the 1920s and 1930s Wall Street financiers and arms manufacturers were widely depicted as manipulators of public opinion, concerned less with making the world "safe for democracy" than with profits and the protection of their interests. World War I turned out to be more complicated than an evil Germany versus virtuous Allies; and the mobilized wartime idealism took on the appearance of a sham.

These views, Cold War propagandists concluded—whether prompted by Senate investigations such as the Nye Committee (the mid-1930s Senate panel that looked into business influence on our involvement in the war) or spread by the popular media—made "Americans become isolationist" and thus "basically indifferent to world developments."[66]

In the early Cold War years, shifts in key words and ideas signaled a sweeping process of ideological transformation. Psychological warfare experts, for example, thought it was fine to laud "American freedom" and "American ideals," but they drew the line at "American civilization." To speak of "Western civilization" and of the United States as the leader of the "Western world" was acceptable, but calling the United States a civilization, as the Beards had, would remind Americans of the particularities of their culture and history and of longstanding debates over what, exactly, the "spirit of the American people" was. There could be a French or a Chinese or an Indian civilization, but Cold War American exceptionalism demanded that the United States be imbued with ideals appropriate for all humanity. Henceforth the phrase "American civilization" all but disappears from official rhetoric, and the United States becomes the embodiment of humanity's universal longing for freedom.

A highly particularized construction of "freedom" became the key ideological weapon. The "idea of freedom is the most contagious idea in history . . . peculiarly and intolerably subversive of the idea of [Soviet] slavery," a classified 1950 document proclaimed to managers being initiated into the national security culture. In addition to "opposition to the communist goal of world conquest," freedom meant "free enterprise," the "rights of the individual," and the right of the United States to organize the "free world" against Communism.[67] This freedom had great emancipatory powers for the individual from repressive regimes and traditions of all kinds, but it was abstract and largely unconstrained by other values. It was what political economist Max Weber once described as the freedom of capital: liberating for some individuals, breaking the bonds of the old, attacking tradition, using whatever it can on the way to profit.[68] It should be no surprise that "freedom" was the supreme value in Cold War national security documents: the nascent "ordering" of the world was inseparable from American-style capitalism. Freedom and the market are ultimately inseparable in these documents; indeed, the international market is the only force capable of promoting freedom's further development.

Encoded in the word "freedom," then, was an agenda that stood apart from and often against such other core values as equality, community, solidarity, and redistributive forms of justice. In the war of ideas against Communism and other radical faiths,[69] "freedom" made for a crusading ethos expressed in a language of good-versus-evil, white-versus-black, free-versus-unfree—all variants of us-versus-them.[70] To turn aspects of humanity's great emancipatory traditions against one another, to use freedom to attack a plethora of diverse values and appeals for social justice—this was what the national security managers' war of ideas was all about. They were fond of arguing that "populist Manichaeanism reflected the propensity of the masses to demonize foreign affairs,"[71] but in reality they were the Pied Pipers leading the procession at every step.

Before the 1940s it would have been hard for such a singular vision of freedom to triumph. But World War II, and then the Cold War, changed the picture. In the depths of the Great Depression, as the historian William Leuchtenburg put it, "the businessman had lost his magic and was as discredited as a Hopi rainmaker in a prolonged drought";[72] now his path to resurrection lay in a "consensus society" speaking the language of freedom and free enterprise as a cornucopia of consumer goods beckoned it forward.[73] Business leaders were deeply fearful that the popularity of the New Deal at home and the spread of socialism abroad signaled drastic changes to the American economic system, and they organized enormous financial reserves to fight back.[74] They also relied on the new reach of mass communication. "We have within our hands the greatest aggregate means of mass education and persuasion the world has ever seen—namely the channels of advertising communication. . . . Why not use it?" asked the director of the War Advertising Council during World War II.[75] And Big Business did—sometimes subtly, sometimes boldly, crafting an updated "business creed" whose hallmark of productivity and free enterprise was partly designed to ward off criticisms of unfair distribution and corporate concentration.

And not just Big Business. When during the war government propagandists in the Office of War Information's "Project America" program set out to define America, they, too, immediately gravitated toward a vision of freedom that stressed the homogenizing, standardizing, advertising-based consumerism of a business civilization.[76] "Our sympathies are universal," argued Robert Sherwood, then a speechwriter for FDR, "because we are ourselves composed of many racial and national strains." Freedom "makes us one." And if the "American idea" embraced a "nation of nations," uniting diverse ethnic, religious, class, and racial backgrounds, then American freedom could be "increasingly able to reach the non-elites of the world."[77] The possibilities for foreign relations were breathtaking because "the extraordinary development of electric communication has made foreign relations domestic affairs," Archibald MacLeish said.[78] With new ways to penetrate other societies appearing, most notably radio and the attractions of mass consumerism, elites were no longer the sole targets of propaganda; the masses could be reached as well.

From a propaganda point of view, the language of markets, advertising, rights, mass media, and law offered powerfully simplifying and formulaic descriptions within which American power could pursue quite specific agendas. Such "universalism," however, was never about just any culture but specifically a market-driven one; never about a civilization except one with "universal" traits; never about what was difficult to communicate among cultures but only what could be easily expressed. "The unprecedented American opportunities have always tempted us to confuse the visionary with the real," Daniel Boorstin warned.[79]

Anticommunism adeptly and shrewdly fused two overlapping but distinguishable aims: the efforts of Big Business to advertise its way back into the good graces of American public opinion after the Great Depression and the needs of the new national security managers to discredit rival visions of America.[80] Tolerance among classes, religious freedom, and individual freedom were part of the emerging catechism. The new consensus had significant emancipatory qualities and would prove itself amenable, in time, to a greater acceptance of civil rights, social diversity, women's rights, and racial justice. Yet this vision of freedom came at a cost. When Gunnar Myrdal's *An American Dilemma*, the classic study of racism and the American creed, entered intellectual debate in the mid-1940s, it did so largely stripped of its impassioned warning that only a powerful reaffirmation of equality could counter the "unbridled freedom" that in the United States so often "provided an opportunity for the stronger to rob the weaker."[81]

Myrdal was not alone. James Truslow Adams, who in the depths of the Depression popularized the phrase "the American Dream," had urged his fellow citizens to take control of the processes unleashed by the industrial and corporate organization of America.[82] Like many of his contemporaries—Lewis Mumford, Van Wyck Brooks, John Dos Passos, Sinclair Lewis—Adams saw the American Dream as a humanizing vision at war with a business civilization that was subordinating everything to the dictates of profit, destroying the natural resources of the land, and turning its back on equality, cultural vibrancy, even the guarantee of basic social securities.

The swift replacement of these essentials by anticommunism and by dreams of an America-centered world underlines just how powerful the globalist vision had become. There is no question that in an America scarred by racism and sexism, an individualistic vision of rights had deeply appealing and profoundly emancipatory qualities. But locked into a globalist ethos, it encouraged a new American exceptionalism that would, in time, turn the United States from a soulful city on a hill into the glittering capital of the world.

HOW TO CONVINCE THE HAVE-NOTS?

If anticommunism legitimized the fundamental assumptions of the national security establishment, it was far less effective in providing a positive message for the rest of the world.[83] Fear was the organizing emotion of anticommunism: fear of a terrifying other, of conspiracy at home, of nuclear nightmare, of near apocalyptic conflict. "The negative task of exposing the gigantic hoax of Soviet Communism is important, and in many ways, more persuasive than any honest picture that can be painted of democracy and freedom," said Assistant Secretary of State Edward Barrett. "Hatred of a devil" has usually proved more potent than any affirmative element.[84]

Anticommunism was, so to speak, a negative ideology.[85] It functioned well enough to mobilize Americans at home and to justify the promotion of the evolving global order. It gave the United States a bludgeon with which to threaten European elites into overcoming their "parochial nationalisms," and it justified alliances with dictators as well as covert activities throughout the world. What it did not, and could not, do was promise the good life to desperately poor countries that rejected Communism. The United States "appeared to offer the status quo against the announced world-wide revolution of Communism," declared a Defense Department study of ideological warfare. "In attempting to counter this positive ideology of Communism, the United States has been forced into a defensive posture. Since our attitude is defensive, it also is negative. Being negative, it is weak."[86]

Invoking freedom was simply ineffective. "There is a 'World Revolution' going on 'out there,'" General George Marshall, former secretary of state and soon-to-be secretary of defense, warned in 1949; the Communists "were riding on the flood of the have-nots," as the triumph of the Chinese Communists—"the most have-not nation of all the have-nots"— made terrifyingly clear.[87] Washington's anticommunism, he continued, too often placed the United States in opposition to a worldwide revolution so desperate, so sweeping, and so motivated by hatred of Western colonialism that the Communists merely needed to channel this tumultuous process to their own ends. "I think it is easier for a camel to pass through the eye of a needle than for a country like our own to find language and approaches to people who have very little,"[88] George Kennan conceded.

Confronted with the Chinese Revolution, widespread postwar suffering, disintegrating but still determined colonial powers, and the declining legitimacy of capitalism overseas, Washington's fear of worldwide upheaval mounted to a fever pitch. In a world "economically divided roughly into two classes, the privileged and the underprivileged nations, the underprivileged must strive for change, any kind of change, as a chance to improve their condition," Kennan warned. That made for "an ideological terrain completely disadvantageous to us."[89] An assistant secretary of state under Truman laid out the problem more starkly:

You Washington people, from Truman on down, ought to quit prat-
tling so much about "liberty"—at least so far as my area is concerned.
What does it mean to the mass of people out my way? Not a blooming
thing. They are hungry. While we talk about liberty and freedom,
some Commie agitator comes along and says: "Under Communism,
you'll have plenty to eat. You'll own the land you now farm for someone else." The poor little native brightens up and says: "Oh, so that's
Communism. Well, I'm a Communist."[90]

Washington found itself torn between Asian demands for independence and European efforts to retain its colonial influence. "The deepest paradox of American foreign policy," complained an NSC task force,
was the United States' "anomalous position of being identified in Asia
as imperialistic and the supporter of Western European colonialism
and in Europe as hastening the break-up of colonial relationships."[91]
Even American generosity toward Europe posed problems with respect
to the colonial world: Washington was condemned for indirectly giving
the Western powers the means to regain control over their colonies. As
one Psychological Strategy Board study noted, "The Marshall Plan sub-
sidy was calculated in such fashion that the French could cover the
trade deficit of their colonies and carry out their investment programs
overseas. . . . The Marshall Plan consolidated, therefore, the fabric of
the French Empire."[92]

Even as colonization receded, the question of the have-nots and
staggering inequality remained. "The United States has been branded a
completely materialistic nation, as the exploiter of the world, grasping,
selfish, colonialistic, opposed to any relief for the world's economically
oppressed," concluded a national security study of U.S. ideological strategy.[93] Simply appealing to freedom reminded the have-nots of American
materialism—and often served to reinforce a belief that America's freedom and democracy flourished in part because of the West's ill-gotten
wealth.

To portray the United States as a developing cornucopia of modern
inventions often simply reinforced the stereotype that "Americans are
only interested in automobiles, electrified washing machines, TV and

automatic toasters."[94] While consumerism might tempt Europeans, who might soon be able to afford it, for the desperately poor it merely "calls attention to all the millions of cars, radios, bathtubs . . . we produce," one national security study observed.[95] After a meeting with Prime Minister Jawaharlal Nehru of India in 1949, Ambassador Loy W. Henderson reported to Washington, with considerable exasperation, that Nehru believed "the US was an overgrown, blundering, uncultured, and somewhat crass nation, and that Americans in general were . . . more interested in such toys as could be produced by modern technique and in satisfaction of their creature comforts than in endeavoring to gain an understanding of the great moral and social trends of the age."[96]

Further, the Soviets had long recognized "what we Americans have been slow to learn—that there are many nations where 'culture' isn't a politically abhorrent term and where intellectuals wield substantial power."[97] While America had a burgeoning popular culture and mass entertainment to offer the world, its high culture seemed dwarfed by that of other civilizations. America could vigorously promote its cultural exchange programs, and work to elevate the general comportment of Americans ("If American tourists must chew gum, they should be told at least to chew it as inconspicuously as possible"),[98] but in the early Cold War American cultural exports were more often part of the problem than the answer. Third World intellectuals, one official observed, feared they might "be swamped by American 'cultural imperialism'—by a way of life characterized by Coca Cola, cowboys and comics." They viewed Americans as "a brash, young, uncultured people." Hollywood, he added, "has not helped."[99]

Meanwhile, increasingly nationalistic countries were showing an unfortunate proclivity to challenge Washington's "global" vision— demanding, for example, control of their own natural resources and the operations of foreign capital in their lands. Throughout the non-Western world, these issues were increasingly posed in terms of imperialism versus freedom, or the status quo versus revolution, or a discredited capitalism versus state planning; in each case, the United States was on the side standing against social justice. And while opposition to revolution might make a convincing argument for Americans at home, "for most of the rest of the world it is no argument at all," a 1954 Department of Defense study pointed out.[100] The Communist doctrine of revolution was "positive and enthusiastic. Because it is positive, it also is inspirational. It generates fervor, hope, intense energy, and a will to fight." America might stand for freedom, but Communists were evoking equality, independence, solidarity, and community in the fight for independence and social justice.[101]

Consequently, the term "revolution" needed to be reappropriated. "No greater disaster could overtake us than that America should be made to seem to have lost—even rejected—its own revolutionary leadership in the world," the chairman of the Psychological Strategy Board warned. Americans, not Soviets, were revolutionizing the world, national security managers liked to say—its economic ways so dynamic, its ideas, science, and technology unsettling to traditional societies. True, Washington initially offered no *revolutionary* methods for countries to transform themselves, but this did not mean that the United States needed to tolerate the accusation that it was the antirevolutionary power. He went on to argue "that the industrial revolution beginning in England, and the democratic revolution, beginning in America, merged to form one continuous revolution—the twentieth century revolution—in which the individual remained free to express his creativeness wherever his motives, capabilities and choices led him." That put the United States "in the business of revolution."[102]

But merely recasting terms only went so far. A more positive ideology—an alternative capable of justifying an ever-deepening American penetration and transformation of other societies—was still needed. Such a doctrine would have to counter the Communists' "pseudo-scientific explanation of the plight of the under-developed world," a particularly difficult task because the Soviets could hardly be blamed either for the plight of peoples under colonial rule or for the promotion of an imperial economic global order. Third World leaders recognized Stalin's bloodthirstiness and the repressiveness of the methods with which the Soviets had industrialized, but this knowledge did not keep them from questioning America's global ambitions. When

U.S. Information Agency Director George Allen asked various Indians during a trip to New Delhi if they condoned the "ruthless colonialism" of the Soviets or their totalitarian internal policies, they told him no—

> but two wrongs never make a right. You Americans are shocked when we are neutral between the two of you. We are not neutral as between freedom and slavery, democracy and dictatorship, but we are neutral as between great power rivalry. We don't see the Russian fleet in Oriental waters. We see only the American fleet. We don't see the Russian Army in mainland China, but we see a good deal of the American army in Formosa, and Japan, and Korea, and Okinawa and the Philippines.[103]

MAKING ANTICOMMUNISM MODERN

Washington's response to these ideological challenges was to project the vision of a benevolent America as the pivot of a world ever more closely linked by "modern technology and communications, the common language of English, and the cosmopolitan customs of the younger generation."[104] A modernizing ethos dressed up anticommunism and freedom concretely and attractively in the garb of order, development, and munificent assistance on the part of the United States. Ideas batted around during World War II days—America's universality, the appeal of its popular culture, and the effectiveness of its mass communications, the creation of one world through the increasing flow of goods and ideas—were again taken up. Between the early Cold War and the 1960s the United States scored remarkable success in recasting itself as the embodiment of modernity.

By the end of the Eisenhower administration, modernization was being trumpeted everywhere as a new and progressive means by which to transform the poor and backward nations of the world.[105] Traditional imperialism had employed the language of power, conflict, and exploitation. Empire and conquest were what they were. (The conquered, it was often argued, were better off under civilized rule than left to themselves.) In contrast, the anticommunist modernizing ethos employed the vocabulary of international order, worldwide development, and foreign aid. American power—manifest in its military bases, its nuclear might, its triumphant economic system—was unique in the nonexploitativeness of its international but wholly magnanimous agenda. The global organizations America had created or supported (the International Monetary Fund, the World Bank, the United Nations) were there to assuage the "explosiveness of the modernization process."[106]

Once the Truman-Eisenhower years had successfully integrated the core capitalist regions of Western Europe and Japan into a Free World led by America, the pressing challenge for the Kennedy and Johnson administrations was to open this structure up to the Third World. From Cuba to Vietnam, demands for revolutionary change had to be confronted by the revolution of modernization that would expose the tyrannies and failures of Communist models of development. The domino theory suggested that the success of Chinese industrialization would threaten the West's interests in India;[107] a successful guerrilla war in Vietnam would threaten the rest of Southeast Asia; and any model of revolutionary social transformation (Cuba, Vietnam) was a menace everywhere. The danger was acute. As Lyndon Johnson put it, with the haves of the world becoming more affluent and "everybody else being impoverished," the have-nots "are going to take it home under their dress. They will come and get it in the nighttime. They will tear the window down to get it because women are not going to see their children starve."[108]

Communism, Walt Rostow noted in a 1962 NSC policy memo, offered "compelling strategies of development, for industrialization, for taking poor countries and making them over into self-reliant powers—however draconian the cost."[109] Yet Communism was not the fundamental issue—nor was anticommunism truly the point. The real challenge was the orderly development and incorporation of all nations into an America-centered globalism. "Even if Marx and Lenin did not exist, we would still have a problem," one Kennedy-era assessment echoed longstanding NSC opinion.[110]

Modernization offered the most sophisticated strategy yet. By using the American market to influence the character of development in the south, American officials hoped to create a single world economic system that would bridge the gap between north and south—and east and west. Reformist elites (with American support in updating their military and security forces) would gradually transform their homelands through trade with the United States and other capitalist nations, injections of foreign aid, and infusions of Western finance. Modernization offered Washington an alternative to supporting either the tottering colonial regimes or the forces organizing against them—a kind of third way. European colonialists, anticommunist modernizers argued, had opposed legitimate demands for independence while standing in the way of an emerging global market system. Now massive American backing for those seeking a path between feudal reaction and revolutionary transformation would help undermine potential alliances between revolutionaries and reformists, intellectuals, and technically educated professionals. Helping Western-inclined elites to modernize their societies would also draw them into the international marketplace—and revolutionary solutions would lose their appeal. This was, in essence, the Freud–plus–Santa Claus theory of foreign relations: persuade countries that underdevelopment was endemic to a society rather than foisted on it by a world system, then play up the benevolence of an America bestowing aid and technical assistance on them.

In effect, modernization took visionary globalism's proclivity toward reform, orderly process, and the rule of law—its hostility to revolution and populist nationalism—and fashioned these traits into a new fighting faith against mass mobilizations. Then it added an enticing array of additional ideological arguments. Being modern implied, for example, that self-interest was the most direct path to collective good; that development required full integration into an America-centered global order, rather than local control over resources and developmental patterns; that "closed societies" fueled the flames of nationalism that economically open societies assuaged.

For Washington this modernizing rhetoric became the perfect globalizing simplifier against revolutionaries of all kinds: radicals, extreme nationalists, anti-American leaders, mass-based populists, state centralizers. It provided updated code words with which to label all those who sought (some mildly, others strongly) to separate themselves from "healthy, moderating" inclusion in an American-led international system.[111]

The missionary ethos, Walt Rostow noted, lived on among his national security colleagues. "As individuals, most of us felt, I suspect, some kind of moral or religious impulse to help those striving to come forward through development. In that sense we were in the line that reached back a century and more to the missionaries from Western societies who went out to distant and often obscure places, not merely to promulgate the faith but also to teach and to heal."[112]

This was dazzling hubris. Leaders who knew little about change in the Third World (as a massive Johnson-era national security study of Asia stated, our "manipulators are sometimes crucially ignorant of those elements they seek to manipulate") and far less about "modernizing" other countries saw themselves as champion "nation-builders," ready to apply the strategies of political warfare and counterinsurgency to achieve their ends.[113] Modernizing in the face of the Communist enemy, in short, legitimized a far more pervasive and varied penetration than anything that had been available to early Cold Warriors.

A modernizing ethos presented another useful tool: a way to cope more effectively with the exasperating problem of intellectuals. As the ever-definition-prone NSC explained in the early 1950s, intellectuals were "a class of persons who were concerned critically and theoretically with and in behalf of certain social, political, philosophical and economic ideas, as differentiated . . . from those who are engaged in the actualities of direction or administration."[114] Touchy and hypersensitive to slights, they were psychologically drawn to the vistas of personal power that socialism and Communism promised. They were volatile, ideology prone, inclined to support state power, and emotional about the needs of the masses. Their attraction to simplistic ideas of equality, community, development, and fraternity even as they derogated freedom (a "common commie tactic") made them potentially dangerous opponents of American power. While intellectuals looked outward for the means to change their society, they were all too likely to turn inward to mobilize their people with revolutionary or at least intensely nationalistic methods. Communism's ideological persuasiveness—its vision of rapid state-directed development and local control over resources, its stress on education, women's rights, and health measures—appealed "to intellectuals in backward areas" in ways that left the national security managers near despair. Perhaps the "saddest fact of all" was that so many of "the greatest intellects should still side against us."[115]

But with modernization, the traditional role of the intellectuals could at last be challenged.[116] They could be marginalized, their generalized thinking about systemic problems dismissed as utopian and antimodern. The modernizing ethos was in fact largely crafted to appeal not to intellectuals but to the emerging middle class of professionals, bureaucrats, military officers, technocrats, academics, and businessmen. The real hope, as Arthur Schlesinger Jr. declared in a report on Latin America to President Kennedy, lay in a "middle-class revolution where the processes of economic modernization carry the new urban middle class into power . . ."[117] These pragmatic thinkers and problem solvers, market-attuned business leaders and professionals could lead their countries into the modern world.

Finally, modernization helped address another Cold War quandary: the taint of capitalism. "We are still having to suffer for the sins of 1850s capitalism in England," an early Cold War analysis lamented.[118] If capitalism in Europe had been largely discredited by the Depression and two world wars, in the underdeveloped world it was inseparable from the history of colonialism. As George Kennan told President Eisenhower in 1953, the Western powers (including the United States) were seen as "greedy and blind and disunited, bound eventually to fall out among themselves and to make a mess of things in those areas in which their influence is felt."[119] To address this perception, propagandists argued, "Our system needs a name," and for a few years during the Eisenhower era "People's Capitalism" was invoked—"Our side's answer to *Das Kapital*."[120] But only domestically did such rhetoric show much promise. In February 1956, some twenty-five thousand visitors passed through Washington's Union Station to view the much publicized U.S. Information Agency (USIA) exhibition on People's Capitalism, in which, for example, the sparseness of a 1776 house was contrasted with the prefab wonders of a modern American home. "The people themselves are the capitalists," USIA proclaimed.[121]

But an affirmative vision of capitalism was a tough sell in the rest of the world. A 1956 USIA survey of entrepreneurs in India reported distinctly unfavorable attitudes: capitalism, for them, was a system marked by exploitation, high unemployment, and a general lack of social responsibility. American propagandists thus set out to distinguish European capitalism ("cartel-like and feudalistic") from America's mixed economy, downplaying the capitalist vocabulary and instead stressing such words as "productivity" and "stability."[122] For this purpose modernization proved ideal. The Western business corporation, skilled in combining capital, technology, organization, and management, was turned into a model for drawing these nations into the global economic order.[123]

Significantly, though, modernization did not automatically mean democracy. While no one should doubt how dimly the United States viewed dictatorships in the long run, the short run was something else again.[124] "Too many people have been deluded by the theory that in the relatively underdeveloped countries the people value liberty more highly than physical security and their daily bread," a presidential committee on overseas communications wrote in 1960. "Such is not always the case. They in fact tend readily to tolerate a governmental structure that provides the latter even if it limits their liberties."[125]

In many transitional societies, conditions were "insufficiently advanced to recommend broadly-based political democracy."[126] Too many governments were "weak and inexperienced; they lack the attitudes and the administrative machinery to meet the problems of effective national unity, class discord, religious strife, tribal enmity, and economic growth."[127] In the modernization era these failing governments had to be propped up however possible in order to ward off Communist and other insurgencies.

This lament over the weakness and folly of indigenous forces of change runs like a red thread through national security reports. "I may be wrong," Kennan remarked in the Truman years, after examining Ho Chi Minh's leadership of the Viet Minh, "but I have not seen the evidence to make me conclude that these people are fit to govern themselves. I don't consider people fit to govern themselves who can't keep their own nationalist movement out of the hands of outside forces."[128] It was agreed that these forces of change could not be left on their own lest they become pawns of the enemy or of brutal anti-American elites. Thus Henry Kissinger's remark to Nixon on the 1973 Chilean election: "I don't see why we need to stand by and watch a country go communist due to the irresponsibility of its people. The issues are much too important for the Chilean voters to be left to decide for themselves."[129]

Lack of respect for others' sovereignty even extended to geographical unity. "The preservation of the unification of a country can have danger," Eisenhower warned the newly appointed U.S. Ambassador to Indonesia, adding that between "a unified Indonesia, which would fall to the Communists, and a break up of that country into smaller segments," he would choose the latter.[130] Or as Dulles complained, "We finally got a territorially integrated China—for whose benefit? The Communists'."[131] When American human rights leaders later questioned the necessity of territorial integrity in Yugoslavia, they were carrying on Cold War tradition.

The Cold War, then, was never about protecting—or even accepting—the sovereignty of other nations or the sanctity of the state but rather about finding ever more effective ways to break down barriers to American influence. It was always about penetrating other nations, which is why weaker nations were insisting then upon the principle of nonintervention in another country's internal affairs and have been ever since. Today such penetration no longer requires the Communist enemy that modernization did. A human rights or a democratizing ethos combined with nation building is usually sufficient. And it no longer needs to be quite so covert; it's part of the helping hand, no longer the hidden one.

UPDATING THE WEAPONS IN THE WAR OF IDEAS

Modernization, of course, no more eliminated international criticism of the United States than anticommunism had. The efforts of the 1950s and 1960s failed to save Washington from accusations that it had become the global center of an unjust economic order. "We are facing a revolt of the have-nots, particularly in Asia, Africa, and Latin America . . . ," complained a presidential task force toward the end of the Eisenhower administration. "They are largely immune to persuasion."[132]

One way the managers tried to strengthen the impact of the modernizing ethos was by pathologizing its opponents. Thus anti-imperialism was scorned as a disturbed projection onto Washington from a past that no longer existed. Anti-Americanism was a psychologically distorted response by intellectuals to the demands of a modernity more responsive to technical knowledge than to their sweeping solutions. Extreme nationalism combined xenophobia, anti-Westernism, and anti-imperialism under the aegis of insecurity. Self-reliance was a psychologically misguided ideal, intensely nationalistic and implicitly socialistic, that shut societies off from the international community. A closed mind was "frequently characterized by neutralism,"[133] itself a "symptom of only partially successful adjustment to living with far-reaching social, economic and political changes . . ."[134] Attraction to revolution and other radical solutions signified an irrational fascination with violence and a refusal to acknowledge that gradual change within a context of stability was a far more practical means of social development. And so on. Eisenhower wondered whether Nehru's blunt criticism of the United States might indicate he was "suffering from an inferiority complex," even "schizophrenia."[135]

In reality, the language of the oppressed reflected a fierce reaction to the appalling poverty and injustice in much of the post-1945 world. The fight for basic needs was often at odds with the "rule of law" and gradual reform. Some of the national security managers were occasionally attuned to these struggles; one wrote of "a vast reservoir of revolution" and added, "Nobody knows exactly what these . . . silent men and women think, feel, dream, or await in the depths of their being."[136] But such momentary understanding never led to much wider empathy for the emancipatory traditions opposed by Washington.

That is not to deny that revolution and violent change are frightening, cruel, and often intensely nationalistic. The weapons of the weak are seldom palatable: the car bomb, the explosion in the officers' club, the blade to the throat of the real or suspected collaborator. But such violence often arises from the desperation of people driven to the edge of survival, people who are seeking less to create a paradise than to destroy a hell. Mao wrote: "No one at the time of his birth was told by his mother to go for communism. . . . One was driven by circumstances. . . ."[137] Or, as Frederick Douglass once said, "To understand, one has to stand under."[138]

The writings of Washington's national security managers suggest they could hear the rumblings in the world they were managing. But, like the rulers and the privileged intellectuals among the Romans, they attributed these portents to the carping of the uneducated and the discontented, of troublemakers and extremists, rather than to the desperate, contentious, sometimes frightening and embittered efforts of the multitudes toward a more just and equitable order. The great Irish historian William Lecky once noted how strange it was that the rise of Christianity "should have taken place under the eyes of a brilliant galaxy of philosophers and historians [and] that all of these writers should have utterly failed to predict the issue of the movement they were observing, and that, during the space of three centuries, they should have treated as simply contemptible" the sweeping changes that were to come[139]—a demonstration of obliviousness that might give pause to imperial managers. But of course being insulated from such elemental realities is partly what imperial management is about. As J. M. Coetzee wrote in his novel *Waiting for the Barbarians*: "One thought alone preoccupies the submerged mind of Empire: how not to end, how not to die, how to prolong its era."[140]

By the late 1960s, the America-centered capitalist order had become immensely powerful, economic integration of the north and the south had advanced substantially, and the world was modernizing at a rapid pace. All of these developments once again called out for a major ideological updating of old Cold War nostrums. Fortunately, a critical change at home—the rise of the civil rights movement—provided the national security establishment with new ideological warfare possibilities. For decades, racism had been America's weak point.[141] "We cannot effectively champion noble causes abroad" without addressing the "shortcomings of our own society," went a typical lament.[142] International criticism of American racism had undoubtedly motivated earlier administrations to take a few steps toward desegregation, and U.S. information warriors used every little step to argue that things were improving. But before the rise of a mass civil rights movement, not much could really be done. Washington agonized over racial issues, but it was all it could do to get the State Department to begin to integrate itself.

The changes of the 1960s weakened segregation in the South and expanded over the next decade to a veritable rights revolution—black rights, women's rights, gay rights, minority rights, consumers' rights, prisoners' rights, and on and on. The USIA quickly molded these developments into an appealing vision of a rights-based individualism, a freedom to pursue one's opportunities in an affluent consumer culture. For decades Cold War propagandists had wanted to laud American "individualism" but knew that the word often conveyed a sense of narrow self-interest opposed to public and community spirit. Starting in the late 1960s, however, USIA campaigns began vigorously projecting an image of the modern individual freed from traditional constraints and outdated social hierarchies. Not surprisingly, though, the mass mobilizations of the civil rights struggles that had forced the expansion of individual rights never found much of a place in the USIA vision.

By the early 1970s, half the planet was within Washington's reach. Though the national security establishment had been shaken by the Vietnam War, the foundations of American power were still firm, and its globalist assumptions were increasingly public and seldom questioned by those under its sway. With the ending of the war, an even more audacious effort to order the planet waited in the wings. Its implementation required a new idealism—a "globally resonant message of a great power," as Brzezinski wrote to Jimmy Carter. And that was human rights.

2

THE CARTER YEARS:
AMERICAN FOREIGN POLICY
FINDS A SOUL

"Human rights is the soul of American foreign policy," President Jimmy Carter proclaimed in December 1978, on the thirtieth anniversary of the signing of the Universal Declaration of Human Rights.[1] In his inaugural address he had invoked human rights—"our commitment to them is absolute"—three times, more than all his predecessors in all their inaugural addresses combined, thus signaling the most important ideological transformation in the American foreign policy establishment since the rise of anticommunism.[2] Hawks and doves, Kennedy liberals and Goldwater conservatives applauded Carter's calls for a renewed American idealism and his crusading determination to move beyond the trauma of the Vietnam War. "The human rights issue is something you should hold onto without compromise," Rev. Billy Graham wrote him. "It is the first time since the War of Independence that we have really had an ideology."[3]

Carter's call for a new idealism based on human rights was a response not only to popular and congressional revulsion over the Vietnam War but also to pressing ideological needs in the national security establishment. "Holding high the banner of human rights" became a way to quiet the growing alarm that America's "arrogance of power," in Senator J. William Fulbright's phrase, reflected a global imperial ethos. The United States would again become a nation "for others to admire and to emulate," Carter promised, with human rights as a "beacon of something that would rally our citizens to a cause."[4]

Apparently "holding high the human rights banner" did not require looking too closely at the nation's actions in Vietnam. As president, Carter largely avoided mentioning war crimes and human rights violations in the Vietnam War—even such egregious ones as free-fire zones (where soldiers could shoot unidentified civilians at will), tiger cages (cramped cells in which prisoners were tortured), Operation Phoenix (for assassinating NLF members and sympathizers in the South), or the massive bombings of Vietnam, Laos, and Cambodia. Nor did he ever question American intentions: "we went there to defend the freedom of the Vietnamese," he insisted, "without any desire to impose American will on another people." Vietnam was "a moral crisis," he said, because we "stooped" to acting like Communists, "abandoning our own values for theirs";[5] but by reaffirming our values in the light of human rights, we could reestablish our claims to moral leadership. According to Anthony Lake, Carter's director for policy planning in the State Department, "this human rights business" was the "centerpiece of our effort to restore America's post-Vietnam, post-Watergate image around the world."[6] Henry Kissinger added his own approval, praising Carter for drawing on "a wellspring of American patriotism, idealism, unity and commitment" after the "traumas of Vietnam and Watergate, a renewed sense of the basic decency of the country, so that [we] may continue to . . . remain actively involved in the world."[7]

Human rights policy was a "no lose political issue," Carter's chief campaign speechwriter noted enthusiastically: "Liberals liked human rights because it involved political freedom and getting liberals out of jail in dictatorships, and conservatives liked it because it involved criticism of Russia."[8] It enabled Carter himself to reach across a Democratic Party split over whether to focus on the Soviet Union or right-wing dictatorships. Polls showed it was popular with the public; it made Americans feel good about themselves again. "[I] felt a particular need to reassure people that we were honest and benevolent and moral," Carter said.[9]

The ideological and strategic transition from the bipolar world of the Cold War required far more than simply recasting once again the old anticommunist ethos. By the late 1960s the motivating power of traditional anticommunism and its modernizing claims had faltered even within the national security world. "The old ideologies are losing much of their impact," a CIA study warned in 1968.[10] The Soviet Union had become economically inefficient, ponderous, and uninspiring to Third World countries. As one national security study pointed out, "the familiar rationale of American involvement—containment, dominoes, the Munich analogy, etc.—no longer fit the facts nearly as well as in a simpler period of East-West confrontation."[11] "We live in a complex age, and complexity does not lend itself to simple explanations," Brzezinski warned Carter in 1977.[12]

The human rights tack quickly demonstrated its ideological value. At the same time, its rhetoric reinvigorated a vocabulary of power suitable to extending American global dominance after the crises of the Vietnam years. From this point on, national security studies would argue both that human rights are universal and that they constitute the very foundation of American life. They turned America into a nation— indeed the only nation—whose "internal structure and dynamics make it organically congenial to lead that emerging process."[13] The binary vision of the Cold War—Free World versus Communist world—was breaking down. Now a plethora of rights, regulations, and laws were replacing the once relatively undifferentiated and abstract "freedom" of the Cold War years.

What is most fervently idealized often hints at what is most intensely repressed. The free-fire zones in Vietnam, the destruction of crops and forests, the search-and-destroy missions, the forcible removal of civilian populations, the terror bombing of undefended villages, the Phoenix program—all these outrages were decried by some political leaders and opinion page commentators as a betrayal of American ideals. Repelled by the waning old Cold War rationales ("dirty hands and good intentions"), critics began to direct human rights language against American as well as Soviet policies. Members of Congress, journalists, and antiwar activists documented the atrocities of American-backed military regimes from Chile to Guatemala, the Philippines to Angola.

Long-secret CIA operations to penetrate European and Asian governments, not to mention American political movements, were energetically exposed. Yet the more fervent their denunciations, the more passionately these critics trumpeted American ideals.

Whereas Soviet human rights abuses were systemic, ours were "mistakes," and the strength of our freedoms showed in their coming to light. Different frameworks materialized to evaluate the parties committing the atrocities. Human rights advocates saw the United States as a promising friend of the abused but withheld their sympathy from frightening revolutions and struggles whose claims might be just but whose methods were brutal. In this dynamic lay the origins of the first current of human rights, which viewed Washington as a global protector and the embodiment of human rights aspirations everywhere.

Paradoxically, as more and more ugly American deeds came to light, human rights advocates appeared less and less willing to regard them as reflections of anything endemic to American power. On the contrary, the growing popularity of human rights signaled the rise of a new faith in an idealistic American government.[14] Human rights seemed uncannily tailored to appeal to every political perspective. Cold War hawks invoked the notion against the Soviets, while doves invoked it just as enthusiastically against right-wing dictatorships. Senator Daniel Patrick Moynihan of New York recalled proposing that conservative and liberal Democrats compromise on their party's 1976 platform: "'We'll be against the dictators you don't like the most,' I said across the table to [activist Sam] Brown, 'if you'll be against the dictators we don't like the most.' The result was the strongest platform commitment to human rights in our history."[15]

Of course, there were a number of more critical voices. By the late 1960s, the Vietnam War had become the touchstone for a systemic critique of American power. Stripped of anticommunist rationales, America appeared to its most penetrating analysts less like a befuddled giant that had betrayed its ideals than like an imperial center surrounded by an obfuscating haze of good intentions. The criticism came not just from radicals. Cold War anticommunism, Senator J. William Fulbright had argued in 1966, cloaked a profoundly misguided drive for American global preeminence.[16] How could we even discuss these issues, he later asked, if "we cannot face up to this arrogant sense of our own superiority, this assumption that it is our God-given role to be the dominant power in the world?"[17] Referring to our highly militarized economy, he observed that "violence had become the nation's leading industry."[18] Fulbright urged Americans to turn away from invocations of America as "a city on the hill," a "beacon light," the incarnation of "the self-evident truths of man"—such rhetoric pointed toward "a superiority complex," he warned. "What this means in plain language is that we think we are better than anybody else."[19]

The dissenting voices—Fulbright, Noam Chomsky, Daniel Berrigan and Philip Berrigan—were diverse and compelling, but none was more eloquent than Martin Luther King Jr. Though King occasionally used the term "human rights," he insisted that the issues of aggression abroad and civil rights at home were indivisible. Indeed, the two currents of human rights, in his vision, were inextricable aspects of the demand for greater equality and justice. The Vietnam War itself was "but a symptom of a far deeper malady within the American spirit." Like Fulbright, King spoke of the deepening militarization of the economy and argued that when "machines and computers, profit motives and property rights are considered more important than people, the giant triplets of racism, materialism, and militarism are incapable of being conquered."[20] Because these were interrelated problems "deeply rooted in the whole structure of our society," a vision of human rights limited to the first current could barely touch them.[21]

The New Left protest movements had used little of the nascent human rights vocabulary—which is not to say that the language of the Universal Declaration on Human Rights was unknown to them or that there were not public invocations of human rights. Consider, for example, the minutes of a May 1967 meeting of the Student Non-Violent Coordinating Committee (SNCC):

> In our staff meeting held during the past week, the organization voted that the Student Non-Violent Coordinating Committee is a human rights organization, interested not only in human rights in the United

States, but throughout the world; that, in the field of international relations, we assert that we encourage and support the liberation struggle of all people against fascism, exploitation, and oppression. We see our struggle here in America as an integral part of the worldwide movement of all oppressed people, such as in Vietnam, Angola, Mozambique, South Africa, Zimbabwe, and Latin America.[22]

But such views were largely drowned out in the early 1970s, when the notion of America as the guardian of human rights began taking hold in the media and Congress. Although many who now adopted the language of human rights had strongly opposed the Vietnam War, they shrank from arguing that it represented, in Susan Sontag's words, the "key to a systemic criticism of America."[23] They preferred instead to see the war as an aberration, not a telling event with deep roots in American history.

WASHINGTON'S GLOBAL VILLAGE

Numerous labels—"postindustrial society," "information age," "global village," "consumption community," to name a few—contended to encapsulate the arriving era. They all entailed versions of a global "implosion," as Marshall McLuhan liked to call it, in which psychic, social, economic, and political parochialism would disappear. "Transnationalism," as Samuel Huntington (soon to join Carter's National Security Council) wrote in 1973, was not only the "in term" but also the preeminent "American mode of expansionism."[24]

The writings of the national security managers in the 1970s show a growing excitement about a new and unprecedented porousness between the nation-state and the world. They examined the spread of mass communications, computers, and consumerism for their potential to overcome earlier problems of "development" and "modernization" and break open previously restrictive or "closed" nation-states. At times their observations recalled the great nineteenth-century American revival movements. "Society, the world, must be melted down in a common crucible, or else the moral elements will still remain heterogeneous, disassociated, and discordant,"[25] one shrewd observer had written in the 1830s, in words eerily compatible with 1970s visions of American "universality."

"This country's commitment to international affairs on a global scale has been decided by history," Brzezinski argued.[26] The United States was the first and so far the only "global society," its "cultural and economic boundaries difficult to delineate."[27] Third World intellectual elites could now be encouraged to develop stronger ties to a global "nervous system" than to their own nations, to think in more "individualistic," "cosmopolitan," and "consumer oriented" ways. Radical intellectuals habitually defended the sovereignty of their people; now a more cosmopolitan spirit could be attractively packaged to promote individual rights in those societies for professionals and members of the middle class.[28] The revolutionary intelligentsia, who had embodied one of the most perplexing challenges of the first three decades of the Cold War, with their "simplistic methods" and their nonmarket economic solutions to their countries' staggering problems, had now been effectively "left behind."[29]

Al Jenkins, an old CIA China specialist, had prophesied to Walt Rostow in 1968 that "the electronics-communications explosion will increasingly riddle curtains, I'm having interesting talks on this, as will the coming *world* stock market (faster and cheaper travel), and truly futuristic *personalized* global communications. . . . Pressure for global cooperation should prove immense . . . and should in time affect the Communist faiths where they play fancy with fact. Even Mao (or his successors) will have to succumb to the 'revisionism' of the modern world of communications, science, and info flows."[30] Now American influence had acquired a "porous and almost invisible quality," Brzezinski declared. "It works through the interpenetration of economic institutions, the sympathetic harmony of political leaders and parties, the shared concepts of sophisticated intellectuals and bureaucratic interests. It is, in other words, something new in the world, and not yet well understood."[31]

NSC studies explored how such changes could enable the United States to penetrate closed societies resistant to incorporation in the global market. "Closed" was a marvelously useful word. It could refer to countries seeking greater economic independence from the United States (creeping autarky) or to those continuing their contacts with the Communist bloc. "Closed" might also suggest resistance to American mass-media influence or efforts to control local resources and patterns of investment. As Secretary of State Edmund Muskie said in 1980, "Human rights and closed societies are incompatible . . . the contrast between our system and the closed societies of our adversaries is dramatically visible."[32] From a national security perspective, no nation could be open if it was free from American influence. And nothing bred closedness faster than revolutions, nationalist movements, expropriation of foreign corporations, and populist authoritarianism.

"Openness," on the other hand, was code for the burgeoning operations of the multinationals. "Down with borders," a revolutionary slogan from the 1968 Paris uprising, became a slogan of IBM. Washington viewed the rapidly increasing prominence of transnational corporations as the linchpin of an emerging "global community." It supported corporate campaigns for a global marketplace opposed to rigid national borders and protectionism, and it sought to calm popular fears of transnationals. The scholar-activist Richard J. Barnet's pathbreaking series of articles in the *New Yorker* in 1973 on the rising multinational corporations shrewdly depicted an emerging corporate elite attacking the barriers of the old nation-state with advertising campaigns leveled against cultural differences, protectionism, and hostility to border-crossing businesses. In this new world, goods, capital, and ideas needed to flow easily. The goal, said Barnet, was a "global shopping center" geared to "a world customer."[33]

Yet even if Communism was losing its appeal by the early 1970s, radical nationalism and sweeping demands for change were not. Nationalism, warned the CIA, could bring with it the "nationalization of foreign-owned enterprises, reservation of key economic sectors for government; or local control, demands for employment of indigenous personnel in foreign-owned firms, increasing controls over new foreign investment, restrictions on profit remittances, rising tax rates, demands for reinvestment of a rising share of profits, and so on."[34] Human rights organizations often speak of challenging state sovereignty, but Washington has long known that the real issue is a people's demand to determine its own future—especially if it is hostile to American power.

THE FIRST STIRRINGS

Human rights issues had first attracted impassioned attention a few years earlier. By 1968, a small movement was developing in the Soviet Union. The Soviet dissidents were a galaxy of courageous, determined, and articulate individuals with an impressive range of views. They compiled evidence of rights violations by the oppressive and repressive Soviet system in graphic detail, speaking not just for intellectuals but also for Jewish refusniks (Jews denied emigration), Pentecostals, and others. They wrote often—and extremely well. CIA studies conceded that the group was tiny and elite; nonetheless, these suffering scientists, intellectuals, writers, and artists were inspiring to the West.

Several developments heralded the growth of the movement: the creation of the Initiative Group for Human Rights; the Trial of the Four, instigated by the Soviets to stop the publication of dissident materials; yearly demonstrations on Moscow's Pushkin Square; and a growing *samizdat* tradition of underground literature. In 1968 the Soviet nuclear physicist Andrei Sakharov's *Thoughts on Progress, Peaceful Coexistence, and Intellectual Freedom* was smuggled to the West and published, and this event—not responses to atrocities in Vietnam—marks the real beginning of the human rights ethos in the United States. *Samizdat* became the backbone of the Soviet movement,[35] and the *Chronicle of Current Events*, a *samizdat* journal that offered meticulous information on political prisoners and other persecuted figures (Alexander Solzhenitsyn, Pyotr Grigorenko, Vladimir Bukovsky, Anatoly Marchenko), documented "the history of the total moral defeat of [Soviet] organs of power,"[36] as Sakharov later wrote. The *Chronicle* fearlessly named names, identifying KGB interrogators and presiding judges. Individual accounts of courage and protest circulated widely in Europe and quickly made their way back into the Soviet Union, in part through traditional CIA-funded apparatuses like Radio Free Europe/Radio Liberty in Munich.

What really brought these events to American public attention, how-ever, was the issue of Jewish emigration, which emerged after the Israeli victory in the June 1967 Six-Day War. The American Jewish community had organized for decades against the Soviet government's harsh restric-tions on Jewish cultural expression; but now the right to emigrate became the center of debate in the United States and the subject of numerous articles in the *New York Times* and the *Washington Post*.

In 1968 the *Times* published eighty-four items on human rights, nearly half on the plight of Soviet Jews. By 1971 the number had risen to 430, some 80 percent related to Soviet Jews. Congressional leaders, aca-demic organizations, and professional societies began to speak out.[37] "As you read this newspaper," one ad addressed the plight of the Soviet Jews, "live with the knowledge that [the Soviet] government would rather have them liquidated. Think about that for a minute. They live with the knowledge that their government would rather have them liq-uidated."[38] Senator Jacob Javits of New York called for justice for Soviet Jewry as a precondition for expanded trade with the Soviets. But it was Senator Henry "Scoop" Jackson of Washington and his aide, Richard Perle, who fused the issues of trade and emigration into a formidable attack on détente itself. At a meeting with Jewish leaders in September 1972, Jackson announced his plans for legislation linking the two issues and called upon his listeners to challenge Nixon's policies toward the Soviet Union: "You want to know what you can do? I'll give you some marching orders. Get behind my amendment. And let's stand firm."[39]

The Jackson-Vanik Amendment pushed human rights to the fore-front of the growing Congressional debate over U.S. relations with Moscow. Sakharov wrote an open letter to Congress in the fall of 1973 (the same year Solzhenitsyn's *Gulag Archipelago* was published) arguing for the withholding of trading rights while repression con-tinued, and warning of massive reprisals against Russian Jews if the world ignored their plight. Members of Congress who favored détente and trade found themselves on the defensive. "This is the most emo-tional issue I've ever been involved in," Florida Democrat Sam Gibbons said.[40] Nixon himself pleaded for "quiet diplomacy" ("Look here!" Nixon told Arthur Burns. "If we'd raised that issue . . . they'd say, 'All right, we're going to talk about your Negroes!'"),[41] while Jewish leaders (often quietly) applauded the increasing numbers of Jews allowed to leave the USSR. Jackson's real goal, Fulbright later argued, was "sabotaging Nixon's détente," and in this he achieved a "sterling success."[42] He had astutely mixed power politics, the SALT negotiations, détente, and Jewish emigration, and once he did, the anti-Soviet cast of the official human rights world came into full focus.

Meanwhile, another area of human rights concern was developing. In August 1973, shortly before the U.S.-backed coup against Salvador Allende in Chile, Congressman Donald Fraser of Minnesota initiated a series of hearings in his House Subcommittee on International Organizations on the relationship of human rights to U.S. foreign policy. The subcommittee eventually examined massacres in Bangladesh in 1971 and Burundi in 1972; widespread torture in Chile, Brazil, Uruguay, and South Korea; and South African apartheid. In all these cases, it found Washington's response "lacking in view of the magnitude of the violations committed."[43] The "prevailing attitude" of the administration, it said, favored "power politics" at the expense of human rights, leading Washington "into embracing governments which practice torture and unabashedly violate almost every human rights guarantee pronounced by the world community."[44]

Congress, led by Fraser and other liberals, but with the support of conservatives who saw human rights as a way of challenging Communist governments (and reducing foreign aid), created a broad legislative base for U.S. human rights policy over the next four years. In 1973, it passed a sense-of-Congress resolution that the "President should deny economic or military assistance to the government of any foreign country which practices the internment or imprisonment of that country's citizens for political purposes."[45] Three years later it passed the Harkin amendments, withholding assistance from any country regularly practicing human rights violations (unless granted a presidential waiver) and obliging the United States to cast its vote against loans to such regimes by the Inter-American Development Bank and the African Development Fund.

The State Department objected, offering its standard rationale that the United States never interfered in the internal affairs of other nations, but pointedly adding its real concern—that the United States traditionally "avoided active intervention in foreign countries' affairs for the sole purpose of promoting these rights."[46] A government's human rights violations "are seldom clear and beyond reasonable dispute."[47] Thus the State Department tried to circumvent legislation requiring American officials in any country receiving American aid to report on the local human rights situation by arguing that such violations were so rampant that there was "no adequate objective way to distinguish which countries were more reprehensible than others."[48] Still, Congress wrote these reports into the law. The tide was turning. Even Henry Kissinger began inserting human rights language into his speeches—some fifty times in 1976, his last year in office.[49] But his memoirs convey a more accurate gauge of his interest in the subject: there are only two references in the index.

The issues raised in the early congressional hearings have reverberated ever since. Were rights universal and thus to be applied across the board in American foreign policy? In principle, double standards were deplored repeatedly in committee discussions and congressional debates. Yet, as a former U.S. Representative to the UN Commission on Human Rights testified before Fraser's subcommittee, "we speak out against violations of countries we are not particularly close to or where we feel we can do so with some measure of safety politically, and we are largely silent, as are other countries, when human rights violations occur on the part of our allies or friendly countries we do not wish to offend."[50]

By the same token, when Communist and Third World leaders criticized the United States for violating human rights in its treatment of Allende and its support of right-wing regimes, congressional leaders were quick to write these attacks off as opportunistic. By what right did nations with political prisoners criticize the United States—or Israel? "We should rip the hides off everybody who presumes to talk about prisoners," UN Ambassador Moynihan admonished—"shame them, hurt them, yell at them."[51] A commitment to human rights was becoming a form of patriotism, a higher kind of loyalty. When Representative Fraser and 104 other members of Congress wrote Secretary of State

Kissinger urging him to take gross violations of human rights into account in his foreign policy calculations, they cited "the traditional commitment of the American people to promote human rights."[52] Professions of a renewed faith in America appear in almost every congressional report on the country's involvement in human rights abuses, including the Church Committee's 1975 report on Chile.

To Nixon and Kissinger, the threat of Chile had lain in its relatively democratic effort to radically transform its socioeconomic structure—to free itself from the economic domination of the United States by nationalizing key industries, and by mobilizing poor and progressive groups. This was a policy of development that sought, however contradictorily, to bring the two great currents of human rights together. "I don't think anybody ever fully grasped that Henry saw Allende as being a far more serious threat than Castro," one former Kissinger aide reported. "Allende was a living example of democratic social reform in Latin America."[53]

In its 1975 report, the Church Committee charged the Nixon administration and the CIA with imitating "KGB tactics," adopting "the methods" and "the value system of the 'enemy,'" and employing "all the dark arts of secret intervention—bribery, blackmail, abduction, assassination."[54] Broadly speaking, U.S. policy had sought to "maximize pressures on the Allende government to prevent its consolidation," to limit its ability to "implement policies contrary to US and hemisphere policies," and thus to destroy "its attractiveness as a model" of sweeping reform. Nixon, it found, had ordered CIA Director Richard Helms to bar the popularly elected Allende from taking office or, failing that, to "bring the Chilean economy under Allende to its knees."[55] "Not a nut or bolt will be allowed to reach Chile under Allende," the American ambassador in Chile had told Kissinger. "Once Allende comes to power we shall do all within our power to condemn Chile and the Chileans to utmost deprivation and poverty, a policy designed for a long time to come to accelerate the hard features of a Communist society."[56]

But for all its bluntness, the Church Committee remained largely silent about the reasons for these strategies. The CIA operations were noted, yet human rights advocates in Congress and the media largely avoided probing too deeply into the reasons for Washington's antipathy to Allende's attempt to combine the two currents. "Why Chile?" asked Church. "The country was no threat to us. It has been aptly character-ized as a 'dagger pointed straight at the heart of Antarctica.'"[57] The question remained unanswered.

What the Church report does underline, however, is the waning ability of the old bipolar worldview to justify—or at least overlook—human rights abuses. "Deniability" became less and less effective as images of atrocities from faraway places flooded the American media. In Congress, unlike the national security world, "ideology" was not a favored word. Instead a "new morality" was needed to replace discred-ited Cold War thinking. "The remedy is clear," Senator Church con-cluded. "American foreign policy . . . must be made to conform once more to our historic ideals, the same fundamental belief in freedom and popular government that once made us a beacon of hope for the downtrodden and oppressed throughout the world."[58]

EARLIER CONCEPTIONS

Calls for this "new morality," for a "reinvigorated idealism," fostered the idea of America as a rights-based nation, its influence great enough to bring an international human rights regime into being. With virtual unanimity, human rights advocates in Congress and the media insisted the United States was so exceptional that if Washington actually com-mitted itself to human rights it would rise above that "arrogance of power" that had corrupted all great powers in the past.

The national security managers now came up with a new narrative of American history—as a step-by-step triumph of human rights. Admittedly, these rights had had "a long hard climb," Carter's deputy secretary of state, Warren Christopher, told a Senate subcommittee. We had progressed "from religious freedom through the Bill of Rights, the abolition of slavery, universal suffrage, the four freedoms, the civil rights movement and the struggle against poverty to the equal rights amendment"; our course was now "firmly set" and offered an "example to the world."[59] American rights and the UN covenants "are identical in spirit,"[60] Carter maintained at the UN in 1977. The United States was no longer simply the leader of the Free World; it had become the embodiment of an international society reflecting all that is best about a commitment to rights.

In reality, this vision of a rights-based nation was both propagandistic and ahistorical; it effectively erased any appreciation of America's earlier, more contentious, sometimes quite radical uses of the phrase "human rights," rooted in challenges to the inequalities of American life, the power of corporations, and the dangers of uncontrolled capital. Early religious thinkers and the Founding Fathers, abolitionists and suffragettes, opponents of corporate power and of the money trusts, and presidents and the media had all, at one time or another, invoked "human rights."

Revolutionaries and foes of slavery and other forms of tyranny, for example, had advocated rebellion and even violence in the name of rights and justice. "Are the people ready to say no chains ought to be broken by violence, and no blood spilt in defense of inalienable human rights, in any quarter of the globe?"[61] demanded the abolitionist William Lloyd Garrison in 1842. "I do not harbour the feelings of revenge. I act from principle," thundered John Brown in 1859. "My aim and object is to restore human rights."[62] Brown's contemporary, the theologian Theodore Parker, wrote that "one held against his will as a slave has a natural right to kill every one who seeks to prevent his enjoyment of liberty."[63] All these calls for radical struggle presented a frontal challenge to the nonradical cast of the emerging human rights movement. "John Brown was right," concluded W. E. B. Du Bois at the end of his magisterial biography of the abolitionist. Only civil war, violence, and radical struggle would rid the nation of slavery.

That Brown became such an iconic figure provides food for thought. His cause was taken up by some of America's most famous intellectuals and writers—Emerson, Thoreau, Theodore Parker, Eugene V. Debs, Clarence Darrow, Langston Hughes. His biographer, David Reynolds, has pointed out that not even Washington or Lincoln was as widely recognized in drama and song.[64] When Julia Ward Howe wrote "The Battle Hymn of the Republic" to the tune of "John Brown's Body," changing

"His soul goes marching on" to "His truth is marching on," she blended the idea of a just god and the acts of a radical reformer into a trope of American folklore.[65] The concept that one man's terrorist is another man's freedom fighter is not alien to the American tradition. It haunts it for good reason.

Human rights were invoked both for and against an American empire—a debate again largely dropped later on (along with the term "empire"). In 1900 the Republican Party platform resolutely defended the struggle in the Philippines as a "war for liberty and human rights," while William Jennings Bryan warned that such "imperialism disregards human rights"[66] and Massachusetts senator George Sewall Boutwell denounced the view that the Filipinos were uncivilized and incapable of independence as "a criminal view of human rights."[67]

Presidents embraced the same language to justify their foreign policy objectives. When Woodrow Wilson declared war on Germany, he spoke of "the entrance of our own beloved country into the grim and terrible war for democracy and human rights which has shaken the world. . . ."[68] His praise of America as the embodiment of human rights was at least as bold and assertive as Jimmy Carter's would be sixty years later. "America will come into the full light of the day when all shall know that she put human rights above all other rights, and that the flag is the flag not only of America, but of humanity," Wilson declaimed. "What other people has devoted itself to this exalted ideal?"[69]

Capital and property rights were often contrasted with human rights—a dichotomy rarely invoked after the mid-twentieth century. Indeed, it was once so commonplace that in 1910 even Theodore Roosevelt could state, "We must place human rights before property rights."[70] Congressman Charles Lindbergh wrote in 1913 that we must "unsaddle from our back the system of capitalism that now dominates the world in conflict with human rights."[71] A former senator charged in 1922 that lawyers were, by means of the Constitution, the laws, and the courts, promoting a system of "property first" against "human rights."[72] Emma Florence Langdon, a founding member of the International Workers of the World, complained in 1904 that the "domain of human rights has been contracting under the arrogant and untrammeled sway of corporate might, and pirates of the sea of commercialism, drunk upon the wine of opulence."[73] Capital, the critic William Allen White weighed in in 1910, "opposes all the restrictions placed upon it essential for the enlargement and protection of human rights. . . . As the rights of man enlarge, the rights of property in so far as they are antagonistic to human rights are clipped."[74] This chorus from the American past would send no echoes into the debates of the 1970s.

Just how narrow and constricted the view of human rights later became is clear in the light of questions that the French thinker and activist Simone Weil raised in her pathbreaking 1942 essay, "Against Human Rights." Rights, she argued, were Roman, contractual, bound to the power of the state. When divorced from the fulfillment of human needs, they become all too useful to the imperium of law in extending its sway over multitudes. (By contrast, "the Greeks had no conception of rights . . . they were content with the name of justice.")[75] The tradition of rights, she warned, emerged from a world of exchange and measurement; they entailed a "bargaining spirit," a "commercial flavor, essentially evocative of legal claims and arguments." Rights may be easier to envision individually, but they are less encompassing than "human needs," which involve more complex challenges of equality and fraternity, a deficit that "was already implicit in the notion of rights which the men of 1789 so unwisely made the keynote of their deliberate challenge to the world."[76] Rights thus remain tied to traditions of law, power, and the state, making them in the end unable to cope effectively with "injustice, lies, and ugliness." They are alien to Christian inspiration in its opposition to Roman power. ("One cannot imagine St. Francis of Assisi talking about rights.") They are, indeed, about power—whether state or individual—and not about love, fraternity, and compassion. To say "I need this" has a different tone and draws on different qualities of experience than to say that something is "my right." Rights, Weil concluded, are fueled more by indignation than by compassion, more by anger than by love.[77] There remain fundamental dimensions of human goodness that confer respect, that involve feelings and actions unspecifiable when confined to the civic and legal language of rights.[78]

In the civil rights and peace movements of the 1960s, both rights and needs became briefly interwoven in challenges to the established order. But by the mid-1970s, the language of needs and the mass mobilizations that set out to transform the structures of wealth and power had receded.[79] Hence the Carter administration marks a sharp movement toward rights talk and away from a commitment to greater equality. Carter never sought to echo Lyndon Johnson, who said: "We seek . . . not just equality as a right and a theory, but equality as a fact and as a result."[80] The New Deal ethos was now under full-scale attack, the safety net weakened, the zeal for a Great Society gone. If the new human rights ethos embodied a new idealism, it was an impoverished one that tacitly accepted the growing extremes of wealth and power at home and abroad.

THE NEW IDEOLOGICAL WARFARE—AND ITS LIMITS

At first the Carter administration deemed only bits and pieces of a human rights agenda suitable to draw on. The concept, Brzezinski told the president, "lacks intellectual depth."[81] But soon enough he recognized its potential for a revitalized assault on the Soviets and their Communist doctrine. The United States "would no longer be seen as defending the status quo nor could the Soviet Union continue to pose as the champion of greater equity."[82] Human rights had become "the genuine historical inevitability of our times," Brzezinski argued—a new doctrine essential for providing "a rebuttal to the Communist doctrine of the historical inevitability of class revolution."[83] History, in short, was on our side.

"Freedom" had been a single, highly generalized word during the early Cold War. "Human rights," by contrast, became the center of a phalanx of ideas: economic and social rights, the rule of law, a free press, respect for ethnic diversity, the integrity of the individual and of elected governments. It offered a way to break freedom down into discrete parts and then codify them, developing new buzz words, analogies, and legalisms that could all claim to reflect American universalism. Not everyone was free, but every individual had rights, and these could be set forth with a precision never before possible.

A handful of Carter's advisors recognized that human rights violations flourished in societies with especially grotesque levels of economic inequality, and that these issues of deprivation also needed to be addressed. Those "forced to live in poverty, hunger, and sickness" cannot really be free, said Andrew Young, Carter's ambassador to the UN. While advocating for the importance of civil and political rights in his 1978 speech to the General Assembly, Young stressed their secondary importance for populations threatened with starvation and destitution. He soon found that such views were not appreciated in Washington.

Prioritizing the first, essentially legalistic, current of human rights was one way of handling a world that was hurtling into greater inequality. At the beginning of the Carter administration the CIA had pointed to the "driving force of egalitarianism"[84] as a potentially disruptive phenomenon both within and among nations. The size of the gap between rich and poor nations had doubled since 1960 and was still increasing. Demands for equality might lead to nationalization of corporate holdings, to local claims on resources, to state-driven development. Non-Western nations were calling for a "new economic global order"—a serious threat, the CIA warned.[85] The drive toward egalitarianism presaged a growing conflict between "ethnocentric nationalism and geocentric technology," in the words of one 1971 report, and thus a serious challenge to multinational corporations.[86]

To make matters worse, the explosion in mass communications was creating, in Brzezinski's words, a "heightened awareness of global inequality" that was bound to "unleash intensified social strife."[87] The mass media offered a vision of a world community enveloped in a spreading consumerism, but only for those able to participate in it; most of the world's population had no hope of getting the kind of jobs that would give them access to such consumption.

The first current of human rights offered a way for a wealthy, consumerist society to still associate itself with what Brzezinski called "a vital human concern." Otherwise, he wrote Carter, "America runs the risk of being perceived" only as "a consumption-oriented society, making us the focus of envy and resentment."[88] The challenge was to shift attention from increasing inequalities to political and individual rights. There was a bonus to this strategy: pontificating about "rights" as such did not require the United States to *do* anything about them. "I am skeptical about announcing far reaching new initiatives re world health or economic development," Brzezinski continued. "The world already expects too much of us and too little of rich Arabs."[89]

The language of rights, then, came to legitimize a penetrating, moderating approach, an ideological alternative to radical changes of all kinds. An emphasis on rights was seen as a way of defusing rightist repression—and thus of undermining radical responses to such repression, ensuring a future for peaceful, "constructive" transformation. Individual human rights became, in the words of a Carter administration document, a "shock-absorber for change."[90] At the same time, this rights vision served to de-legitimize various nationalist and economic challenges to American power. It also offered the means to share an ethos with elite groups in a range of societies—businessmen, scientists, religious leaders, educators, women's rights advocates, journalists—who in turn could reinforce trends toward a "global community." All this was very much in the interest of the United States, and it had some practical advantages. In the past, the United States had had to develop links with opposition figures covertly and quietly. Now political dissidents and human rights advocates had excellent reasons for frequent and overt contact with American officials.

The Soviet Union was an early test case of this new strategy. "The Carter administration," Robert Gates, a former CIA director and the current secretary of defense, has written, "waged ideological warfare on the Soviets with a determination and intensity that was very different from its predecessor" by attacking "the legitimacy of the Soviet government in the eyes of its own people."[91] CIA studies and national security memoranda pointed out that dissident intellectuals, Pentecostals, and Jewish refusniks were starting to support one another, and other religious and ethnic groups were showing signs of increased political activity. In Eastern Europe, Moscow faced rumblings of renewed nationalism, the lure of Western consumerism, and increased dissident activity;[92] in

Western Europe, there were increasing attacks from Eurocommunists who had themselves taken up human rights issues and support for dissidents.

The CIA was not in any doubt about what was aggravating Soviet domestic problems: the president and his administration's personal appeals on behalf of Soviet dissidents.[93] "Spurred by a sense of Soviet vulnerability to Mr. Carter's policies," one analyst observed, the Soviets— "disoriented" and "unsure how to react"[94]—were attacking him more fiercely than all his recent predecessors.[95] Dissidents were becoming "endemic to Soviet society."[96] "Stalinist terror" was no longer a viable strategy, but détente was rife with dangers, too. A 1977 CIA memorandum summarized the situation: "The emergence of dissident activity throughout Eastern Europe since the beginning of 1976 has added a new dimension to the problems of East Germany and Poland. It is linked in the Soviet view with the behavior of dissidents in the USSR as a single challenge which the West is encouraging against the existing order in the East."[97]

Carter administration officials were divided, and Carter himself torn, over how to level their ideological attack while negotiating with the Soviets on other issues. There was a kind of doublethink in Carter's conviction that invoking human rights did not infringe on Soviet "internal affairs." He could have argued that of course they did—and rightly so. But he shrank from this admission, even as he increased budgets for Radio Free Europe/Radio Liberty and supported Brzezinski's intensification of covert warfare in Eastern Europe (hand in hand with Pope John Paul II, a Pole committed to human rights). Carter criticized the Nixon–Kissinger notion of "linkage"—of making progress in one area dependent upon progress in another—yet his own policies were a commonsense form of linkage through human rights.

The national security managers were also willing to pressure right-wing as well as left-wing dictatorships—as long as they were not facing serious radical challenges. Carter repeatedly attacked Nixon's support for Pinochet's Chile, and his administration took some limited steps to rein in Pinochet's human rights atrocities. Similar efforts resulted in the release of some political prisoners elsewhere. Assistant Secretary of

State Patricia Derian proved a highly articulate voice seeking action in Indonesia, Argentina, and a number of Central American nations, often making far more vehement arguments than most of the Carter administration wanted to hear—or act on. As Assistant Secretary of State Richard Holbrooke put it, "a small but vocal group of people now sought to carry out far-reaching changes in the world structure. . . . They sought change we could not control, with potentially dangerous results both for our national strategic interest and in fact even the interests of the people involved. By their excesses they gave the opponents of true human rights a certain unfortunate claim to legitimacy."[98]

The cases of Pinochet's Chile, Argentina, Brazil, and South Korea all support the notion that even modest human rights pressure came from Washington only when the stability of a regime was not seen as endangered. By contrast, those of Nicaragua and Iran starkly illuminate how such pressure could transmute into clashes with nationalistic revolutions, whether from the right or from the left. When Carter took office, the revolutionary Sandinista movement was threatening the right-wing regime of Anastasio Somoza in Nicaragua. Somoza was a corrupt, brutal dictator, but Washington was reluctant to end its support because he was a pro-American counter to the left-wing Sandinistas.[99]

The question was whether to pressure Somoza to reform or simply push him out of office. In the latter case, Carter's initial hope was to keep the Sandinistas from taking power, exclude them from a transitional government, and marginalize them in a post-Somoza coalition under a middle-class reformist leadership. If Somoza were removed, Secretary of State Cyrus Vance explained optimistically, "the Sandinistas would probably lose their basic appeal and become a marginal splinter group."[100] Assistant Secretary of State for Inter-American Affairs Viron Vaky elaborated: "perhaps some outside catalyst might be able to promote this process so that the choice does not develop into that radical polarization of just Somoza on one hand and the extremists, who are willing to take violent action," on the other. The goal was a "moderate third choice"[101]—a "middle way" that, Carter thought, would be far more attuned to his vision of human rights. But the middle class proved too weak and too compromised by its links with the Somoza regime to provide a viable alternative to the popular Sandinistas. Time had run out.[102]

A few voices within the administration spoke out against suppressing the Sandinistas. Neither Patricia Derian nor Andrew Young, who had both been leaders in the civil rights movement, feared the revolution, nor did they believe the Soviets or Cubans could easily manipulate it; besides, they argued, instability and revolution were unstoppable at any acceptable cost, and Central Americans should be allowed to forge their own political futures. As Young pointed out, self-determination was a critical part of any concept of human rights. But such views were dismissed by officials worried that a Sandinista victory would extend leftist influence in the region and that the administration's conservative critics could then proclaim Nicaragua "the new Cuba of the Western Hemisphere."[103]

Once the Sandinistas came to power, Carter sometimes adopted a more conciliatory public tone. At the same time, he quickly signed an intelligence finding that provided for covert action, as Gates later wrote, "focused primarily on propaganda, exposing what the Sandinistas were all about, and the Cuban role in supporting the Nicaraguan revolution."[104] As an increasing number of officials denounced the Sandinistas for human rights violations, the United States began building up the military and intelligence infrastructure to engage in a war against them and support the right-wing counterinsurgency movement in El Salvador.[105] In Gates's words, "The foundations of U.S. policy and actions in Central America in the 1980s were put in place by Jimmy Carter—and well before the [Soviet] invasion of Afghanistan."[106]

Left-wing revolutionary movements were not the only challenge to Washington's emerging human rights doctrine, as its reaction to the Iranian revolution—waged by a coalition of religious fundamentalists, leftist radicals, and middle-class reformers—vividly illustrated. The Shah of Iran was a notorious violator of human rights, yet on New Year's Eve 1977 Carter toasted his great leadership of "an island of stability in one of the more troubled areas of the world."[107] The Iranian Revolution erupted a week later. As it gained momentum, the Carter administration became deeply involved in keeping the Shah in power. Presidential advisors were split between Brzezinski's "iron fist" call for the Shah to institute martial law and Vance's more accommodative conviction that repression would prove ineffective.

As the revolutionaries triumphed, Carter announced that "it is our hope that these troubled people will create a stable government." As with Nicaragua and Vietnam, he argued that past American actions and policies had little to do with current relations: "We have done nothing for which any American need apologize,"[108] he insisted. "We have never tried to decide or to determine for the Iranian people or any other people on Earth who their leaders ought to be or what form of government they should have since I've been in office."[109] He left unmentioned CIA involvement in the 1953 Iranian coup as well as the wasteful, corrupt "development" over which the Shah had presided for decades with enthusiastic American support. Nor did Carter show any empathy for Iranian anger or understanding of the injustice that was fueling revolution. He spoke instead, as national security managers long had, of the regrettable "ability of the relatively few militants, who had deep and fervent commitments, to succeed against an all-powerful military force and an entrenched government."[110]

In Washington, Senator Jackson joined a growing chorus in attacking the new Iranian leadership for its application of summary justice and other human rights violations. Kissinger agreed, blaming Carter's human rights campaign for undermining the Shah's regime.[111] The travesty the Shah had made of human rights, however, was barely acknowledged. When asked in 1978 by Bill Moyers about the Shah's police state, Carter blandly replied: "I think the Shah has had that criticism, sometimes perhaps justified—I don't know the details of it."[112] He offered no real explanation to Americans as to why the Iranians had rejected not just the Shah, but American influence as well. After November 4, 1979, when the U.S. embassy in Tehran was seized, the Carter administration quickly came up with the terms in which to frame the issue of the hostages and their incarceration: it was a "flagrant violation of elementary human rights."[113]

THE INTERNATIONAL RIGHTS REGIME

An effective ideology requires that its advocates be capable of ably wielding it both at home and abroad. In the words of Anthony Lake, U.S. human rights efforts were shaping "a growing international lobby which combines its influence with our own."[114] The Carter administration promoted numerous international human rights treaties. Carter signed and sent to the Senate the International Covenant on Economic, Social, and Cultural Rights, the International Covenant on Civil and Political Rights, the American Convention on Human Rights, and the Convention on the Elimination of All Forms of Discrimination Against Women; he also urged the ratification of the UN Genocide Convention and the Treaty for Elimination of All Forms of Racial Discrimination. The Senate had acted on none of these treaties by the time he left the White House, but his advocacy nonetheless advanced what administration officials called an international rights regime. Carter's support for strengthening the UN Human Rights Commission and for creating a UN High Commission for Human Rights were understood as useful steps in Washington's new rights agenda.

The creation of independent human rights groups to complement Washington's concerns had clear benefits from the American point of view. In a speech before the American Bar Association, Deputy Secretary of State Warren Christopher proposed setting up an international human rights database, adding that since the data collected by any one country, including the United States, would be "suspect," what was needed was "an objective, widely respected clearinghouse for human rights information on all countries of the world."[115] His speech was a trial balloon based on discussions within the administration that gained urgency after the London-based Amnesty International received the Nobel Peace Prize in 1977.[116] The issue was not control over human rights groups per se so much as influence. Brzezinski wrote Carter laying out the reasons for setting up a human rights foundation that could deal with congressional concerns when Washington did not support human rights in a specific country. After all, he pointed out, American government exhortations on the topic "often conflict with other legitimate foreign policy objectives." But mobilizing private American groups and establishing a quasi-governmental organization funded by Congress could create a "*positive, action program for human rights* comparable, say, to the activities of AID to promote economic development." (The comparison with the U.S. Agency for International Development is illuminating: few agencies have more busily involved themselves in the internal affairs of other nations.) The overall strategy, as Brzezinski summarized it, was to spread the concepts that needed to be nourished in the national security bureaucracy via the "echo chamber" of foundations, academia, existing organizations, and international groups.[117]

In Brzezinski's view, human rights required a "solid intellectual base" as well as basic research on "the varieties of human rights" and their promotion in "diverse social and cultural contexts"—not to mention research on the ways various rights interacted with one another, the relevance of each in different countries, and feedback on how well policies were working. The government could not effectively do all this on its own. Conferences, consultants, academic and university research centers, and think tanks all had a role to play in Washington's emerging human rights strategy. A nongovernment but government-funded foundation could develop ideas and provide "the central direction, support and motivation for a successful, and relevant, scholarly effort."[118] It could also "funnel money to international human rights organizations, as well as to national human rights organizations operating in other countries and in the US based on the value of their work."[119] Human rights groups could act where it would be "inappropriate" for the government to do so. Of course, the NGOs, while deserving support, had to be "insulated from direct dependence" on the U.S. government to better promote "a worldwide constituency for human rights." The United States Information Agency could publicize materials about appropriate situations, but credibility would be far greater if "sponsored by an institution with some autonomy from the U.S. government," Brzezinski went on, echoing long-standing propaganda practice. Such institutions, along with a growing number of NGOs, could "provide direct help and psychological support for dissidents within their own societies . . . helping to finance the publication and distribution of suppressed works."[120]

"Multi-lateralizing," as this strategy was termed, did not mean losing control of the agenda. Just the opposite: American foundations and NGOs could energize the UN Human Rights Commission, help evolve harmonious policies with other Western nations and NGOs, promote regional human rights groups in Africa, and provide a voice "independent from, and in some cases more credible than, the U.S. government" in the Third World. Annual prizes could be given, a "clearing house for information" established, annual reports on trends issued, and international and national conferences supported.[121]

There were more subtle benefits as well. Decades before human rights leaders called for a "broad concept" of rights to encompass economic and cultural issues, key national security leaders had seized on the ideological utility of such an approach—though some Carter administration officials remained skeptical, warning that if the definition of rights "ever gets so broad that it also includes milk for Hottentots, its usefulness will be lost."[122] This was not a difference between hawks and doves; hawks like Brzezinski were advocates of the broadest definition of rights. Human rights, he wrote, "means also certain basic minimum standards of social and economic existence. In effect, human rights refer to all three (political, social, and economic). . . ." Appearances to the contrary, he was not embracing the second current but rather recasting needs as rights in precisely the legalistic, power-affirming sense that Simone Weil had warned against. This broader definition, Brzezinski wrote, was "highly advantageous" in that "it would retain for us the desirable identification with a human cause whose time has come, and yet it would avoid some of the rigidities that are potential in the narrower political definition."[123] With everything now becoming a question of "rights," the old dichotomies between political rights and revolution, individual rights and economic needs—between the first and the second currents—could be replaced by an all-encompassing vision that stressed change through the evolutionary, gradualist methods of the first current alone. All these basic human needs had been codified in the UN covenants, all could be classified as "rights"—and so all could fit into the language of legal obligation and lawful process, reinforcing the underlying sense of step-by-step, nonviolent, nonradical change.

Almost all these ideas were in place by the Reagan years, which saw the creation of the National Endowment of Democracy and a host of other government initiatives. Foundations, think tanks, NGOs, and universities were thus encouraged to fund human rights work and to facilitate its intellectual development, promote conferences, encourage journals and publications, and develop a global network of rights workers. Washington's promotion of a global human rights constituency fit quite smoothly with its image of the United States as the preeminent rights-based nation. This promotion was quite bold in its frank acknowledgement of its benefits to American foreign policy interests, but it was also subtle in the way it perceived that even fierce debates in the United States over human rights could shape international debate in a manner ultimately favorable to the United States, turning the first current of human rights (however much Washington might violate it in practice) against the second.

THE NEW AMERICAN ORGANIZATIONS

Of the various human rights groups that came to flourish after the Carter years, two are particularly significant for the scope of their work: Human Rights Watch (which began as Helsinki Watch) and Amnesty International.

In 1975, thirty-five nations signed the Helsinki Accords, aimed at improving relations between the Communist bloc and the West. Thereafter a number of conferences were held to oversee their progress. Carter appointed Arthur Goldberg—former Supreme Court justice, UN ambassador, lawyer for the AFL-CIO, and longtime advocate of human rights—as his ambassador to the 1978 Belgrade Review Conference. Goldberg returned in great frustration. While a wide range of issues had been discussed, he had found few of his European counterparts willing to confront the Soviets about their obvious abuses of human rights in violation of the Helsinki Accords. The conference ended with little more than an agreement to meet again in Madrid in 1980.

Goldberg set out to foster different results the next time around. None of the long-standing U.S. organizations that had spoken of human rights, like Freedom House, were independent enough of the government to operate effectively. The world's leading human rights organization, Amnesty International, which had been founded in 1961, was not even American—it was based in London. Goldberg approached Robert Bernstein, the president of Random House and an outspoken advocate of the freedom to speak and publish, with his idea: "What this country needs is its own Helsinki Group. Would you folks be willing to form one?" Bernstein declined, explaining that raising the necessary resources for his Fund for Free Expression was challenging enough. Goldberg next approached McGeorge Bundy, former national security advisor and by then the president of the Ford Foundation, to which he had brought his own interest in funding human rights work. In the summer of 1978, after meeting with "dozens of people in the government and in the nonprofit sector to get their views," the foundation came up with a small planning grant to set up a U.S. Helsinki Watch Committee.[124] In January 1979, it granted another $400,000. Once the funding was in place, Bernstein came aboard as cochair.

Over the years Helsinki Watch expanded into regional committees (Americas Watch, Africa Watch, Asia Watch, Middle East Watch), and in 1988 these committees united to form Human Rights Watch. From its beginnings the group has been emblematic of the American human rights organizations that formed in the late 1970s and early '80s.[125] It was not mass based; tactics associated with the civil rights and antiwar movements of the 1960s, and with the earlier struggles to organize labor and to obtain women's suffrage, had no place in its evolving strategies. Rather, it was an elite organization, an NGO with a board of directors and a paid staff quite unlike the movement organizations of a decade before. Its natural constituency was to be found in the worlds of power and influence—among politicians, journalists, jurists, union leaders, and academics. Its principal aim was to pressure the United States and Soviet governments into acting in accord with the organization's human rights objectives. As sociologists like to say, it lived by "tree-topping" tactics aimed at other elites, not grassroots mobilizing of large constituencies. Its leaders were primarily upper-middle-class professionals—from publishing, law, journalism, and Wall Street—with highly developed communications skills and discretionary time and income to devote to international issues. Most of them traveled widely, especially in Europe, and moved amid the elites and intellectuals of many countries. They generally felt comfortable with the idea of multi-culturalism and had long supported civil rights.

They shared another trait with many of those in the top reaches of American power. As Jeri Laber, executive director of Helsinki Watch, later wrote, "We had something in this country that we were proud of, our freedoms, and we could without any embarrassment export them to the rest of the world and we were so happy to see a government, a President [Jimmy Carter] who recognized this and was going to take the moral high ground, which we felt we deserved."[126] Such an organi-zation might have seen in this kind of idealization of America a systemic ideological problem. It might have combined support for the genuine freedoms that do exist in the United States with an investigation into why American power often operated so brutally and exploitatively. It might have acknowledged that America was no more immune than the great powers of the past to the "arrogance of power." It might have explored the flaws in a system that had supported the Vietnam War for a decade. And it certainly might have raised—even years later—issues of accountability, war crimes, and reconciliation vis-à-vis Vietnam, as they would be raised in other nations for other crimes. But while some members undoubtedly shared these concerns, the organization's official view was quite different. "It's hard to recreate how idealistic and how exciting it was," Jeri Laber has written, "because we really felt we were on the side of the gods. We were creating a new ideology from precepts we believed had long been forgotten, a belief in the essential dignity of the human being as defined in our country's founding documents."[127] Or as Robert Bernstein said in congressional testimony in 1981: "[We] believe that the entire ideology of the United States depends on human rights. . . . We should be exporting our ideology. It's not obnoxious to speak about our ideas, and to tell people we think they are great and that other countries should follow them."[128]

Helsinki Watch had another characteristic in common with many American leaders: its anticommunism. Laber had worked as foreign editor of the *Current Digest of the Soviet Press* and then as publications director of the covertly funded Institute for the Study of the USSR.[129] The Soviet dissidents often sought out the assistance of foreigners, and they added a fillip to the human rights leader's anticommunist idealism. Repelled as they were by Soviet power, they found it hard to be critical of American power. (Vietnam looked different from the perspective of Moscow and St. Petersburg: Solzhenitsyn said in his 1978 commencement address at Harvard that American antiwar resisters had "became accomplices . . . in the genocide and the suffering today imposed on thirty million people there.")[130] The Helsinki agreements had changed their status, for by signing them Moscow had made itself *legally* liable when charges of abuse were lodged by Western governments and activists. The Kremlin continued to declare such charges propaganda, but now it was harder to dismiss specific accusations as nothing more than reflections of U.S. government interests.

Still, as Helsinki Watch worked closely with dissidents in the USSR and Eastern Europe (particularly Poland and Czechoslovakia), it found itself emulating long-standing American government practices. To use a word that became popular later, this dynamic raised issues of transparency. The Kremlin often accused Soviet dissidents and Western human rights organizations of having links with British intelligence and the CIA. There was little mystery for those who really wished to know where Radio Free Europe and the Eastern European and Soviet émigrés who nourished its broadcasting and translating operations got their funds. Moscow dealt constantly with the smuggling of *samizdat* materials out of the USSR—which were then broadcast back into the Soviet Union over CIA-controlled radio stations. Journalistic accounts of the dissident's trials, which received little publicity in Eastern Europe and the USSR, were aired in detail on the Voice of America and Radio Free Europe.

Memoirs and comments by some Soviet dissidents make it clear they were well aware that they were receiving help of various kinds from Western governments—creating problems of integrity that have bedeviled rights activitists ever since.[131] Understandably, few dissidents chose to discuss these issues. The KGB was eager to accuse them of precisely

such collaboration, from the passing of *samizdat* all the way to treason-
ous cooperation. Some foreign reporters certainly knew the score, but
they rarely included it in their stories. As one former CIA member put
it, "East European and Soviet dissidents didn't have a problem with CIA
backing."[132]

In this case, transparency was to no one's benefit except that of the
Soviet authorities. Was it appropriate for Helsinki Watch representatives to accept American government aid while entering Eastern Europe
under false pretenses in order to establish connections with local dissidents? Was it wise to use U.S. embassy facilities to further human rights
work? The list of questions is long, but the problem is clear: independence from Washington. Helsinki Watch worked more or less openly
and in parallel with U.S. government strategies, and knowingly or not,
it and other human rights groups had the strong support of some of
Washington's shrewdest operatives. They may have sought to embody
the conscience of an era, but their origins were not entirely free of John
le Carré intrigue.

And another odd note: Helsinki Watch repeatedly claimed that the
abuses it documented had been largely ignored. But in fact there was a
vigorous tradition, still thriving in the 1970s, of exposing the ugliness
of the Soviet system and its oppression of Eastern Europe. AFL-CIO
publications, *Reader's Digest*, Radio Free Europe and its associated radio
stations, Jewish publications detailing Soviet anti-Semitism, books and
articles cataloguing the horrors of the Stalinist past and its bastardized
forms of repression in the present, congressional hearings, the *New
York Times* and the *Washington Post*—the list goes on and on: none
were shy about reporting the plight of countless beleaguered individuals or publicizing Solzhenitsyn's views after he received his Nobel Prize
in 1970. There was never any lack of awareness about the repressive
nature of the Soviet regime. So why did activists trumpet Helsinki
Watch as a rousing new call to arms? Partly because it offered an inspirational appeal that seemed to go far beyond the old Cold War ethos; by
claiming human rights as a new and moral approach, it could set itself
apart from earlier arguments and tactics.

Compared with the publicity long accorded Soviet acts, the right-wing abuses that Donald Fraser's congressional subcommittee exposed in the 1970s—and the involvement of U.S. advisors in so many of them— received little attention, though there was more reason for them to be shocking to Americans. "The Uruguayan Government couldn't survive 24 hours if it were left alone before the people," a former Uruguayan leader testified against the military regime there. "It survives because it is being kept in power artificially." This was not a matter of simply suspending American military assistance but of the United States "ceasing to be the aggressor."[133] Such testimony rarely made it into the media, and when it did it was simply overwhelmed by all the Soviet repression stories. Moreover, Soviet and Eastern European dissidents emerged as *individuals* far more than did those from other lands. Few Americans could name any dissidents from Latin America, South Korea, or the Philippines. Even those who were briefly prominent, such as the Argentinean journalist Jacobo Timmerman, had no impact comparable to that of Sakharov, Solzhenitsyn, Natan Sharansky, or Yuri Orlov. No other dissident group ever fit in quite so well in Washington—or in the American media.

There was, in fact, another path that human rights organizations could have taken—the one that Amnesty International did take. Amnesty was, significantly, European. (An American branch, Amnesty USA, was created in 1966 but was not fully functional until the early 1970s, and even then, Americans who joined tended to see themselves as part of the London-based group.) The story of its founding is now legendary. In 1961 Peter Benenson, a British barrister active in political causes, was moved by the plight of students incarcerated for speaking out under the right-wing Salazar dictatorship in Portugal. His call for an amnesty for political prisoners led to a firestorm of public response, and with it the beginnings of the organization. Its complicated subsequent history has been told several times[134]—the internal conflicts that soon developed; the funds from British intelligence, for which one of its early secretaries had once worked.[135] Yet despite these problems, the group retained a powerful inspirational quality.

Amnesty's creators saw great-power rivalry and Kennedy-era calls for fighting for freedom as deeply cynical. Benenson and his colleagues sought to stand apart from those attitudes by raising their voices against torture and the incarceration of political prisoners everywhere. They were speaking for those "who are tired of the polarized thinking which is the result of the Cold War and similar conflicts but who are deeply concerned with those who are suffering simply because they are suffering,"[136] Eric Baker, another founder, later said. Amnesty's objective was not to answer the question "Why are people suffering?" but to help the sufferers. Torture was a particular focus; since few if any governments sought to justify it, it could be opposed across the entire political spectrum. Like genocide, torture was in a different category from other violations. "No great political subtlety is required in order to oppose it."[137] Nor was an exact definition of the term necessary for it to be grasped, at least in those days.

The word "amnesty" is revealing. Benenson had considered "armistice"—a noun more directly attuned to ending the Cold War and overcoming its stultifying mind-sets. Yet "amnesty" drew on other provocative associations that are noteworthy in light of the later human rights emphasis on accountability, criminal responsibility, and legalistic language. While "amnesty" implies that a crime had been committed (the ruling authority can pardon past offences), "armistice" suggested for Berenson an intentional putting to rest of past disputes, a resolution possible only by letting go of old battles, "a unique worldwide opening of the prison doors for those jailed for their beliefs."[138]

The sad fact, Benenson argued, is that "there is no area of the world where people are not suffering for their beliefs and no ideology which is blameless."[139] This conviction was enshrined in the early Amnesty years by the requirement that local groups balance the political prisoners they campaigned for—one from the West, one from the Communist bloc, and one from the Third World. A scathing 1978 editorial in the *New York Times* attacked this rule that no more than a third of the victims championed could come from Communist countries as a "parody of evenhandedness . . . worthy of George Orwell."[140] But to Amnesty's founders, any other stance would have betokened a return

to the debilitating immorality of the Cold War. Amnesty further stipu-
lated that its members could not campaign for prisoners from their own
countries—an effort both to gain greater freedom from Cold War distortions and to bring in a perspective from the outside. There was, in
Amnesty's view, a moral equivalence among prisoners—a perspective
reinforced by its insistence that it took no position on the nature of governments, only on their actions against nonviolent political prisoners.

The concept of "prisoners of conscience" perfectly fit this idealism.
As Benenson wrote a friend, Amnesty was about "rekindling a fire in
the minds of men," creating "a sense of belonging to something greater
than oneself, of being a small part of the entire human race." For those
who had witnessed the "eclipse of socialism," for youth searching for an
ideal, for those weary of the bleak Cold War, Amnesty was an organization that sought to free not only prisoners in jails but also those
"imprisoned by cynicism, and doubt." The term "prisoners of conscience,"
suggesting something more than being jailed for the right to speak or
protest, captures this spirit. "Conscience" implies at least some awareness by the prisoner of having done something knowingly. The moral
weight is on the side of the prisoner, who attains a certain moral stature
by standing in judgment of the society and the government that has
done the imprisoning. It is contrary to hate and wrath; when one is
conscience-stricken, the impulse to act springs less from anger than
from love. This was not the rights-based individualism that was to blossom in later years, but language that echoed Gandhi, Martin Luther
King Jr., and Saint Francis: empowerment that comes with a sense of
connection with others through action for others—a notable founding
sentiment.

What, then, constituted a "prisoner of conscience"?[141] The term does
not appear in the 1948 Universal Declaration of Human Rights, a document on which Amnesty, in any case, did not much draw in its early
years. Prisoners of conscience could not be advocates of violence—such
advocacy, Benenson believed, led back into sterile Cold War disputes.
But this definition posed problems, like the painful controversy over
Nelson Mandela, who did plan acts of sabotage and who defended at his
trial in 1964 the right of the African National Congress to violently

overthrow apartheid. He did so not "in a spirit of recklessness, nor because I have any love of violence. I planned it as a result of a calm and sober assessment of the political situation that has arisen after many years of tyranny, exploitation and oppression of my people by the Whites."[142] Thus, by Amnesty's definition, he could not be a prisoner of conscience. Neither could the Berrigan brothers, who had burned draft board files as an act of opposition to the Vietnam War.

Benenson himself worried that the refusal to acknowledge anyone as a prisoner of conscience who "advocate[d] or condone[d] personal violence" might be going too far. Wasn't the implication that "we deny anyone the right to express a view which is intended to stir up violence or antagonism? We don't go so far as that, do we? All we mean to say is that we see no reason to rub the flesh off our knuckles getting a man out of gaol, when his purpose is to put other people into gaol."[143]

What then, of civil disobedience? Was a refusal to pay taxes to be supported? (Yes, taxes for the military.) Was a refusal to carry out military orders to be defended? (Yes, as in the case of Capt. Howard Levy, the American dermatologist who refused to train Green Berets for service in Vietnam.) What of dissidents who were not jailed yet faced dismissal from their jobs, disruption of their correspondence, verbal threats, police interrogation, and character assassination in the press? (No, as in the case of Sakharov, who became a prisoner of conscience only when placed under detention.)

"Purity of heart is to will one thing," wrote Kierkegaard. Perhaps in the end this sentiment is what still resonates from the admirable passion so evident in the founding years of Amnesty. Benenson left the organization in the mid-1960s, and the views of its new leader, Seán MacBride, leaned less toward advocating for prisoners of conscience than toward turning Amnesty into a kind of "Red Cross for political prisoners."[144] Still, the group's animating vision was never reducible to the language of rights. Amnesty, conscience, the search for a stance above (not between) two warring parties, avoidance of ideological wars and old animosities—these notions are of a purity not to be dismissed. But the contradictions that flow from such a stance are more illuminated than resolved by such purity—as is evident from the way the emerging movement dealt with the aftermath of the Vietnam War and the mass killings that were unleashed in Cambodia.

A NARROW VISION

Vietnam and Cambodia exposed the limitations of these new organizations. Few of their leaders focused much on the long-term issues posed by the Vietnam War. None looked back to Nuremberg to raise the charges of crimes against peace or war crimes. It fell to other groups to raise the issues of mass slaughter and nonviolence vis-à-vis the war, most notably the American Friends Service Committee (AFSC), whose Quaker spirit recalls that of the early Amnesty.

Founded in 1917 and the recipient of the 1947 Nobel Peace Prize, the AFSC had long been committed to social justice, peace, and humanitarian causes. The Vietnam War posed a particularly acute challenge by bringing up key questions that the human rights movement had assiduously avoided. Should all violence be condemned? Should the response be a call for a plague on both houses? How could one relate the war to other struggles in the Third World, such as the battle against apartheid? The AFSC's executive secretary spelled out the challenge in 1975: "All too frequently, in human experience, wars of liberation have been fought with lofty courage and high idealism only to result tragically and ironically in the rebirth of tyranny with new tyrants in charge." Revolutionary violence would not build a new, just society; but the answer was not to simply denounce violence but to advocate for a kind of revolutionary pacifism. "The necessity to be nonviolent must be urged with passion, and persuasion, *not* upon the oppressed revolutionaries, but upon those who oppress them, and upon the accomplices of the oppressors." Many of the governments that were fighting rebellions in the Third World were corrupt, vicious states employing far greater violence than that leveled against them. "To put it simply: We believe in nonviolence and in revolution and therefore in the possibility of nonviolent revolution. We understand that the oppressed do not share our faith in nonviolence. We have given them little reason to do so."[145] The task, in part, was to reduce direct American "domination and/or

American support for their oppressors, and this, in turn, will serve to minimize the violence which they feel compelled to use to reach their goal." The AFSC did "not support the violent means used by the NLF and Hanoi, but we do support their objective in seeking the liberation of Vietnam from foreign domination. . . . Clearly one has to distinguish between the violence of the Americans—which is criminal—and that of the people of Vietnam—which, by contrast, is tragic."[146] Few human rights leaders enunciated comparable views.

If the issue of aggression and war crimes in Vietnam was largely ignored after the war, in the case of Cambodia Washington altogether washed its hands of responsibility for what transpired. The national security managers dismissed any connection between the bloodbath caused by the American war and the campaign of mass murder by Pol Pot's Khmer Rouge that followed. Cambodia, for them, was an instance of "autogenocide"—the suicide of a people in the name of revolution— and it encapsulated all the dangers of radicalism, ardent egalitarianism, and Third World nationalism that the United States insisted it had been fighting throughout the Cold War.

Not surprisingly, Carter hardly mentioned Cambodia in his memoirs. The word "hypocrisy" barely begins to cover his administration's support for Pol Pot's insurgents as they fought the Vietnamese invasion in 1979, followed by support for the Khmer Rouge's retention of Cambodia's UN seat—even as it denounced Khmer Rouge genocide. As one historian concludes, "nothing indicates that the administration gave any thought whatsoever to trying to prevent Pol Pot from resuming his murderous role."[147] Indeed, when Assistant Secretary of State Richard Holbrooke, testifying before Congress in March 1979, called for the withdrawal of Vietnamese forces from Cambodia, he said nothing about how the Khmer Rouge would be prevented from resuming control. Instead, attention became focused on the flight of the boat people, a great embarrassment to Vietnam. That many of the Vietnamese refugees were fleeing from Cambodia was largely ignored.

It was easy enough for human rights leaders to denounce the crimes of the Khmer Rouge. What was far harder was acknowledging American responsibility for what had happened. And yet already at the time of the American invasion and bombing of Cambodia in 1970, witnesses of the flight of peasants to Phnom Penh to escape the B-52s and the shattering of their traditional livelihoods were warning of the horrors such brutalization might bring in its wake. In the end, this was another awful chapter in the very old story of how savage warfare not only destroys a society but also opens the way for the rise of a small, fanatical, brutal leadership capable of horrific atrocities rationalized by ideology. Lenin's and Hitler's rise to power is grim evidence, if any is needed. To unleash wars of such ferocity without taking responsibility for the consequences is to fail to understand what Nuremberg was all about—and why aggressive war is the supreme crime.

Senator Fulbright was one of the few in the Washington establishment to speak about the Vietnamese and the war in the former Indochina with compassion:

> We ought not to be punishing them. Our conscience should impel us to conciliation at every opportunity. The argument that what happened since the end of the war shows the harsh, totalitarian nature of the regime we were fighting misses what is important. The real point is that what happened was largely the *result* of the war. It destroyed the old, traditional government and customs and practices. The war came close, politically if not physically, to doing what General LeMay once proposed—bombing them back to the Stone Age. I think what has happened is a direct result of the war and of what we did in that war.[148]

Carter never spoke in such terms. The Vietnam War was "embarrassing"; our reputation was "soiled," our "cleanness and decency" blemished. "Mistakes" had been made. Nothing more need be said. And by and large the new human rights leaders followed Carter's lead. There was a chilling precedent, of course. Europeans spoke tearfully of human rights after the Holocaust and then utterly ignored them in the colonial wars of the 1940s, 1950s, and 1960s. In both cases, the rise of human rights left plenty of room for historical amnesia.

On the other hand, many human rights leaders echoed Carter's impassioned attack on the Soviet invasion of Afghanistan in 1979, which he charged with "violating human rights in the grossest kind of way. Hundreds of Afghan freedom fighters are dying every week. . . . Entire villages are being wiped out. . . . Terror tactics, including the use of chemical weapons, are the trademark of the ruthless attempts to crush Moslem resistance and to install a Soviet form of peace—a peace of brutal armed suppression."[149] "Virtually every known crime of war is taking place there, and on a scale so vast it defies imagination,"[150] added Helsinki Watch leaders. Such language would have been just as suitable to Vietnam. But as the mantra went, Vietnam was an American "mistake." Afghanistan was what the Soviet Union was all about. Once again, the statements of American human rights organizations about Afghanistan offer little that resembles Fulbright's verdict: "the truth of the matter is when you look at our actions, as distinct from our loftily expressed self-conceptions, it is difficult to see much difference between our actions in Vietnam and the Russians in Afghanistan."[151]

At the crux of the matter is power, its operations in the world, and what it would mean to expose its ways consistently and without partiality. As the human rights ethos came to the fore during the 1970s, Congress, the media, and the fledgling organizations preferred not to take too hard a look at how American power really operated. This was a formative beginning. For, as James Baldwin warned, "Ignorance, allied with power, is the most ferocious enemy justice can have."[152]

3

THE REAGAN ADMINISTRATION:
DEMOCRATIZATION AND PROXY WARS

During the presidential campaign of 1980, Ronald Reagan specifically attacked Carter's human rights policies. They had "undercut our friends," he charged, by demanding unrealistic reforms; they had weakened the Shah when he most needed our help, failed to prevent the rise of a "Marxist left" government in Nicaragua, and distracted American attention from the dangers of Soviet military power. His own administration came into office with no clear conception of what to do about human rights. As Assistant Secretary of State for Human Rights and Humanitarian Affairs Elliott Abrams later explained, the thinking on human rights was dismissive: "This is no good—throw it out." But after toying for several months with Secretary of State Alexander Haig's recommendation that "anti-terrorism" be made the moral center of American policy (because, he reasoned, "terrorism is the ultimate abuse of human rights"),[1] Reagan opted for folding Carter's human rights policies into what the new administration termed "democratization."[2]

Just as the ideology of anticommunism had brought national security strategizing and American idealism together at the beginning of the Cold War, democratization linked human rights and American national interests in the Reagan years. For too long, Abrams later testified, U.S. human rights policies had proceeded "almost exclusively along a negative or reactive track" that focused on individual violations rather than the undemocratic systems that encouraged them. "The goal of human rights deserves more," Reagan said; it deserves a more positive-sounding "second track": democracy promotion. As Abrams explained, "democracies have the best human rights records." Going down both tracks, he said, would take us beyond the symptoms so that we could treat the disease itself, "promoting the formation of democratic systems in which human rights abuses simply are not tolerated."[3]

By transmuting the old anticommunist vocabulary into the language of democratization, Reagan's national security managers adeptly justified a number of once covert methods of infiltration and penetration, such as payments to influence elections and the local media, as simply what an overt commitment to democratizing required. Building new institutions was the key: free universities, a free press, trade unions, free elections. "Civil society," "leadership training," "international networks," "community action organizations," "going to the core of other societies through NGOs," an "architecture for democratizing human rights," "democracy promotion efforts"—all these terms appear prominently in the national security documents of those years.[4] Funneling funds to political parties was now "opening up the political process"; training security forces was "democratic crowd control"; the Contras in Nicaragua and the Mujahideen fighting the Russians in Afghanistan were "freedom fighters" battling for democracy against "totalitarian forces."

Democratization and "dirty hands"—the new National Endowment for Democracy and William Casey's CIA—went smoothly together. Promoting American operations as enhancements of other countries' "civil society" became a wonderfully pliable way to aid only select political and business groups, unions, media outlets, and electoral monitors while appearing to offer wide support to democratic values and to a "transnational" network committed to their implementation. It was a reaching out, as Reagan liked to say, that reflected a long American tradition of voluntarism. The encounter of like-minded people and volunteer organizations through the free flow of ideas—and the promise of a cornucopia of goods produced by "the continuing revolution of the marketplace"—heralded a new democratic age in which human rights could triumph. Countries were to enter the great "energizing global marketplace" and work with a plethora of American NGOs and U.S.

government programs to create the "infrastructure of democracy." Everything that stood in the way of this free flow of goods and ideas, be it the state or restrictive social mores, would in the end give way. "The industrial age is over," Secretary of State George Schultz declared, "society is beginning to reorganize itself in new ways. Closed and compartmentalized societies cannot take advantage of the information age. People must have their human rights."[5]

In the narratives usually bandied about, after the Vietnam War traditional Cold War anticommunism was finally challenged, its methods repudiated. But in reality the opposite happened. Exposing Cold War interventions in the internal affairs of other nations led not to their being discarded but to their being, in many cases, ideologically recast—and often made more overt. The mechanisms of Washington's drive for global preeminence became increasingly visible. Carter's invocation of human rights had re-idealized American power. But that wasn't enough for the demanding tasks the national security managers of the Reagan era saw ahead.

In the Kennedy–Johnson era, the American role in political warfare was kept secret in planning and execution. As one NSC memo of the time made clear, political warfare was "warfare—not public relations. . . . It embraces diverse forms of coercion and violence including strikes and riots, economic sanctions, subsidies for guerrilla or proxy warfare and, when necessary, kidnapping or assassination of enemy elites."[6] Meanwhile, "nation building" was publicly disassociated from covert warfare and its secret programs for training security, police, and counterterror forces. Democratization did the reverse: it dressed up the fight against Communists and radicals with an insistence that local security forces were actually being trained in the ways of human rights—even as they continued to receive covert training in counterterror methods.

In the Bay of Pigs, for example, Kennedy had sought to conceal how deeply involved the United States was in running the invading military force. During the Reagan era, U.S. ties to many (though not all) such operations would be openly acknowledged in such countries as

Guatemala, El Salvador, Afghanistan, Nicaragua, and Honduras. The defeat of left-wing insurgencies was considered a laudable goal, as were proxy wars, the "democratizing" penetration of Third World countries, and the reversal of Communist gains in Afghanistan, Angola, and Ethiopia. The Nicaraguan Contras, for example, were openly a proxy force (their funding and their method of operating, as the Iran-Contra scandal revealed, were largely covert). These efforts were characteristic of the Reagan Doctrine, under which anticommunist guerrillas and resistance movements received all manner of aid in the effort to roll back Soviet-supported regimes. What had once been highly secret payoffs to political parties, local bureaucrats, journalists, and media organizations were often now openly touted as part of the fight for democratization—which would ultimately protect human rights. Aid to murderous regimes in Guatemala and El Salvador to help them "reform," hold elections, and defeat Communist insurgents was espoused as a necessary counterinsurgency strategy, but covert support for less palatable forces remained effectively obscured in endless debates as to whether death squads were rogue operations or organs of United States–supported regimes.

Human rights groups sometimes speak as though there were an explosion of rights atrocities in the Reagan years. What was really escalating, though, was the way that rights and abuses were coming into the public spotlight together. The earlier anticommunist vision of the Free World had never required any particular nation to be free—its acceptance of American leadership was sufficient. But a human rights policy exposed Washington to uncomfortable questions about its connections to the more thuggish aspects of numerous United States–backed regimes. In an era of human rights, therefore, Washington's challenge was to insulate the operations of American power from any *fundamental* responsibility for such local atrocities. Washington's least palatable methods, of course, could still be publicly denied or explained away as "mistakes," "excesses," the result of rogue elements—and of the lack of adequate U.S. programs to train local troops in the importance of human rights and democratization.

But as the fear of Communism by itself proved insufficient to filter out

American responsibility, the national security managers also came to understand how useful it could be to depict the world as a place of countless human rights violations, of individuals being tortured everywhere—the South, especially, was a cauldron of murderous mayhem—a world, in short, where ever-widening American involvement was a noble response to "moral impulses." Revolutions, insurgencies, violent protests, mass mobilizations of the discontented, "extreme nationalism" and "fanaticism" could all be blurred together as the "breeding grounds" of countless human rights violations. In such a world, the United States could portray itself as one of the few powers that could make a positive difference.

DEMOCRATIZATION AS POLITICAL WARFARE

Reagan was a masterly ideological warrior. He took long-standing national security simplifications and forged them into weapons for a fierce campaign of political warfare. Drawing on Cold War anticommunism, he called the USSR an "evil empire," reviving the old Manichaeism that was always useful for arousing popular support. But he also updated anticommunism, lambasting the Soviet Union for embodying the worst excesses and brutalities of an undemocratic, human-rights-violating state, qualities that made it, in Reagan's eyes, even more evil.

Such simplifications were not just for the public. As usual, the documents intended to galvanize the innermost circles of power were themselves full of simplistic formulations. CIA reports and analyses describe in near apocalyptic tones the expansionism of the Soviets, their brutally successful infiltration and domination of their surrogates, the consolidation of their power through their proxies in Cuba and in Nicaragua. In the words of one 1981 CIA report, "communist exploitation of trends in Central America constitutes the most serious challenge to US interests and freedom of action in the hemisphere since Cuba became allied with the USSR." The region could become "a battle ground over the next few years which would distract, weaken, and undermine the United States in other parts of the world . . . spreading leftist insurgency elsewhere in the region."[7]

As always, the national security establishment saw the global task as two-tiered: first, confronting the Soviets and other countries insistent on charting their own political and economic paths, and second, building a "world order." As one Reagan-era CIA memo acknowledged, "the severe instabilities that exist in many settings in the Third World are chronic, will not soon be overcome, and in many instances would continue to exist regardless of the USSR."[8] Radicalism and nationalism would continue with or without the Soviets: "Revolutionary violence lies near the heart of a general contradiction facing U.S. policy in much of the Third World: how best to defend U.S. interests and to support peaceful change where the choices are between 'friendly' but ineffective regimes and other parties that might come to dominate tomorrow's scene but are radical in nature and often hostile to U.S. interests."[9]

Despite alarmed public pronouncements about the threat of Communism—Soviet military power and expansionism in Afghanistan, the revolution in Nicaragua, the collapse of the Shah, and the Vietnamese invasion of Cambodia—some of Reagan's national security managers (and Reagan himself) sensed a growing vulnerability in the Soviet Union. The United States might be able to change the "correlation of forces." While the Soviets were capable of manipulating Third World discontent against the United States, Reagan argued, "the mystique of communism has, at long last, been shattered."[10] The "Soviet policy of unparalleled global expansionism" had, notably, coincided with the decreasing appeal of "Communist ideologies throughout much of the world."[11] "Widespread disenchantment with communist ideology" was seeping into Soviet society, too. Corruption, violent crime, a feeling of malaise, and a sense of foreboding appeared to be spreading. CIA Director William Casey told Reagan bluntly, "Ideology is virtually dead as a means of inspiring loyalty to the regime."[12] Détente had brought increased access to Western media and, with it, a growing awareness of the consumer cornucopia of America and Europe, which was eroding faith in the old promises of socialist well-being. Even if Leonid Brezhnev's successors changed course, "to embark on reform in any circumstances would be to court disaster."[13]

Ideological warfare against the USSR, to be sure, was not actually causing these changes in the USSR, but the United States believed it could significantly shape them toward its own ends. The Soviets, numerous CIA studies suggest, fully agreed. "Our society is developing . . . not in isolation from hostile surroundings," one CIA report quotes Yuri Andropov (who in 1982 succeeded Brezhnev), but in conditions of "psychological warfare unleashed by imperialism."[14] That he feared such ideological penetration might "shake the ideological foundations of society" says a great deal about the decrepitude of the Soviet regime.

In its political warfare against the USSR, Washington had long sought to promote ethnic and regional enmities, and in the Carter years Brzezinski had called for a special committee to oversee such efforts. But Reagan was far more forceful. With the war in Afghanistan raging, the Soviets found themselves on the receiving end, as one Soviet publication put it, of a campaign of "unprecedented magnitude" to subvert Soviet Muslims and "spark a 'Muslim bomb.'"[15]

"The Soviet Union has failed utterly to become a country," declared the vice chairman of the National Intelligence Council; it was a "demographic basket-case."[16] Breaking it apart was a goal that went back to the earliest days of the national security establishment, but now that the USSR had "entered its terminal phase," it seemed within reach. He continued, "Not a single nationality group is content with Russian control. All yearn for their political and economic freedom."[17] Reagan responded with massive military spending and expanded economic warfare. As he wrote in his memoirs, "The great dynamic of capitalism had given us a powerful weapon in our battle against Communism—money. The Russians could never win the arms race; we could outspend them forever."[18]

Pope John Paul II was further shaking the foundations of a once feared Soviet power. As Casey told Reagan, "if they go [into Poland], they will get economic crisis arising from the debt, a slowdown of the whole Polish work force, and millions of Poles conducting a guerrilla war against them. If they don't, they are open to the West . . . which could unravel their entire system." In short, one analysis observed, "the Free World has out-distanced the Soviet Union economically, crushed it ideologically, and held it off politically." The only serious arena of competition left was military. From now on the Cold War would become "more and more of a bare-knuckle street fight."[19] Hence the utility of the Reagan Doctrine, with its enthusiastic espousal of proxy wars and its public advocacy of various once covert means of support to "anti-Marxist insurgencies" around the world.

Democratization and the Reagan Doctrine were not particularly linked. "I view them as almost completely unrelated," Elliott Abrams said. "I view the Reagan Doctrine as the method of resisting and defeating communist expansionism without risking American lives. Whereas, I think, the expansion of democracy was only partly related; related in that it was obviously a tool to use against communists, to hit them where they were weakest, but it was also a manifestation of simple idealism."[20] Reagan, as usual, provided ideological direction. "We must not break faith with those who are risking their lives on every continent, from Afghanistan to Nicaragua, to defy Soviet supported aggression and secure rights which have been ours from birth," he declared. "Support for freedom fighters is self-defense."[21]

Of course, not everything was out in the open. The Reagan strategy had its own special blend of covert and overt operations.[22] The administration channeled assistance to a variety of nonofficial, often private military, advisory, and civilian supply operations. Retired general John Singlaub wrote CIA Director William Casey in 1986, for example, that he was working behind the scenes to arm anticommunist insurgents by creating "a conduit for maintaining a continuous flow of Soviet weapons and technology, to be utilized by the United States in its support of Freedom Fighters in Nicaragua, Afghanistan, Angola, Cambodia, Ethiopia, etc."[23] Such obfuscations required the development of highly complex interrelationships between U.S. military and intelligence agencies, on the one hand, and private operators, the military, and the intelligence apparatus of other states (Saudi Arabia, Argentina, Taiwan, Israel) on the other.

Democratization provided an excellent banner under which to conduct at least the most public of these activities. First, it offered a superb moral weapon against the brutalities and repressions the Soviet regime visited on its own citizens as well as on Eastern Europeans. Second, it invoked the old either/or of freedom versus repression in an updated form that served to justify the Reagan Doctrine. It provided a defense for funding and coordinating "anticommunist" insurgencies from Afghani-stan to Angola (despite their admittedly miserable human rights records) since they were "freedom fighters"—Davids battling Soviet-supported Goliaths. Third, it discredited the idea that the Vietnamese struggle had had anything to do with self-determination and the rights of peoples to find their own way. "Democratization" implied precisely the opposite: that incorporation in an America-centered world would help countries alter their internal processes in democratic directions. Finally, as Walter Raymond, the CIA operative who coordinated the NSC's democratization program, observed, it sounded positive and progressive, not negative or simply anticommunist[24]—a useful impression for garnering both public and private support.

Taking the high road of democratization, in brief, erased any moral equivalency between two sides that were both guilty of widespread human rights violations. Secretary of State George Schultz said it was "naïve to believe" that democracy's mere "existence somewhere in the world is sufficient incentive for its growth elsewhere." At times covertly but preferably overtly, he argued, it was America's duty to promote democratization and human rights throughout the world. The United States had to stop being morally isolationist and lend the helping hand that would transform others so that they, too, could share the ben-efits that Americans enjoyed.[25] As the *Washington Post* editorialized, "democracy is America's national ideology and the national pride"[26]—and therefore, as the *New York Times* added, "there is no reason to keep the Americans' ideological preferences in the closet, like a shaming secret."[27]

THE IDEOLOGY AND ORGANIZATION
OF DEMOCRATIZATION

"Let us be shy no longer," Reagan declaimed. All other "isms" had their "missionaries"—why not the United States?[28] The "objective I propose is quite simple to state," he announced before the British Parliament in June 1982: "to foster the infrastructure of democracy—the system of a free press, unions, political parties, universities . . . It is time we com-mitted ourselves as a nation—in both the public and private sectors—to

assisting democracy development."[29] In the language of a contempora-
neous national security directive, democratization was to become the
"ideological thrust which clearly affirms the superiority of U.S. and
Western values of individual dignity and freedom, a free press, free
trade unions, free enterprise, and political democracy over the repressive features of Soviet Communism."[30]

Promoting this "infrastructure" of democracy sugarcoated a key
Reagan administration agenda. For democratization was never just
about exploiting human rights (or explaining away violations) to achieve
strategic aims; it was a highly sophisticated program designed to discredit alternative models of social and economic change. "This isn't a
question of East versus West, of the United States versus the Soviet
Union," Reagan proclaimed. "We are witnessing today a great revolutionary crisis—a crisis where the demands of the economic order are
conflicting directly with those of the political order" to bring about
"rejection of the arbitrary power of the state, the refusal to subordinate
the rights of the individual to the super-state, the realization that col-
lectivism stifles all the best human impulses."[31]

That Reagan's anti–big government ethos encountered so little resistance among human rights leaders was all the more impressive in an
age when the weakening of state sovereignty around the globe masked a
strategy for increasing the power of the American state itself. Democratization sought to weaken the autonomy of states in both the Third
World and the First, to force them open culturally, economically, and
ideologically by delegitimizing the role of the state as the regulator of
national economic, cultural, and political affairs. Europe and Japan
posed particular challenges. "Anti-American, neutralist, and pacifist
views have gained increasing influence in a number of NATO countries," one NSC report complained—a "shift to the left on the part of
European political and intellectual elites" evident in an "increasing
hostility to free enterprise."[32]

Attacking state regulation over domestic economies was a critical
step in undercutting alternatives to the U.S. economic model. Reagan's
promotion of privatization—attacking the safety net, eradicating social
programs, weakening unions, loosening regulations on capital flows and

corporate practices—was hardly welcomed by many human rights activists. But in other ways Reagan's view of the state as the enemy allowed Washington to co-opt the anti-statist language of various rights organizations. The state as regulator of the domestic economy, controller of local resources, and distributor of wealth became a decreasingly important issue. While human rights activists often favored sweeping changes in poor countries, the movement's leaders, in contrast, tended to decry any state role in distributive justice—or any sense of economic democracy at all. "The concept of economic and social rights is profoundly undemocratic," warned Aryeh Neier, the executive director of Human Rights Watch. "Rejection of the idea of economic and social rights reflects a commitment to democracy not only for its own sake but also because it is preferable in substance to what we can expect from platonic guardians."[33] Reagan administration officials couldn't have said it better.

NSC committees worked out the details for realizing these diverse aims of democratization, leading in 1983 to Congress's creating the National Endowment for Democracy (NED).[34] In itself, the NED was really just a highly visible part of a proliferating network of organizations that funded and operated the various aspects of the administration's public diplomacy program. Some of these groups had existed since the Cold War and were relatively autonomous. Others were designed as front groups for political warfare. They shared board members, funded one another's projects, and generally kept the issue of whether projects were funded directly through the government or through quasi-governmental or private sources shrouded in secrecy.[35]

Their purpose, one administration official explained, was to implement "aid, training and organizational support for foreign government and private groups to encourage the growth of democratic political institutions and practices." Democratization assistance, national security managers argued—"the support and cultivation of political groups and forces abroad that may serve the long-term interests of the United States and the West generally"[36]—was no more interventionist than humanitarian or economic aid. Such timely external aid might tip the balance toward bringing pro-democratic leaders to power, defeating leftist groups, and shoring up human rights with "systemic support."

In the main, the NED distributed grants to organizations headed by the Republican and Democratic parties, the AFL-CIO, the Chamber of Commerce, and various women's and youth organizations; the idea was for private institutions to help their counterparts abroad.[37] "We're engaged in almost missionary work," stated the head of the National Republican Institute. "We've seen what the communists do for each other. And now we've come a long way and we have a broadly democratic movement, a force for democracy."[38] Of course, these nongovernmental groups often worked in coordination with the State Department, the CIA, and local U.S. embassies.

The administration had little to fear from the independence of these groups. As Paul Bremer, then executive secretary of the Department of State, wrote to William Clark, Reagan's national security advisor, "democracy promoting institutes and foundations cannot as a practical matter stray very far from government policy, or from what each party in or out of office approves."[39] Former CIA director William Colby concurred: "It is not necessary to turn to a covert approach. Many of the programs which in the 1950s were conducted as covert operations now are conducted quite openly and consequently without controversy."[40] Overt funding, in short, cut the long-standing Gordian knot. "It would be terrible for democratic groups around the world to be seen as subsidized by the CIA. . . . That's why the Endowment was created," its director declared.[41]

The NED could allocate funds for specific projects without specific congressional approval. But few who looked closely would have considered the institution independent. Senator William Proxmire of Wisconsin proposed an amendment to ban anyone who had been with U.S. intelligence in the preceding twenty years from serving on the NED board or staff; it was rejected after Casey simply promised not to use the new agency for intelligence activities. Congress was hardly likely to question the independent-mindedness of the directors of the NED or similar operations when they included such insiders as Walter Mondale, Henry Kissinger, Lane Kirkpatrick, Dante Fascell, and the chairs of the Republican and Democratic National Committees.

Helsinki Watch thought it inappropriate for human rights groups "that exist to criticize governments to accept government support."[42] Not that the NSC hadn't offered it. In the Carter years, shortly after the Ford Foundation made its initial grant of $45,000 to establish the International Helsinki Federation for Human Rights, State Department and NSC officials offered the group's leaders ten times that amount. They turned it down.[43] Once the NED was created, Helsinki Watch remained uneasy about such quasi-government funding for its work, but, notably, it never challenged the NED's mandate or its panoply of overt methods for extending America's reach.

In many ways the NED brought to fruition Zbigniew Brzezinski's ideas for the creation of a human rights foundation. Funds would go to NGOs, foreign individuals, conferences and groups, as well as awards for human rights leaders. In the coming years, direct and indirect government support would cover a multitude of activities. As the State Department reported to the NSC in the early 1990s, democracy promotion's toolbox had come to include

> civic education, civic organization, civic-military relations; conflict prevention/resolution; ethnic, racial and religious diversity programs; human rights education and training, information exchange, legislative training/development; media training and development; political party development; public administration development; rule of law; support for elections/election reform; and trade union development.[44]

DEMOCRATIZATION AND HUMAN RIGHTS BATTLES:
WARRING OVER THE FACTS

The shift in Washington's tactics significantly changed the environment within which American human rights organizations operated. "The Reagan administration shaped our course," Neier later wrote; we "had an easy time scoring points against the administration for failing to live up to its rhetoric." Moreover, "what made our efforts effective was our insistence on holding the United States accountable for abuses by governments of other countries that held power because of U.S. support. Though U.S. officials were not the authors of those abuses, in circumstances where the United States acted as an apologist for torture, disappearances, or murder, we treated our government . . . as a 'surrogate villain.'"[45]

Human rights groups insisted that U.S. government advocacy of human rights was not only morally right but also very much in Washington's own strategic interests.[46] "Indeed, it could be argued," the leader of Americas Watch remarked, "that if the United States spoke out consistently and evenhandedly to criticize human rights abuses wherever they occur, the possibility of a conflict with strategic concerns would be diminished or eliminated."[47] Or as William Schulz of Amnesty International USA said, "The right thing to do is not only *not* at odds with U.S. interests, but . . . a good deal of the time the two go hand in hand."[48] U.S. power was to be "redirected rather than resisted," another Amnesty organizer added.[49] "In accepting, at least rhetorically, that efforts to promote human rights are central to U.S. foreign policy, and that such efforts should proceed evenhandedly," Neier argued, "the Reagan administration effectively ended debate over those issues."[50] The outcome was a great boon for human rights: "the United States," Neier said, "was a force worldwide for the human rights cause."[51]

But this espousal of Washington's own rhetoric was a two-edged sword. The national security managers opted for a human rights strategy not because human rights groups were pressuring them, but because human rights were proving useful in dealing with some otherwise intractable ideological problems. Human rights leaders thought they could shape the use of power through human rights; the national security managers knew better. They were quite willing to live with the criticism of human rights organizations and skillful enough to turn their critics' ammunition to their own ends.

Human rights leaders spoke as though Washington had actually taken up the cause of human rights—as opposed to adapting human rights language as part of an ideological war of ideas, which is something quite different. They convinced themselves that Washington was actually interested in human rights rather than in an ideological vision of "rights-based power" that would nourish the idea that American values were universal. They repeatedly praised the Reagan administration for "vigorously pursuing" the cause of human rights in Cuba and the USSR, for example, as though such advocacy were a principled stand rather than a political strategy.[52] They lauded its support for "civil society" throughout the Soviet bloc and challenged it to extend its support elsewhere, while refusing to acknowledge how that support was fueled by Washington's national security interests.[53]

Reagan's view, human rights leaders argued, was simply too narrow; he "missed opportunities" to support "the rule of law and those civilian institutions which are required for real democracy to flourish: an independent judiciary, a free press, functioning trade unions, opposition political parties."[54] One side saw human rights as a constraint on power, the other as a weapon of power, and rights, but in the end their language blended to such an extent that when the Reagan administration left office human rights leaders could praise it for having "persuaded" the nation "of the rightness of human rights as its goal."[55] Yet the course of their marriage of convenience never ran smooth.

Helsinki Watch was often on the same side as the administration in denouncing Soviet abuses,[56] but its insistence that rights be universal in their application—including such United States–backed right-wing regimes as those of South Korea, the Philippines, Chile, and Argentina—led to bitter acrimony. Turkey, a NATO ally, was a case in point. Helsinki Watch accused Turkey of denying defendants the right to legal representations, of routinely using electric-shock torture in interrogations, of arresting young people arbitrarily on terrorist charges, and of operating a prison system that was "possibly the most horrifying hellhole in the world."[57] Abrams vehemently dismissed such criticism, waxing eloquent about the need to appreciate the "unique historical, social and geopolitical conditions of a particular country," matters that were often "simply ignored" by rights advocates. "The clamor of ill-informed and self-righteous critics," he wrote in a letter to the New York Times, "does not help but hinders in the building of the modern, Western-oriented Turkey in which human rights will be fully guaranteed."[58]

Helsinki Watch fired back immediately: "The fact that Mr. Abrams has been clamoring about Helsinki Watch's reports on Turkey while he has never found 'shallow analysis' in our many reports condemning human-rights abuses in the Soviet bloc countries seems to reveal his own political agenda: to promote U.S. geopolitical interests with regard to Turkey, a 'loyal member of NATO.' "[59]

For Washington, the exposure of egregious human rights abuses among allies was embarrassing and politically messy—but ultimately worth it. The Soviets would have loved to be able to portray Amnesty and Helsinki Watch as agents of the American government, making it all the easier to label their own dissenters disloyal—or worse. Some "rights groups" once funded by the CIA, like Freedom House, were easier for the Soviets to discredit, but the very independence of Helsinki Watch and Amnesty, evident in their disputes over U.S. support for regimes that tortured, made them a boon to the national security managers. Learning to live with the sharp criticisms of human rights leaders paid off so handsomely that Reagan himself lauded Amnesty in glowing terms on its twenty-fifth anniversary for its ability "to mobilize the world, government officials and private citizens, on behalf of political prisoners and in defense of human rights."[60]

Central America occasioned the fiercest debates between human rights organizations and the national security managers of the Reagan years. Americas Watch was founded in 1981 and immediately became involved in the most bitter struggle with Washington that the movement had yet seen. Both Americas Watch and Amnesty savaged the Reagan administration for its commendation of governments that were systematically abusing human rights and for claiming dramatic progress in Argentina, Chile, Paraguay, and Uruguay. UN Ambassador Jeane Kirkpatrick's praise for the "moral quality" of the El Salvadoran government even as death squads were roaming the country; Reagan's praise for President Efraín Ríos Montt of Guatemala for being "totally dedicated to democracy" even as his armed forces were slaughtering tens of thousands in counterinsurgency operations; the administration's praise of the Nicaraguan Contras as "freedom fighters" even as they were committing massive atrocities; Washington's decision to normalize relations with Chile's dictator, Augusto Pinochet—all these outrages were challenged in some of the most blistering human rights criticism ever aimed at Washington.

Several reports in the early and mid-1980s accused the administration of using democratization as a smoke screen for its support of murderous anticommunist regimes. Washington, in turn, attempted to explain away such human rights violations as it was willing to acknowledge as regrettable but temporary: the short-term costs of fighting "communist insurgencies" had to be paid in order to achieve the long-term goal of democratization so that rights could then flourish. Americas Watch dismissed this transition-to-democracy argument as little more than a claim "in which a non-democratic and unpopular government that abuses its citizens systematically is said to be on the road to elections."[61] Not surprisingly, the administration denounced critics who documented these regimes' participation in torture, massacre, aerial bombardment of civilians, systematic displacement of peasants from their lands and so on as unconstructive and biased.[62]

The character of human rights debates over Central America was quickly established. As the Reagan administration zealously defended murderous regimes there, human rights organizations exposed practices that few in the media or in Congress could comfortably support. In meticulously well-researched reports, they showed how the yearly State Department human rights reports were tailored to serve political ends, how "facts" were often gross distortions, how carefully chosen language exculpated favored leaders. "The amount of argument, the amount of battle that goes on in these [government] reports is unbelievable," Richard Holbrooke testified to Congress in 1983. "They are by definition false, because they are always calibrated to meet the existing overall bilateral relationships. The battles over the exact adjective with which to describe something that all of us privately know is appalling is unspeakable."[63] Exploding these verbal minefields in the government's face in order to expose horrific rights abuses and then seeking to shame Washington into mending its ways was the fundamental human rights strategy of these years.

In the case of El Salvador, progress toward human rights had to be deemed sufficient in order for Congress to approve military assistance. Congressional action in 1981 required the president to certify every 180 days that the government of El Salvador was making a "concerted and significant effort" to comply with internationally recognized human rights, that it was achieving "substantial control" over elements in the armed forces that were torturing and murdering civilians, and that it was making progress in land reform, free elections, and good-faith efforts to investigate the cases of murdered Americans. Americas Watch and Amnesty produced painstaking reports disputing the administration on the facts in all these areas,[64] and, citing Washington's own global invocation of human rights, they charged it with hypocrisy, double standards, and complicity in abuses in El Salvador and elsewhere in Central America.

On January 26, 1982, two days before the presidential finding on El Salvador was due, the recently formed Americas Watch released a devastating account of the horrendous human rights situation there. It created a brief news sensation.[65] The administration's stance, as usual, was simply to deny the facts while attacking the messenger. Nothing was more "democratic" (and in the long run more useful for human rights), it would argue in response to such criticisms, than an election, and there was one approaching in El Salvador. As is well documented, the administration then intervened massively in the March 1982 El Salvadoran election, which gave José Napoleón Duarte the presidency, and heralded the results as proof of the popular will for democracy.

Human rights leaders often despaired over the evident effectiveness of using such elections to legitimize the continuing brutality of local regimes. Congressional leaders not only let themselves be persuaded that these elections were democratic but also lauded them as a step in the direction of human rights. Once there was general agreement in Congress that the survival of the Salvadoran government was important to U.S. national interests, the certification debates, as one scholar activist has written, "amounted to little more than putting the best face on a bad situation."[66] By leaving the power to certify up to the president, Congress essentially assured that certification would go through. The process allowed Congress to avoid blatant support for criminal regimes without undermining in any serious way U.S. material support for them. Thus, although national security managers faced fierce and sometimes embarrassing criticism in these battles over certification, they usually won their larger policy objectives. "If the Duarte Government fell, human rights would suffer; if the guerrilla forces obtained power, far worse would come," Abrams testified before Congress. "To acquiesce in this, to withdraw our support from the Government of El Salvador, would make a mockery of our concern for human rights."[67] Congress bought the argument.

But even if human rights leaders were frustrated by the ease with which Congress could be placated, they never effectively challenged the labels that Reagan attached to groups his administration opposed— "Communists," "totalitarians," "terrorists," "Marxist-Leninists." Some human rights leaders even endorsed them. Others chafed at the president's insistence that the Soviets were behind every left-leaning government and local insurgency in Central America, and some questioned traditional globalist mantras about falling dominoes. But when the administration labeled a movement Communist, or denounced the Nicaraguans as another Cuba or a burgeoning Marxist-Leninist regime, they failed to come up with arguments to counter these mobilizing but misleading characterizations.

Only a handful in Congress seriously questioned Reagan's portrayal of the enemy; the rest were afraid of appearing soft on Communism. As Robert Gates, then deputy director of the CIA, later wrote, "one of the enduring characteristics of Congress, especially on foreign affairs, is its eagerness to avoid clear-cut actions that will leave the Hill unambiguously responsible if something goes wrong, especially if they have acted contrary to the wishes of the President."[68] Some in Congress argued that Nicaragua was just a local issue, but not many wished to lock horns with Elliott Abrams when he framed the matter: "Call the effort to consolidate communism in Nicaragua a 'local conflict' and you can oppose U.S. intervention. Call it a 'Latin issue' and you can urge a 'Latin solution.' But what if you call it what it is, an effort by the Soviet Union to become the dominant power in the region that lies between the Panama Canal and Mexico? Then, whose responsibility is it to act? Only the United States had the power to deal with the Soviet Union."[69]

A congressional consensus developed not to challenge Reagan on the issue of Communism in general or Nicaragua in particular. It was joined by leading members of the Democratic foreign policy establishment—Brzezinski, Richard Holbrooke, and Samuel Huntington—who signed a statement in the *New York Times* calling on the United States to prevent "the consolidation of the first Marxist-Leninist state on the American mainland" and urging a massive campaign of public diplomacy to discredit any notion that Nicaragua might be moving in a more "humane and progressive direction."[70] Some Americas Watch reports raised doubts that Nicaragua was actually "exporting revolution" or "subverting its neighbors," claims that were not only "yet to be proven" but in fact had been contradicted by a former member of the CIA. Further, they found claims of abuses there exaggerated; the administration had "used human rights arguments with a profound cynicism and disregard for the truth."[71]

Yet human rights groups tended to talk more about the facts the administration was distorting than the policy motives behind these distortions. Their laserlike focus on specific violations became both a strength and a weakness of the movement. It was a strength because challenging the administration on its facts allowed human rights leaders to take the initiative—reproaching, exposing, shaming—while protecting themselves from accusations of anti-Americanism, left-wing bias, or softness on Communism. It was a weakness since it provided no context as to why opposition forces felt compelled to take up arms or why they might commit human rights abuses themselves. Because human rights leaders adopted the language of facts and law, they were unable to confront the simplistic labels and rationales of the national security strategists with anything more convincing than a fragmentary vision of rights. They could provide no empathetic vision of what kind of society that oppositional groups might be seeking to create. Nor could they explain why popular forces might want to be free of U.S. influence. Consequently, they had little sense of how to respond effectively to Washington's support for entrenched rulers, or to American hostility toward struggles for radical change.

Similarly limited views arose in reaction to Vietnam. Human rights leaders did dismiss Reagan's rhetoric that the Vietnam War had been a "noble cause" and warned he was seeking to overcome "anti-interventionist" sentiment and reassert American power by accentuating East-West conflicts.[72] But they often concurred with Reagan's view of postwar Vietnam as a nightmare of human rights abuses: hundreds of thousands in flight from the new tyranny, the exodus of the boat people, "reeducation camps" as centers of hard labor and indoctrination, repression of Buddhists and students. Once again, they made little mention of the context for these abuses—the legacy of American aggression and the aftereffects of war and invasion, the continuing American hostility and embargoes on trade that compounded the country's problems and set the stage for myriad abuses.

Vietnam provides a textbook case of the link between U.S. power and human rights abuses. And yet the selective human rights vision of the time paid attention to only some types of violations, which were blamed almost entirely on "communists"—a view shared by Congress, the media, and the administration. If human rights leaders largely avoided any discussion of Washington's strategic policies and its adept labeling of its enemies, insisting that a human rights violation was a human rights violation, period, such a stance came at a price—especially in Central America, where key aspects of the operation of U.S. power that were vital to any real understanding of the larger context of abuses often receded from view.

CHALLENGING DEMOCRATIZATION:
THE MACBRIDE COMMISSION REPORT

There was one sustained challenge to Washington's democratizing vision of the world—but it didn't come from the human rights world. In 1974, the UN General Assembly adopted two pathbreaking resolutions concerning development: first, a declaration that endorsed a right to nationalize industries and to place restraints on the intervention of multinational corporations in local politics; and, second, a call for sweeping institutional reform of global economic organizations such as the International Monetary Fund. This was a brief if heady moment, when OPEC's growing power emboldened the nations of the South to think they might finally have the leverage to renegotiate a wide variety of economic, cultural, and political arrangements that had heretofore benefited the wealthier nations. In the resolutions' wake, UNESCO created a commission to study "communication problems," with Seán MacBride, a former chair of Amnesty International and a Nobel Peace Prize laureate, presiding over a prestigious group of intellectuals, writers, and social scientists.[73] Their report, *Many Voices, One World*, released in 1979 and widely debated in the early years of the Reagan administration, made clear what kinds of issues were being left out of discussions about the United States's global role, in the mainstream media, in Congress, and, even more strikingly, among human rights groups.

The MacBride report called for a "new world information and communications order," but this was hardly a technical matter. Civil, political, and individual rights, the commission argued, can neither theoretically nor practically be separated from the tasks of protecting communities from aggression, safeguarding ecological and cultural integrity, basing models of development on a community's definition of its own needs, or implementing economic and social justice. And communications had an essential role to play in guaranteeing those rights. Ironically, the MacBride Commission and Reagan's national security managers saw the same processes under way: the Western-dominated corporate centralization of privately owned communications, the spread of an advertising-based consumerist lifestyle, the weakening of cultural cohesion in communities, along with a deepening loss of local control over resources and development. But their perspectives were very different. As the national security managers well understood, media images simplify and dramatize reality, "disrupting the context of politics by focusing on an instantaneous present, and encouraging emotional reactions to events rather than reflective consideration of them," in the words of one NSC report. Effectively utilized, the West's powerful communications network could be a "serious threat" to recalcitrant "governing elites in the Third World and the Communist world alike."[74] The MacBride Commission saw this threat to elites from a different angle: the Western media's tendency "to splinter the national audience into many mini-audiences." That was why "every country should develop its communication patterns in accordance with its own conditions, needs, and traditions, thus strengthening its integrity, independence, and self-reliance."[75]

In an age of increasingly powerful new communications technologies, such as satellites and instantaneous worldwide transmission, the report continued, the "free flow" was turning into a "one-way flow," reflecting the "life styles, values and models of a few of the most advanced countries, and certain consumption and development patterns" that could not possibly provide sustainable models for others.[76] A commercialized mass culture was being disseminated via highly concentrated, profit-driven, corporately owned global communications networks that were extolling "acquisition and consumerism at the expense of other values." These developments threatened to undercut popular cultures, leaving individuals "more cut off from the society in which they live as a result of media penetration into their lives,"[77] and destroying their capacity to think in nonmarket, nonprofit terms about human needs and human rights.

The problem was further complicated by the fact that peoples of different nations in the South largely learned about one another through the Western media; "news flows tend toward a North-South direction," thus inhibiting the needed exchanges of information among Third World countries that is essential for a greater understanding of their mutual problems. Western countries and corporations, moreover, often had far more knowledge of the economic and technical aspects of countries than did native elites,[78] further limiting the ability of governments to control their own developmental destinies.[79]

For America's national security managers "one-way flow" was, as one might expect, about overcoming "anti-commercialism" and warding off restrictions on the expansion of Western information technologies and services.[80] Human rights groups, for their part, had talked so much about defying state sovereignty in order to support individual human rights that they had largely ignored the scope of cultural penetration and commercialization. But to the MacBride Commission, the global communications system was essentially a "monologue" of the West to the rest, and it had to change. "Communications, nowadays, is a matter of human rights," and critical among these rights was "the right to be heard." Quoting the Universal Declaration of Human Rights, the commission stressed that "this right includes freedom to hold opinions without interference, and to seek, receive, and impart information. . . ."[81] A unilateral, commercialized approach had wrongly turned freedom of the press and communication into the "right to receive" the West's messages—in contravention of "the rights of peoples . . . to comprehensive and true information," the right of each nation to inform the world about its affairs, and "the right of each nation to protect its cultural and social identity against the false or distorted information" embedded in so much Western reporting.[82]

Human rights organizations dealt with the awkward challenge of the commission's report by ignoring it. The mainstream media and the Reagan administration, in contrast, attacked. A "freak, rotten as a whole," one Reuters executive called the report.[83] The "right to be heard" would "impose on newspapers and broadcasters the obligation to give [away] space or airtime," thus interfering with freedom of the press, the *New York Times* argued.[84] To Elliott Abrams, the report was an "ideological assault on the very free press values which UNESCO is mandated to defend."[85] These attacks were part of a far broader onslaught against a South struggling to rewrite the economic and political rules of the global order. The "free flow" was largely a code word for commercialization. As H. L. Mencken observed, "Freedom of the press is reserved for those who own one."

From the perspective of the MacBride Commission, Reagan-style democratization was about pulling people from diverse societies into transnational webs, already existing networks in which Americans and other Westerners could feel comfortable—and moral. As the nations of the South continued to resist economic and cultural incorporation into a global market system on Western terms, the West, the commission concluded, was increasingly portraying the South as a world of despots, torturers, and terrorists, a veritable wasteland of backward cultures and brutal regimes. Of all news reports on the South disseminated in the North, 50 percent focused on violence, disaster, backwardness, follies, excesses, and other negatives; the equivalent for the developed countries was under 10 percent.[86]

Such portrayals of the South served powerful interests in Washington and Europe, for an atrocity-ridden South seemed to legitimize a Western helping hand without calling for any transformation of the Western structures of wealth and control. And it could seem that with so many human rights violations all over the world, those few that served Washington's strategic interests were only a small part of the bleak big picture. But the "right to be heard"—promulgated as a human right—challenged the fundamental organization of Western power in the South.

THE RIGHTS OF NONCOMBATANTS

The human rights movement may have had its limitations, but in the 1980s at least one of its achievements was beyond dispute—or so it seemed. Breaking with previous practice, human rights organizations began focusing on the rights of noncombatants, noting abuses by guerrilla movements and reporting the crimes of both state and non-state actors.[87] But in fact some of the shrewdest national security managers had long supported such a widening of focus. Brzezinski had led the way by lumping economic and social questions together as issues of rights, positing a rights-based reformist alternative to revolutionary change. Now the national security managers took up the cause, applying the "laws of war" to guerrilla insurgencies. Their goal was to strip the revolutionary movements that Washington opposed of their moral stature and their claims to justice by imputing a range of "terrorist acts" to them, and to portray such crimes as inherent in any revolutionary struggle.

Americas Watch certainly did not see its censure of human rights violations on all sides of a conflict as a vision parallel to Washington's. From Amnesty it had inherited an awareness of the savagery into which all sides in a conflict could descend; hence its concern for noncombatants and the suffering of the innocent. When Washington spoke the same language, however, it had different ends in mind.

For decades the national security managers had been exasperated by what they regarded as the press's one-sided focus on American atrocities and its blindness to the "terrorism" of insurgents. While the Kennedy, Johnson, and Nixon administrations had eagerly spoken of

the terrorist component of Vietcong tactics (such as the assassination
of village leaders), their efforts had been overwhelmed by accounts of
American military savagery, bombings, and assassinations carried out
by both the Americans and the South Vietnamese. Washington turned
out massive studies of Vietcong terrorism, compiled detailed figures on
terrorist attacks, released countless accounts of the murders of women,
children, and other innocents; and still, from Washington's perspective, the media all too often described this brutality as the work of so
many Robin Hoods resorting to the "weapons of the weak." Using the
language of human rights to condemn "violations by non-state armed
groups" offered a solution.[88]

Washington wanted "non-combatants" to be viewed in a new way—
not as the seas in which guerrillas swam (which they often were) but as
"human shields"—civilians unfairly exposed to danger, neutral innocents forced by insurgents to take sides. Viewed from this perspective,
many aspects of guerrilla warfare were war crimes and thus in violation
of the laws of war. Both national security managers and human rights
leaders eagerly promoted this new view—which, paradoxically, allowed
Washington to shape the ethics of such situations to its own advantage.

During the 1970s and 1980s, for example, the Guatemalan government was slaughtering Indian peasants considered "subversive" for col-
laborating with the guerrilla opposition. As a high-ranking government
military advisor explained:

> The problem of war is not just a question of who is shooting. For each
> one who is shooting there are 10 working behind him. The guerrillas
> won over many Indian collaborators. Therefore, the Indians were sub-
> versives. And how do you deal with subversion? Clearly you had to kill
> the Indians because they were collaborating with the subversion. And
> then it would be said that you were killing innocent people. But they
> weren't innocent. They had sold out to subversion.[89]

With anticommunism wearing thin as a rationale, accusing enemies of
using noncombatants as hostages or pawns was a highly useful tack,
especially since it often made opposition forces and the populations

from which they arose appear deeply antagonistic to one another. True, the local government might still be committing human rights atrocities— but wasn't everyone?

In this new ideological era, the national security managers saw a long-sought opportunity to turn the tide against insurgencies of all kinds by invoking what Jeane Kirkpatrick called the semantics of human rights.[90] Kirkpatrick and Abrams led the way, denouncing Americas Watch and Amnesty—and various members of Congress—for failing to shine a spotlight on the crimes of guerrilla movements and insurgency groups.[91] Human rights advocates "must not hesitate to condemn the mounting abuses against noncombatants," Kirkpatrick insisted; they can no longer highlight government repression "while ignoring guerrilla violence."[92]

Guerrillas, Kirkpatrick remarked acidly, "may massacre half of the inhabitants of a hamlet, dragging them from their beds in the middle of the night," but that is "not a violation of human rights by definition: that is a protest of a national liberation movement." She acknowledged that repressive governments often responded aggressively to the violence "created" by the guerrillas who hid among the people, but she blamed the insurgents. "The essence of their strategy [in El Salvador] is provocation: through persistent attacks which disrupt society and make ordinary life impossible, such revolutionaries challenge authority and force repressive countermeasures in the expectation that such repression will undermine the legitimacy of the regime."[93]

Reagan administration officials did not deny that social and political upheaval might arise from the desperation of the downtrodden. "The government headed by Ronald Reagan has not the slightest tendency to imagine that the political turmoil in Central America has no roots in social and economic problems," Kirkpatrick acknowledged. "We know the people of El Salvador, Honduras, Nicaragua, Costa Rica have been ill-fed, ill-housed, ill-clothed, illiterate for centuries. . . . We know that there existed . . . neglect, unmet needs, unfulfilled hopes and that these gave rise to movement for reform and revolution. We understand, broadly speaking, how it happened."[94] Washington, of course, also knew that fighting an insurgency movement entailed attacks on "noncombatants," a veritable "counterterror," as military counterinsurgency manuals have long phrased it. (When the local populace appeared to support local guerrillas, as one CIA cable observed, "the soldiers were forced to fire at anything that moved.")[95]

The new focus on the laws of war was part of a broader tendency in the human rights movement to make law itself the paramount means of institutionalizing human rights. A dense network of legalese, of rules and laws of war, offered a new vocabulary of judgment and morality that provided a new "mark of legitimacy—and legitimacy has become the currency of power,"[96] one legal scholar remarked. But "we should be clear," he warned, that "this bold new vocabulary beats ploughshares into swords as often as the reverse."[97] For their part, the national security managers were delighted, since accusations of criminality could strip the struggles by insurgents, the mobilized poor, and the dispossessed of any claims to justice. Labeling such enemies Communists was still useful, but condemning them for violating the laws of war helped deflect public attention from the far more blatant violations of the repressive governments Washington backed.

There is little in the human rights literature of the 1980s that sheds light on why guerrillas (and their supporters) might be engaging in so many acts of violence ("war crimes"). Consider a few snippets of Americas Watch charges against the FLMN in El Salvador: It used "targeted assassinations" in the rural areas to combat army infiltration, as well as "summary executions, kidnapping, and the destruction of public and private property."[98] "To avoid being press-ganged into joining the guerrilla forces, thousands joined the refugee population in Honduras or crowded into the slums around San Salvador and into displaced-persons camps."[99] It was imperative that the FLMN cease sabotaging such nonmilitary targets as "public transport, commercial establishments and telephone lines" and stop using "catapult bombs" aimed at military targets because of their excessive toll on civilians. While open to some debate, all these instances could now be cited as violations of the laws of war. Though Americas Watch put vastly more weight on the crimes of the regime than on sporadic guerrilla attacks,[100] to Washington it didn't matter—it was enough to be able to cite reports by groups like Americas Watch to point to the criminality of insurgencies.

In the acrimonious debates between Washington and human rights organizations over the rights of noncombatants, the notion of fighting oppression slipped further and further into the background. El Salvador's archbishop, Óscar Romero, had said shortly before his assassination in 1980 that "when a dictatorship seriously violates human rights and attacks the common good of the nation, when it becomes unbearable and closes all channels of dialogue, of understanding, of rationality—when this happens, the church speaks of the legitimate right of insurrectional violence."[101] Human rights groups took no position on whether conditions could ever grow so intolerable that they justified insurrectional violence.[102] In the end, the gathering of more and more facts about more and more violations, though useful in many ways, provided no real insight into oppression or what to do about it. Reports documenting atrocities do not necessarily lead to an understanding of what causes uprisings, or how to weigh the justice of various kinds of direct political action, whether radical, religious, or reformist. However important the rights of noncombatants—and they are critically important—the commitment to them that was now unfolding was proving highly useful to Washington as the brutality of repressive states was increasingly countered by reports on the brutality of insurgents—however modest their brutality might be in comparison.

THE FAILURE OF CERTIFICATION

When human rights groups refused on principle to take a stand on American global policies and geopolitical questions, they chose to ignore the history of the national security establishment's standard operating procedures. Some human rights activists and members of Congress were well aware of long-standing U.S. military programs in counterinsurgency and counterterror operations, which brought military and intelligence officers from other countries to the United States for training.[103] But few leaders spoke of or to this history. Thus all the newly uncovered facts about ongoing atrocities were reported with little background on decades of political warfare strategies. Human rights groups never much addressed Washington's policies, certainly not in a way that effectively discredited the rhetoric of democratization. Meanwhile, the weakness of relying on "certification" to bring the facts to light became ever more evident.

The 1976 law decreed that no aid be given to governments that were grossly violating human rights. By certifying relative improvement in a government's human rights record, however, a president could waive the proscription and authorize continued assistance. The administration was to take into account "the relevant findings of appropriate international organizations, including nongovernmental organizations . . . [and] the extent of cooperation by such governments in permitting an unimpeded investigation by any such organization of alleged violations."[104]

The procedure was deceptively simple. American diplomatic missions around the world were to produce the initial drafts of the country reports; these were then to be coordinated by the Bureau of Human Rights and sent on to senior State Department officials. To generate the reports, members of local U.S. missions were expected to meet with human rights monitors on the ground, attend trials, visit prisons, and hold discussions with government officials. (Such a process ensured contentious and ongoing debates: Were there more political killings by the government, or by insurgents? Were death squads rogue or government operations? Were the armed forces killing innocent noncombatants or guerrilla supporters—and in what numbers?)

Notably absent from the process was any requirement that ongoing Defense Department, CIA, or other covertly sanctioned programs and counterinsurgency operations with bearing on human rights be reported and assessed. There were no calls for reports on indirect or tacit American support for the training of local forces by other governments, or for accounts of "private" but officially encouraged groups (long a CIA and Pentagon specialty). There were no demands for detailed evaluations of training by U.S. military advisors, or of the counterterror aspects of counterinsurgency practices encouraged by U.S. military assistance; or for information about covert funding through governments friendly to Washington. Investigations were largely focused outward, on gathering information about other countries and contacting dissident groups that might be helpful in the future, rather than inward, on accounts by American officials about U.S. government links with groups involved in rights violations. Not surprisingly, a large number of internal government communications, assessments, directives, and accounts were completely classified—the very ones, of course, that would have provided persuasive evidence of Washington's participation in human rights atrocities. The standard claim to this day is that nothing in the available documents reveals any pattern of military, CIA, or quasi-private involvement. The operative word is "available."

After the 1979 coup in El Salvador led to the rapidly escalating ferocity of the civil war, the United States implemented a counterinsurgency program reminiscent of its involvement in Vietnam. In the early 1980s Americas Watch, Amnesty, and the Lawyer's Committee for Human Rights, drawing on newspaper accounts and sources in El Salvador and the United States, provided a searing indictment of the part U.S. aid and American experts were playing in the training of Salvadoran troops.[105] The result was a horrifying level of mass murder. In the rural areas, sweeps to "clean up" areas of suspected guerrilla sympathy wiped out whole peasant villages, forcing the survivors to flee, many to refugee camps. As one Amnesty researcher wrote in his own study, the evidence suggested "an intent to kill as many inhabitants as possible in targeted villages, and to kill entire families so that children would not grow up to avenge their parents."[106] "It's a brilliant technique," a former marine said. "By terrorizing civilians, the army is crushing the rebellion without the need to directly confront the guerillas." "The subversives like to say that they are the fish and the people are the ocean," El Salvadoran officers told a group of visiting congressmen. "What we have done in the north is to dry up the ocean so we can catch the fish easily."[107]

Human rights groups well knew that there were targets in El Salvador in addition to the guerrillas. The wave of assassinations and executions was directed at any suspected collaborators or sympathizers with insurgents—indeed almost all critics of the government's repressive methods were subject to attack. Human rights reports recounted staggering carnage in the urban areas: "legal trade union members; professional, religious, and political activists; students; indeed almost anyone who might have any inclinations to promote a political settlement, and many who had no such inclinations at all."[108]

As human rights groups tenaciously exposed Washington's lies, the national security managers felt that they often had little choice but to keep lying about counterinsurgency "excesses" when they came to light. Thus the U.S. government denied any knowledge of who had assassinated Archbishop Romero (when the U.S. Embassy in El Salvador had cabled Washington, identifying the killers); insisted that there had been no massacre at El Mozote in 1981 (the UN Truth Commission Report in 1993 concluded that at least two hundred victims had been slaughtered); and so on. Years after leaving his post in Honduras, where he was accused of supporting the local death squads, Ambassador Nicholas Negroponte dismissed all such allegations: "Frankly, I think that some of the retrospective efforts to try and suggest that we were supportive of or condoned the actions of human rights violators is really revisionistic."[109] The reality was closer to "don't ask-don't tell," author Thomas Powers has pointed out: "Officials don't ask the CIA what its counterparts are really doing, and the agency doesn't tell. Of course, everyone knows."[110]

Yet human rights leaders found it difficult to challenge Washington effectively on these issues. Even as they revealed fact after horrendous fact, both the slaughter of noncombatants and the American commitment continued to escalate. Human rights groups denounced Washington for failing to control the murderous excesses of the regimes it supported; they wrote of rogue operations, locally run death squads, and the utter lack of restraint by the native military commanders who ran the counterinsurgency operations. National security managers knew better. They understood that all this killing was an inherent part of counterinsurgency. They also knew that the widespread slaughter was, to a large extent, achieving its objectives—after which Washington would be able to point to the decline in the murder rate as proof that its "training" to overcome local excesses was working.[111] The core issue, then, was never primarily the excesses that human rights reports tended to focus on but, rather, the very nature of counterinsurgency as political warfare and the methods of counterterror that were so unabashedly laid out in U.S. military manuals.[112] On these matters human rights organizations had little to say.

Democratic Party critics were in a bind as well. In El Salvador as elsewhere in Central America, they opposed a victory of "Marxist guerrillas," shrinking no less than Republicans from any reduction of aid that would risk "losing" the country. "We do not want to see a guerrilla victory," New York Representative Stephen Solarz said. "But we do not want to see the United States provide assistance to a government whose security forces remain responsible for the abduction and torture of thousands of people."[113] The congressional debate never broke free from the straitjacket of such positions, and presidential certification proved an ideal way to ensure that it would not. Human rights organizations could report endlessly on the crimes of the Salvadoran armed forces, but to those who wanted to turn the discussion to the more insidious operations of Washington itself, they had far less to say, and would in any case have found little support in Congress.[114] Nor did anyone express much empathy for the grassroots radical forces—they were "insurgents," or worse.

The existence of death squads in El Salvador, Guatemala, and Honduras goes directly to the issue of the restraints that human rights organizations imposed on themselves. The question they focused on was: Are the death squads directly linked to the El Salvadoran, Honduran, and Guatemalan governments, or are they rogue operations? If the former, then the aid the United States was providing made a mockery of the certification process; if the latter, then aiding the regimes could be justified. But the far more important question was whether parts of the U.S. military, private contractors, or other foreign military and intelligence groups were advising, supporting, and in diverse ways sustaining the death squads and comparably horrendous covert counterinsurgency methods. And on this question, they wavered.

In private, many of Reagan's national security managers showed few illusions about the "murderous thugs" they were aligned with. In public, they lauded moves toward elections and praised El Salvador's efforts to control its death squads, but they knew that those squads were part of the government apparatus and that some of their personnel were on the CIA payroll. This is not to say that American officials controlled the regime or the death squads; control in such situations involves a complicated dynamic among diverse, shadowy instruments of power. But in the gloomy words of one Rand Corporation specialist, "As I was told repeatedly by U.S. military and intelligence personnel who were as clear-eyed as they were aghast, the dirty little secret shared by those determined to prevent an FLMN takeover, a group that included both the Salvadoran armed forces and the United States government—was this: the death squads worked."[115]

Americas Watch and Amnesty International astutely assembled details of death squad and counterterror operations into a picture that suggested they were run from the highest levels of the Salvadoran, Honduran, and Guatemalan regimes. Reagan, Abrams, and the rest insisted there was no proof of such involvement. Reagan even got so inventive as to theorize that the left wing was running the death squads so that "the right wing will be blamed for it."[116]

Reporters filled in some of the blanks with stories on CIA-taught techniques, computer systems for tracking dissidents, and so forth.[117] In Guatemala, the *Boston Globe* reported, "agents of the death squads were paid, assisted, and instructed by the Central Intelligence Agency. CIA helicopters, communications equipment, and special firearms were placed at the disposal of G-2 agents while they were liquidating human rights activists, students, judges, and other inconvenient people."[118] Local leaders were on the CIA payroll; the CIA (among others) was providing hit lists of subversives to the regimes; "trainers" were taking part in counterinsurgency operations; some death squads had received training in Texas. The Lawyers' Committee for Human Rights alleged in a letter to Defense Secretary Dick Cheney that the killers of six pacifist Jesuits at the Central American University in El Salvador had been trained by U.S. Special Forces as recently as three days before the assassinations.[119] Human rights groups kept arguing that the death squads operated as part of the local governments; Washington kept insisting there was no proof. The problem was framed again and again in terms of rogue versus local control—neatly deflecting the larger issue of American backing.

One Amnesty report on death squad activity in Honduras pointed explicitly to U.S. funding for Battalion 3-16, the leading death squad. Members had been trained in the United States, where plans for model interrogation centers (including the layout of cells) and the role of psychological coercion had been discussed. Some prisoners had been interrogated in the presence of U.S. government agents. Amnesty cited articles in the American press that reported direct involvement in the creation and functioning of the death squads. Indeed, one of Amnesty's chief investigators wrote a devastating history (though not under Amnesty's aegis) of the police and military strategies linked to U.S. officials and advisors that "helped create the 'death squads' in the first place":[120]

> The pool of 'A&A'[assassination and abduction] talent within the U.S. armed forces is clearly considerable, and these assets at one remove may be even more numerous and used more regularly. U.S. contract employees of Hispanic origin played a major part in the more complex of the sabotage and raiding operations in the undeclared war with Nicaragua. Termed "UCLAs," these "Unilaterally Controlled Latino Assets" were disposable personnel whom the U.S. government could (and would) deny if caught out; and so they were free to use the full range of special operations skills their Special Forces trainers could impart. But this was almost a sideshow to the Special Forces training relationships with foreign military and paramilitary forces.[121]

By and large, though, Americas Watch preferred not to turn its investigatory powers in this direction. It could have put a spotlight on the training of torturers and death squad members, probing the chain of command all the way up through Washington's shadowy world of covert warfare. If it had done so and publicized the results, it could have almost certainly brought a body of evidence from the post–World War II period to light, enabling it to demonstrate a vast, systemic pattern of activity.[122] But it did not do so.

Instead, some human rights leaders simply decided that the administration was not involved. "Unquestionably, Washington has also tried hard to stop the murders and disappearances," Aryeh Neier wrote. "These practices are impervious to United States pressure, however."[123] To argue thus did not break the rules of the game, while arguing that the United States was deeply implicated would have linked the crimes that human rights groups were uncovering to the national security establishment in a way far too likely to discomfort members of Congress, funders, and foundation supporters. Besides, what would have qualified as solid proof? The testimony of shadowy characters, reports based on backgrounders, the off-the-record comments of various observers—all this was easily dismissed.

American officials reacted with outrage to the very idea that the administration might be involved in any such activities. Abrams ridiculed the claim that U.S. officials "condone, if they do not actually participate in, murder, rape, torture and mutilation." Writing in response to questions raised by the *New York Times* columnist Anthony Lewis, he complained there was "no evidence too flimsy, no charge too scurrilous, no personal attack too unfair for Mr. Lewis, if it serves the purpose of instructing readers that American policy and those who carry it out are a force for evil in the world."[124] His rebuttal, as is so often the case in public national security arguments, rested on an appeal to American good intentions—"Americans know that their country does not fit his ugly description."[125]

On October 15, 1984, six days before the second presidential campaign debate between Ronald Reagan and Walter Mondale, news accounts appeared of a CIA-written manual for the Contras, *Psychological Operations in Guerrilla Warfare*. Its ninety pages laid out how "Armed Propaganda Teams" could build political support for the Contras through deceit, intimidation, and violence, and recommended "selective use of violence for propagandistic effects," including "neutralizing" (i.e., assassinating) government officials. The Contras were urged "to provoke riots or shootings, which lead to the killing of one or more persons, who will be seen as the martyrs; this situation should be taken advantage of immediately against the Government to create even bigger conflicts." Further: "Carefully selected, planned targets—judges, police officials, tax collectors, etc.—may be removed for PSYOP [psychological operations] effect in a UWOA [unconventional warfare operations area] . . ."[126]

Americas Watch meticulously dissected the manual and cited it as "evidence that the United States directly solicited the Contras to commit war crimes"; it could "properly be described as a manual for terrorists." It could also be described—though it was not—as standard operating procedure in numerous covert U.S. counterterrorism operations.[127] By and large, though, human rights groups used the existence of the manual for shock effect; and shock without follow-up can deflect attention from systemic patterns of abuses. In any case, congressional investigations quickly relegated the issue to the sidelines, concluding that "negligence, not intent to violate the law, marked the manual's history."[128]

In the end, the issue of the death squads points to what human rights organizations ultimately did not seek to do: convey an understanding of the methods Washington was really using and what they meant for the notion of human rights in general. In their reports there was little acknowledgment of Washington's modus operandi over the preceding half century, little sense that persuading Washington to stop trying to control indigenous processes of change was either viable or just. Nor did they take a position on whether conditions in El Salvador or elsewhere were desperate enough to justify rebellion against the government—a key issue in the concept of human rights, nowhere more so than in the American Revolution itself.

THE CASE OF NICARAGUA

The Reagan administration's campaign against the leftist Sandinista government in Nicaragua presents a political dynamic of a different sort—a proxy war against an established government. In national security eyes, anticommunism had long legitimized covert proxy wars. With Nicaragua, however, Washington combined overt military strategies with covert political warfare. Proxy armies run by the CIA no longer required total deniability, though many of their methods certainly did. An economic embargo designed to cripple development, a military strategy aimed at destroying both urban and rural goods, forcing up Sandinista war expenditures, and intimidating the population—these methods were to prove quite successful. As in the waging of counterinsurgency and death squad activities, all that had to be obfuscated were various aspects of Washington's involvement.

Americas Watch denounced Reagan's "deceptive and harmful use" of human rights issues to attack Nicaragua's Sandinista government. Based on a "core of fact" about the Sandinistas' "serious abuses," the administration had constructed an "edifice of innuendo and exaggeration." The group argued that the November 1984 election victory by the Sandinistas represented an important democratic advance over the previous five decades of Nicaraguan history. Whatever the government was guilty of, clearly "the most violent abuses in human rights in Nicaragua today are being committed by the Contras."[129]

Such findings, however, never challenged the group's self-imposed "mandate" that it "does not take a position on U.S. geopolitical strategy in Central America . . . Whether or not other American interests are legitimate is not the province of Americas Watch."[130] Nor would it take a stand on the general question of whether the United States ought to fund the Contras: "We opposed aid to non-governmental forces such as the 'contras' to the extent that it may be demonstrated that they engage in systematic gross violations of human rights."[131] If the Contras were not committing war crimes and otherwise violating human rights, U.S. support for them would not be an issue for Americas Watch. Amnesty International agreed. Amnesty "does not take a position on questions of foreign policy," though it might address "secondary governments" who funded or provided logistical support to groups that committed human rights violations.[132] This determined neutrality on the issues of invasion and proxy war suggests how great the divide was between the mainstream human rights organizations and the peace movement. It testifies as well to Washington's continuing success in turning the two currents of human rights against each other.

Human rights leaders did occasionally speculate on geopolitical matters. For example, the director of Americas Watch once suggested positing the worst—that Nicaragua had become "another Cuba," a fully

Communist state; did that mean the United States should "launch a war to overthrow the government?" But wasn't that what the Russians were doing in Afghanistan? "Should we behave like them?" His conclusion was revealing. "We don't have to bully small countries that we consider obnoxious. Our side has more options. We dominate the world, not by flexing our muscles, but economically, technologically, ideologically, linguistically, and culturally."[133] Waging war on countries to promote human rights was out, but the promotion of democratization and human rights was rapidly gaining favor.

Rights leaders seldom confronted American policy directly.[134] Their reports raised doubts about the administration's claim that Nicaragua was arming the El Salvadoran rebels, a key rationale for its proxy war; but such skepticism did not challenge policy per se. Their mantra was "Take no sides in a conflict." Yet in Nicaragua, as Neier commented, the United States "used human rights information as an instrument of warfare"—it highlighted Sandinista abuses in order to gain public support. Thus the dilemma: "We didn't want to fall into the trap of overstating them," yet had to "make sure we didn't understate abuses, as that would make us an apologist for them."[135]

The executive director of Americas Watch charged that the Sandinistas "have aligned themselves with the Soviet Union; they are not democrats; they have shown no respect for freedom of expression"—charges about which many human rights activists were dubious. However, he continued, "as Amnesty International's report demonstrates, they have largely—though not entirely—avoided the worst cruelties practiced by the government that preceded them and by the governments in nearby El Salvador and Guatemala."[136] The conclusion may not have been the one Washington wanted, but it could live with it well enough because the terms of the debate were exactly what it wanted.

Attacking the Contras became a safe way for congressional opponents of the proxy war to debate the issue of Nicaragua. They repeatedly challenged the legality of Reagan's undertaking—its dubious funding (temporarily cut off by the Boland Amendment), the illegal mining of the harbors, the illicit CIA involvement. As Neier argued, "there would be no war in Nicaragua except for the United States. We organized, recruited, trained, guided, financed, and supplied the contras, and we speak to the world in their behalf."[137]

Yet despite such arguments, Americas Watch still concluded that the Contras were non-state actors rather than components of a U.S. military operation. (In the rare instances that this standing was disputed, it was quickly dismissed as irrelevant to the focus on the rights of noncombatants.) Had it ever been acknowledged that the invasion was run almost completely by the United States, using a mercenary force armed by Washington, responsibility for the human rights atrocities would have fallen directly on the Reagan administration.

In 1986, the International Court of Justice ruled in the case of *Nicaragua v. the United States* that "by training, arming, equipping, financing and supplying the *contra* forces or otherwise encouraging supporting and aiding military and paramilitary activities in and against Nicaragua," the United States "has acted, against the Republic of Nicaragua, in breach of its obligations under customary international law not to intervene in the affairs of another state."[138] The U.S. had "encouraged" the Contras to act "contrary to general principals of humanitarian law."[139] The court found further that the United States attacks had violated "international law not to use force against another state."[140]

Not only did the Reagan administration ignore the court's findings; little of the decision made its way into congressional testimony by Americas Watch or Amnesty (or into a more general public debate). Yet these groups could have easily insisted that while such issues were outside their mandate, they nevertheless warranted investigation by a citizens commission—or an international group—to assess Washington's legal responsibility for crimes against peace and its accountability for the war crimes they themselves had been documenting. They could have warned, as they did about leaders in other countries in later years, that American leaders could face charges for violating the laws of war even under the U.S. government's official interpretation. They chose not to do so.

They ignored a further aspect of the court's ruling. In the 1940s, non-Western countries had successfully insisted on nonintervention in the internal affairs of other countries as part of the UN charter—a demand reflecting their histories of colonization. When the court lambasted the various U.S. arguments as essentially proposing a "new principle" of the right of "ideological intervention," a "striking innovation" that had no basis in law,[141] many human rights leaders should have had reason for pause; for Reagan's entire promotion of democratization could be seen as a form of the ideological intervention that the court was dismissing as baseless in international law. The dismaying truth, however, was that U.S. human rights leaders were coming to accept it.[142]

THE CO-OPTATION OF THE MOVEMENT

The human rights groups' stand of refraining from comment on foreign policy was anything but consistent. Some leaders might have disliked the democratizing methods the United States brought to bear against the Sandinistas, but in the end they found much that was positive in the overall approach. In Chile, for example, Washington was becoming increasingly concerned that Pinochet's ruthless dictatorship was likely to give rise to a resurgent left. After 1985, the U.S. Embassy in Santiago and the National Endowment for Democracy (along with more covert entities) sought to ensure a transfer of leadership to a political center opposed to any radical ideas; they applied pressure to achieve a "no" vote in the 1988 plebiscite Pinochet had called to legitimize his continuation in office. Washington's objective was to isolate the left, weaken the radical demands of labor groups, and, as far as possible, wean the right away from the dictatorship.[143] Promotion of civil society (as opposed to community action), backing of electoral politics (as opposed to labor organizing), and support of multinational corporations were all aspects of Washington's strategy.[144]

Of course, it can be plausibly argued that the various democratization activities intended to weaken Pinochet were also a viable way to promote human rights—developing links with business leaders, supporting the press, labor groups, key academics, and so on.[145] The actions the United States took against Pinochet, Neier later wrote—among them the National Endowment of Democracy's funneling of money to the Chilean opposition—represented Washington's acknowledgment, at least in principle, of the importance of "promoting human rights as a foreign policy goal." Reagan's (and later George H. W. Bush's) policy toward Chile, Neier continued, was a victory for human rights—an "acceptance of the view that our policy should be applied evenhandedly." This growing alliance with Washington did not involve any violation of principle, human rights leaders argued; it was a pragmatic one of sharing certain ends.[146]

In Nicaragua there was practically no form of democratizing that human rights leaders found unacceptable. Yet such "ideological intervention" was (and remains) a charged issue. Was funding by the National Endowment for Democracy and other American sources for a Nicaraguan paper, *La Prensa*, to promote calls for the overthrow of the Sandinista government, already under siege, an example of the free press in operation? Does freedom of the press extend to a paper's right to support armed, externally controlled forces (the Contras) attempting to overthrow an elected government? Human rights reports rarely delved into such questions.[147] In 1975, the Senate's Church Report on CIA operations against the Allende government in Chile had pointed to the funds that flowed to *El Mercurio* so that the paper could spread CIA-planted rumors and propaganda,[148] showing how the CIA made Allende's censorship of the paper a centerpiece in a highly orchestrated campaign to accuse him of suppressing "freedom of the press." Did human rights groups assume such standard operating procedures of ideological intervention were myths? Irrelevant? Unworthy of investigation? They simply took no position.

Yet they had not always deflected questions about the impact of hostile attitudes on human rights. In its 1975–1976 report on Cuba, Amnesty argued that the "persistence of fear, real or imagined, of counterrevolutionary conspiracies" was "primarily responsible for the early excesses in the treatment of political prisoners. By the same token, the removal of that fear has been largely responsible for the improvements in conditions."[149]

There were few comparable statements about Nicaragua. Americas Watch leaders often found connections between American hostility and human rights lapses questionable: "We have no way of knowing whether the Sandinistas would be more repressive or less repressive if there were

no war. Too many factors enter into the equation to make any calculation that can be defended,"[150] Neier wrote. Such views fit with the prevailing media norms. A 1986 *New York Times* editorial, "The Sandinista
Road to Stalinism," argued that the "Sandinistas ask us to believe that
Congress's full support for the Nicaraguan 'contras' is forcing them to
crack down further on free thought and speech. We don't believe it. The
depredations of the C.I.A.-sponsored army neither justify nor explain
the totalitarian trend in Managua."[151] There was "no reason to swallow
President Ortega's claim that the crackdown is the fault of the 'brutal
aggression by North American and its internal allies.' "[152]

The Sandinistas, who had often cooperated with Americas Watch
and Amnesty on their numerous visits, allowing monitors wide access
to much of the country (in sharp contrast to what these groups encoun
tered in El Salvador, Guatemala, and Honduras) saw it differently. In
the words of one progressive Nicaraguan group, "It is impossible to discuss human rights in Nicaragua without taking a position against the
war, since that is the principal source of human rights violations and
arguably very nearly the exclusive one." The rights to work, health, education, and national independence were all being "systematically and
deliberately violated by the government of the United States, which,
through its contra proxies, is far and away the leading abuser of human
rights in the country."[153]

Yet a discussion that ignored the context of the war is almost exactly
what human rights groups proceeded to conduct. The electoral defeat of
the Sandinistas in 1991, Americas Watch concluded, removed "the pretext that had given rise to the violations . . ."[154] "Pretext" is a notable
choice of words: "something that is put forward to conceal a true purpose." In the comments of various human rights leaders, there is a
double standard: the Sandinistas' repressive acts reveal what they are
really up to, and yet Washington's hostile acts do not reveal the truth
about America. The rights to self-determination, sovereignty, cultural
integrity, education, and health slide into the background, less important than the civil rights that these groups were charging the Sandinistas with violating. As usual, the first current of human rights was
swamping the second.[155]

Reagan in his public diplomacy used words somewhat differently from his predecessors', but the script was much the same. Cuba had long provided the paradigmatic testing ground for hostile action in the Americas—embargoes, proxy warfare, assassination attempts—with each instance of reactive countermeasures singled out as one more example of Communist repression. Our hostile acts, it was claimed, forced our enemies to reveal their innermost repressive selves. And so in Nicaragua the (nationalist, revolutionary) leadership was not really driven to commit abuses by the United States; they were die-hard Marxists all along, just waiting for the chance to take the country down the one-party totalitarian path. The United States had been patient, waiting to see what direction the new regime would take. And in any case there was little the United States could do, since the *fundamental* reasons for abuse and repression—as in Cuba, China, Vietnam, Guatemala, and Iran—arose straight out of the ideology of the regime.

These campaigns against almost every nationalistic or revolutionary force the United States has confronted since the Cold War began reflected the innermost tenets of the globalist faith. Turn the accusations inside out and the beliefs of the national security managers emerge with stark clarity. Most of them never doubted that the Nicaraguan Revolution was a dangerous example. As CIA Director William Casey told Bob Woodward, "Let's make the bastards sweat"[156]—level an embargo, commit economic sabotage, use proxy war to make government expenditures skyrocket.[157] And unnerve them with the ever present possibility that the United States might invade—"perception management," as the psyops warriors called it.[158] Such hostility would bring out the regime's truly repressive character, thus justifying the United States's highly interventionist policies of democratizing.

Little wonder, then, that human rights leaders sometimes wondered whether the Contras had been created to bleed Nicaragua "as an object lesson to anyone else with thoughts about establishing a leftist government in the Western Hemisphere."[159] But such thoughts never led them to find a war against the social advancement and economic well-being of a nation a violation of human rights. Their obliviousness further bound them to a single current of human rights and implicated them in

Washington's use of that current for its own quite different ends. So interchangeable had their approach become with Washington's political warfare strategies that some human rights leaders concluded that, with the Reagan administration, "concern with human rights appeared to have secured a permanent place in the formulation of our policy toward other nations."[160]

Not everyone was convinced. The Nicaraguan government established solidarity organizations worldwide; by 1988 there were more than seventy-seven sister-city relationships between Nicaraguan and American communities alone. Religious and peace organizations developed a "Pledge of Resistance," eventually signed by some seventy thousand, to engage in acts of civil disobedience and nonviolent demonstrations at the White House and the Capital in the event of an American invasion. Such defiance was anathema to many human rights leaders, some of whom openly condemned leftists for undermining the universality of human rights principles. Neier again: "Much of the left did not speak out against abuses of human rights by governments aligned with the Soviet Union, particularly in the Third World and above all in Nicaragua." He acknowledged that the movement had initially drawn most of its support from progressives opposed to the Vietnam War and outraged at U.S. complicity in the coup in Chile. Now, in failing to take a principled stand against *all* rights violations, what he called the left was abetting Reagan's "simplistic" claims of democratization and thus aiding "Reagan and company" in taking control of "the political capital of the human rights cause."[161]

Rarely has the divide between human rights leaders and activists been so stark. The leaders often reined in the activists whose ideals had been forged in the upheavals of the 1960s and whose tactics they feared were incendiary. They did so in the name of "consistently applying principles," of "not taking sides," of "taking no position on foreign policy" or on aggression or on war itself. Unfortunately, their self-imposed impartiality was a moral-sounding stance that Washington could easily live with; after all, it was an outcome of Washington's long-standing psychological-warfare strategy of turning the two currents of human rights against each other.

4

HUMAN RIGHTS AND CHINA

Just as the Cold War was coming to an end, China erupted as one of the most contentious and long-lasting issues in the history of human rights. On June 4, 1989, tanks rolled into Beijing's Tiananmen Square, and overnight the notion of the Chinese government as an interesting anomaly—a Communist state experimenting with economic reforms— was replaced by the image of a corrupt clique of octogenarian hard-liners clinging to power by brute force. For twenty days China dominated the nightly network news (which devoted 25 percent of its air time to the situation), and CNN came into its own, continually replaying graphic footage of the terrible events as they unfolded. Tiananmen's "goddess of liberty," a ten-meter-tall stature created during the crisis that quickly became seen in the United States as a replica of the Statue of Liberty, was constantly invoked on the air as a testament to the universality of American freedom and human rights.

In Congress, the word "barbaric" was repeated again and again. The Chinese government's acts were "barbaric," its behavior "barbaric and reactionary," its vision the "very depths of barbarism." "The civilized world is repulsed by what we have witnessed," declared Senate Minority Leader Robert Dole.[1] "The tanks in Tiananmen stand as mute but mov-ing testimony of the moral bankruptcy of a government that can main-tain itself in power only by killing its own people," Senate Majority Leader George Mitchell stated.[2] Within a week, the *Congressional Record* had printed three thousand pages of denunciations. Almost every member of Congress spoke, most demanding that Washington act.

For nearly fifteen years China had been called the "great human rights exception"—a nation that enjoyed "an inexplicable immunity" from human rights criticism.[3] Of course, for national security managers the reasons seemed obvious enough. Ever since the Nixon administration, U.S. policy had been guided mainly by security concerns that saw China as an important counterweight to the Soviet Union. Although both presidents Carter and Reagan spoke out about human rights violations in other Communist countries, toward China they maintained a pointed silence. Instead, they emphasized Beijing's strategic importance and the gradual improvements its new market-oriented reforms were yielding an approach most famously evident in Reagan's reference to "so-called Communist China."[4] Only after the Chinese Communist Party itself spoke openly for the first time in 1978 about the massive rights violations during the Cultural Revolution did the State Department issue its first full report on human rights conditions there.[5]

But why did human rights groups follow Washington in largely avoiding human rights issues as they related to China? Their leaders have offered a number of reasons.[6] The "paucity of information" and the difficulty of gathering accurate statistics made hard data scarce. Journalists, often a source for information on rights violations elsewhere, feared expulsion. Human rights advocates conceded that some of their reports were inadequate. For example, a 1985 report from the Asia Watch section of the Fund for Free Expression, focusing largely on China's economic and social advancements, devoted only a single sentence to the suppression of political rights.[7] Moreover, Chinese Americans, unlike refugees from the USSR and Eastern Europe, never constituted much of a pressure group; few wanted to "embarrass the PRC" and risk impeding normalization and their ability to travel to China. Since Washington had no diplomatic, commercial, or foreign assistance leverage to exert over Beijing, human rights advocates in Congress also remained subdued; as even one conservative congressman said bluntly, once economic reforms had made "the Chinese seem increasingly 'ours,' their lack of human rights is not an issue."[8] Far more than Amnesty, American human rights groups believed, like the Cold War anticommunists before them, that their work required not just U.S. pressure on a recalcitrant government but access to dissidents and local activists as well. The latter were urging reform within the bounds of socialism; they showed little interest in cooperating with Western human rights groups to publicize abuses they were exposing themselves, and so those groups by and large held back.

Still, the situation was changing by the mid-1980s. As Human Rights Watch pointed out, increasing economic contacts meant a developing potential both to positively influence China and to pressure it. Chinese students had started coming to the West. Tibet was attracting more attention, and in 1985 impetus for the formation of Asia Watch came from an aide to the Dalai Lama.[9] The increasing prominence of a "Tibet lobby," worldwide protests against Chinese actions in Tibet in 1987, and statements by the Dalai Lama all attracted congressional interest. Finally, in 1988, just a year before Tiananmen, the Soros Open Fund Society (the precursor of the Open Society Institute founded in 1993) became active in Beijing. But the events of Tiananmen put an abrupt halt to these gradual changes, and soon there was bitter acrimony between human rights organizations and the Bush administration over how to handle China.

CHINA IN WASHINGTON'S GRAND STRATEGY

Contrary to all the claims of human rights scholars and advocates, China was never *really* the great "human rights exception." There as elsewhere human rights organizations broadly followed in the wake of Washington's global strategy—a hidden history that once again reveals just how tied into U.S. national security concerns the evolution of human rights attitudes has been. An overview of Washington's grand strategy toward China since 1949 shows this process at work and what was really at stake in it.

From 1949 on, Washington's policy of isolating China went hand in hand with its strategies for a new economic and political order in Asia.

China might have been contained (as British, Indian, and Japanese leaders, among others, had advocated) by promoting a realpolitik balance of power system in Asia. But containment was not enough to accomplish Washington's global strategy. China had to be isolated, in order to prevent other Asian and European nations from recognizing it or having any economic and cultural contacts with it, or negotiating over such issues as China's entrance into the UN and the future status of Taiwan.[10] Washington's policy, in short, was about far more than just containing the Chinese Revolution; its far greater goal was to integrate the rest of Asia into an America-centered world.

In Europe, a line denoting containment of the Soviet sphere could be drawn across a region that was relatively stable in military, economic, and ideological terms. But until the mid-1960s the new Asian order was still weak and highly vulnerable; traditional colonial trade patterns were altering very slowly. Japan had not yet been tightly drawn into an America-centered global economic system, and though the traditional economic ties between China and non-Communist East Asia had largely been broken, the United States feared they could still be mended, with devastating consequences for its Asian policies.

Washington's approach to China was thus very different from its policy toward the Kremlin. By the late 1940s, containment without isolation had come to be largely accepted as the best way to deal with the Soviet Union. In the months after Stalin's death in March 1953, the Eisenhower administration began a debate over expanding contact with the USSR, which the new Soviet leadership eagerly sought. Repeated discussions weighed the pros and cons of cultural exchange and of negotiation, their urgency fueled in part by increasing concern over the Soviet Union's new nuclear capability.[11] Without those interactions, it is hard to see how the emerging bipolar world could have come to be quite so compatible with the key interests of the two great powers.

But for decades American policy toward China was far harsher. The United States monitored in great detail the contacts of overseas Chinese— its own citizens and those of other nations—with China. American diplomats noted who went to China and why, and what they did and said upon their return. Even in internal discussions, government officials rarely suggested that drawing Chinese leaders into diplomatic talks would serve any purpose other than the negative one of legitimizing them. The vaguest nods in that direction were attacked as undermining Taiwan, to which the Nationalist Chinese under Jiang Jieshi had fled in 1949 after the triumph of the Chinese Revolution.

Cultural exchanges were forbidden. Few business contacts were permitted either, especially compared with the checkered but persistent relations between American businesses and the Soviet Union after November 1917. Businesses suspected of dealing with the PRC were carefully monitored and financial transactions in Hong Kong reported in detail by the Treasury Department as part of the ongoing American embargo against trade with China. The United States allowed no journalist to enter China until Edgar Snow went in 1959. Nor did any literary image of China ever match the way the Soviet Union, in John le Carré's novels, challenged the West in a deadly game with intricate rules. The Chinese seemed to be beyond such games, beyond rules. Hence Secretary of State John Foster Dulles's refusal to shake Zhou Enlai's hand at the Geneva Conference in 1954; it was a minimal civility that had not been denied even the Soviets.

Many Western histories and human rights accounts of China argue that Beijing was at least as hostile to Washington. The reasons given are varied: the inflexibility of the repressive Communists; the reinforcement of Communist dogma by American intervention in the Chinese civil war after 1945; resentment over centuries-long humiliation at the hands of the West; lack of experience in dealing with other states as equals; China's pride—which is to say, its xenophobic nationalism; the very nature of the Communist system, which was said to require a demonic enemy to promote domestic revolutionary goals, and so on. Whatever one makes of these arguments, they all tend to ignore the obvious: that Beijing would have responded to recognition by Washington, that it would have taken its seat in the UN had it not been blocked, that it would have willingly traded goods (on however limited a basis), possibly with the United States, certainly with some of its allies.[12]

President Eisenhower and Secretary of State Dulles believed they were holding the line against China to gain time—not just for animosity between the Soviet Union and China to grow, but also for a new Asian system of power to emerge that China would ultimately have to conform to. Eisenhower and Dulles often spoke in private of the long-term likelihood of a split between China and the Soviet Union; the pivotal question for them was whether the West could stand firm and wait for a new Asian order for as long as twenty-five years. If the Sino-Soviet split came too early, the situation in Asia might even deteriorate. To focus only on the way they intensified military pressure on China as a means of provoking a split, therefore, is largely to ignore Washington's underlying strategic concern. Isolating China and developing the rest of Asia—economically, politically, and militarily—were always inextricably bound.

In later years American officials and human rights leaders liked to say that China had isolated itself, but the real story is that by the mid-1960s China's isolation from a rapidly developing Asia no longer fully served U.S. strategic objectives.[13] Washington's tactics were starting to change in these years. In a widely heralded 1967 article for *Foreign Affairs*, Richard Nixon noted that "taking the long view, we simply cannot afford to leave China forever outside the family of nations, there to nurture its fantasies, cherish its hates and threaten its neighbors. There is no place on this small planet for a billion people to live in angry isolation." In reality, he was echoing the Johnson administration when he argued that "a policy of restraint, of reward, of a creative counter pressure designed to persuade Peking that its interests can be served only by accepting the basic rules of international civility" could pull China "back into the world community."[14]

Washington well understood what this policy would require. From the Eisenhower administration on, its argument had been that the American market was a vehicle for shaping economic relations with the South, and particularly for encouraging select allies—Japan, Taiwan, South Korea—to develop and integrate their economic systems with the United States and thereby reap the rewards of the global marketplace. The Western business corporation, skilled in combining capital, technological know-how, organization, and management, was the ideal institution for drawing these nations into the global economic order.[15]

Even the Soviet Union was a candidate. A year earlier, Kennedy's secretary of defense, Robert McNamara, had echoed widely shared sentiments when he stated that "peaceful trade between the United States and the USSR would tend on the whole to mold the Soviet Union in the Western image."[16] All this was possible because, as one governmental task force on development phrased it, the United States was the only genuinely "universalist" power available to order the planet.[17]

In the long run, these hoped-for changes could apply just as fully to China. William Bundy suggested in a 1966 memo to Secretary of State Dean Rusk, "A chance to begin developing an export market in the U.S. would have the most attraction for the Chinese Communists, and we could expect them sooner or later to test our willingness to accept their goods."[18] A massive interdepartment government study of the same year echoed the idea: if the United States were to lift its trade embargo, "the greatest gain to China would be in its opportunity to earn dollars by selling in the rich US market . . . [and this change] could contribute substantially to Peking's ability to import grain and industrial equipment."[19] It could have further political implications as well: "Once engaged in selling to profitable U.S. markets, even via third countries, Communist China would be less free to act in ways which might threaten to cut off that source of scarce foreign exchange. As a result, China might gradually acquire a practical interest in developing and maintaining a measure of detente."[20]

"Opening" involved several steps, the first of which was Nixon's triangular diplomacy with China and the USSR. That pointed toward the second step, itself prefigured in the integration of Japan and other Asian economies into the global marketplace. As the Pentagon's draft study for post–Cold War policy put it, Washington's visible victory had been the triumph over Communism and the Soviet Union, but the "less visible one, the integration of Germany and Japan into a U.S.-led system of collective security," was what had truly consolidated the "leadership necessary to establish and protect a new order."[21] No new rivals now stood in the way, and Washington would prevent any potential competitors "from even aspiring to a larger regional or global role." The United States—as balancer, manipulator, preeminent military power—

would be the ultimate adjudicator of power relations and developments in every region of the globe. That included China's incorporation into the global market.

CHINA AT THE END OF THE COLD WAR

If Tiananmen had erupted a number of years later, Washington's response might have been to punish Beijing far more than it chose to, even to push for regime change. But in 1989 the events in China appeared largely as a distraction from a more pressing and volatile geopolitical issue: Mikhail Gorbachev's call for an end to the Cold War. His push for new policies in Europe was an audacious challenge to President George H. W. Bush, who warned that the United States seemed to be "losing the battle . . . over influencing the direction of Europe."[22] With Eastern Europe breaking free of Russian control, the overwhelming preoccupation was increasingly: Whither Germany and, thus, whither Europe? The future of East Germany and the question of whether reunification would take place inside or outside NATO emerged as the main battleground on which the continuation of American preeminence would be decided. Washington's closest European allies, Great Britain and France, opposed a reunified Germany;[23] Bush advocated for a reunified Germany within NATO, since an independent Germany outside NATO might lead to an independent Europe, a more multipolar future, and thus an abortive end to Washington's four-decades-long effort to fashion a world order of its own making. By the mid-1990s these issues were significantly under control. As Paul Wolfowitz observed much later, globalization "refers primarily to the increasing interconnectedness of the world economy [and] occurs within the context of the global dominance of American economic and political ideas, accompanied by the spread of American mass culture"; unipolarity describes the same phenomenon.[24]

But in 1989, as one NSC staffer explained, "The whole world was flying down, straining every resource we had. . . . We had no interest in pushing China over the edge."[25] The reshaping of Europe and the breakup of the USSR brought too much volatility to Washington's global agenda to risk further instability in China. Tiananmen briefly made national security managers nervous that China might become a focal point for discontented nations; Beijing could then seek to position itself as the leader of the world's poorer states in opposition to an American-European-Japanese-led coalition defending the status quo.[26] These considerations lay partly behind President Bush's wariness of pushing the hard-liners too far. His hard-liners did not include Deng Xiaoping but other leaders who might be tempted to pursue a more autonomous economic development plan. This "China at the crossroads" argument echoed throughout the 1990s—China as a nation poised between inward-looking nationalism and outward-looking economic integration.[27]

Tiananmen provoked an outpouring of outrage in the West, rousing human rights leaders to challenge Bush's China policies. He was fiercely attacked for supporting the "bloody Butchers of Beijing," as Bill Clinton put it. But for the national security managers, once the immediate Tiananmen crisis passed and the Chinese government consolidated its power, the question again became how to handle China. In a still-globalizing world, China needed to be tied down in an intricate web of integration, a web not spun by the world's one superpower alone but made up of countless tiny threads of soft power, like the thousands of Lilliputian threads that bound Gulliver—each one insufficient in itself, but all of them together achieving their goal. Washington's objective was clear enough: China was to be "incorporated" into the "norms and rules" of the international order. Beijing would gradually abandon its doctrinal vestiges, "choosing to become a member of the global establishment."[28] With Beijing now learning the rules, Washington could spend time negotiating with it over issues of nuclear proliferation, support for the Gulf War in the UN Security Council, and so on—critical concerns for the United States that could not be advanced by embargoing China. In the meantime, the national security managers quietly continued to reinforce American links with Japan and Taiwan. Almost everyone was uneasy about China, for it always "loomed" large, a potential superpower if only in its capacity to turn the international system upside down.[29]

The national security disputes, as is so often the case, were mainly over means and timing, less about the objective than the tactics to achieve it. Broadly put, starting in the late 1980s the national security managers sought a stable but relatively weak and pliable China. The problem was that a weak China would not be stable, and a stable China would not be weak. Few of them wanted to see China become a failed state, which would bring risks to American power by destabilizing the international system. But no more did they wish to see a powerful, autonomous, self-determining nation asserting its right to formulate the rules along with the other great powers. According to one observer, two basic camps emerged—an "open door" constituency seeking "constructive engagement" and a "closed door" constituency. Both groups sought to change China, to undermine the Communist Party's hold on power, and to accelerate the pluralization of the Chinese polity and the marketization of the economy. The debate was over methods, not purpose.[30]

This debate continues. A 2008 congressional study identified its two poles: a Blue Team of hard-liners who rejected cooperation and engagement, and a Red Team eager to draw China into the international community. The former stresses the malignity of China's growing military menace and favors links with Taiwan and a strong alliance with Japan. So does the latter, but more quietly, and it is uneasy about making Taiwan an issue.[31]

Ultimately, the ideological dispute within the national security establishment was not really about human rights versus corporate interests, hawks versus doves, idealism versus realpolitik. The human rights ethos has always had a strong constituency among some of the most hard-line anticommunist national security managers, from Senator Henry Jackson to Zbigniew Brzezinski to Richard Perle, for whom human rights remained a potent ideological weapon of last resort toward China. Rights formed the very ideological core of democratization, of soft power, of the "rule of law." As the hawkish historian Robert Kagan has written, seeking improvements in human rights behavior "is really the only way out of the looming prospect of endless confrontation."[32] A "broad program of human rights," Perle has argued, is something the Chinese Communist Party "could not survive."[33] For hard-liners like these, human rights represented a weapon to be brought out as needed to challenge Beijing while ensuring American public support for "containing" China.

RIGHTING CHINA: THE HUMAN RIGHTS
MOVEMENT AFTER TIANANMEN

For human rights leaders, the end of the Cold War called for a fresh conception of American foreign policy. With superpower competition a thing of the past, the Bush administration now had the chance "to move human rights to center stage in US foreign policy"[34] and make "respect for the rights of the individual" the very "basis of the world order of the 1990s."[35] No longer would it be necessary—if it ever had been—to subordinate human rights to security interests. Human Rights Watch called for the administration to make "human rights a critical element of a 'new world order.'"[36] Globalization was a portent of things to come; against its apparent triumph, China now stood virtually alone, the last great holdout to an encircling capitalist system.

In the immediate post-Tiananmen days, human rights organizations published detailed accounts of scores of "people who have disappeared into the Chinese gulag." The group attacked Bush for having raised "hypocrisy to new heights by coupling public expressions of concern with behind-the-scenes efforts to patch things up with those responsible for the slaughter and arrests following the June 4 crackdown."[37] Again Human Rights Watch insisted that Bush's policy of "constructive engagement" was a failure. They accused Bush of a rigid Kissingerian realpolitik: "Rather than even considering the use of trade sanctions, President Bush ensured the Chinese leaders understood that their friend in the White House would block any more severe sanction than a private finger-wagging for their continued imprisonment and mistreatment of democracy advocates."[38] When Bush's deputy secretary of state, Lawrence Eagleburger, chastised senators for their preoccupation with Tiananmen ("In the real world, we need to see that China is less completely charming than the land of panda bears and the Great Wall and also less completely evil than a night in June when the Goddess of Democracy was crushed by tanks in Tiananmen"), Human Rights

Watch condemned his comments as a reflection of the administration's continuing "role as apologists for China."[39]

The administration responded, "Some argue that a nation as moral and just as ours should not taint itself by dealing with nations less moral, less just. But this counsel offers up self-righteousness draped in a false morality." Like Nixon before him, Bush preferred the practical, hands-on language of geopolitics. ("We often seem to lecture and confront other nations publicly on issues such as human rights," he later wrote. "I tried to avoid becoming the pedantic lecturer.")[40] The "vision thing" was never congenial to him. In this instance, though, he invoked a language of freedom through commerce: "I think as people have commercial incentive, whether it's in China or in other totalitarian systems, the move to democracy becomes more inexorable."[41]

In linking freedom and commerce Bush set the context for much of the debate during his administration. What gradually emerged went a step beyond Reagan's recasting of human rights as democratization. Now a business ethos and a corporate-based vision of globalization would be even more prominent features in America's war of ideas. Human rights leaders initially opposed the shift in emphasis, but as with the battle over democratization, they gradually if contentiously came to accept the administration's view that corporate power and the market were of critical importance. Out of their angry debates with national security managers evolved a way of dealing with China—and the larger world—that combined a rights-based ethos that could support democratization with a corporate-friendly culture that spoke the "universal language" of human rights.

At first Congress seemed like the ideal forum for publicizing the Chinese government's human rights violations. Since the 1970s, the American human rights movement had drawn on various tenets of American nationalism that members of Congress passionately espoused. As the preeminent rights-based nation, the United States was inextricably identified with human rights and advanced freedom whenever it lived up to its ideals. Promoting human rights would succeed through orderly reform, not revolution or violence. These rights were understood to exist within the realm of the civil and political, not the cultural or the economic. And of course the United States had a particular responsibility to respond to other countries' human rights violations. During the events of Tiananmen, all this thinking was projected onto the Chinese dissidents, who were immediately perceived as being moved by "our ideals," fighting for "what we have"—they, too, "want the American Dream." "Uncivilized" tyrants might "try to stem the tide," but in time the Chinese people would come to enjoy "our freedoms."[42]

Congressional debates were impassioned and ongoing. Proliferating committees examined various concerns from various angles, each appealing to a different constituency: forced sterilization and abortion, high mortality rates in state-run orphanages and female infanticide, religious persecution and anti-Christian violence, suppression of labor unions, denial of free speech, forced confessions, psychiatric detention, the harvesting and sale of organs, prison labor in the gulags, repression in Tibet, and so on. But though all this activity in the name of human rights attracted a lot of media coverage, it was far less successful at engendering trade sanctions. Unlike congressional discussions of the Soviet Union—which had never had an enticing market and where issues of Jewish immigration, and thus Israel, shaped the debates—the discussions of China showed just how interwoven issues of trade and human rights could become. According to Senator Kent Conrad of North Dakota, trade would "increase the presence of American and other Western firms in China. It will open China to the Internet and other advanced telecommunications technologies that, over time, will expose average Chinese to our thoughts, values, and ideals on human rights, workers' rights and democracy."[43] Senator Dick Durbin of Illinois: "Flood a nation with modems . . . [and] no government can bridle the expansion of thought that will flow."[44] Senator Orrin Hatch of Utah: "There is a relationship between China's barbarism and economic autarky that cannot be denied."[45] Senator William Roth of Delaware: "The forces unleashed by American and other foreign participation in China's market opening will help sow the seeds of democracy and human rights."[46] Senator Christopher Dodd of Connecticut: "there is much to do for

China to meet the standards we expect of civilized nations, [but] trade will make a difference."[47]

A minority on both the right and the left dissented. "Businesses exist, quite frankly, to make money. I certainly have no problem with that," conceded Senator Jesse Helms of North Carolina, a conservative. "But let's be honest on the process of what we are doing here in this Senate Chamber. American businesses, even if viewed in the most charitable view, are not likely to lift a finger to promote democracy in China."[48] Liberal Senator Paul Wellstone, teaming up with Helms in support of a religious freedom act for China, agreed: "the rush for the money and the focus on the money to be made by our trade policy with China has trumped our concern with human rights; trumped our concern about a country that is equivalent in the gulags to the Soviets in their worst years."[49]

Gone was the more pristine, less commercially based human rights idealism of the Carter era. A dynamic, energized corporate vision of the world was coming into its own both within Congress and beyond. From this perspective, denouncing China's human rights violations could go hand in hand with supporting investment there. Bush could be openly condemned for backing the Chinese government; Democrats were delighted to do so. But human rights organizations that insisted on embargoes and trade restrictions found themselves pushed aside even by fervent congressional allies, who argued that the incorporation of China into the world capitalist marketplace was a logical and essential next step.

Human rights groups fought back tenaciously, pressuring Congress to impose economic sanctions and deny China the most favored nation (MFN) status normally accorded other nations. Making MFN an issue ensured that China's human rights record would be debated each year in Congress. (Human Rights Watch hoped that its China drive would become a model for how to pressure other countries in the region.) Rights leaders thus spoke of a "linkage" according to which everything from China's admittance to international institutions to its hosting the 2000 Olympics to visits by American delegations and leaders would be dependent on demonstrations of human rights improvement—which, they warned, would be unlikely to occur "without sustained international pressure."[50]

U.S. human rights leaders argued that nothing about improved economic relations or increased trade led inevitably to political liberation and recognition of human rights. They did not buy the Bush administration's arguments that "building a free market" would lead to "building democracy," "as if promoting a capitalist economy was all that was needed to bring about a democratic system."[51] They argued that China was dependent on the international economy for growth and that Western governments had both the leverage and the responsibility to force concessions.

But Bush's national security managers knew that embargoing China was simply not in the cards. Even if Washington had wanted to, neither the Europeans nor the Japanese had any intention of clamping down on investment. Nor did the overseas Chinese community support such a move.[52] And leading congressional figures, however much they attacked Beijing for rights violations, fully agreed. As with the congressional battles of the 1980s over certification of human rights progress, there was a kind of slow motion inevitability to the outcome.

As the Bush administration mobilized behind the argument that China's expanding economy would open it up to democratization and human rights, Fortune 500 companies also argued against sanctions. For more than a decade Big Business had worried that human rights might be invoked on behalf of labor and better working conditions, leading to various kinds of restraint on "free trade." But now, along with the national security managers, it embraced the language of human rights with a passion, echoing the argument that rights could just as well emerge out of growing trade and an expanding market. As one national security analyst put it, "the purposes to which information technology is put—decentralizing operations and decision-making, creating horizontal links, improving producer-consumer contact, sharpening external awareness and adaptability—correspond with strong market forces and distribution economics. They pave the way for democratization."[53] This development left human rights groups virtually alone in seeking sanctions, and once Tiananmen disappeared from daily newscasts, the corporate onslaught proved unstoppable.

Human Rights Watch condemned both the Bush and the Clinton administrations for "maintaining relations at any cost and sacrificing human rights in the process."[54] Yet increasingly it found itself ensnared in the ongoing debates. What was most likely to advance human rights in China? Did pressure work? Were embargoes really useful? Was Washington selling out human rights by refusing to downgrade China's most favored nation status? Or would improvement come inevitably with widening capitalism and the country's increasing incorporation in the "global order"? If China was an example of "market Stalinism," as some human rights leaders argued, should more be done to open it? There were no easy answers. More revealing, perhaps, is that there was no essential challenge to the benefits claimed for a developing capitalism in China.

Bill Clinton, too, proved quite comfortable with policies that promoted American corporate involvement in the name of human rights and democracy. After considerable debate, his economic and strategic advisors poured forth a stream of praise for the benefits of globalization, and once again Congress echoed them. "Exposure to democracy and capitalism" and to "information and telecommunications" and "web based communications technology," argued Senator Pete Domenici of New Mexico, would increasingly influence the course of Chinese development in "our direction. Imagine what Internet success means to a one-party, authoritarian state such as China."[55]

Over the course of the 1990s, human rights leaders gradually acquiesced to these arguments. "Rail against capitalism as you will," wrote William Schulz, the executive director of Amnesty USA, "but recognize that since we are stuck with it, the test now is to make it work for the largest number of people."[56] Few observers believed that greater corporate involvement per se world make China *more* repressive, or that it was morally wrong or fortified the Chinese government. Some did: dissident Harry Wu argued that "trading with this government and putting investment in this country is like the blood transfusion to a dying regime."[57] But most insisted that sanctions only aroused the antagonism of ordinary Chinese and thus fueled "increasing nationalism which ultimately hurts the human rights cause."[58]

As one human rights leader said, Congress "needed ideological cover to allow them to backtrack from their own linkage of trade and human rights. . . . And that's what the business community gave them. They not only gave them a reason to do it, they gave them a rationale to justify their own change of heart."[59] But he might have been speaking of the movement itself, which was beginning to espouse a more market-friendly ethos. In Schulz's words, "Whether the commercialist argument that economic investment improves a country's human rights record is true, what is hard to dispute is that respect for human rights is good for business."[60] Developing states unrestrained by democracy, movement leaders argued, tended to suppress labor unions and violate workers' rights; legal reforms were essential for advancing both economic development and human rights. A democratic government could enforce contracts and be a better economic partner, Amnesty International USA argued—perhaps half-heartedly.[61]

Faced with the widely agreed upon strategy of a rights-based "commercial diplomacy," human rights leaders turned their focus to enlisting multinational corporations on behalf of human rights. Don't become complicit in repression, they now warned them; promote human rights by encouraging unions, opposing compulsory political indoctrination, standing up for political prisoners, and defending freedom of expression, association, and religious belief.[62] Restrictions on these freedoms "could constrict your bottom line. And how governments handle human rights can tip you off as to what you might face in the event of a corporate dispute."[63] This was not just a strategy for China, to be sure, but an expression of the growing commitment by human rights groups to infusing "commercial diplomacy" with appeals for stability and rights of all sorts—a major step toward corporatizing human rights across the world, of which China was just a part.

As the decadelong debate over China came to a close, human rights leaders concluded that seeking constraints on trade was simply beyond their capacity;[64] the pressures of commerce and corporate interests were too powerful. What they would do instead was infuse the market-place with human rights concerns. Their decision would have reverberations for years to come, in the partial "corporatizing" of human rights—a way for the movement to live, however reluctantly, with Big Business in the global marketplace.

A look at the creation of the Congressional-Executive Commission on China in 2000 graphically illustrates just how compatible human rights groups, business interests, Congress, and the national security establishment had become. The commission was an elaborate apparatus to monitor China's compliance with all sorts of rights—among them freedom of religion, freedom of movement, workers' rights, rights associated with democratic governance, intellectual property rights, Tibetan rights, Taiwanese democracy, and the treatment of political prisoners. Databases of persecuted individuals were developed to track all government-to-government and all government-funded cooperative programs between China and the United States, with the results made available in both classified and unclassified versions for members of Congress and the public.[65]

By the beginning of the new century, then, grand geopolitical strategy and human rights interests each had a logic that kept them on parallel, mutually reinforcing tracks. With Taiwan, Tibet, and Hong Kong, the national security managers were continually probing China's vulnerabilities even as they spoke of cooperating with Beijing. Tibet in particular became a focus of human rights constituencies worldwide.[66] There was even a special coordinator in the State Department "to promote substantive dialogue between the government of the People's Republic of China and the Dalai Lama and his representatives."[67]

The ongoing struggle over the evolution of Hong Kong's democracy appeared far less often in the media, but it was part of the debate over "peaceful evolution" and "democratization" in China as a whole.[68] One of George H. W. Bush's last acts as president was to sign into law the U.S.–Hong Kong Policy Act, which empowered Washington to treat Hong Kong as a nonsovereign entity distinct from China for purposes of U.S. domestic law. Funding for pro-democracy political parties and organizations in Hong Kong, calling attention to the deteriorating political rights situation, helping critics with image building and media presentation skills—all these were part of the programs that Washington often quietly promoted along with human rights groups.

EXPORTING BENEVOLENCE

"Help meant making China more like the West, bringing change that by definition was understood to be constructive," the historian Jonathan Spence concludes in *To Change China*, his account of more than 350 years of Western advisors in China. In each generation they "had presented their expertise as the wrapping around an ideological package, trying to force the Chinese to accept both together."[69] Compelled by their sense of "moral rightness,"[70] they brought something from outside that they believed the Chinese could not arrive at by themselves. They identified with those Chinese who seemed most like them—those willing to be trained in their ways, thus less alien. These advisors, in Spence's account, all sought to fashion China's destiny, only to realize in the end that they had been used by the Chinese for their own ends rather than as gatekeepers to the modern world.

By the beginning of the twenty-first century, the scope of Western-backed democratizing projects and the human rights apparatus in China was indeed impressive. Working with a wide range of groups inside and outside the country, NGOs and governments often overlapped in their goals as they encouraged systemic reforms and sought the release of various political prisoners. Washington itself employed multiple strategies, observed a 2004–2005 State Department overview, including "bilateral diplomatic efforts, multilateral action, and support through government and nongovernmental channels."[71]

The language of human rights groups had grown strikingly similar. Human Rights in China (HRIC), established in March 1989 (before Tiananmen) with the assistance of Robert Bernstein, the cofounder of Human Rights Watch, contributed to human rights work "by implementing programs to generate institutional, systemic change in China while also engaging in critical advocacy strategies on behalf of individuals in China." The organization pursued "policy interventions" that addressed "human rights, technology, legal and administrative reform," including expanding Internet access and curtailing abuse of the rural population, migrant workers, women, ethnic minorities, and children. The goal was to build a "technology platform" that used proxy server technology to reach hundreds of thousands of subscribers in China.[72]

Since the mid-1990s, more than five hundred international NGOs and foundations have given more than $100 million a year for projects in China. In 2000, at least 700 grant-making foundations, 70 advocacy groups, 200 humanitarian organizations, and 150 faith-based charitable organizations were working on China in some capacity.[73] Most have described their mission as advocating for "good governance," "reforming the system of law," seeking "transparency," and supporting "human rights" and the development of "civil society." Again, all these phrases resonate with the language of Washington. USAID, for example, explains that the democratic governance it promotes is "more likely to advocate and observe international laws, protect civil and human rights, avoid external conflicts, and pursue free market economies essential to international trade and prosperity."[74] The Ford Foundation uses similar language (as do the Carnegie Endowment for International Peace, the Asia Foundation, and the Himalayan Foundation): "Law-based strategies serve as an important tool of Ford grantees for advancing human rights, equitable and sustainable development, civic participation and governmental accountability."[75]

Beijing has been both welcoming and wary of these American and Western NGOs. Publicly, the Chinese government has embraced a wide range of advice and assistance—for example, in educating and training provincial and local government officials in charge of WTO rules, in promoting the "rule of law," and in reforming the criminal justice system. But some Chinese critics accuse the NGOs of essentially training "spokesmen for U.S. interests among China's political and cultural elite," supporting reforms that encourage particular directions of economic development, and creating a "culture of compliance" with American ways.[76] They worry that the Internet will ignite the passions of dissatisfied individuals, especially those unable to withstand the allure of American lifestyles. (The MacBride Commission report continues to be relevant.) Internet users tend to be younger, with less "political and ideological education," and are thus prone to believe that "individualistic endeavors lead to personal success" and to favor the "individualistic will to succeed" over community ties.[77]

Such responses are to be expected. Human rights advocates inside and outside the U.S. government were all too aware that they were part of a calculated bargain between Beijing and Washington, the former seeking to learn Western methods and norms, the latter hoping to influence internal developments in ways to its liking. Both sides knew they could not always get what they wanted. But in another updated version of aligning with elites to bring about change, from the late 1980s on Washington and various NGOs attempted to influence the direction of the Chinese government by cultivating the "reformist wing" of the Chinese leadership, much as they had once supported dissident individuals and groups in Eastern European countries. Human Rights Watch was particularly proud of its role in Eastern Europe, where "clients" it had once defended won high posts in the new governments.[78] Tiananmen was all the more shocking because the opposite happened there. The "main political casualty of the post–June 4 repression in China," Human Rights Watch lamented in 1990, "has been the very considerable constituency of reform-minded intellectuals, policymakers and senior Party and government officials that was previously moving steadily towards a commanding position,"[79] a group that represented "the main hope for future democratic reform and economic renewal in China." The organization bewailed the "indifference" of the Bush administration and angrily suggested that it might, "by default and inaction, rest content to convey the message that the US people and its government are but fair-weather friends."[80]

Some old-time Cold War propagandists, with ties going back to the Psychological Warfare Board of the Truman years, had offered words of caution as China was first opening in the 1980s. Chinese students, they pointed out, had long gone abroad to learn the skills of the Western world, and the old Chinese elite was astute in sending them out to learn new techniques "and search out new words" to explain China's perilous situation. Washington's quiet attempt to influence such students with

American ideas was all well and good, but, as one of these Cold Warriors argued, it was also risky: "If perceived as intrusion, the adverse reaction is likely to be broad and determined, from Chinese sympathetic toward those ideas as well as Chinese who reject them or are unable to understand them."[81] His advice was blunt: "Whatever happens, it must take place in China and be done by Chinese. . . ."[82] One searches in vain for this kind of perceptiveness in the human rights reports.

THE DISSIDENTS AND THEIR SUPPORTERS

A group of particular interest to the human rights community was the dissidents who fled China after Tiananmen; they quickly became central to the movement's challenges to the Chinese government's human rights record. The word "dissidents," as in Eastern Europe, has a political edge to it. It is about more than just abuse; it is about an abusive system, and, at bottom, regime change.

Some national security managers, by contrast, were skeptical of these "radicals with radios."[83] They looked askance at the burgeoning infrastructure of the dissident movement, its independent links with opposition groups in China, and the propagation of its views through such outlets as the United States–funded Radio Free Asia.[84] But as was often the case with opposition movements, the real issue for Washington was not whether to support a movement they had not created but how to channel its energy and keep it as a strategy in reserve.

For a time, the dissidents were taken up by the media, human rights groups, and Congress. They embodied "our" ideals, and the label "pro-democracy" stuck—partly because it captured certain truths about the movement, partly because of its usefulness as a mobilizing vision for various constituencies. It was not, however, uncontested. Nor were reformers universally appreciated, as an intelligence report from the time of Tiananmen suggests: "Reformers in the course of one year have managed to alienate all their natural constituencies—intellectuals, who complain of meager salaries and repression; students, who gripe that only officials and their children get ahead; and local officials and rural entrepreneurs, whose enterprises are pinched by retrenchment."[85]

Other reports raised doubts that the 1989 protests were truly widespread and that democracy was truly their animating ethos.[86] What was clear was that bitter disputes over the succession struggle among China's leaders had created an opening for protest as elite elements sought to manipulate the crisis for their own ends.[87] Some Chinese appeared to have had "ties with Taiwan and the exile association China Alliance for Democracy."[88] Such ties were hardly surprising. And there is an argument to be made for open assistance and funding, in China as elsewhere. But it has been offered only selectively, and neither the dissidents nor rights organizations have expressed much concern over the issue. To use the current language, transparency has been limited.

Human rights leaders routinely insist that they don't take money from Washington, that they are independent. But the true situation is considerably murkier. The NED, for example, began funding "democracy seminars" in China in the mid-1980s; after Tiananmen it extended its support to the dissident exile community and its numerous publications. In the 1990s alone, the NED awarded $4,974,505 to media in the exile community, including almost every major dissident magazine in the United States. Its beneficiaries included sophisticated and informative magazines like *Beijing Spring*, whose editorial board was composed of leading Chinese and Western intellectuals; many were also regular commentators or hosts on the United States–funded Radio Free Asia.[89]

The NED, along with various American foundations, also funded labor groups in Hong Kong. More than $2.5 million went to the Asian-American Free Labor Institute (AAFLI) to build a support network of labor activists to assist organizers in Hong Kong, Taiwan, and China. Funding also flowed to Harry Wu's Laogai Research Foundation for a database on China's forced labor prison camps and publicity about their use as detention centers for political prisoners. It went as well to Human Rights in China, a group that is independent yet often—not without reason—blurred together with Human Rights Watch.[90] In the 1990s the NED granted it $1,133,000, and in 2004 it received $486,561 to develop "benchmark indicators to assess China's human rights progress" up to the Olympics.[91]

American association with Chinese students and dissidents is not new. In the 1930s, the journalist Edgar Snow assisted Chinese revolutionaries and critics of the regime, including the great writer Lu Hsun, and helped smuggle Zhou Enlai's wife, Deng Yingzhao, out of Beijing.[92] But help from organizations, including those funded by Washington or influential foundations that can be seen as representing the American establishment is not quite the same thing. Old-time CIA operatives, even those highly supportive of dissidents, such as former ambassador and senior CIA official James Lilley, have been uneasy about quasi-governmental support and too-obvious monitoring. Of contact with dissidents, "I think it is very important that you handle this with some subtlety," he has warned. "I know at times past we've tried to have our Assistant Secretary for Human Rights" see various dissidents. "It would look good back in the States, but you really hurt them."[93] Pro-democracy forces should support democracy in Taiwan and Hong Kong as a challenge to the PRC, he advises, but they should soften the rhetoric about changing their system.

Lilley's suggestion that proximity to American power and influence may in the long run be of little value to critics of injustice, however, was quite simply beyond most American human rights leaders. The fact that they now spoke much the same language as Washington further blinded them to the consequences of their activities for those on the receiving end. Human rights organizations often worked on the periphery of various covert worlds—Washington's, Taipei's, Beijing's—a development barely noted in human rights reports. That some of these organizations' leaders came from the national security establishment or maintained close affiliations with it received hardly a comment. Yet the contradiction between the shadowy John le Carré world of mistrust, uncertainty, and covert and overt struggle in which these groups operated and their bright idealism was inescapable.

Beijing, for example, was certainly aware that many leaders of Human Rights Watch came from national security circles. Former NSC members, Pentagon and State Department officials, ambassadors and special assistants to Bush and Clinton—all were involved, as was the Pentagon official who had picked bombing targets in the first Iraq war and became the organization's advisor on military affairs. From Beijing's perspective,

Human Rights Watch and much of the rest of the U.S. human rights world seemed very much a part of semi-official Washington. (The trend continues: In 2010, the editor of *Foreign Affairs*, the official publication of the Council on Foreign Relations, became the new chair of Human Rights Watch. Earlier the long-standing executive director of the Human Rights First Committee joined the Obama administration as Assistant Secretary of State for Democracy, Labor, and Human Rights. The new executive director of Amnesty USA was no novice to the intricately interwoven worlds of foundations, power, and the movement, either, having worked for more than a decade in the Ford Foundation's Human Rights Unit.)

Support for Chinese dissidents who become American citizens and then return to their homeland to propagate their views almost certainly feeds these organizations' semi-official appearance. When dissidents with new American passports have returned to China to investigate human rights, distribute materials, and, often, make contact with dissident groups, and have then been arrested by the Chinese government, they have demanded the full protection of the American government, knowing that their actions were not only political but in fact a direct challenge to Beijing. Their arrest, or news that their relatives have been questioned or harassed, then generates headlines in the American media. Would the arrest of a Caucasian American who had secretly contacted dissident groups and distributed highly political materials occasion equal outrage?

The NED itself has always seen regime change as part of its mission. No funding operation has more actively fostered ties between human rights organizations in the United States and such Communist Party foes in China as the Chinese Democracy Party (CDP). Human Rights Watch had decried the imprisonment of CDP members and government attacks on party members who have worked with overseas dissidents[94]— fully aware that the CDP was partly funded by the NED and was dedicated to ending the leadership of the Communist Party.[95] The CDP's leader in the United States wrote (in somewhat difficult-to-follow English) that since so many members of the CDP were both American and Chinese citizens, "they will bring the society's value's viewpoint and the society system of America to China, the party, the government and the congress will set up a best diplomatic relations between China and America. This is the biggest and long term country interests of America."[96] It seems safe to say that the Chinese Communist leaders do not share such views.

Such highly political undertakings and their blurring with the exposure of human rights abuses are suggestive of nothing so much as earlier forms of propaganda warfare. Human rights groups have often derided the Chinese government for its "apprehension that so-called hostile foreign forces are bent on destabilizing China"[97]—a goal the NED has frankly acknowledged. Can it be any wonder that Beijing discredits dissidents in China and in Hong Kong by maintaining that they are beholden to American support—"begging in front of foreigners to save them"?[98]

In the years after Tiananmen, Chinese dissidents also offered what some Russian dissidents once had: a glowing vision of the United States. They were not innocent of political theory, but they tended to employ it in doctrinal utterances about the free market and American democracy. Critics of "anti-Americanism" have often argued that American intellectuals see nonexistent positive qualities in China (or elsewhere) because they transform their dissatisfactions at home into virtues projected onto other countries. The same argument can be applied to Chinese dissidents looking toward America. And of course the obverse can be just as true—that an excessive idealizing of our own country can project onto other countries a not-so-subtle disapproval for failing to be like us.

JUDGING CHINA

"By what right did they go?" Jonathan Spence had asked of several centuries of Western advisors in China. "A clue to the answer surely lies in the fact that the advisors themselves did not think of posing the question. They were sure that their civilization, whatever its shortcomings, had given them something valid to offer, something that China lacked. They had the right because they had the ability, the faith, and the drive." And Spence added: "The story of these men is more a cautionary tale than an inspirational tract."[99]

In its modern variant, the question is how much self-idealization is involved—"beautifying oneself while making others appear ugly" in the Chinese phrase. The condescending and moralizing tone often used in discussions of China is revealing. We have to "teach China how to behave." "We have put them on notice." They have to learn to "live up to basic standards of decency," and that certain actions are "just unaccept-able in civilized nations." "We issued a report card today," Amnesty USA announced in 1999, and "we feel that China did not make any prog-ress."[100] There is the hard-line approach: "we must pressure them to cre-ate better behavior." And there is a softer approach: "coaxing them to better behavior," creating "incentives for China to improve." China is on a "learning curve." Its progress is to be closely "monitored." "Sustained international support is clearly necessary" to improve the situation;[101] it is "very important to say, good," when China does the right thing. But we need to "urge China's leaders to move to the right side of history";[102] we have to press for the reforms they don't undertake.

"The more *we* bring China into the world, the more we bring change and freedom into China," President Clinton said in language often echoed in human rights discussions.[103] The debate has never been over the appropriateness of bringing outside pressures to shape and change China but over what configuration of forces would work most effec-tively. The language has grown deeply encoded, a blending of national security and academic social science jargon. How do we get "greater traction" through "engagement"? There are questions of "time frames," "concrete benchmarks," "indicators," "metrics," "toolboxes."[104] How do we help "build the scaffolding" for protecting rights?[105] The "tools for leverage" are many and diverse, including "trade and security baskets."

The United States "retains an ability to function as a gatekeeper to respectability." Washington is the "role setter." In time China may acquire the "ability to behave as a responsible international stakeholder," but it is not yet a "fully responsible" one.[106] The "open door" would enable the Chinese to "undergo a process of socialization that will make them more amenable to hearing and discussing the views of others."[107] We have to ensure that a "paranoiac" response does not occur in China, but also that the Chinese "lose face" when they "act badly." After all, they carry a great deal of "historical baggage." Though the country may start "acting nervous," we "should not provide fodder for Chinese nationalism."[108] Still, we cannot turn away from efforts to "help channel China's growing influence in a positive direction." Washington is committed to "working hard to ensure that China recognizes its own interest in supporting the international system."[109]

Such words and phrases are usually one-way; they are not intended to be applicable to the United States. The United States is not said to be on a "learning curve"; there are no "incentives" for Americans to improve their behavior. In the 1940s and early 1950s American intellectuals devoted much anguished questioning to whether the United States was still in an "adolescent" and immature phase.[110] But thereafter the language changed; it was other nations that had to learn to act in a "civilized" way and "grow up." This is self-idealizing language. We are the "architects"; we have the plans, we have tools, we are the responsible managers of the company in which others are stakeholders.

THE HUMAN RIGHTS MOVEMENT'S VIEW
OF THE CHINESE REVOLUTION

Though the Bush administration was in no hurry to see the Chinese Communist government overthrown, many in the human rights community certainly were. Because the regime relied on repression, they argued, the implementation of full civil and political rights would likely lead to the government's collapse, a prospect few of them were troubled by. Nor did they show much sympathy for the view of Chinese Finance Minister Liu Zhongli: "The United States maintains a triple standard. On their own human rights problems they shut their eyes. For some other countries' human rights questions they open one eye and shut the other. And for China, they open both eyes and stare."[111]

After Tiananmen China seemed to become a veritable cauldron of abuses with little improvement in sight. *No One Is Safe*, Amnesty titled its 1996 report. Human Rights Watch's yearly roundups found the situation consistently dire—"human rights deteriorated" (1995); "significantly deteriorated" (2002); "deteriorated significantly" (2006); "slipping backwards" (2007); "steadily deteriorating" (2008).

This relentlessly sober view does not, however, provide all that much insight, since it is partly an aspect of the long-standing certainty that practically nothing positive came out of the revolution itself. From this perspective, Mao was a "monster," a "tyrant" like earlier Chinese emperors, or worse. The rectification campaigns against intellectuals, the Great Leap Forward, and the Cultural Revolution are lumped with the horrors of Stalin's Russia and Pol Pot's Cambodia, more ugly chapters in the black book of Communism. As a result, human rights accounts shed little light on the most momentous revolution in history; the gains in health and education and the emancipation of women are treated as by-products of a totalitarian regime whose real objective was utter control. The respect for Mao that Westerners sometimes observe in China today they dismiss, as often as not, as xenophobic nationalism or a symptom of a still deeply disturbed society.

And so a conviction has come to flourish among human rights advocates: the further China moves away from its revolutionary traditions and ideals, the more rapidly it can create a freer and more equitable society. They credit little of China's transformation since the 1980s to its complex revolutionary tradition, even though the rapid implementation of market reforms (and the opposition today to some of them) have grown out of earlier revolutionary transformations. Such a view is badly skewed, for rights advocates, by dismissing the revolution's achievements, have come to see their inability to change China as their movement's greatest defeat, while failing to perceive that the drives for greater social and economic justice in Chinese society are, in fact, deeply rooted in the revolution.

Some earlier observers were more sensitive to the underlying issues. In his classic 1949 account, *China Shakes the World*, Jack Belden shrank from the ideological dogmatism of the revolution but pointed out that only the Communists had successfully attacked the age-old bondage of the peasantry and the exploitation of women: "The Communists pulled down the proud and raised up the humble. They freed women from men, the child from the father, the tenant from the landlord."[112] China would continue to favor the "social right over the individual right" as long as its staggering problems remained; the revolution, Belden stressed, is "not finished." The West had failed to bring a better way of life to China. Foreigners had plundered the country for more than a century under the doctrine of free enterprise, leading more and more Chinese "to reject the doctrine of individual liberty because they came to believe it was a weapon of the strong to oppress the weak."[113] The staggering problems China confronted demanded the utmost empathy from Americans. Today the Communist Party is, for better or worse, often still seen within China not as a decaying elite feeding off a brutalized populace but as a political force that retains considerable legitimacy from the radical changes it has spearheaded—as well as from its frank acknowledgment of past failures. The widespread spirit of criticism and challenge to authority so evident today cannot simply be placed at the door of a relatively recent human rights revolution when an earlier and greater revolution played a far larger role.

In the language of human rights today, views like Belden's can seem like condescending apologetics. For some, to fail to emphasize the primacy of individual rights is to suggest that liberties are just for white Europeans and Americans—that there is indeed a double standard, "one for the Russians, who are Europeans, and another for the Chinese, who are Asians." Such an attitude is viewed as demeaning—as saying that non-whites don't want freedom, that the "great hordes of Chinese simply are not to be judged by the same human rights standards applicable to Europeans and those Third World people raised in the Western tradition."[114] It is also a way of saying that economic and social rights should not be privileged over individual rights. But the opposite argument has important elements of truth as well; the prevailing human rights view fails to fully take into account the excruciatingly painful and frightening reasons for revolutionary upheaval, and to a great extent ignores the diverse struggles for justice and social transformation that are part of China's cultural traditions. Further, it conveniently disregards how Washington's determination to isolate the revolution added immense burdens to the building of a new China.

Interwoven with the impassioned argument of rights advocates that the Chinese have as great a claim to individual rights as anyone else is the notion that meaningful change will not come without considerable pressure from the outside. If we don't pressure them, they won't get there. Or as Human Rights Watch has insisted, "Only by ensuring that China pays with its reputation for its misconduct is there any chance of encouraging better behavior."[115] This is not a stance that displays openness to a variety of Chinese efforts, however alien in some ways to Western eyes, to find justice and social transformation.

China is certainly home to enormous human rights abuses. Yet it is also home to frequent protests, to inchoate but widespread demands for greater respect and a wide assortment of rights amid skyrocketing levels of inequality. There are increasing calls for improved medical care, regulation of pollution, and a brake on massive corruption. None of this suggests more need for outside help—or that without it the situation will only deteriorate. The Chinese are not cut off from the world; they can and are learning from others. But they are as able as anyone in the world to find their own way.

CHINA VERSUS INDIA

"Tens of thousands of political prisoners, including prisoners of conscience, were held without charge or trial under special or preventive detention laws. Torture of detainees was routine throughout the country and scores of people died in police and military custody as a result. Scores of political detainees 'disappeared.' Hundreds of people were reported to have been extra-judicially executed by security forces."[116] So begins Amnesty International's 1994 report—on India. Yet there was little public reaction to it in the United States, while denunciations of China never ceased. Why the difference?

Part of the answer lies in the political systems under which the abuses occurred. "China," in the words of a 2006 Human Rights Watch report, "remains a one-party state that does not hold national elections, has no independent judiciary, leads the world in executions, aggressively censors the Internet, bans independent trade unions, and represses minorities."[117] A description of India by the same organization reads: "despite an overarching commitment to respecting citizens' freedom to express their views, peacefully protest, and form their own organizations, the Indian government lacks the will and capacity to implement many laws and policies designed to ensure the protection of rights."[118] U.S. government human rights reports offer much the same view: India "held steadfast to its distinction as the region's most stable and vibrant democracy," begins the Department of State's 2001 report on Indian human rights.[119] By contrast, its 2006 report on China begins: "The Chinese leadership's preoccupation with stability in the face of continued economic and social upheaval fueled an increase in human rights violations accompanied by tightened controls on fundamental freedoms."[120] In laying out human rights problems in India, the State Department report adds that the abuses "were generated by a traditionally hierarchical social structure, deeply rooted tensions among the country's many ethnic and religious communities, violent secessionist movements and the authorities' attempts to repress them, and deficient police methods and training."[121] The language accorded China is more accusatory, less explanatory: "the Government continued to commit numerous and serious abuses." India is treated more gently because its violations are believed to point to its lack of development rather than to systemic faults, while the persecution of each and every dissident in China is taken as evidence of systemic oppression.

How much does the nature of a political regime tell us about human rights under it? In its early years Amnesty International would have answered, "Not very much." Regime labeling was too closely tied to Cold War stereotyping—which is why Amnesty insisted on defending prisoners of conscience according to the trinity of one each from a Western, a neutral, and a Communist country. But today such labeling has become a preeminent method for assessing practically every aspect of human rights.

The stances of the U.S. government and human rights groups on Tibet and Kashmir provide additional contrast. "China and Tibet" was an entry title in recent reports by both Human Rights Watch and the Department of State, an implicit demarcation of separate areas/countries. (Amnesty does not separate them this way.) Kashmir received several paragraphs on rights abuses, but the entry was not headed "India and Kashmir." Tibet had its own subheading; Kashmir did not. Human Rights Watch officially takes no stand on issues of self-determination and independence—a plausible position, given the highly explosive and historically complex nature of such issues. But Beijing has never shed its conviction that the heartfelt support of human rights leaders for Tibetan dissident and overseas groups (including the Dalai Lama) is highly political and implicitly pro-independence. Certainly the CIA's long history of ties with the Tibetan resistance has not been forgotten in Beijing.[122]

For China and Tibet, there has long been an elaborate, highly sophisticated monitoring apparatus in Washington and among human rights groups. Nothing comparable has existed for India—and Kashmir has barely been a blip on the news compared to Tibet. Perhaps because India is democratic, Human Rights Watch did not hesitate to write to the Indian prime minster in 2006, urging him to raise China's human rights record in Tibet with the visiting Chinese president: "The situation inside Tibet is worsening, and your government's deepening relationship with China offers an unprecedented opportunity to press China for change."[123] The presumptions are notable. Human Rights Watch has not asked Chinese leaders to raise Kashmir with Indian dignitaries. The organization takes seriously the claim that India has "entered into a partnership with the US to promote democracy."[124] It saluted the commitment to human rights in Tibet India exhibited by hosting Tibet's government-in-exile. A democratic but rights-violating India versus a reforming but still rights-violating one-party system: this contrast revealed a fundamental ideological orientation of human rights leaders, with roots in a long tradition of "exporting benevolence" to China.

BEIJING'S VIEW OF HUMAN RIGHTS
IN THE UNITED STATES

In the early 1990s, Beijing launched attacks against the crescendo of human rights criticisms by raising its own voice against American rights violations. At the same time, it argued that China was developing an understanding of human rights that necessarily differed from the West's. In short, Beijing began debating the principles and assumptions behind the emerging human rights regime.

Many of Beijing's issues formed a mirror image of Washington's, their implications all the clearer for being set within Washington's war of ideas. The Chinese conviction that Western human rights advocates were regime-change proponents was hardly paranoid—there was plenty of evidence to support it. Nor was China being "hypersensitive" with its allegations of foreign involvement; that involvement was deep, long-standing, and backed by radio, satellite TV, and Internet diffusion of antigovernment materials. Western organizations sensed no conde-scension in their words and actions, no moralizing bent, no intrusive-ness into China's internal affairs. They were merely lending a helping hand, encouraging others to understand their universal human rights; in Beijing such talk sounded very different, especially in the context of Washington's ongoing discussion of "changing China." After all, it was not Beijing that first spoke of culture, entertainment, models of the good life, and human rights as tools of "soft power" and penetration; it was Washington. And it was Human Rights Watch that called human rights an "ideology," with all the implications that term carries in China.

What gave Washington and Western organizations the right to judge all other countries of the world, Beijing began to ask? By what right did they claim to speak for the needs of entire populations, and to privilege some kinds of abuse over others? How could they presume to know best how other countries should transform themselves?

"If you disguise yourself as a 'human rights judge,'" commented one Chinese diplomat, "and go all over the place to point out and criticize the human rights situation of other countries, touching on all 190-odd countries, and say nothing about your own human rights situation, it is like holding the torchlight to shine only on others and not on your-self."[125] Another added that "to talk especially about others" but not about oneself was "an example of hegemony and power politics."[126] That American law mandated such reporting did not mean the United States had the moral authority to carry it out. Moreover, the language of human rights, Beijing noted, disappeared when Washington spoke of its own house—then the talk was of "civil rights." Western human rights groups liked to think that such criticisms from Beijing and governments in the South were an attempt to deflect attention from their own human rights abuses. But Beijing was well aware of the international resentment over Washington's "human rights diplomacy."

What interests, Beijing asked during the Bush and Clinton years, were being served by Washington's invocation of human rights? Beijing saw "human rights diplomacy" as both a direct and an indirect attack on the Communist Party: "The crux of the problem is that as long as China does not change its socialist system, the United States will see it as an 'authoritarian state' with no human rights."[127] Despite well-documented improvements in rights, Beijing argued, China continued to be vilified owing to human rights organizations' hostility to the Communist Party. Because the regime was judged to be structurally flawed, human rights required systemic transformation—whether rapidly (via the overthrow of the government) or slowly (via peaceful evolution spurred by human rights diplomacy).

Beijing also saw this mode of diplomacy as part of a much broader global agenda—a determined drive by Washington to consolidate its status as the preeminent global power and stave off the emergence of a multipolar world. More and more the United States was inserting itself into the internal affairs of other countries under the legitimizing guise of "humanitarian interventionism." Beijing was alarmed when NATO intervened in the former Yugoslavia without UN sanction. In its eyes, "human rights diplomacy" was diplomatic parlance for an attempt "to guide and also to regulate China, a long term process of 'engagement' to make China conform to Washington's rules." As one Chinese critic charged, the purpose was "to control China's economy and politics from within through the process of globalization" and to weaken its national spirit.[128] Washington used human rights to give a "halo of idealism" to realist preoccupations; "carrots" in attractive wrappings concealed the designs of power.[129]

Some Chinese analysts pointed to the way human rights diplomacy and the character of American society were increasingly feeding upon each other. America's commercial culture, they argued, was at the core of a quite distinctive "civilization," one far more capitalist than any other. (European concerns and values were at least not entirely motivated by profit.) They acknowledged the popular aspects of America's "soft power" (Hollywood, the media, fast food) but warned that this popular culture cloaked corrosive ideological messages.[130] There was nothing wrong with contrasting cultures and clashes of ideas, Beijing insisted—but this was exactly what Washington sought to deny. American soft power was about an Americanizing globalization, not about adjusting America's institutions and its ethos to a varied, multipolar world.

Recent Chinese polls have found the nation's popular view of the United States mixed: considerable admiration for America's advanced science and technology, less for its legal system, and even less for its affluent wastefulness. Few see the United States as a "friendly country"; most see it as a "rival in competition." A large percentage believe it is trying to "contain" China. When asked why the United States keeps raising the issue of human rights, 43 percent thought that it was to "destabilize China," 10 percent to "demonize" China, 19 percent the result of "failure to understand the situation in China," and only 15 percent that it was to promote "democratic construction."[131]

Few Chinese doubt that the United States sees their country as its "greatest potential challenge," though most think war is unlikely. Many Chinese commentators point to the restraints the Iraq War placed on Washington after 2003. Yet they have also observed recent leaps in Washington's power—including the "historic breakthrough" in U.S. influence in Central Asia and Afghanistan, part of a "grand plan" to make "America omnipresent in the world."[132] Others have noted how U.S. Central Asian policy has promoted democracy and the free market to facilitate American encirclement of Russia and control oil and gas resources; and how the color revolutions of the Clinton and George W. Bush years were more successful at toppling regimes than improving governments.[133]

"Easy to disintegrate, hard to Westernize," some Chinese analysts have encapsulated the possible effects of regime change in fragile nations.[134] Disintegration and westernizing all too often go together.[135] Nevertheless, Washington, they believe, is overreaching, its democratizing ethos impelling it to do more than it can actually achieve. They suggest that China has no comparable ideological blueprint to change the world, no ideological message except that countries need to find their own way. Multipolarity stands against U.S. unipolarity but is not anti-American per se.

It is unlikely that Beijing sees the global order today as any less predatory than in the days of the Opium Wars a century and a half ago. Some Chinese warily note how easily legalism, human rights, and moralism have all blended together in American thought, a concern George Kennan raised more than a half century ago when he warned that America's legalism was not simply the invocation of law but a projection of American moralism as well.[136] Calls for the United Nations to play a greater international role have become increasingly prominent in Beijing, partly to offset the predatory nature of the world they see around them. But few Chinese commentators have much confidence that the aspirations of powerful states will soon be constrained by rules that are "international." As some wryly note, the term "international community" as it is typically used in human rights reports leaves out China, India, and much of the South, with the result that it represents little more than some 20 percent of the peoples of the globe.

CONDEMNING WASHINGTON

Beijing's understanding of power also informed its perceptions of American human rights violations. From its objections to American behavior in the 1990s (the use of depleted uranium bombs in the Gulf War, the manufacture and export of instruments of torture, the "illegal" war against Serbia) to its condemnations of more recent American wrongdoing (Abu Ghraib, rendition, the clandestine system of prisons in Afghanistan and elsewhere, Guantánamo, torture), Beijing has linked what it considers American-instigated atrocities and human rights abuses to Washington's global ambitions and its "unilateralism."[137] Its criticisms have not been all that different from those of American human rights groups—except for the broader context in which they have been placed. In Beijing's view, the abuse of Iraqi prisoners was not an isolated act nor Abu Ghraib a rare exception; instead, such transgressions were indicative of the way the United States has come to flout "international norms" in its quest to sustain its sole-superpower status.[138]

Unlike Western human rights groups, Beijing argued that the invasion of Iraq "has produced the biggest human rights tragedy and the greatest humanitarian disaster in the modern world today."[139] In addition, it has closely chronicled the "innocent civilians" killed by U.S. military forces in Afghanistan and the use of torture in United States–run prisons there. Again unlike Western human rights groups, China has raised the issue of aggression and has challenged Washington on numerous wars widely judged outside the United States to be aggressive, from Nicaragua to Panama to Kosovo to Iraq. It has zeroed in on the ways human rights violations follow in the wake of occupations, noting that Western human rights groups narrow their focus to individual war crimes and violations of the "laws of war" instead of considering the possible illegality of occupation itself. Beijing thus offers a *systemic* view of American human rights violations—aggressive war, occupation, the imposition of foreign-backed regimes, denial of national independence and self-determination. Where Western human rights groups find systemic defects in China's domestic human rights abuses, China points to the systemic disorders that follow from Washington's global role.

The Chinese have noted that the United States has ratified only three of the six major UN human rights covenants. (The Chinese have ratified five.) The United States has yet to ratify the Covenant on Economic, Social, and Cultural rights; the Convention on the Elimination of Discrimination Against Women; the International Convention on the Elimination of All Forms of Racial Discrimination; and the Conventions on the Rights of the Child. And the covenants Washington has ratified are limited by so many reservations and exceptions that its commitment amounts to little more than window dressing. Then there are all those covenants the United States hasn't signed. It has adamantly

opposed the Declaration on the Right to Development—the only Western country to do so.

Human rights leaders attack China's insistence on the paramount
importance of protecting national sovereignty, but Beijing counters that
without true independence there is little prospect of creating a regime
rooted in popular needs and human rights. Still, it does not consider
claims of national sovereignty completely inviolable. Beijing has criticized abuses in other societies—apartheid in South Africa, attacks on
ethnic Chinese in Indonesia, and crimes of genocide. By the late 1980s,
articles in the *People's Daily* had begun taking note of "international
crimes of human rights"—racial discrimination, apartheid, genocide,
slave trafficking, refugee situations—and calling upon nations to curb
these violations "in accordance with international legal principles."[140]

TWO VIEWS OF HUMAN RIGHTS

In the early 1990s, Western human rights leaders spoke of the enormous threat to the universal vision of rights that was coming from the
East: Asian leaders were proclaiming Asian values and an Asian way,
challenging the "indivisibility of human rights," promoting "cultural
relativism," and even denying that rights applied "equally to all people."
This was not Beijing's position, however; a nation that had "sinified"
Marxism was acutely sensitive to the necessity of particularizing "universal" ideas and ways of thought.

Beijing agreed that human rights and universality could go together
conceptually—*if* the state of a country's economy and its historical
and cultural traditions were fully taken into account. Advocates of the
Western human rights regime maintained that rights, in the words of
Human Rights Watch, are "not luxuries to be enjoyed only after a certain level of economic development has been reached"[141]—and also, as
we have seen, that "the abuse of human rights impedes economic development."[142] Yet this stance hardly obviates the need to envision civil
and political rights concretely or relate them to economic development
and social transformation in highly varied contexts. Beijing insisted
that there were no ready formulas for doing so.

None of Beijing's views in fact refuted the argument that civil free-doms improve economic development or that political repression may work against development. But Beijing did suggest that such notions rested on historically dubious propositions that idealized the West's actual course of development. Chinese historians point to the brutal, centralizing, and repressive methods the Western states used to develop their wealth and power as historic examples of human rights atrocities. They see Western development less as a triumphant evolution of human rights than as a process wherein high-sounding ideals were repeatedly invoked to legitimize a long series of horrors. They accuse human rights advocates of suggesting there are now far different and more humane ways to develop, though the West never practiced them during its own rise. Their intention is not to claim that China, too, should proceed like the West, with "colonies, genocide of the natives, expansionism, exploit-ative trade relations," as one report characterized that history. Rather they are calling attention to a certain hypocrisy in the eagerness with which critics of China conveniently turned against the very methods the West itself had used to create the wealth, affluence, and power in which its vision of rights now flourishes.[143]

Chinese accounts point out the role of slavery in American develop-ment, the racism that continues to this day, and the settler culture that seized the Indian lands—hardly useful methods for dealing with Chi-na's own ethnic minorities. Noting how America's great natural wealth combined with the benefits of being free of feudalism at its founding, Beijing contends that human rights conditions are "closely associated with how developed the country's economy is."[144] If it is bogus for dic-tatorships to justify suppression of rights under the guise of develop-ment, these critics argued, it is just as bogus to trumpet human rights arguments from the center of the greatest concentration of wealth known to history—while manifesting amnesia about the methods used to achieve it, and often to sustain it today.

Fundamentally, then, Beijing believes the United States enjoys more rights because of its wealth, power, and history—not because of its greater virtue, empathy, or understanding of others. It argues that an individualizing of human rights pervades the Western human rights stance largely because of such affluence; that basic subsistence, national independence, economic and cultural transformation are often simply taken for granted. The United States sees itself as a "mentor," concluded one Chinese observer, when it is really just ignoring the "unique conditions that have made the democratic system in the U.S. more advanced than in many other countries."[145] Of course, such considerations are not entirely alien to American observers. "We tend to overlook the fact that our social and political system was established upon probably the richest, most productive, most desirable piece of real estate in the world," Senator J. William Fulbright cautioned. "If our system had been implanted on the bleak areas of Siberia, I doubt it would have been so productive."[146] But such comments have been few and far between in Western human rights discussions.

In this context, Beijing asks, is it not a form of human rights violation for a nation that constitutes 5 percent of the world's population to consume 30 percent of the world's oil, gas, and coal? If China, with a population of 1.2 billion, consumed what the United States does, "it would have surpassed the world's total consumption figure by 140%."[147]

Beijing notes as well that Americans were spared the threat of foreign invasion (though Native Americans were not) for hundreds of years, while China, like many other countries, suffered the "humiliation of being carved up by foreign aggressors and has experienced the tribulations of long-time wars." Western powers, including the United States, came heavily armed with literal as well as religious and ideological weapons, justifying the unequal treatment they imposed with the most uplifting and self-righteous words. American human rights leaders like to emphasize that the UN has been committed from its birth to human rights over sovereignty; China prefers to note that the UN has always been committed to both rights and sovereignty, for reasons any former colonized or semicolonized people can appreciate.

Are the Chinese and American human rights visions simply too far apart? Perhaps. Yet—for argument's sake—what if each side accepted the plausibility of the other's perspective and then used it to rethink human rights globally and at home? What if human rights challenged every society equally (as any system of justice really should in the end), if in different ways? For Beijing, it is America's power, not its rights-based ethos, that continues to play the central role in upholding a violent, ugly, and irrational world economic and political order.[148] For Washington—and not only Washington—the Chinese government is not democratically restrained; its repressive mechanisms are potent and effective. Neither view is invalid. That Beijing feels itself under assault by Washington and Western human rights groups does not make their charges false—just truths in the service of power, which is what propaganda is so very often about.

BEIJING'S VIEW OF HUMAN RIGHTS IN THE UNITED STATES

On human rights issues, Beijing has essentially refused to set itself up as a judge of others—with one exception. Though China is a developing country, it "can still afford to buy a mirror to give to the U.S. so that they can get a good look at themselves,"[149] remarked one Chinese ambassador. So in the 1990s Beijing began issuing detailed and wide-ranging reports on life in America, a kind of "tit for tat," as Zhao Qizheng, the minister of information, put it.[150] What it found amiss would startle few observers of American conditions: a steady rise in homelessness and below-the-poverty-line populations; grossly unequal access to health insurance and medical care; racial disparities in wealth and education; rampant violence reinforced by some 235 million guns; illegal detention and systems of surveillance; continued inequality of women, domestic violence, and sexual offenses. The list is long and extremely well documented.

Chinese critics asked how the growing inequalities between rich and poor in the United States could be compatible with a human rights spirit. Why were 36.5 million Americans living in poverty in 2006? Why is the wealth of the richest growing exponentially, widening the already huge earnings gap between the rich and the less well off? Why did payments to corporate CEOs that were some 475 times higher than those to ordinary workers go unchallenged by human rights advocates?

On another subject, was the control of patents on medicines for AIDS and other diseases that would help enormously in poorer countries an intellectual property right—or a human rights violation?[151]

America's harsh penal system attracted special attention. Why, the Chinese asked, did the United States have the largest prison population in the world, nearly 2.26 million men and women in prison in 2006—counting those on probation and parole, some 7 million, one in every thirty-two adults? Why did the number of prisoners increase 7.3 percent annually throughout the 1990s, more than doubling the 1985 total? Why did blacks, who comprise only 12.1 percent of the population, comprise 40 percent of all inmates sentenced to more than one year?[152] What accounted for overcrowded prison conditions, the high percentage of the mentally ill behind bars, rampant AIDS, and the sexual victimization of prisoners? Why did the federal government allow states to use attack dogs in dealing with prisoners? And why, especially, when the American media cover these issues, do they virtually never do so under the rubric of "human rights," when their coverage of China's prison and labor camp conditions is always so categorized? Why, if the plight of a Chinese prisoner can "epitomize the state of human rights in China today,"[153] in the words of the Lawyers' Committee for Human Rights does no American prisoner evidently epitomize the state of human rights in the United States? Why do Western human rights groups argue that, while the United States certainly needs "reform," Beijing needs "regime change" and "the rule of law"?

When the subject shifts to the second current of human rights, the differing orientations of the United States and China come through even more starkly. Although Amartya Sen is often quoted in human rights literature pointing out that, unlike China in the 1950s, no country with a free press has suffered a famine (India being his most famous example), the Chinese question the deductions he draws from this observation. And they are not alone—critics in America and abroad have pointed out that the issues of justice and a free press are not so simple. As far back as the 1850s, Frederick Douglass, looking at the unquestionably vibrant press in the United States, asked how it could coexist with one of the most cruel systems of slavery the world had ever known. Why was a people so moral about some issues able to live face-to-face with such evil? And why did segregation last for another century after slavery? The issue was not the absence of a free press or of the free flow of ideas or of criticism. How and why blatant injustices are accepted and lived with as part of the commonweal is, as the American abolitionist John Brown warned, the key question of human rights.

While American human rights groups call for democratization in other countries, Chinese critics focus on the electoral process, a "game for the rich people where politics are so highly commercialized."[154] How are the $3 billion cost of presidential campaigns, the marketing of candidates, negative campaigning, and the influence of "soft" donations any different from the abuses Washington and human rights leaders are so fond of pointing out elsewhere? Are the concentration of ownership in the media and the advertising, sound-bite ethos of contemporary American democracy irrelevant to its functioning? Does it not matter that reporters, who once saw themselves as paragons of independence, "maintain their jobs, salaries, and promotion opportunities by catering to the value and viewpoints on 'international and political affairs' of the wealthy and powerful in American life?"[155] In short, do human rights advocates holding up the United States as a rights-based society actually find a thriving, vital democratic ethos functioning there?

Chinese analysts note the absence of the word "equality" in the Constitution as it came from the hands of the Founders. Even the Bill of Rights does not venture beyond civil and political rights. The Constitution itself does "not include economic, social, and cultural rights."[156] It includes no mandate to "have the basic needs of people satisfied." To these commentators, the preoccupation with individual rights mitigates against equality, weakens a sense of the common good, and furthers an individualism rooted in a spirit of competition over a spirit of cooperation. American historians, of course, are not unaware of this absence. "We have yet to read a substantive meaning of equal protection into the realm of economy," noted Henry Steele Commager in the early 1990s. "Neither the court nor the Congress is at this stage prepared to say the equal protection of the laws means an equal right to a job, means equality in housing, means equality in medical care, means equality in prison and penal conditions, means equality in all those nonpolitical, non-legal, and we might say, nonsocial areas. Thus a century after we got rid of the paradox of freedom and slavery, the paradox of equality and individualism persists and may indeed be getting more aggravated."[157]

THE FUTURE

In 2004, China amended its constitution to include this declaration: "The state respects and safeguards human rights." The invocation of the phrase "human rights" represented the end point of a shift that had taken several decades to accomplish. The concept had been ideologically suspect as bourgeois, and it was strongly denounced in the Cultural Revolution. Then in 1985 Deng Xiaoping raised the question: "What are human rights? Above all, how many people are they meant for?" He cautioned that "we see the question from a different point of view" than the West, but he left open the answers to his questions, thus legitimizing discussion in elite circles.[158]

After Tiananmen, while adopting a hard line to defend the repression of popular movements, Deng supported efforts to explore the issues of human rights from a "socialist perspective." On November 1, 1991, the State Council of Information issued a white paper, "Human Rights in China"—the first human rights document ever released by the Chinese government. "If the name is correct," remarked one Chinese official, "speech will be heeded; if the speech is heeded, something will come of it."[159]

The language of human rights in China was emerging from quite different constituencies. The "lawless years" of the Cultural Revolution—during which many members of the Communist elite had also suffered acutely—provided a genuine incentive to respect the "rule of law." There is an element of orderliness in rights—an aspect of nonviolence, a reformist quality. Invoking rights in post–Cultural Revolution China was a "radical" step, but Chinese leaders are also showing that human rights can cut various ways, and not simply as propaganda.

Some Chinese writers see the evolution of human rights as a work in progress that only began with the individualistic visions of the American Declaration of Independence and the French Declaration of the Rights of Man. But these early liberating statements failed to restrain European colonialism and racism in the non-white world or rampant inequality at home. Only with non-Western struggles against colonialism, racism, imperialism, and economic exploitation did the concept of human rights move beyond individual rights toward the UN covenants that today codify cultural and social rights and especially the right to a decent standard of living. But this, Beijing insisted, was not where progress should stop. Additional human rights standards needed to evolve, the collective aspect of human rights to more fully develop, the social obligations of individuals to be more carefully considered, and the use of civil and political rights as a perennial prism for economic, social, and cultural rights to be divested of its ideological aspects.[160]

This view highlights the traditions of revolution and struggle. Its heroes include Toussaint L'Ouverture leading the uprising against the French in Haiti in the name of the rights of man; the forces of the Mahdi uprising rebelling against General Gordon in Sudan in the name of universal equality before Allah; Simón Bolívar leading the struggle for independence in Latin America; the Taiping movement seeking a more equitable society in nineteenth-century China; Mustafa Kemal enacting radical reforms in Turkey; Gandhi leading the struggle for independence and dignity in India; Augusto Sandino rising up against U.S. domination in Nicaragua.[161] Contrast this list with the ones that are the norm in Western human rights histories: John Locke, Thomas Jefferson, Eleanor Roosevelt—remarkable thinkers or leaders all, and very much part of a world of law, courts, charters, and covenants. The divide between the traditions is what gives pause, a divide that underlines, once again, the differences between the two currents of human rights.

In China today the contractual contentiousness of individual rights finds less intellectual traction where collective rights challenge the idea of the isolated individual and reflect the deep anxiety that an antagonistic, self-interested struggle among individuals is far from the best way to meet human needs. Nor is there a strong belief there that "human rights" really reflect a genuine transformation in the brutal workings of the world order that has evolved out of centuries of Western power. To merely expand the human rights currently defined by the Western world would be to keep rights far too insulated from true universalism— locked into a Western provincialism that has found so much so universal so quickly because highly selective aspects of rights are already embodied in its own familiar ways.

Measured against the standards of the past three hundred years, Chinese citizens now enjoy an unprecedented degree of economic and personal freedom. Inequality is still staggering, progress uneven, the challenges enormous; but the monumental effort to change China continues from within, even if it does not fit easily into the Western human rights vision of change. Neither the national security establishment nor the human rights community has shown much sense of the Chinese people struggling to better their own society in their own way and within their own particular historical context. They seldom acknowledge that this struggle might be growing out of long traditions of protest in a culturally sophisticated society that has been undergoing continual transformation for well over a century. But what a multipolar planet without a proselytizing center might mean for China and elsewhere is not necessarily a weakening of the quest for justice but rather a vision of human rights more challenging and less comfortable for all the great powers. As well it should be.

5

POST-REAGAN: HUMANITARIANISM
AMID THE RUINS

With the collapse of the Soviet Union, Washington faced a tough new ideological challenge. The old enemy was gone. "The operative problem of the moment is that a bunch of smart people haven't been able to come up with a new slogan, and saying that there aren't any good slogans isn't a slogan either," Bill Clinton lamented. "We can Latinize and analyze all we want, but until people can say it in a few words we're sunk."[1]

"Globalization and human rights" didn't quite do it. Neither did "a strategy of enlargement . . . of the world's free community of market democracies."[2] Still, potentially useful new code words and catch phrases were emerging—"failed states," "rogue states," "chaos," "terrorist," "genocide." Anthony Lake, Clinton's national security advisor, observed that "ancient cauldrons of animosity" were being released—ethnic barbarism, virulent nationalism, terrorism, factional and religious hatreds—the dark underside of globalization. As the world was becoming "more connected, it had become more hazardous," the authors of a USAID document noted.[3] "Weapons, germs, drugs, envy, and hate cross borders at accelerating rates."[4] Lake was pithier: "Look around you. Listen. You can hear the locusts munching."[5]

Rights advocates by and large agreed, talking once again about a "disaster ridden" South in a way non-Western countries disputed and often deeply resented. Amnesty, sounding little different from Washington, warned that "a spate of local wars, often accompanied by the virtual disintegration of state authorities, have spread turmoil and terror. . . .

Nationalist, ethnic, and religious conflict, famine and repression have led to massive movements of refugees. . . . These horrific events illuminate the interdependence and indivisibility of human rights more powerfully than any abstract argument."[6] U.S. human rights leaders spoke out against "isolationism" and American withdrawal as fervently as national security managers had been doing since 1945. In a world so threatened by violence and suffering, how could we pull back? The answer, if one was a moral being, appeared to be that one could not.

Yet the absence of a clear enemy laid all the more bare the real ideological impetus of American policy as almost all forms of intervention—"humanitarian" measures against atrocities and genocide, "democratization," economic "shock treatment," rebuilding of "failed states," promotion of "regime change"—became sanctioned in Washington. With the Soviet Union and the threat of its responses gone, "intervening almost anywhere" was safer, a Rand Corporation report noted with relief, "because there is no danger of escalation to apocalyptic levels."[7]

Despite general optimism over American preeminence, a few of the old-time national security managers were growing uneasy, sensing increasing problems in the operations of the global order itself. Among them was Zbigniew Brzezinski, who saw dangers lurking in the perception of America around the globe and the great disparities in the world's wealth. "Procedural freedom, without substantive freedom from basic wants, may not be enough," he cautioned in 1993; "the cultural hedonism of the West may appear to be less proof of the inherent superiority of the free market and more the consequence of wider global inequality."[8] Expressing sentiments largely missing from human rights literature, he warned that America's internal social and cultural dilemmas were generating a twofold danger to Washington's power: "on the one hand, the image of a society guided largely by cornucopian aspirations devoid of deeper human qualities tends to undermine the global appeal of the American social model, especially as the symbol of freedom; on the other hand, that image tends to generate highly exaggerated material expectations among the vast masses of the world's poorer majority, expectations that cannot conceivably be satisfied yet the frustration of which is bound to intensify their resentment of global inequality."[9]

Ten years on, Brzezinski would speak of what seemed to be a rising countercreed among desperate and dispossessed populations, "a combination of the widespread revulsion against globalization as a self-interested process of the relatively few rich to disempower the poor along with an intensified anti-Americanism which views the US as not only the motor of that unfair globalization but also as the source of political and cultural imperialism."[10]

America's national security managers were well aware of the dark side of globalization. Some managers liked to argue, at least in public, that a rising tide lifts all boats. Others recognized the wreckage that would inevitably be left behind as some boats sailed briskly out to sea.[11] "Global elites thrive," a CIA-sponsored study pointed out, "but the majority of the world's population fails to benefit from globalization."[12] "Sharpening inequalities in income"[13] and "sharpening internal social cleavages" would further intensify widespread rage, elevating "the problem of inequality into the central issue of our times."[14] Globalization might well tear some nations asunder, particularly given the "more than 2,000 ethnic and indigenous groups, which are minorities in the states in which they live." Or to put it bluntly, "increased communal tensions, political instability, even conflict" were inseparable from the glittering promises of globalization.[15]

Yet Washington's managers were not too worried. They judged that "the widening income and regional disputes" would not be "incompatible with a growing middle class and increasing overall wealth," a situation not inimical to American power.[16] If their guardedly argued economic predictions held true, CIA-funded task forces foresaw a planet of 2 billion somewhat-well-off people—enough to sustain the globalization process—living amid 4.7 billion others.

If globalization was augmenting inequality, then it was all the more critical to counter "the conflation of globalization with US values," that, the CIA observed, had "fueled anti-Americanism in some parts of the world."[17] Separating out Americanization from globalization in

Washington's message to the world was imperative. The chosen means was to promote the image of a transnational middle-class world of shared universal values and civilized interests rather than an America-centered one, all the while proclaiming the nation's desire to promote human rights, to do good, to do more, to confront the suffering, and even, if necessary for humanitarian reasons, to wage war.

THE CYNICISM OF THE TRUE BELIEVERS

The national security establishment spends an enormous amount of time researching and evaluating a vast number of issues, occasionally with great insight, but all too often with shockingly little. U.S. government documents of the fifty years preceding the Clinton era reveal a near unceasing stream of simplifications, debate-limiting abstractions, and sweeping generalizations about American credibility and its "global role." And true to form, human rights advocates repeatedly point out that Washington is "misperceiving" the world and that if only Washington understood its true interests it would consistently promote human rights. Other critics join in arguing that U.S. intelligence fails to provide analyses of the world "as it is," as though the CIA had not been from its origins an agency designed to analyze the world from the perspective of American state interests, and to assess how to further those interests by covert and analytic means.

After a half century of critics' and historians' listing innumerable misperceptions and mistakes, some pause might seem to be in order to consider who is misperceiving what—and whose interests these "mistakes" serve. Nowhere is this dynamic more illuminating than in the triumph of the national security managers' ideology of interventionism, a faith in an America-centered globalism so intense, so omnipresent, and imbued with such near messianic conviction that human rights leaders widely accepted it provided that human rights were included. There is little sense that the vision of an American-centered order might itself be the source of a profound misperception of the world.

When a noted human rights advocate argues that "the biggest flaw in the U.S. approach" to foreign policy is not its "unilateralism" but its "a la cartism," she is really paying a backhanded compliment to the managers' often cynical realpolitik.[18] The incessant complaints that Washington was never doing enough in support of rights, never working consistently around the planet, never using its power sufficiently for good causes, were all well and good ideologically. Yet by the onset of the Clinton years, the calls for doing more, intervening more, helping others to transform themselves in ways that American human rights leaders believed possible and just, joined them to national security leaders like Siamese twins—their movements connected more to each other than to local nationalisms or to struggles for a more multipolar, culturally diverse world.

Operationally this interventionist ethos often appears ineffective or myopic. Reform efforts never quite succeed, shock treatments in Russia and elsewhere leave staggering gaps between rich and poor, living standards decline, corruption spreads. World Bank, IMF, State Department, NSC, and human rights memoranda and reports find breakdowns, chaos, lack of progress—and then insist upon doing more, far more, of basically the same thing. Challenges and crises, then, demand not that the ethos of interventionism be changed but that it be continually refined, updated, and propagated precisely because its operationalized form is often in flagrant contradiction with its own globalist faith. Failures, in other words, end up revitalizing the faith: they have to be explained away, and then they demand renewed, ever greater efforts.

The process in which defeat becomes a reason to redouble the application of more of the same also pervaded U.S. policy surrounding "failed states." Officials occasionally acknowledge that there are really no models for nation building, that the link between economic and political development is murky, that all sorts of compromises with the real world are necessary. "Nation building is at best an imperfect concept," concedes one CIA-supported study, echoing decades of similar laments.[19] "The accepted international practices to promote democracy . . . haven't proved to be all that satisfactory," warned the head of the very office that oversees transitions in failed states. "The simple fact is that we do not know how to do democracy building."[20]

In 1994, the CIA set up a State Failure Task Force; it was followed by a

Failed States Index, an intricate series of assessments that ranked states and the signals of their possible "failure."[21] The dire predictions and calls for "preventive" diplomacy heralded later calls for "preventive intervention." When early studies suggested that the number of failed states was relatively modest, new criteria promptly allowed for the inclusion of "revolutionary wars, ethnic wars, adverse or disruptive regime transitions, and genocides or policides—of varying magnitudes." Such an expansive definition soon encompassed some 113 "failures" and a terminological new world to match—"fragile countries," "failing countries," "failed countries," "recovering states," "humanitarian countries," and so on.[22]

Washington continues undaunted by complaints from its human rights critics. They warn (again) that its actions are lowering American prestige, or (again) causing us to lose the "war of ideas," or (again) leading to a serious weakening of our "credibility," or (again) ignoring human rights ideals at the cost of embarrassingly blatant hypocrisy. Variants of such rhetoric plied almost daily for more than six decades are not, however, empty verbiage. They really amount to an impassioned call not to challenge or rethink global assumptions. Through the various policy fiascos of one sort or another runs a common thread: the need to assert, reaffirm, or consolidate American globalism. The vision pushes toward involvement, deeper commitment, rarely toward pulling back. Failures simply demand that we "learn the lessons"—of how to do more, better, extending our helping hand once again.

Concluding that the ideological message is not quite getting across is crucial to the way the process works. "The higher priority now accorded to nation-building has yet to be matched by a comprehensive policy or institutional capacity within the U.S. government," concludes a 2005 report from a committee headed by Samuel Berger and Brent Scowcroft[23]—after more than forty years of nation-building efforts by the national security establishment. This is simply par for the ideological course. For such reports, studies, and appeals are really always in part about the need for continued ideological mobilization to undertake these tasks, however discordant the results and however obvious the failures.

Even a cursory historical look at the way the United States has "employed strategies for moving countries along the path of development" might suggest some caution as to the results.[24] Yet however great the failures, the opposite conclusions are drawn. Washington's tool kits are ready at hand to go to work, and operational failures are again interpreted as reason for deeper and deeper involvement in the internal dynamics of other countries. This is no longer about the Cold War, where Washington's nation-building initiatives could be held up as a bulwark against Communism. It is about the promotion of an architecture of power that allows Washington greater latitude to pursue its own interests—promoting structural readjustment programs, pushing privatization and its attendant cutbacks in public programs of health, food, education—all the while espousing a vision of American "humanitarianism," a "rights based developmentalism," and supporting the far less well funded efforts of humanitarian, human rights, and developmental groups to help fill in where they can.

HUMANITARIANISM AS A FIGHTING FAITH

"We feel your pain" was Clintonism not only at home. It was a call to mobilize around a politics of suffering and victimization, prompting the transformation of a humanitarian ethos into a fighting faith. Those who struggled against Communism had been able to identify a clear enemy behind much of the carnage in the world. Now at the end of the Cold War accounts of social injustice, poverty, and economic failure threatened to swamp Washington's progressive globalism.[25]

Humanitarianism became the post–Cold War zeitgeist in part because it offered a response to the atrocities and "messiness" that the Cold War no longer explained. The Cold War had projected superpower conflicts into the remotest areas of the world, but it affirmed, at least outwardly, state sovereignty. Humanitarian interventionism, by contrast, was to blossom amid withering attacks on state sovereignty as it sought to root a penetrative dynamic of globalization in a rights-based, corporate-driven development process. The Cold War had condensed all the disruptive forces of an era into Communism and its support of nationalist and radical movements. It was an age of national self-determination, revolution, and anticolonial struggles. The new era was one of democratization, human rights, and humanitarianism. In the former era Washington organized half the planet; in the latter it sought to organize the whole.

For human rights leaders this development was more an opportunity than a problem. A "responsibility to protect," the construction of a legal apparatus to try those guilty of genocide and war crimes of all kinds, and the promotion of humanitarian intervention to stop other atrocities all came together by the end of the decade. With no ideological alternatives at hand to rival an American-backed global economic order, and with local states weakened, rights advocates called for a vast new effort to infuse Clinton's "democratic moment" with a more expansive vision of human rights. In the process, human rights became "one of the world's dominant ideologies"[26] and the movement itself more inclusive, developing, in the words of one Human Rights Watch official, into "a substantial mosaic that includes large professional NGOs as well as thousands of regional, national, and local organizations working on issues ranging from self-determination to the rights of children, and from access to HIV medications to the right to water."[27]

Human rights, the theory went, are "universal"—they are what Americans embody and others have fought for. As Clinton put it, "There is no them; there is only us."[28] Making others into what they really wanted to become meant emancipation, not manipulation. Democratic forms might vary; the operations of the market economy might manifest themselves differently depending on levels of development. But rights were set forth in international law and shone with the clarity of law itself. No Cold Warrior ever envisioned fashioning such a penetrating ethos.

To the calls for democratization of earlier years was now added an even more morally imperative cry—the responsibility to protect the rights of others, wherever they might be, even if that meant waging war, and by so doing infusing human rights into traditional humanitarianism. Human rights organizations often speak of their efforts to defeat the claims of state sovereignty in order to defend a population from atrocities. They point to the brutal dictatorships that have invoked sovereignty to protect themselves and repress their subjects. They speak of rights trumping sovereignty, and of the urgent need to become more deeply involved in what were once sacrosanct internal affairs. They embrace the language of globalization while warning, as well, of the dark underside that demands redress through human rights. And in the process they find almost no area of any nation's internal concerns off limits to them. As Mark Twain might have put it, they may have derived from their experience of several decades of human rights struggles far more wisdom than was in them.

An expanding human rights mandate went hand in hand with the decline of Third World developmentalism. With states less and less able to deal with local socioeconomic issues, human rights leaders spoke more and more about "rights based developmental strategies." The Clinton years saw a growing convergence of those groups that promoted economic and social development with those that defended human rights.[29] This was a significant step beyond Reagan's vision of democratization, in which democracy and the marketplace reinforced each other and U.S. involvement focused largely on local political, business, and security questions. Just as Washington had coupled its earlier interventions with efforts to change societies by restructuring their economies, now human rights organizations rapidly extended rights into almost all areas of development and social change. Formerly they had focused largely on civil and political issues such as torture, political imprisonment, and the rights of noncombatants; now they were addressing underlying social and economic problems.[30] Nonstate violence opened up yet more arenas for action.[31] Women's rights, tribal rights, gay rights, civil rights of all kinds would be advanced with the "building blocks of a rights respecting society—a free press, an independent judiciary, education in human rights, and tolerance and civilian control of the military." Human rights leaders argued for a decisive shift "from needs-based, welfare and humanitarian approaches to a rights-based approach to development."[32]

Amnesty embraced this holistic vision of rights more slowly than Human Rights Watch, but in August 2001 the organization voted to "adopt a new mission, which included all the rights" in the Universal

Declaration of Human Rights,[33] joining the emerging Washington-backed consensus. Amnesty officials also spoke of overcoming the artificial divide between civil and political rights on the one hand and economic and social ones on the other; there was no justification, they said, for prioritizing either set."[34] And yet, with Amnesty as with Human Rights Watch, the first current quietly reasserted itself, much as Washington knew it would, because by insisting that, in the end, all the rights embodied in the first current had to be recognized in order to realize those embodied in the second current, the first remained the prism for viewing the second.

THE VICTIM

In the 1950s, Albert Camus sought to appeal to the best in his time by writing *The Rebel*. The title in the 1990s could have been *The Victim*. No word better captures the spirit of the age in the United States. Human rights had become the very "language of the victim and the dispossessed,"[35] commented one historian. "It harvests the hopes of the victims,"[36] added another. The issue of financial compensation for crime victims had briefly emerged in American courts in the 1960s and early 1970s but quickly faded. More and more, victims' rights came to mean the opportunity to speak out in court, a privilege compatible both with the goals of hard-line prosecutors and judges seeking more stringent punishments and those of progressives seeking to protect people in need.[37] Both sides singled out the individual who has been wronged: the rape victim, the pedestrian hit by a drunk driver, the old couple robbed of their life savings, the bystander shot during a holdup. Who could be anti-victim?

The imagery was of harm individualized, atrocity narrated through the biographies of the innocent, accompanied by demands for remedies, empathy, a helping hand. As Canadian Michael Ignatieff astutely observed, this attitude was "a weary world away from the internationalism of the 1960s," when political causes could be supported or opposed on the basis of struggles over different ways to develop societies. Now there were "no good causes left—only victims of bad causes."[38] The sentiment "I'm at one with the victims," another writer noted, conceals a humanitarian anti-politics—"a pure defense of the innocent and the powerless against power, a pure defense of the individual amidst immense and potentially cruel or despotic machineries of culture, state, war, ethnic conflict, tribalism, patriarchy, and other mobilizations or instantiations of collective power against individuals."[39] Political movements and mass struggles had all become tainted. Supporting victims, by contrast, was beyond causes, beyond politics.

The humanitarian spirit calls for us to be our brother's keeper; failing to come to the aid of those in need makes us complicit in their harm. One may not be directly responsible for what is happening in the world; America may not be responsible for much of the ugliness and chaos in the world. The real complicity, from the humanitarian perspective, lies in not responding. This perspective reinforced the efforts of human rights groups to move away from an exclusive focus on state action (torture, disappearance, political imprisonment) to include, as one report put it, "the culpability of state inaction in the face of known abuses by private actors."[40]

But what of situations that call on us to aid the "victims" by rebelling, as Camus once wrote, against what we have become? That the new humanitarian interventionism called for no transformative changes in the United States was an ideological gift to Washington. It demanded great changes of others, but of us only that we become the well-intentioned humanitarians we really were all along. It made Americans look everywhere except—fundamentally—at ourselves.

HUMANITARIANISM AND INTERVENTION

"Human rights and humanitarianism are two sides of the same coin," Washington now argued.[41] No longer was it enough to deal individually with the wars, failed states, and atrocities of Africa and the South; there had to be strategies for the long run: disaster requires development, development is the answer to disaster, government studies declared.[42] In addition to addressing immediate needs, developmental relief also had to "contribute to sustainable development and peace."[43] Development and human rights could no longer be isolated from this "broader context" or from a creative use of "market forces" and multinational corporations. Human rights thus became a far more assertive ethos: an anti-state centric "nation building" committed to linking up markets, elites, and NGOs on a globe-spanning scale.

In this new world, traditional humanitarian aid was too limited; it reached too few of the war-affected populations, often reinforcing an oppressive ruling elite or a local warlord. The goal for Washington was not to intervene less, USAID said, but for the state to use as many other groups as possible to do more: "The changing face of development, combined with shrinking budgets, has shaped a need for greater collaboration among government, business, and civil society."[44] This change "necessitates a new kind of collaboration—one that enables the public and private sectors to transcend the traditional boundaries that have hindered cooperation in the past and to work together towards common goals."[45]

The decentralized world of NGOs made it all the more necessary to promote a common lexicon ideologically suited to Washington's objectives. Victims became "rights holders," humanitarians their advocates. Developmental strategies and humanitarianism were to be "people-centered," "empowering." Out was impartial, needs-based emergency relief that respected state sovereignty; in were both aid predicated on clear legal, political, and moral judgments against abusers and rights-based development.

For far too long, USAID complained, traditional aid efforts had been a substitute for "more concerted action" to address desperate need. "Humanitarian intervention cannot be impartial to the Serb militiaman and the Muslim civilian, or the machete-wielding Hutu and the Tutsi victim." Washington particularly objected to a 1994 International Red Cross (IRC) code of conduct that reaffirmed the independence of humanitarian groups from governments. The Red Cross view, complained a 2002 USAID report, "has internal inconsistencies: for example, local societies must be respected, even if their values and practices violate human rights and humanitarian law. And . . . it ignores the existence of predatory political actors in most complex emergencies. . . . The IRC's doctrine of discretion and silence . . . has shaded into complicity with war crimes." The result, it declared, was the "well-fed dead."[46] Aggression had continued, and vulnerable civilians had been kept alive by the Red Cross only to then be "brutalized by war, human rights violations, and other forms of abuse." That was why force might be necessary—and legitimate. Such "blurring of the distinction between humanitarian and military operations" held enormous promise for Washington. It might turn traditional humanitarianism upside down, but in Washington it was now being proclaimed as the modern way to deal with the post–Cold War world of failing states.[47]

Traditional humanitarianism was a response to a world of suffering too enormous and unjust to overcome in any foreseeable future, and so its guiding ethos was compassion, charity, and a helping hand extended, where possible, without taking sides. During the Cold War such humanitarianism, whatever its benefactions, had not proved a particularly useful ideological weapon for Washington. The United States had used the necessity of fighting Communism to excuse the difficulties of modernizing in perilous contexts, while pointing to atrocities and famines in Communist areas as evidence of the draconian character of the ruling regimes.

For much of the Cold War, the divide between politically neutral humanitarianism and state-led developmental aid was relatively clear— and the clarity wasn't always to Washington's advantage.[48] In the Third World in the 1960s and 1970s, famine and war were widely blamed on Western power and its influence over the character of its client states. But with Third World state-centric developmental strategies discredited by the 1990s—nowhere more so than among leaders of the human rights community—Washington began to challenge traditional humanitarianism and its principles of neutrality and universality, its willingness to keep silent and work in conjunction with repressive states to reach victims. Now a developmental politics could be clothed in a muscular new humanitarian garb. International NGOs need no longer feel compelled to work "at arm's length" from Washington and other governments, a 2003 USAID report urged. The relationship could become "intimate." "Forceful humanitarian intervention," Washington liked to say, was something new under the sun.[49]

The idea that NGOs and human rights groups might involve themselves in efforts to overthrow or reconstruct authoritarian regimes had once been anathema to them. "We have not the slightest intention of dabbling in the domestic affairs of other nations," Peter Benenson wrote in June 1961 in the first Amnesty newsletter.[50] But as times changed, Washington saw its opportunity to draw these groups in. The world's sole remaining superpower had "a moral obligation to take a stand against human atrocities whenever and wherever they occur."[51] NATO's intervention in Kosovo epitomized this "close new relationship between humanitarian, political, and military interests," a USAID overview asserted as the 1990s came to an end.[52]

Victims were everywhere—in disasters, failing states, regime-sponsored atrocities, and genocide—and in all these cases, their suffering legitimized intervention, or so the argument went. Humanitarian war marked the apotheosis of a new "altruistic" spirit. From the early 1990s on, leading American human rights groups applauded the new humanitarianism Washington and London were espousing. They could have argued that in extreme cases military intervention could reflect a crass pursuit of national interests and still be morally necessary: thus Vietnam's invasion of Cambodia in 1978, which ended the Khmer Rouge atrocities; India's attack on East Pakistan in 1971, leading to the creation of Bangladesh; and Tanzania's invasion of Uganda in 1979, which destroyed Idi Amin's murderous regime. But they did not make this argument; those invasions, all opposed by Washington, had been largely ignored by human rights leaders.[53] The new era of humanitarianism grew out of something else: Washington's need to keep refurbishing faith in the singularity of its moral status. An America-centered order did not demand that Washington accept responsibility for the state the world was in but only that it help those it judged in need—or, when possible, rout the perpetrators of atrocities and violence.

Human Rights Watch shared this view, even to the point of endorsing

military intervention in humanitarian crises. The most "dramatic development in 1999," it reported, was the use of military force to "stop crimes
against humanity." Intervention in Kosovo by members of the international community signaled a "new readiness" to use "extraordinary
resources, including troops," to address such crimes.[54] Washington's
interests were not dissected; its motives were left shrouded in a cloud of
inspiring rhetoric. "Broader approaches" had become the new orthodoxy.

Few groups stood quite so distinctly outside this new consensus as Doctors Without Borders (Médecins San Frontières, or MSF), which was
awarded the Nobel Peace Prize in 1999. Founded in 1971 in the aftermath of the Biafran secession, MSF broke with other relief organizations: "When we saw people dying on the other side of the frontiers, we
asked ourselves, 'what is this border? It doesn't mean anything to us.'"[55]
MSF sought "to bear witness to the fate of populations as precisely as
possible, not as defenders of human rights, but simply as direct witnesses to the suffering of the sick and injured and to the stolen dignity
of so many men, women, and children all over the world."[56]

In doing so, it questioned the validity of any "universal moral conscience" based on the operations of a handful of states.[57] "We are invited
to believe that ethics and politics have become reconciled on the initiative of a handful" of powerful states, warned an MSF leader.[58] The very
same powers that have enshrined humanitarian principles into law are
subverting them; they are cloaking their political agendas in humanitarian language and co-opting the humanitarian ideal into the service
of other causes,"[59] the director of MSF-US argued in 2003.

MSF cautioned against the current thinking among many NGOs
and UN groups that humanitarian action ought to become part of an
integrated system: "But integrated into what? Integrated into policy in
the same way as are the use of force, economic development or even
justice in a global quest for consistency and effectiveness?" While these
groups may find such a vision seductive, "whether because of conviction, lack of financial or political independence or simple pragmatism,"

ultimately "the integration of humanitarian action into a system is tan-
tamount to the disintegration of its very humanitarian values."[60] Of
course, "not for one minute" does such an outcome "trouble those who
want to make humanitarian action into a simple tool at the disposal of
politics"[61]—that is, Washington. The right to intervene, MSF concludes,
simply does not exist in international humanitarian law; the very idea
"may even, in a monstrous misinterpretation, mean killing in the name
of humanitarianism."[62]

Speaking for others poses further moral contradictions, for the
unheard are not, in fact, unable to speak. "To put it another way," MSF
explains, "when institutions like the UN Security Council approach aid
organizations and ask what can be done for the Liberian people, these
organizations would be better advised to refer them to the parties most
affected by the conflict—the Liberians who have attempted to express
their grievances, by piling up bodies in front of the US Embassy in
Monrovia, for example." Giving the powerless a voice in the public
arena, hearing rather than speaking for, transforming pity into the
demand for justice—these aims require that rights advocates separate
themselves from "all forms of power and politics, however respectable
they may be." Otherwise, confronted by desperate suffering, they end
up simply absorbing and recycling it in preconceived conceptions of
what is just and what is unjust.[63]

Humanitarianism, argues MSF, cannot be "traded or made condi-
tional"; to do so inevitably leads to the sacrifice of the most vulnerable.[64]
The group calls for a massive paradigm shift. Consider, for example, the
pervasive business practices in which defense of patents rewarded not
invention but corporate profits and that, in aiming at increasing profits
rather than the alleviation of suffering, have contributed to a veritable
"denial of medicine for most of humanity. . . . Only 1% of medicines
brought to market treat diseases like tuberculosis, malaria, and sleeping
sickness that most affect people in developing countries."[65] In challenging the profits of pharmaceutical companies and the skewed priorities
of medical research, MSF stepped into the second current of human
rights.

RIGHTS AS A SYSTEM OF POWER

More than any previous president, Clinton called on NGOs to strengthen civil society abroad. He established Democracy Corps, which sent teams of Americans throughout the former Soviet Union "to overcome bottlenecks to democratic development." He called for cooperation among American business, labor, political, and volunteer organizations to develop the needed "independent, civil, and services sectors in the new democracies." His often cautious secretary of state, Warren Christopher, was far from cautious about these audacious efforts: "We have to help others build up the institutions that make democracy possible," he said.[66] His State Department colleague, Morton Halperin, director of the Democracy Project, was blunter: "We divide the world in two. Those countries who choose democracy, we help. In those countries which do not choose, we create conditions where they will choose it."[67] Later an important ancillary was enunciated in a Council for Foreign Relations study headed by Christopher's successor as secretary of state, Madeleine Albright: "Unconstitutional actions that threaten democracy from within a state should be resisted by a collective international response as readily as are external aggressions against a sovereign state."[68]

By the early 1990s, the shift toward the new paradigm of economic-based democratization was well under way,[69] a framework designed to offer a "common vocabulary" and a "lens though which a developing country's political environment is analyzed and evaluated."[70] Since then, a wide array of groups (AID; the State, Treasury, and Commerce Departments; the Trade and Development Agency; the Export-Import Bank; the Overseas Private Investment Security Council; the African Development Foundation; the Inter-American Foundation) have codified it. Here, as elsewhere, the rapid rise in funding has been impressive. In 1980, the United States and the European Union together spent some $20 million on "democracy-related foreign aid." By 2001, the figure had risen to $571 and $392 million, respectively, and by 2006 to some $2 billon for the United States and $3.5 billion for the EU.[71] And these sums do not even include funding by corporations, nongovernmental foundations, and quasi-governmental groups like the NED, not to mention billionaire activists such as George Soros.

By insisting that everything was related to everything else—civil and political liberties to the market, a free press to civil society, privatization to transparency and accountability, electoral politics to the media—national security managers sought to legitimize almost every kind of involvement. For Washington it was the opening of a new ideological era. In the words of a 1999 State Department report, "We are rapidly moving toward a global network of government officials, activists, thinkers, and practitioners who share a common commitment to democracy, the universality of human rights, and respect for the rule of law."[72]

While human rights groups may have been convinced of their influence on policy, in fact Washington had often defined these issues to suit its own interests years before. Almost every area the groups now took up—the role of NGOs, of women, of the media; of civil society; of child soldiers; of the "rule of law"—had already been considered in an outpouring of government studies and funded research that dwarfs independent human rights literature. The need to ensure that civil freedoms were not subordinated to economic policies was already a leitmotif of USAID's 1991 Democracy and Governance programs, which themselves drew on a wealth of preexisting national security discussions. When Human Rights Watch cautioned in 1995 against "the unbridled pursuit of economic development in the absence of the vigorous promotion of human rights,"[73] Washington had a plethora of reports already at hand arguing for an "integrated developmental agenda . . . inextricably linked to democratization and good governance." When rights groups began to link the rule of law, or freedom of the press, and women's rights with progress in human rights,[74] when they began to laud the role of NGOs in building up civil society and to focus on corporate operations and "good governance," Washington was ready with studies designed to promote NGOs, transparency, and democratization. When Human Rights Watch protested the "conceptual attack launched by abusive governments against such basic principles as the indivisibility and universality of human rights" and invoked "the duty to ensure that international assistance does not underwrite repression,"[75] Washington was ready with reams of reports underwriting just such a position.[76] Human Rights Watch's position that "respect for civil and political rights is the best guarantee of the economic rights that abusive proponents of development-first theories purport to champion"[77] had far earlier advocates in the national security establishment. Washington had concluded that calling rights "indivisible" would ensure the primacy of "individual rights" far more effectively than arguing that civil and political rights took precedence over economic ones.

By seeking to make Washington live up to its rhetoric, human rights organizations were once again spotlighting the "enforcement gap" between ideals and policy. But the deeper question is one of language and definitions—not only what can be done about the evils of the world but why those problems are defined as they are and, especially, who gets to do the defining. Reading national security documents takes one into a world of think tanks, consultants, and task forces who share a vocabulary, code words, and analogies. On one level, this overlapping language may have signaled Washington's growing acceptance of ideas about human rights. But since it is the business of the national security managers to develop, propagate, and fine-tune this language, at a deeper level it marked a diminution: proximity to power wore down the biting edge of the human rights world and led it, almost inevitably, to buy into too many assumptions at too high a price.

CIVIL SOCIETY: NOBODY IN CHARGE

"Civil society"—meaning, in general, lawyers, academics, journalists, ministers, managers, and other professionals[78]—has been a much favored term both of human rights groups and of Washington since the Clinton years. (Washington dropped its late 1960s to mid-1980s predecessor, "civic society," out of worry that it might suggest an unwanted "society wide mobilizing" of groups.)[79] The new buzzword was hard to define with exactitude and contentiously fought over in academic literature, but highly useful to Washington for all that.[80]

Both Washington and human rights leaders applauded the rise of civil society as the best alternative to centralized state power. As one USAID report explained: "Civil society—from human rights organizations to the media—are often the leading voices for change around the world. And they often bear the brunt of the pushback we are seeing by those in power who feel threatened by reform."[81] It is the "domestic counterpart" of the "transnational networks" that encourage "interaction" and "global outlooks"[82]—which is why democracies must speak out when the international links of local NGOs are challenged and why the Department of State must partner with NGOs "to defend their work worldwide." For Washington, NGOs are nothing less than "America's invisible sector" of influence.[83]

Washington's views have policy implications, of course. "The emphasis on transforming the structures of governance in the polity is the functional equivalent of structural adjustment programs in the economic arena," explained one USAID report.[84] "Participation, thoughtfully handled, can be quietly subversive," moving nations "from statist to free-market economies."[85] A weakened state serves this end beautifully—the devolution of power undercuts future demagogues, reducing the temptation to revert to centralizing authoritarianism.[86] A large number of groups as well as a lack of vertical organization also undermines any possibility of state control—which, for Washington, is the ideal situation. When "nobody is in charge,"[87] its economic and political influence encounters less effective resistance.[88] This is what Washington understands by an "open society."

Yet what is to be done if the "political will for decent governance and structural reform is lacking" in a nation singled out by Washington? During the Clinton and the George W. Bush years, the answer was unambiguous: "Reform minded elements"—a much favored Cold War phrase—in the upper echelons should be "encouraged to link up with pressures from below in civil society, persuading ruling elites of the need for institutional reform to improve governance." Outside influences (Washington, other governments, NGOs) might then "tip the balance through persuasive engagement with the rulers and the society."[89] Thus the United States "should identify and try to strengthen the hand of reform-oriented ministers, agency heads, and provincial governors." Even if backing these reformers does not immediately succeed, it represents an "investment in the future, when a political shift gives reformers real power."[90]

Local NGOs, USAID commentaries pointed out, are not classic domestic political operators or movement groups. They depend largely on outside financial support. Very rudimentary groups need assistance in setting up a "governing board" and a "formal personnel structure." At first, they are often small and unstable,[91] but as they develop a management structure, they can participate in "learning networks" and conferences that enhance their fund-raising abilities. At this point, they can be "selected" as "partners," receiving umbrella grants from external actors, whose role is to build them up and "to bring the international perspective"[92]—hardly a peripheral concern.[93]

This point of view is sometimes criticized within the bureaucracy. "'Civil society,' I really hate this term," one USAID worker stationed in Africa complained in 1996. It sets up a construct of "inherently evil governments versus inherently virtuous civil society. We tend to romanticize that the way forward in this region, which is so beset by tumult and conflict, is through the empowerment of civil society. . . . In fact, civil society has the same vulnerability as government." Others have pointed to the chaos of hundreds of NGOs pouring into a country (like Rwanda) with no coordination at all. What are the implications of a small country's having two hundred international NGOs? Do they squash growth?[94]

The Department of State's own "guiding principles" on NGOs, issued in 2006, make explicit a set of long-held assumptions. Other governments have no right to repress these groups—a hospitable environment free from intimidation is imperative. So are the rights to receive funding from foreign entities, to have unrestricted access to foreign-based media, and to cooperate with foreign governments. When these principles are violated, "democratic nations" must rise in their defense.[95]

A "free media" is, of course, essential to civil society. But how to build it in places that have never had an independent press, and how to ensure that anti-American views do not predominate?[96] A 1999 USAID report laid out the strategy: the local U.S. Embassy, sometimes in partnership with European powers or NGOs, might advise on needed laws, run seminars, provide a wide assortment of "U.S.-based training to media lawyers and assistance," and offer rewards for excellence in reporting, including trips to the United States and additional funding. These tactics all require close personal contact—offering connections and access to "the world."[97]

As detailed in the report, the approach is impressively hands-on. Representatives on the ground are asked to catalogue the various media outlets along with number and types of journalists, their areas of interest, levels of professional training, salaries, bonuses, and political orientations. They are charged with gathering information on a wide range of topics: What kinds of professional associations are there? With whom do journalists affiliate and what are their goals? Who might be the best "local partner" for a "sector development program"? Which NGOs should be encouraged to aid journalists? What foreign countries have a presence in the local media, and what influence do they have? What are the media attitudes toward international NGOs? Is the content "balanced"? Is civil society receiving the kind of coverage it deserves?[98]

The report stresses the importance of direct funding of local media and strongly encourages the use of advertising. In Washington's view, commercializing the media and democratizing go hand in hand. Commercialization undercuts state control of the media and increases the role of the market. Funding of nongovernmental newspapers and periodicals is essential for creating "alternative media."[99] If direct U.S. funding is too "complicated," Washington can support such intermediaries as Freedom House, the International Center for Journalists, and Internews to "distance the local actor from U.S. policies."[100]

"Removing barriers" is just part of the free flow of ideas and information, the report explains; media restraints, after all, are "violations of international human rights conventions." Bringing local, regional, national, and international networks together ensures the "credibility" of local news and promotes "international understanding." What Washington really has in mind, however, is evident in the cases of using local media to support oppositional groups that it repeatedly invokes as triumphs—Solidarity in Poland, the anti-Sandinistas in Nicaragua, opponents of Milošević in the former Yugoslavia, and various players in the color revolutions.[101]

Finally, the report advises, Washington should not focus only on the media. Local think tanks (sometimes with American and European connections) should be funded as "content providers," university programs augmented to sustain their work, and polling agencies, policy institutes, and advocacy groups joined in a complex package—always with "new technology gatekeepers offering training, advice, software, investors."[102] As with so many areas of intensive involvement in the 1990s, who could possibly object to such admirable aims?

THE "RULE OF LAW" AND CORPORATE RESPONSIBILITY

National security managers and human rights leaders often call for the rule of law—yet what is it? A legal regime can implement a wide diversity of policies, after all. Laws do not just protect against unreasonable search and seizure or cruel and unusual punishment; they support markets, corporate rights, and, often, astronomical profits. They can also stipulate what can be privatized and how—not to mention ways of controlling local resources, mandates for wide-ranging health programs, the implementation of taxes to redistribute wealth, and so on.

In the human rights world, though, rule-of-law rhetoric often increases as interest in social transformation wanes. The words seldom appear in the same paragraph with "redistribution." A focus on law suggests a calmer, gentler sense of change and transformation—of rules followed, bills enacted, and bitter political and economic debates diminished. As law prevails, radical economic change recedes; in the words of one observer, "political choices fade from view—as do choices among different economic ideas about how development happens or what it implies for social, political, or economic life."[103]

To assert that legal formalities increase rights, an argument is required—as to how, for example, assets in the hands of a foreigner rather than a local investor will encourage growth, or how property under the control of the title holder rather than the squatter will lead to

economic growth or justice.[104] Is due process served when interpretations of law stress the rights of those with inordinate power in a society?
Is clarity of law always a benefit? Max Weber's account of the English
exception—the puzzle that industrial development arrived first in the
nation with the most confusing and least formal system of property law
and judicial procedure—comes to mind.[105]

Along with a focus on the rule of law, groups like Amnesty and
Human Rights Watch also began to adopt language similar to that of
national security managers and World Bank publicists on "corruption,"
"good governance," and "transparency." For example, in 2001 the executive director of Amnesty USA declared, "When it comes to business
interests, the 'rule of law' encompasses three things: combating corruption, providing transparent regulations for the conduct of business, and
guaranteeing the fair enforcement of contracts."[106] The policy of privatization and liberalization was embedded in the overlapping discourses.
A human rights approach, explained one report, does not seek "to shut
down global trade and investment, only to invoke broadly accepted
rights to define the limits within which commerce should proceed."[107]
Moreover, added another, "far-sighted companies" were coming to
understand "that the same strong judiciary and rule of law needed to
protect dissidents also safeguard their own commercial interests." They
were increasingly aware that human rights problems are "bad for business,"[108] that a "healthy civil society and democratic society are the best
guarantor of the long-term stability that business needs to thrive."[109]
"Rogue" companies might still be a problem, but "for hard headed busi-
nesspeople, the smart move is to face up to global human rights standards early and make them work by making them stick."[110] Human
Rights Watch pointed out that companies would "want something
better than a kangaroo court" to deal with business issues. Amnesty
International created a "corporate responsibility project." "The observation that human rights are actually good for business," the leader of
Amnesty USA noted, fell into the category of "startling but true."[111]
Washington agreed.[112]

Major foundations espoused similarly rosy visions of NGOs, corporations, and the market coming together, with "NGO's influencing

economic forces (which means private forces) for the better—working with and within corporate structures in order to bring pressure for less exploitative ways of operating." Former NGO officials were "becoming advisers to multinational corporations (MNCs), with MNCs approaching NGOs for 'certification,' and campaigns for fairer trading and better terms for producer groups." In 1998, the director of the Governance and Civil Society Unit of the Ford Foundation said, "I think the foreseeable future will be dominated by attempts to reshape capitalist processes to reduce their social and environmental costs while not killing incentives to growth."[113]

In all these areas, human rights organizations typically ended up once again judging specific situations, not the general organization and operation of American power. They came to accept transnational corporations, arguing that their operations could be infused with a rights-based ethos; they insisted that the World Bank and the IMF could be turned from obstacles to indigenous democratic struggles into organizations relevant to human rights pursuits. Such institutions were criticized, often strongly, for "not factoring in human rights concerns" and for focusing on "narrow economic considerations." What was talked about far less was whether these institutions could really adopt the changes human rights groups were advocating without altering their basic modes of operation.

THE COLOR REVOLUTIONS

By the end of the 1990s, in Eastern Europe and in the Newly Independent States (NIS) of the former Soviet Union, an influx of NGOs and of nongovernmental financial support for opposition groups, selected media, and democratization programs signaled a quiet but obvious shift: the involvement of an increasing number of human rights activists in attempted "regime change." George Soros, with his enormous funding, promoted this process throughout the region. The Soros Foundation in Ukraine stated it hoped through its programs "to distinguish the brightest minds in Ukraine and to promote the formation of an indigenous elite that will act as the critical mass in effecting the country's transformation into a fully democratic, highly-developed state."[114] For much of the decade, Soros argued, the groups he supported "offered the only alternative vision to repressive state governments fomenting ethnic hostilities."[115] Unlike USAID, he had no need to be diplomatic: "If this isn't meddling in the affairs of a foreign nation, I don't know what is!"[116] Soros's role might not be "identical to the foreign policy of the U.S. government," Deputy Secretary of State Strobe Talbott commented, "but it's compatible with it."[117]

Elsewhere, the National Democratic Institute (part of the NED) organized a briefing in October 1999 for some twenty Serbian opposition leaders in Budapest to persuade them that data provided by Bill Clinton's polling firm showed Milošević could be defeated in the coming election.[118] United States–funded consultants played a crucial behind-the-scenes role in virtually every facet of the anti-Milošević drive over the ensuing year, running tracking polls, training thousands of opposition activists, and helping to organize a vitally important parallel vote count. The United States also paid for the five thousand cans of spray paint student activists used to scrawl anti-Milošević graffiti on walls across Serbia and the 2.5 million stickers with the slogan "He's Finished" that became the revolution's catchphrase.[119] Ukrainian journalists were trained by American-supported groups to deliver "balanced fair reports" on the need to privatize—which of course meant advocacy of market reforms. Later, in Georgia, the United States brought in "democracy trainers" from Serbia, Croatia, Slovakia, and Russia to offer a rich assortment of lessons from the developing color revolutions—Serbia's pro-democracy innovations of 2000, Ukraine's Orange Revolution of 2004, Kyrgyzstan's Tulip Revolution of March 2005.[120]

If public money fed into the color revolutions is not hard to trace, neither is the involvement of past and present national security managers. When Freedom House trained some one thousand poll observers in Ukraine (funded through NED), its chairman was James Woolsey, a former director of the CIA. U.S. Ambassador Richard Miles was deeply involved in anti-Milošević operations; later, in Georgia, he worked to bring down Eduard Shevardnadze. Ten months after the success in

Belgrade, the U.S. ambassador in Minsk, a veteran of comparable operations in Nicaragua, was involved in a similar campaign against Alexander Lukashenko, the authoritarian leader of Belarus.[121] Washington's public diplomacy in these and other instances was pervasive and impressive: "Overt democratic support where we can, covert activities where we must" might well be the slogan.

Washington, in brief, was democracy's friend.[122] "We saw them marching for democracy through the streets of former capitals such as Kiev and Tbilisi," recounts a glowing USAID account. "A vast outpouring of people reaching for democracy stunned the world. One picture summed it up: in the cold dark night of Tbilisi, Georgia, as people marched toward the seats of government to protest a fraudulent election, one firm hand held up a model of the Statue of Liberty. Millions are asking for the rights that statue represents: elections to choose their leaders and freedom of speech, press, and religion."[123]

"There is a conspiracy theory—that what happened was planned in D.C.," USAID quotes a former mayor in Georgia. "It's not true. What this assistance did, it made civil actors [come] alive, and when the critical moment came, we understood each other like a well-prepared soccer team." The United States did not "cause" the color revolutions, argued another Ukrainian activist. Fallen rulers may blame "outside interference" for their defeats, but U.S. aid "only serves as a source of ideas and inspiration"—and funding. Or as USAID puts it: "It is only when citizens and local leaders in each country decide to change things that countries move from authoritarian rule towards democracy."[124]

The United States had a more subtle view of its role. The task, a USAID study said, was to keep the "donor assistance package" from looking like it had been externally imposed. "Legitimating means getting a buy-in from the appropriate people in the country to push the reform process forward." The aim is to foster "the emergence of a well regarded 'policy champion' (an individual or group who believes in the policy) to take on leadership for the subsequent implementation tasks." For intervention "to be smoothly implemented and successful," the assistance to "stakeholders" must be "welcomed or 'owned' by those receiving it." Of course, this is not always possible, the study conceded. Those on the "receiving end" may not actually have proposed the ideas in the first place.[125]

Publicly, human rights organizations greeted the color revolutions with enthusiasm, supporting NGOs, advocating for a free media, and demanding electoral transparency. They praised the Czech Republic's Velvet Revolution as the glorious precursor of those that followed. When the Orange Revolution shook Ukraine, "U.S. pressure for reform and support for Ukrainian civil society and political pluralism played a positive role,"[126] Human Rights Watch declared. Human rights organizations defended United States–funded groups when they were repressed in several Central Asian countries, though usually with little reference to where their money came from. And when such information did become public, it was contrasted with the imperial meddling of the Kremlin, its double-dealing support for repressive dictators. One Human Rights Watch report detailed Vladimir Putin's moves against NGOs in Russia; yet even though it began with Putin's assertion that for some NGOs, "the priority is to receive financing from influential foreign foundations," it offered barely a word about foreign funding.[127]

After a color revolution, human rights groups often issued detailed reports on signs of repression in the new government, calls for greater democratization, demands for further reforms. But Western funding or military assistance were seldom considered much of an issue. Human rights leaders rarely commented on Washington's obvious geopolitical considerations in promoting the color revolutions. (The great powers are "competing not only for influence" in the region, Anthony Lake, Clinton's national security advisor, wrote, "but for oil and potential control over the pipelines that will carry the 'black gold' to the west.")[128] Nor did they balk at the number of former national security people advising such operations: Brent Scowcroft, James Baker, Henry Kissinger, Zbigniew Brzezinski, John Sununu, and so on.

One might well argue that there is nothing wrong with an American ambassador's and various U.S. and EU groups' participating in, even orchestrating, such democratizing efforts. And if things need to be done covertly now and then, well—it's for a good cause; one can't be an innocent in a world of thuggish, murderous regimes. The same might be said of a billionaire like George Soros (though it rarely is)—that it's quite okay for him to promote his vision of democracy by committing funds to certain groups in a foreign country he sees moving in the right direction, regardless of what critics in that country might think.

Occasional qualms over such interventions are assuaged by the conviction that the government in question shouldn't be jailing citizens who are seeking to promote political change and greater freedom. Even if Washington has its own agenda, the outcomes are still worth it. Thus the conviction quietly grows that there is no conflict between self-determination on the one hand and external funding, advice, and training on the other. That some local advocates of change oppose intervention ("Let us find our own way") and don't like having local leaders picked out as "human rights heroes" by their patrons in the West is rarely acknowledged.

Consider, for a moment, the situation in reverse. Let's suppose the "democratization" model of social change had been applied by other countries to the civil rights mobilizations in the South in the 1950s and 1960s. Hundreds of NGOs move in, funded by France, India, England, Sweden, Cuba, and Israel. Critics of such foreign involvement are roundly dismissed in the international press as provincial supporters of the status quo. Certain black leaders are picked out and advised on how to organize and how to fight in the courts against a corrupt nontransparent local government. Individuals deemed suitable for global television are highlighted. Funding proposals proliferate. Foreign governments and NGOs call for local officials who are obstructing justice to be indicted. Certain state governors are accused of crimes against humanity for their brutal and illegal use of state power to block integration and their tacit acceptance of violent, even murderous police tactics.

Let us further suppose that leading foreign figures are not inclined to favor black power advocates like Malcolm X, denouncing them as opponents of human rights. Nor is there much empathetic understanding of protest traditions in the mold of W. E. B. Du Bois, Marcus Garvey, John Henry Brown, or even of Ghandian civil disobedience if it ends in violence. And what of foreign funds coming from quasi-governmental groups abroad? In point of fact, the paranoia over Communist influence was still high in Washington during these years and was used to justify surveillance of Martin Luther King Jr. and civil rights groups.

The possibilities and the complexities in this analogy can be taken further, but the conclusion is clear. It is simply inconceivable that anything like this could take place, then or today, in the world's most powerful country. American laws preclude it, the media would denounce foreign meddling, and Congress and the FBI would immediately investigate.

SOUTH AFRICA

While the color revolutions infused Washington's interests with a democratizing, regime-changing human rights ethos, Africa's terrible poverty, disease, and violence called forth more fervent humanitarian appeals for help. In David Rieff's words, what "we know as globalization will prove to be a catastrophe in Africa."[129] Occasionally human rights reports find a bright spot—steps toward democratization, progress toward the rule of law. Still, the tone and detail of these reports is deeply depressing—of David seeking to slay the rights-abusing Goliaths and getting thrashed in the process.

Only in South Africa, with the triumph over apartheid, did the story really appear different. But here, too, the human rights depiction of events is striking in its selectiveness: the struggle comes through less as a mass mobilization, which included a role for radical violence, than as the self-transformation of a society that recognized the need for a broadened rights base. That the new nation rejected a far-reaching redistribution of wealth and power as it sought to consolidate a constitutional system that would protect it from capital flight and provide confidence to international business is simply elided. To some African intellectuals, the end of apartheid signaled the completion of a long process of struggle but not, regrettably, the beginning of a way out of Africa's desperate plight. In human rights literature, however, there are few regrets.

Given their orientation, it is not surprising that human rights organizations have lauded the Truth and Reconciliation Commission as "one of the most original and positive efforts in Africa and in the world to ensure accountability during a transition process."[130] In its five volumes, the commission captured the pain and injustice of apartheid by focusing on individual violations of human rights. But the term "violation" applied only to specific acts, not to systemic injustices or to the laws passed by the apartheid government.[131] In practice, the Truth and Reconciliation Commission, as Mahmood Mamdani argues, "reduced apartheid from a relationship between the state and entire communities to one between the state and individuals," the very essence of the first current of human rights. The Truth and Reconciliation Commission did not stress apartheid as a "form of power that governed natives differently from non-natives."[132] It excluded "the project of Apartheid, determined that the project itself should be defined as political"—much as Amnesty International had done in the 1980s when it refused to condemn apartheid per se because apartheid was a political ideology and Amnesty was neutral on the subject of ideology.[133]

What human rights groups found particularly praiseworthy in the commission's proceedings was its even-handed approach. Victims and perpetrators could be found on all sides. The struggle of the African National Congress against apartheid was obviously just, but the ANC was nonetheless held "responsible for the commission of gross human rights violations," having repeatedly breached the Geneva Protocols— which is criminal behavior, even in the context of a war against a ruthless apartheid state. "Equal application of the laws" was of paramount importance, wrote one human rights leader to the chairman of the commission, Archbishop Desmund Tutu, after ANC leader Thabo Mbeki criticized the commission. "There was no moral, philosophical, or legal basis for Mbeki's argument that a just war warranted unjust methods of warfare, such as urban bombings ... and the torture and murder of their own combatants suspected of disloyalty. These are never 'legitimate actions.' "[134]

The stance appears self-evident: the use of force must be reasonably tailored to a lawful military end, and there must be a fundamental distinction between combatants and noncombatants.[135] The ANC was morally and politically accountable for having created a climate in which its supporters believed it was legitimate to ignore this distinction in the name of a "people's war." For human rights groups, the matter is simple: Violence creates victims. It is criminal. Their view issues from the bedrock human rights belief in protecting noncombatants and the innocent. There is much to be said in its behalf.

But let us apply these rules to a hypothetical situation from the past: a Jewish group organizing against the Nazis in Berlin in the early 1940s. Group members plant bombs in public places throughout Berlin to disrupt daily life, killing scores of civilians. That's a crime. So is the car bomb they use to attack a club frequented by off-duty SS officers. They blow up a train that carries wounded soldiers—another crime. And another: they kill several turncoats who are judged to be working for the Nazis. The group attacks Goering's home, killing family members, but he isn't there. They seize Eva Braun as a hostage. And so forth. That all these acts might today be judged crimes gives one pause. This is not to say that the human rights critique of the ANC is wrong— but that flickers of doubt start to enter in when the context is systemic injustice.

Human rights groups also praised the commission for its acceptance of the principle of human rights "impartiality": abuses must be fully reported regardless of who committed them. But here, too, the issue is more complicated. Leaders of the ANC accepted the principle, but then challenged the commission to address the "truth" of the South African situation. "The past is another country," Archbishop Tutu said. But was it only a country of suffering and injustice? Of helpless people abused and denied rights? Of victims? Was there no heroism through collective struggle? Was the Soweto uprising simply a "horrendous occurrence"? Tutu's report "tells the truth, but not the whole truth" wrote Jeremy Cronin, a long-standing ANC member. "We are asked to recognize the 'little perpetrator' in each of us, but we are nowhere asked to recognize the 'little freedom fighter,' the collective self-emancipator that we all could be." Victims and perpetrators alone do not make up the past, ANC leaders argued. "There were strugglers. Millions of ordinary South Africans refused to be merely victims; they organized themselves for survival and struggle into stokvels, shop stewards' councils and self-defense units. The silence, even awkwardness, of the commission's report on these realities is a serious impediment."[136]

The commission's approach, in fact, favored one version of the past above another. "If you were on Robben Island, your collective experience is affirmed in a substantial literature," Cronin points out.

> Every visiting international celebrity makes a pilgrimage to the island. You do not need, particularly, to look to the truth commission for acknowledgement. But what if you spent a large part of the 1980s as a guerrilla in Angola? You fought pitched battles against Unita. You understood this as a contribution to a continental struggle for emancipation. . . . But your story has barely been told. And now you turn to the commission's report and, once more, that experience is reduced to Quatro Camp and the abuses (which you do not deny) that happened there. You do not particularly recognize yourself in this past.[137]

It is "precisely the cycle of victim and perpetrator that we must break," Cronin concludes. His point is poignant because it goes to the core of the human rights vision that tends to downplay struggles for liberation. The history of victim abuses and perpetrators is accurate as far as it goes, but where it doesn't go is just as noteworthy—into a world of systemic wrongs, a world of struggle, of collective mobilization against injustice.

RWANDA

Rwanda was two things, according to human rights accounts: genocide and the intervention that did not take place. Genocide it was. Lack of intervention it was not. The *kind* of intervention that took place is the issue, along with why it failed to stop the genocide or possibly even contributed to it. The history of Rwanda in the years leading up to the genocide offers a particularly unsettling insight into the effects of Washington's ideology of democratization and rights-based development as it was applied throughout much of Africa. In fact, USAID had lauded Rwanda as "one of the best examples of first generation Democracy/Governance (D/G) activities to arise out of and be designed under the Africa Bureau's Democracy and Governance Program"[138]—a virtual laboratory of Washington's strategies for promoting an "enabling environment" for economic change.

The events that culminated in genocide are the subject of a growing literature; the bitter disputes between Hutu and Tutsi elites have been extensively examined.[139] The immediate catalyst came in 1990 when the Rwandan Patriotic Front (RPF), made up of minority Tutsi living in exile in neighboring Uganda and Tanzania, invaded northern Rwanda. The resulting civil war between the mainly Hutu regime (with support from France) and the RPF (with support from Uganda and probably the United States) exacerbated antipathies between the Hutus and the Tutsis dating back to the era of German and Belgian colonialization and its divide-and-rule policies. As the French scholar Gerard Prunier writes, Rwanda was a time bomb.[140] Still, in August 1993, after two years of negotiations, the two sides signed the Arusha agreements to put an end to the fighting. But tensions continued to mount, and with the assassination of President Juvenal Habyarimana in April 1994 the genocide erupted: Hutus slaughtered some 800,000 Tutsis in one hundred days.[141]

Washington's democratizing "tool kit" and humanitarian rhetoric were almost pure fantasy for Rwanda—though not for Washington's interests, just as the earlier promotion of the specter of Communism had been an enormous distortion of local realities but quite useful for Washington's pursuit of its global aims. Before the genocide national security managers certainly understood that Rwanda faced an acute crisis, yet this awareness did not shake their confidence in their fundamental grasp of the processes of democratization, i.e., of a way to work successfully with the IMF and the World Bank on a structural adjustment program while opening up the society to greater U.S. influence.[142] The ideological orientation of the United States, the IMF, the World Bank, and the Western European powers is clear: state-driven development was to be discarded—thirty years of "state-centric, authoritarian, one-party rule" had allowed "for little change in the civic culture." But at last a new "civil culture," nourished and sustained by global ties, was emerging as the state's economic role was "being redefined." Department of State and USAID reports document support for multiparty "consensus" and for greater citizen access to government as well as assistance from multinational donors: "Germany and Canada on the electoral law, the UNDP on election planning; the Swiss and the United States on a free press; and German foundations and USAID on private association in civic action to name a few."[143]

Note how much of the vocabulary Washington used elsewhere it applied to Rwanda. Its Democratic Initiative and Governance Project was providing the nation with the "tools" for promoting citizen participation in its "unfolding democratization process." Private associations were helping individuals learn their rights and duties as electors. Support for a dynamic National Assembly would increase citizen access to government and make it more "transparent and accountable."[144] Support for a free press and an "open information regime" would help citizens learn how to act "in both a free and open market economy and in a democratic polity."[145] The press, lacking depth and necessary skills, needed "guidance"; obstacles remained, but "training" a "responsible media" was a key step. New strategies for decentralized development would make local government more responsible. As the Organization of African Unity panel that later examined the genocide reported, the Rwandan government ran "a developmental dictatorship."[146] Foreign aid by the early 1990s, it noted, represented more than three-quarters of the state's capital budget and a significant share of its operating budget as well. "Rwanda was not only the land of a thousand hills, went the local joke, it was also the land of a thousand aid workers."[147]

Central to democratization was a flourishing human rights movement. "Five human rights organizations have formed and are actively monitoring alleged civil rights violations by the security apparatus," USAID reported. Of course, the task ahead was daunting; peace in the wake of the 1990 invasion by the RPF required "ethnic reconciliation." Still, this was a "historic opportunity" with a "more than modest chance of success."[148] Though Washington could not simply impose a "blueprint," it could help "facilitate the social learning process," and "selective interventions" could "leverage the process" with practices that, "through trial and application elsewhere, have proven their mettle in making democracies work."[149]

"Civil society" was once again the pivotal concept behind a dynamic that stood "outside of the formal organs of government, providing countervailing centers of power" to state institutions.[150] A diversity of nonstate actors would be built up "through which the people find voice for their aspirations, their demands, and their political will." Support for the rights of women and marginalized people would transform them into backers of a "liberalized economy." Citizens would thus be "empowered," local NGOs funded, and National Assembly members taught to understand their roles.

As usual, human rights reporting adopted the rhetoric but worried over the "implementation gap." Meticulously documented studies in the 1990s depicted an Africa moving toward democratization on the one hand and chaos on the other.[151] Human rights leaders insisted that the two trends were opposites, but the stark accounts of African misery and the Rwandan genocide suggest otherwise.

These leaders stressed how dependent progress was on international involvement in the "peace process." They spoke in the encoded language of "demands for greater democracy" being "backed by donor nations" that "saw political reform as necessary for economic progress," of an "awakening civil society" and a returning "multi-party system," of events that seemed "to herald a new era of freedom for the press."[152] None of it, Prunier writes, had much to do with what was really happening: "The desperate African struggle for survival is bowdlerized beyond recognition."[153] The OAU panel agreed: "international institutions seemed oblivious to most of the elemental realities of Rwanda society."[154] Democratization, it observed, proceeded with no regard for the explosive internal dynamics of the country. As a result, "the movement ended up inciting malevolent forces within society while alienating even further the majority of the population."[155] Outsiders were "blinded by their faith in multipartyism as a panacea for all Rwanda's woes."[156] In fact, "as with the media, so with politics: unaccustomed freedom of association came perilously close to anarchy."[157]

Before his death in 1999, Julius Nyerere, the former Tanzanian leader, pinpointed the single most corrosive force in recent African history: "We had too much interference. . . . The Cold War took over and we had these externally supported dictatorships everywhere over the continent. I naturally resent some of the implications I get about the 'wrong things' that are happening on the continent of Africa. We never had a chance." No continent, he insisted, had ever been subjected for so long to such shattering violence. The end of the Cold War had not ended the violence; now intervention was simply donning new verbal garments in the name of "so called democracy and the manuals of democracy, the manuals of all the governments which are 'blessed' by the West. The manual has been prepared in Paris, written in Washington."[158]

Africa's devastation makes the failure to transcend the limits of the first current of human rights horrifyingly obvious. By the 1990s the language of earlier struggles for emancipation had largely been replaced by hopes for a rights ethos rooted in the rule of law, civil society, and good governance. Human rights arrived "fully packaged from the West" in the 1980s,[159] notes the scholar and human rights activist Alex de Waal. The ethos sought no legitimacy from Africa's earlier nationalist struggles. In the human rights pantheon Mandela is a hero—but not Nkrumah, Nyerere, Kenyatta, Nasser, or Lumumba. These earlier leaders and their regimes are more often seen as part of the problem than as part of an evolving, useful tradition. Little thought is given to why their secularist regimes failed, or why their failures were, for Washington, Cold War success stories. Yet the consequences were considerable. For de Waal, the "thwarting of the 'primary movements' for social change in Africa in the middle part of the twentieth century was, I suspect, the biggest tragedy that overtook the continent."[160]

Civil society could not provide a countervailing center of power either. The Tanzanian intellectual Issa Shivji has noted that colonialism and neocolonialism required the co-opting of local elites. In an African setting the distinction between state and civil societies, with the state demonized and civil society conflated with the privileged status of NGOs, is a dubious one. NGOs are not really a third sector, he argued; nor are they independent of the state. They are inextricably interwoven with the operations of global power.[161] National security managers hardly disagree. "Transnational civil society," as Thomas Carothers of the Carnegie Endowment has written, was "very much part of the same projection of Western political and economic power that civil society activists decry in other venues."[162]

Rwanda offers an extraordinarily bleak example of a myopic democratizing ethos run amuck. In the 1990s new developmental schemes multiplied, World Bank and IMF reports proliferated, NGOs spread. But Africa's terrible poverty, disease, and violence continued on their devastating course. There was no shortage of explanations for failure; models came and went. But the language and its code words endured to explain the ruins. Yet, as usual, it was not from obliviousness but rather out of the toxic mixture of ideology and hard-headed calculation of interests that Washington opposed UN intervention in Rwanda and the genocide occurred as it did.[163]

Rwanda is the guilt America must expiate, and to do so Washington must be ready to intervene against evil across the globe: that is the lesson of Samantha Powers's 2002 *A Problem from Hell*. Powers argues that the United States did know genocide was happening in Rwanda. Then she examines the reasons for our lack of intervention—"domestic constraints," the absence of American interests, the fiasco of the Somalia "humanitarian intervention."[164] Her conclusion is clear: "American leadership is indispensable. This is especially true because Europe continues to avoid intervening in violent humanitarian crises. And it remains true irrespective of American unpopularity abroad. . . . The United States did not exert leadership during the Rwanda genocide; the rest of the world, conveniently, saw leadership not to act."[165]

As so often, the United States was attacked not for what it did but for what it did not do. Human rights leaders assumed their by now familiar position, insisting that nothing was stopping the United States from acting morally except a lack of clearsightedness and a failure of will. Put off by the expense and the constraints of domestic politics, American leaders had looked the other way. ("I was obsessed with Haiti and Bosnia during that period," Anthony Lake recalled, "so Rwanda was . . . a 'sideshow,' but not even a sideshow—a no-show.")[166] The media, too, had failed. While Bosnia received massive coverage, initially Rwanda barely made it into the press.

But what if Washington was doing what it wished to do—with results that were wildly different from what it expected? What if Washington was pursuing its global geopolitical and economic strategies as usual, only to have them explode this time? As the OAU panel noted, "at no time was consideration given to the likely political or social repercussions of economic shock therapy to a country engaged in armed conflict."[167] To human rights leaders this accusation is largely beside the point: economic and ideological meddling was not "involvement"—at least not their kind. But of course the second current in human rights is as important (and as potentially volatile when it is neglected) as the first. The "politics of economics" in Rwanda proved catastrophic—one more example of how the structural adjustment programs "were at least partly responsible for triggering many of the serious internal conflicts that have wracked Africa since the 1980s."[168]

Great power conflicts continued to play themselves out through overt and covert means. The French, reported the OAU, "never overcame their deep-seated antagonism to the RPF as just another 'Anglo-Saxon' Trojan horse in their African preserve"; they saw RPF leader Paul Kagame as pro-American and President Yoweri Museveni of English-speaking Uganda as the power behind the Tutsi insurgents.[169] France thus did "all it could" to prevent the victory of the RPF by shoring up Habyarimana[170] and providing arms to Hutu forces "right through until June, the third month of the genocide."[171]

While neither Washington nor human rights leaders found it easy to call for investigations into French officialdom's complicity in the genocide, the Rwandan government's 2007 report documents in considerable detail French activities that directly and indirectly aided the genocidaires: "France armed Rwanda's murderous regime, sent soldiers to support it as the genocide was unfolding, and accepted some of its most heinous perpetrators as 'refugees' after rebels forced them from power. Later, France helped the genocidaires regroup in the Congo and launch a savage cross-border campaign aimed at retaking power so they could complete their murderous work."[172]

The report details how some thirty-three French officials, from President François Mitterrand on down, considered the RPF linked with the Americans who were seeking to break France's remaining hold over the region. Mitterrand himself said, "Our presence cannot be limited. We are at the boundary of the Anglophone front."[173] Publicly, Washington downplays such French views, perhaps because they might lead to questions about U.S. actions, which both Washington and the Rwandan government are eager to avoid.[174] Exposing French involvement also risks setting off an outpouring of leaks from government and intelligence agencies in Paris, London, and Washington concerning who was doing what in Rwanda and Uganda prior to invasion—and ever since.

A "sins of omission" approach does not go very far toward explaining why Washington acted as it did in Rwanda. It does not account for the long record of great power manipulation dating back to the Cold War or explain much about the RPF's decision to invade or why it did not regard saving Tutsi civilians as a priority[175] or consider that widespread massacres would be a likely result of its offensives.[176] How, after all, does one mobilize opinion against genocide if the RPF itself "was carrying on a massive campaign of killings . . . using obviously selected killer teams"?[177] The RPF seemed not even to trust the Tutsi survivors in Rwanda; it ruled through "a policy of political control through terror."[178]

Some historians have suggested the United States *did* intervene in Rwanda, via a proxy. "That proxy was the RPF, backed up by entire units from the Uganda Army," Mahmoud Mamdani writes. "The green light was given to the RPF, whose commanding officer, Paul Kagame, had recently returned from training in the US, just as it was lately given to the Ethiopian army in Somalia. Instead of using its resources and influence to bring about a political solution to the civil war, and then strengthen it, the US signaled to one of the parties that it could pursue victory with impunity. This unilateralism was part of what led to the disaster."[179] U.S. and UN intervention might have slowed down the victory.[180] National security documents are spotty, though; little has been disclosed about official or quasi-official links with Paul Kagame and the

RDF or Washington's quiet military and intelligence embrace of his leadership after 1994, including his deepening involvement in the wars in the Congo.[181]

By and large the human rights depiction of Washington's role in Rwanda gives the national security managers the benefit of the doubt. And accounts like Samantha Powers's are not inclined to see standard Cold War practices (the use of proxy armies, the operation of powerful quasi-official private groups often in corporate service, the influencing of local organizations, economic shock therapy, and so on) still at work. With genocide they find a world of good versus evil—and indifference or lack of will in Washington. Though of course there is truth in such depictions, there is also obfuscation of Washington's power and interests.

THE END OF YUGOSLAVIA

"If we know that hundreds of thousands of people are going to die, we should not care if the experts call it genocide or not," an official of Human Rights Watch argued before a House Subcommittee in 2004. "We already know what we need to know to decide to act. We know that innocent lives are being lost. We know who is doing it. And we know exactly what will happen if we do not act."[182] Thus "if we know" is a powerful mobilizing call. But, as the case of Yugoslavia suggests, it tends to highlight certain issues while ignoring others.

In Rwanda, we knew and did not act, it is said. Yet much the same could be said about Yugoslavia. We knew that if the country broke up, it was likely to descend into a frightening civil war. We knew that a multicultural Yugoslavia was a flawed state capable of deeply repressive acts, but that this hardly justified encouraging divisions that might lead to conflict. We knew that the EU was divided, with its various members pursuing their own interests even as they urged an IMF shock therapy that wreaked havoc on the Yugoslavian state. U.S. national security managers were aware that a breakup might come at massive human cost.

The EU, for its part, was having its own moment of triumphalism as the Cold War ended. In the eyes of its own "humanitarian internationalists," Europe stood for human rights, multilateralism, open markets,

and a policy of benign internationalism.[183] This Europe dismissed Gorbachev's plea for "a common European House" and called for the application of shock treatment and privatization to Eastern Europe and the
areas of the former USSR. Existing economic patterns in the East were
to be abruptly cast aside.[184]

On all these matters, human rights leaders remained largely silent.
The deepening crisis in Yugoslavia engendered few appeals to save this
unified multicultural state. Just the opposite: there was open support
for a breakup even as Yugoslavia approached the abyss of civil war.
Human Rights Watch denounced the notion that "a certain amount of
repression by the Yugoslav government is necessary as a practical
matter to hold Yugoslavia's fractious ethnic minorities together as a
nation."[185] The organization encouraged the formation of independent
political parties without much consideration as to whether they would
pursue a breakup. Pressures to end the one party-state and demands for
multiparty democracy and "increased respect for human rights" suggest little sensitivity to the ways such parties could unleash forces that
would destroy any democratic possibilities and, worse, any peace.

Human rights reports lamented that efforts to build democracy
were being overtaken by ethnic struggles. But the two phenomena were
part of the same process. Pluralism in the political arena is not so admirable if it exacerbates ethnic divisions (as it did in Yugoslavia) or fuels
bitter disputes between elites seeking to dominate the state (as in
Rwanda). Was it enough to label this often-contradictory element in the
breakup of Yugoslavia and its rapid slide toward civil war "a trend
toward democracy" and leave it at that? Human Rights Watch and
Amnesty insisted that they took "no position on Yugoslavia's territorial
integration or the claims to independence of its constituent republics,"[186] though they criticized the Bush administration for having
"devoted too much energy in trying to preserve Yugoslav unity." They
dismissed the argument that unity promoted rights—a plausible position, certainly. But disunity hardly promoted rights, either.[187]

These issues were hardly raised by human rights leaders. In November 1990, the executive director of Helsinki Watch asked, "Why Keep

Yugoslavia One Country?" in a *New York Times* op-ed piece: "Why not acknowledge the Government's impotence and offer aid to those republics that will protect the rights of their citizens?" she asked. "There is no moral law that commits us to honor the national unity of Yugoslavia. But there are laws, both moral and statutory, that commit us to deny aid to governments that oppress."[188]

A "student of Yugoslav law and society" presciently responded:

> It seems truly bizarre that "human rights" activists so cavalierly advocate policies that are likely to turn Yugoslavia into the Lebanon of Europe. If the Yugoslav state collapses, the republics are almost certain to fight one another because of the large minority populations that are scattered through the country, each of which will be oppressed by the local majority and seek protection from compatriots in adjoining republics.
>
> At best, we could expect repression, perhaps massive expulsions, the sundering of mixed towns and families, followed by permanent hostility and an arms race—well known from the division of India and Pakistan in 1947. More likely would be such communal violence as to make present human rights abuses in Kosovo seem absolutely civilized. Or perhaps Helsinki Watch views war as not a matter of human rights?[189]

Yugoslavia was cast by human rights groups less as a civil war than as an eruption of wars within the former Yugoslavia by newly independent nations—and thus an "international conflict," with Serbs the aggressors and purveyors of genocidal violence. As Cyrus Vance and Lord Carrington struggled to define the relationship among the emerging Yugoslav republics in 1992, they pleaded for "no Western recognition of the independence of any Yugoslav republic until all had agreed on their mutual relationships." U.S. Ambassador Warren Zimmerman ruefully concluded that "if this simple principle had been maintained, less blood would have been shed in Bosnia."[190] Few such concerns were evident in human rights reporting.

Washington's interests in what was happening in Yugoslavia are still widely debated, but ensuring that the EU would not emerge significantly independent of American power after the Cold War was clearly among them. Expanding NATO and its mission was "an essential consequence of the raising of the Iron Curtain,"[191] Richard Holbrooke argued in 1995. Debates over how to do so proliferated, but in the end the disintegration of Yugoslavia marked the reconsolidation of American military power in NATO.

GENOCIDE, MILITANT HUMANITARIANISM, BOSNIA, AND KOSOVO

Before the War on Terror, Washington had no single mobilizing touchstone to energize its calls for democratization, globalization, and humanitarianism. By contrast, genocide offered human rights advocates the ultimate justification for the priority of morality over realpolitik, law over power, justice over national sovereignty. Yet even the genocide debate demonstrates, once again, how human rights leaders ended up closer to embracing Washington than to challenging its power.

Genocide's moment for human rights organizations was actually quite brief. Writing in 2007, Aryeh Neier pointed out that Human Rights Watch had used the label "only three times in its history: to describe the slaughter of Bosnian Muslims in the early 1990s; of Rwandan Tutsis in 1994; and of Iraqi Kurds by Saddam Hussein's regime in the Anfal campaign of 1988."[192] Though some Human Rights Watch leaders joined the Bush administration in labeling Darfur genocide, the organization itself, along with Amnesty and Doctors Without Borders, refused to do so. Had genocide declined? Had the world changed? Was Darfur really so different from Bosnia? In the 1990s human rights leaders spoke of ethnic cleansing as genocide; later they were more cautious.[193] Why?

"God words," Kenneth Burke once warned, are more effective in arousing the passions than the intellect.[194] This is especially true when they tap into underlying currents in a country's intellectual and political life. Before the June 1967 war between Israel and Arab nations, the

Holocaust had engendered only moderate interest in the United States.[195] But by the early 1990s the climate was different. Broad interest in Bosnia coincided with a blossoming of popular films, books, and academic programs and the opening of the United States Holocaust Memorial Museum in Washington. Bosnia became part of the emotional firestorm in this "Americanization of the Holocaust."[196]

As the Cold War came to an end and the "implementation gap" remained as wide as ever, an increasing desperation underlay the human rights community's preoccupation with genocide. If Washington couldn't be aroused by genocide, then what could sustain the human rights agenda? If American power simply continued to operate as usual, then what was the future of human rights in an America-centered world order? The imagery of victims and abusers, the insistence that criminals be held accountable in international courts formed part of an impassioned call for Washington to live up to its role as global moral guardian. Genocide was not the only or even the central issue; what was at stake was the centrality of human rights for a new era.

In 2007 the World Court handed down a decision on Bosnia's claim that Serbia had committed genocide. The court ruled that the slaughter of some seven thousand men at Srebrenica in 1995 constituted "acts of genocide" but found no broader pattern of calculated genocide.[197] The court did find overwhelming evidence of massive killings in specific areas and detention camps throughout Bosnia–Herzegovina. But its rejection of the sweeping claims of genocide, for which proof of intent is required, shocked human rights leaders, who had long regarded progress in confronting genocide as one of their triumphs.

The Court further rejected the UN General Assembly resolution identifying the policy of "ethnic cleansing" as a form of genocide, concluding that the term "ethnic cleansing" had "no legal significance of its own." Neither the intent to render an area "ethnically homogeneous" nor the operations to implement such a policy "can *as such* be designated genocide." Deportation or displacement of members of a group was not necessarily equivalent to destruction of that group. Such acts constituted genocide only if they could be characterized as "deliberately inflicting on the group conditions of life calculated to bring about its physical destruction in whole or in part." The evidence the court examined did not show that this had happened in Bosnia. A distinction is required between the "physical destruction and mere dissolution of a group." Criminal all this may be, and horrific, but it is not genocide. Nor was the eradication of historical and cultural shrines of particular groups—"cultural genocide" is simply not a category that exists under international law.[198]

Human rights leaders had long argued otherwise. In 1992, Human Rights Watch announced there was prima facie evidence of genocide in Bosnia–Herzegovina.[199] Human rights reports and the media were filled with holocaust imagery—corpses, concentration camps, starving inmates.[200] In this context, human rights leaders began to parse the definition of genocide. Neier concluded that Serbian "ethnic cleansing" in Bosnia fit the definition, since the Serbs "tried to destroy a distinctive ethnic/religious group, the Bosnian Muslims, by deportations, bombardment of civilian towns, internment of civilians in detention camps, destructions of cultural monuments, pillage, torture, summary execution, and rape."[201] The "purpose was to eliminate permanently from controlled territory a segment of the population, just as the Nazis attempted to eliminate permanently all Jews from countries occupied and subjugated by German troops."[202] "Just as the Nazis" is inflammatory rhetoric, but it well reflects what various members of Congress were adding to the incendiary debates over Bosnia in the 1990s. In the words of Congressman James Moran: "There is evil prevalent in Yugoslavia. It is being perpetuated by people for the very same reasons that Nazi Germany initiated its program of ethnic cleansing and became so powerful."[203] Christopher Smith of New Jersey added: "We are confronting here" something "inherently evil, a racist force so irrational that it cannot be satisfied by a positive gesture. Genocide must be condemned, confronted, and stopped, not tolerated and appeased."[204] And Senator Joseph Biden pointedly concluded: "Serbs are illiterates and degenerates."[205]

Truth is an early casualty in all wars, as reading human rights reports on Bosnia certainly suggests. Clausewitz's warning that war tends toward the absolute—and absolutist language—was largely borne out. Partly because human rights groups are preoccupied with mobilizing around atrocities, they rarely reflect on the role of wartime propaganda and media hysteria. Public relations, marketing, and advertising techniques tend to be used rather than dissected in human rights literature. There are no reminders of the distorting debates about U.S. involvement in World War I, for example, or of the many instances in which outrage over atrocities was manipulated by groups to further their agendas.[206]

Comparing Human Rights Watch reports with that of the Dutch government's commission investigating the events at Srebrenica yields up two very different views. The Dutch felt some responsibility for the murders at Srebrenica, where Dutch troops had been in charge of protecting the "safe haven." Their report speaks of "civil war," not genocide, and observes that there "was a more or less equal propensity to instigate violence,"[207] adding that "it would be a rather blinkered view to conclude that the Serbs were responsible for most of it."[208] It questions the black-and-white supposition that the Serbs were brutal aggressors and the Muslims victims—the latter were "unwilling to consider compromises and their long-term prospects were reasonably good. They waged propaganda very skillfully, making themselves the 'victims.'"[209] It acknowledges the villainy of Slobodan Milošević—"among the worst, but only one among several leaders that include the Croats"—but challenges the popular account of the massacre at Srebrenica (though seven thousand men were slaughtered there, the act was "not centrally planned," was in part a response to earlier massacres of Serbs, and was "probably" tied to military activities by Muslim men seeking to break out of the safe area). The report cautions against too facilely blaming the Serbs for the August 1995 mortar attack on the market at Markdale (it is "possible" that the Muslims did it) and challenges the notion of a "concentration camp" at Omarska. ("The footage was not actually of a camp; there was no 'compound' in the sense of an area fully enclosed by barbed wire." The "emaciated semi-naked person depicted had been specially selected.") It is also more nuanced about accusations of Serbians having overrun the Srebrenica "safe area." (Never in its history had the UN used the term "safe areas," as opposed to militarily protected "safe havens." "Safe areas" were more a "warning not to attack," and their existence did not prevent the Muslims within them from sending out military forays to fight the Serbs.) The Dutch report concludes that there was "seldom any deeper analysis of the background to what was happening in Yugoslavia or careful consideration of the main points of dissent."[210]

More than any other atrocity, human rights leaders argued, genocide demands intervening *and* taking sides—and take sides many of them did. Human Rights Watch became increasingly involved in calculating military and diplomatic strategies, calling for air strikes against Serbian forces to protect "safe areas" and urging military action to stop ethnic cleansing in Kosovo. The organization's repeated demand "that U.N. peace negotiations not continue unless a neutral body such as the ICRC certified that grave breaches of the Geneva Conventions had been halted" marked a shift from reporting violations on all sides to negotiating and strategizing.[211]

Human rights organizations were somewhat divided over the use of military force. Amnesty International took "no position" regarding humanitarian intervention, though today it insists that "the UN must be prepared to use force as a last resort to protect people."[212] Human Rights Watch, on the other hand, held that "the human rights movement should urge military intervention when it is the last feasible option to stop genocide or comparable mass slaughter."[213] For some, genocide and ethnic cleansing even trumped the need for UN Security Council approval, thus overcoming one of the main legal objections to the war in Kosovo.[214] War for human rights was an enormous leap, but not one to which Washington had any objection.

The establishment of an international legal rights regime seemed on its face less problematic. In July 1992 Human Rights Watch called for an International Criminal Tribunal to deal with the ongoing atrocities in Bosnia, which, with Bosnia and Croatia gaining recognition as independent states, were now war crimes subject to prosecution. And thus, with UN backing, the precedent was set for this crucial next step in the implementation of human rights.[215] Those guilty of atrocities would no longer be able to hide behind state sovereignty.[216] Yet the ensuing trials illustrate once again how admirable objectives can be closely interwoven with the aims of Washington. The tribunal "was to all intents and purposes, the creation of the United States," observed one historian, "which drafted its original statute, instigated a short-lived war crimes commission to test the water, and shepherded the idea through the United Nations."[217] The results were mixed and controversial then and have remained so. As David Scheffer, Washington's former war-crimes ambassador, phrased it, the court was a "'shiny new hammer' in the 'civilized world's box of foreign policy tools.'"[218] But various critics called the trials, particularly Milošević's, a travesty of justice.[219] It does not help that no American or Western European official or group has ever been either investigated or charged with anything—not even NATO for what Amnesty (though not Human Rights Watch) called the "illegal bombing" of targets in Kosovo and the "criminal" act of using cluster bombs.[220]

GENOCIDE VERSUS AGGRESSION

In recent years, Darfur has exemplified the "supreme crime."[221] There have been calls for intervention on college campuses, in the media, from religious groups, and Congress, and self-excoriations for failing to act. "Never again" seems to have become "again and again." Darfur is a "slow motion" Rwanda. And the "lesson" of each genocide is the same: "the killings really take off only after the murderers see that the world, and especially, the United States, is not going to care or react."[222]

The debate over Darfur, however, essentially masked another issue.[223] Darfur was genocide, while Iraq was . . . civil war, religious conflagration, terrorism—but not Darfur. In the history of human rights, the worst atrocities are always committed by somebody else, never us. "Clearly it is not U.S. policy to commit these horrendous crimes [against humanity]," wrote the director of Human Rights Watch in 1998. Washington need hardly worry, therefore, about the International Court. After all, how could the concept of crimes against humanity be used "to harass democratic leaders who have at worst a few human rights peccadilloes to their record?"[224]

Yet, as Mahmood Mamdani has pointed out, there are notable resemblances between Darfur and Iraq: in the number of civilians killed, in the role of paramilitary killers, in the targeting of groups rather than individuals. "The violence in the two places is named differently. In Iraq, it is said to be a cycle of insurgency and counterinsurgency; in Darfur, it is called genocide.[225] Why the difference?"[226]

The reasons lie partly in the core convictions of human rights groups. However fiercely some of their members opposed the war in Iraq, it is not part of their mandate to challenge war and occupation. And of course as far as Washington is concerned, that's just fine. To compare Darfur with Iraq would be unsettling: the moral polarities might be shaken.

Not that Washington has felt under any obligation to intervene militarily in what it has itself labeled genocide. Under George W. Bush, the 1948 UN Convention on Genocide was interpreted as requiring no military action at all, just a "response" of some sort—like protesting at the United Nations. Secretary of State Colin Powell explained to the Senate Foreign Relations Committee in 2004 that the Genocide Convention committed signatories to "undertake to prevent and punish" the crime, not to intervene: Article XII charges states to "call upon the competent organs of the United Nations to take such action. . . ."[227]

Human rights organizations were appalled. "I have no idea what Colin Powell's game is, but to call it genocide and then effectively say, 'Oh, shucks, but we are not going to do anything about that genocide' undermines the very word 'genocide,'"[228] a Doctors Without Borders official fumed. But Washington's understanding of the limited nature of our obligations in response to "genocide" quickly became entrenched. Barack Obama said during his presidential campaign that if genocide was "the criterion by which we are making decisions on the deployment of U.S. forces, then by that argument you would have 300,000 troops in the Congo right now—where millions have been slaughtered as a consequence of ethnic strife—which we haven't done. We would be deploying unilaterally and occupying the Sudan, which we haven't done."[229] What a long way this position lies from the arguments of the 1990s. Predictably, the major human rights organizations once again followed Washington's lead, largely dropping the word "genocide" in relation to Darfur.

Finally, descriptions of genocide as the "supreme international crime"[230] or "the gravest crime known to humankind"[231] are acceptable to Washington because they alter the meaning of Nuremberg itself. The International Military Tribunal at Nuremberg judged "aggressive war" as the "supreme international crime" out of which all others come.[232] Controversies over American aggression litter the Cold War era (and adventures in Central America and the Caribbean before it). "Aggression" is a term that non-Western critics as well as many Western ones apply to American and European behavior in Vietnam, Cuba, Nicaragua, and Iraq, and to the proxy forces covertly utilized in Guatemala, the Dominican Republic, Panama, and elsewhere. But this is a vocabulary the human rights community shuns. Human Rights Watch, according to Neier, "has never labeled any party to any conflict as an aggressor, holding that the concept of aggression is poorly defined. As Israel and the United States argued at the Rome conference in 1998 when the treaty for the International Criminal Court was adopted, it is impossible to come up with a definition of aggression that is not politically controversial."[233] The organization's executive director adds: "The question of who started any given conflict or who is most at fault invariably leads to lengthy historical digressions that are antithetical to the careful, objective investigations into the contemporary conduct of warring parties in which the organization specializes."[234]

Other nations (and the World Court) argue that "aggression" is indeed definable. At Nuremberg Justice Robert Jackson defined an aggressor as a state that is the first to launch an "invasion of its armed force, with or without a declaration of war, of the territory of another state," or one that provides "support to armed bands formed in the territory of another state," or refuses "notwithstanding the request of the invaded state, to take in its own territory, all the measures in its power to deprive those bands of all assistance or protection."[235] Is it truly more complicated to define and identify aggression than genocide? Human Rights Watch has no difficulty identifying genocide under Hitler; is his aggression any harder to see as paradigmatic, even if it is an extreme case? Extremes can help clarify both aggression and genocide as they occur—far more commonly—in ambiguous situations. Why dismiss one and embrace the other?

If national security managers do not very much like invocations of genocide, they have learned to live with them well enough. They never opposed signing the 1948 UN Convention on Genocide; in fact, long before there was a highly public U.S. human rights movement, they were promoting it. They understood its ideological utility in the war of ideas against the Soviets. Truman had warned that failure to approve the convention would undercut America's credibility. Nixon and Carter both endorsed it. The senatorial opposition that continued for several decades was a boon to Soviet anti-American propaganda, as Reagan perceived; his commitment to the genocide treaty proved sufficient to finally obtain Senate passage.[236]

Today, debates over genocide have the effect of tamping down the moral horror of other atrocities in which the United States is directly involved. And genocide serves another purpose: to raise calls for Washington's global involvement. The "sole remaining superpower has a moral obligation to take a stand against human atrocities whenever and wherever they occur," declares a 2003 USAID strategy document.[237] The 2006 National Security Strategy exhorts, "History teaches that sometimes other states will not act unless America does its part."[238] Congressman Steny Hoyer summed up this view in 2000: "Genocide and mass slaughter debases our nation's principles and insults our collective conscience. . . . [A]s the world's one military and economic superpower, we have the opportunity—and, in my view, the responsibility—to promote an international moral order."[239]

Human rights leaders tend to agree. As Kenneth Roth of Human Rights Watch and Ruth Wedgwood, the former vice chair of Freedom House, wrote in 2002, "The U.S. did not seek its special security role. But given lingering historical suspicions among neighbors in many regions, America's unique role as a guarantor of security has continued for want of a more reliable arrangement."[240] The UN is largely dependent on

American power anyway, the argument goes, and Washington is uniquely qualified to act; not to respond is to violate who we really are.

Ranking genocide above aggression on the scale of evils is not an outcome derived from Nuremberg. It is a contribution of the human rights community, aided and abetted by the national security establishment and the popular rights-based vision of the United States. An emphasis on genocide places the weight of morality on America's side; an emphasis on aggression does not. Neither national security managers nor human rights leaders have ever acknowledged that the United States commits aggression. They simply avoid the issue.

6

TERRORISM AND THE PATHOLOGY
OF AMERICAN POWER

"Terrorism" is a brilliant propaganda word, a grim corroboration of Montaigne's warning that "Nothing is so firmly believed as that which we least know." It blinds even as it appears to illuminate. It energizes leaders, bureaucracies, and the media, and it cows critics. Who, after all, is for terrorists? The very notion is rife with ugliness: innocents murdered, body parts in the marketplace, the burning twin towers. Even more than "Communism," "terrorism" is a label that simplifies. Panic lurks beneath. The dread is no longer of an insidious penetration but of chaos and pathological acts committed by barbarians. Communism was at least a corruption of the good, a cynical manipulation of Enlightenment ideals. Terrorism is the perversion of humanity itself.

The George W. Bush administration fused the aims of democratization, human rights, and regime change with a "War on Terror" to create the most formidable fighting faith since anticommunism. Not since the late 1940s had there been such an emotionally charged enemy to mobilize national security leaders. For more than half a century, such mobilizing efforts had accompanied appeals to "reshape the global order" in a "new era"; Truman, Kennedy, Nixon, Carter, and Reagan all made them. So when Bush, once again, said, "History has given us a unique opportunity . . . to restructure the world toward freedom,"[1] he was drawing on standard national security rhetoric.[2] Yet his administration was to push much further the Clinton administration's ideas about "total penetration," involvement in failing states, promotion of regime change (in the color revolutions in Eastern Europe), and humanitarian intervention. Its soaring rhetoric of freedom and transformational diplomacy was a good fit with the war in Afghanistan and the occupation of Iraq: on one side, American "universality" and the "civilized world"; on the other, the barbarity of suicide bombers.

Terrorism became the new paradigm quite abruptly after 9/11. The great simplifier of national security matters is typically the president, and on this score Bush did not disappoint. Terrorists, driven by "an ideology of hatred and fear,"[3] were "demented, fanatics," "men without conscience," "parasites," "cold blooded killers who despise freedom, reject tolerance and kill the innocent." "Evil but not insane,"[4] they had not yet "taken control of a great power," but "they share a vision and operate as a network of dozens of violent extremist groups around the world, striking separately and in concert."[5] The terrorists were "not protesting our policies. They were protesting our existence"[6] in "a clash between civilization and those who would destroy it."[7] Their strategy "glorifies the deliberate killing of innocents."[8] Their "radical visions— having little to do with policy and much to do with a blinding will to power—reek of fascism, Nazism, and totalitarianism."[9] We were no longer dealing with civilized human beings but with "killers who have made the death of Americans the calling of their lives."[10]

Of course, "terrorism" and "terrorists" had long had a place in Washington's ideological arsenal. Truman lambasted "terrorist" attacks by Communists against the Greek state,[11] Eisenhower warned of the Communists' "highly organized world campaign of deceit, subversion and terrorism";[12] Johnson denounced the NLF "terrorism" that targeted "school teachers and school administrations, health officials, village leaders, schools, hospitals, research stations, and medical clinics."[13] "The evil scourge of terrorism" was one of Reagan's favorite phrases; he often alluded to "state supported" terrorists who "intentionally kill and maim unarmed civilians, often women and children. . . ."[14] During the Clinton years nonstate actors, too, became guilty of "terrorism," though the term remained just one code word competing with others.[15]

Terrorism's rapid acceptance as a paradigm following 9/11 owed something to another context as well. After the founding of the Palestine

Liberation Organization (PLO) in 1964, several conferences in Tel Aviv and Washington had propagated a definition of terrorism as violence targeted at innocent civilians for political purposes, a definition that quickly spread among influential policy makers. National security professionals in Washington and Tel Aviv well knew that since the beginning of the UN there had been competing views over whether struggles for independence and self-determination and resistance against occupations involved terrorism. Amnesty International had long argued that agreement on how to relate issues of terrorism to such struggles was unlikely to be reached. The Islamic Conference of Foreign Ministers on Terrorism added in 2002 that any legitimate struggles ("resistance to foreign aggression and the struggle of peoples under colonial or alien domination and foreign occupation for national liberation and self-determination") had to be differentiated from acts of terrorism—thus rejecting "any attempt to link terrorism to the struggle of the Palestinian people."[16]

This Gordian knot was cut by simply ignoring the complexity and endless legalistic debates. "Beyond all nuance and quibble," the administration's new definition made terrorism "a moral evil, infecting not only those who commit such crimes, but those who, out of malice, ignorance, or simple refusal to think, countenance them."[17] This might not be a legal definition or one that appears in the *OED*—but it was a compelling moral position and excellent propaganda.

MAKING PROPAGANDA OF THE INNOCENT

Historically human rights groups have always focused on protecting innocents—noncombatants, abused women, suffering children. They have marketed their message, raised funds, and galvanized constituencies on this basis. They have produced graphic accounts of the wounded and the dead, rife with images of body parts and limbs torn asunder. These groups also speak of the complex interrelationship of economic, social, legal, democratic, cultural, and civil rights; they espouse such concepts as the laws of war, the rights of noncombatants, the responsibility to protect. But underlying it all has been the sanctity of the innocent victim, and nothing could be a more flagrant assault on this notion than terrorism. Deliberately killing and maiming civilians "is terrorism pure and simple," UN Secretary-General Kofi Annan declared in 2005, in a phrase widely quoted by human rights leaders.[18] No complex legal analysis is required to reach this conclusion. It's what human rights is all about. Terrorism is anti human rights—its veritable opposite, emotionally, legally, and morally.

Terrorism is an attack on innocent civilians: the obvious nature of this equation is exactly what makes it such an evocative instrument of propaganda warfare, a perfect instance of the way specific truths can obfuscate more complex understanding. Over the decades, the focus of human rights had evolved—from prisoners of conscience to the rights of noncombatants to democratization to humanitarian intervention. But nothing quite so emphatically reinforced the individual-centered vision of the first current as the fight against terrorism. As a result, human rights groups found themselves in alignment with Washington, coming together in a shared language. But by making the targeting of civilians the core of their own definition of terrorism, they unwittingly added ammunition to Bush's War on Terror. The protection of innocent civilians that had been their mobilizing call was subtly turned against them.

Washington adeptly packaged itself as the very antipode of those who targeted civilians, especially women and children. Terrorism is not a particular regime, or rogue state, or religion, Bush said; it is the "premeditated, politically motivated violence perpetrated against innocents."[19] Or as the National Strategy for Combating Terrorists put it, terrorism is "premeditated, politically motivated violence perpetrated against noncombatant targets by sub-national groups or clandestine agents."[20] Bush propagated this new paradigm relentlessly. Targeting innocent civilians is wrong, always and everywhere.

American human rights groups used the same terminology. There was little disagreement among them that "attacks on civilians" aimed at the "heart of the entire structure of international human rights and humanitarian law" and drove "the current massive efforts to deter and destroy terrorist capabilities."[21] No cause, no rationale, no act justified doing harm to innocents. "Whatever you believe about anything else," declared Kenneth Roth, the executive director of Human Rights Watch, "the bottom line should be you never deliberately kill civilians," for it is "the fundamental principle of human rights and humanitarian law."[22]

This morally impassioned assertion was strengthening in its purity. Humanitarianism as a fighting faith had been partly fueled by our uneasiness over the responsibility we bore for a world of unceasing atrocities. Terrorism effectively erased this feeling. The terrorist label brought back full force the conviction that whatever else could be laid at our door; at least we didn't act like them. The great human rights battles of the Bush years—torture, renditions, Guantánamo, Abu Ghraib—were largely over the horror of our becoming "like them."

After a half century in which "Communist" had put a stop to critical thinking more effectively than any other word in the American lexicon, some reflection about the consequences of embracing the term "terrorist" might have been in order. But there was little. "Terrorism today poses a serious threat," Human Rights Watch asserted. When the organization warned that violations of human rights were undermining Washington's credibility as the "leader of the campaign against terrorism," it was straightforwardly adopting Washington's language.[23] The "War on Terror" had to be fought with respect for human rights, it insisted, not in violation of them. American abuses provided rallying cries "for terrorist recruiters"; the pictures from Abu Ghraib were "recruiting posters for 'Terrorism, Inc.'" The fight would be won only by extending human rights and thus destroying the "breeding grounds of terrorists."[24]

There were some trenchant criticisms of the concept of a war on terror from these groups. Was it really even a war? The administration "stretches the meaning of the word 'war'" to give itself "extraordinary powers enjoyed by a wartime government," thus breaking down the distinction between what is permissible in times of peace and of war.[25] The "real test of success is whether the administration's approach to terrorism is neutralizing more terrorists than it breeds. Here the available signs are negative."[26] But in the end, the goal was noble even if the tactics were not.

———

For Washington, defining terrorism as the targeting of innocent civilians was a strategic boon. Just as national security managers had embraced the rights of noncombatants as a way to challenge insurgency movements after Vietnam, following 9/11 they seized on the "innocent" to promote certain interests over others, drawing on several handy ideological implications embedded in this definition. A Manichean vision of the world reemerged with a virulence not seen since the height of the Cold War. "We are in a conflict between good and evil,"[27] Bush declared, "and America will call evil by its name." This battle required that a clear distinction be drawn between the targeting of civilians and all other acts in which civilians might be harmed. The former was "intrinsically evil, necessarily evil and wholly evil,"[28] no matter what the objectives or circumstances. To suggest that this view might oversimplify a complicated issue was no more than "false sophistication"—the mark of a broken-down conscience unable to distinguish between good and evil.[29]

From this Manichean vision follows the view that terrorism is the antithesis of the rule of law and of the entire civilized effort to protect the rights of noncombatants and the innocent. The terrorist respects no code of law established for war or peacetime.[30] Violating the prohibition against targeting civilians means "you are left without any norms at all," thus placing all the achievements of the Hague and Geneva Conferences and the entire edifice of the laws of war "in danger of being swept aside."[31] Note that the issue is the line between lawful and illegal violence—not peace, but the regulation of war. The "very raison d'être of al Qaeda is to violate the laws of war by targeting innocent civilians," asserted a former U.S. attorney general.[32] As a result, for Washington and U.S. human rights leaders defeating terrorism and promoting the laws of war were indistinguishable aims.

A related and equally useful ideological implication is proportionality, a concept that prohibits attacks when the harm to civilians is expected to outweigh the anticipated advantages.[33] Military operations are to be directed only at military targets and combatants; they may not intentionally strike at civilians or civilian objects. Thus there is no moral equivalence between, say, a stray missile's killing civilians in a town held by insurgents and a terrorist group's suicide bombings of civilians. One is legal, the other criminal; one is morally acceptable, the other is not. The individuals who attacked the World Trade Center meant to kill civilians, whereas Washington's aim is to kill only "combatants" and minimize injuries to civilians, whose deaths are "unintentional," "accidental." Innocent civilians may indeed be killed, but they are not specifically being targeted. No debate over means or estimates of expected civilian deaths equates morally with deliberately attacking the innocent. Rarely does one find any notion so pure and simple in war—or in life. But terrorism fits the description: it is radical evil.

Human rights groups, too, often discuss the laws of war in terms of proportionality. Was the collateral damage justified? Were too many civilians killed? Was insufficient care taken? Was a hospital targeted, or a radio station, or an electrical generator? Legal parsing inevitably follows. Didn't clause X preclude attacks on Y targets under Z conditions? Terrorists pose no such complexities. The law regarding them is refreshingly simple.[34] They are the other.

"Targeting civilians" has still another useful ideological application: deromanticizing insurgencies and almost all violent acts of resistance. The label "depraved" can be applied to all those who use these methods, and they can no longer be regarded as heroic.[35] However contentious the arguments over the definition of "freedom fighters" in earlier eras, most members of the national security establishment now agreed that the contemporary terrorist's central focus on targeting civilians was qualitatively different—particularly when it came to the Middle East and the Palestinians after the establishment of the PLO.

Earlier freedom fighters, argues one Israeli authority, were bound by certain ethical rules. They "drew a sharp distinction between soldiers and small children, between repressive authorities and helpless women, between governmental agents and ordinary citizens, between a military outpost and a common dwelling place." The contemporary terrorist, by contrast, knows no such distinctions.[36] Suicide bombing accepts few if any moral limits on the choice of targets. To the charge that this definition of terrorism applied equally to the Nicaraguan Contras, Senator Henry Jackson retorted that neither the intent nor the logic of their policy was the same, whatever its costs to civilians. Did one not see the *moral* difference?[37]

Another ideological tool that the "terrorist" label offers derives from the argument that there are simply no grievances that justify the murder of innocent people, nor should grievances ever be invoked to mitigate the evil of terrorist acts. Human rights leaders fully concurred, even in cases where the grievances were real and urgent. For Washington, ideological warfare involved undermining the image of terrorists in their own communities; terrorism had to "be isolated from the context which breeds it" *before* the grievances that gave rise to it could be adequately addressed.[38] American human rights leaders focused more on the *moral* context of terrorism—the inhumanity, the total corruption of means and ends. While it was "beyond Human Rights Watch's scope to work to address political grievances or the conditions that lead to pathologies that lead groups to attack thousands of civilians," a "terrorist pathology" was what the organization saw at work: "Sympathy for such crimes is the breeding ground for terrorism, and sympathizers are the potential recruits."[39] In the end only the mores of human rights offered an alternative. "Let's face it, we're never going to persuade Osama bin Laden to give up and pursue peaceful political change," warned Kenneth Roth of Human Rights Watch, "which means, in the long run, that the war against terrorism is going to be won or lost on the issue of recruitment."[40] Terrorism "will succumb only where peaceful political change is a realistic option."[41] Building a culture in which any disregard for civilian life would be condemned rather than condoned was essential for defeating terrorism;[41] that was why the "fight against terrorism must be understood as a campaign for human rights."[42]

Echoing its earlier Cold War position, Human Rights Watch argued that Washington needed a "positive vision." It was not enough to be against terrorism; the administration "will have to be in favor of the values that explain what is wrong with attacking civilians—the values of human rights." The United States needed to "look at those closed countries and begin to press for the creation of pluralism, or real political opportunities there," since, after all, repression "fuels terrorism by closing off avenues of peaceful dissent."[43]

Washington was more than willing to oblige. "Ignoring human development is not an option. It is imperative that we encourage and nurture democratization," Bush's coordinator for counterterrorism declared. The "destructive task" of "eradicating enemy networks" had to be balanced by the "constructive task" of "building legitimacy, good governance, trust, prosperity, tolerance, and the rule of law"—wording almost identical to that of various Human Rights Watch reports.[44]

Calls for democratization were reinforced in the War on Terror, for terrorism was "the crassest antithesis of democratic values."[45] Where democracies honored the unique value of each individual, terrorism rejected the concept of personal worth.[46] That was why attacking individuals was attacking the core value of human rights, and why the "moral narrative" of our time must be about standing against terrorism. Even more than humanitarianism, terrorism brought into sharp focus the individual-centered outlook that lies at the heart of human rights advocacy.

"It has generally been acknowledged to be madness to go to war for an idea, but if anything is more unsatisfactory, it is to go to war against a nightmare," Lord Salisbury stated in 1877. Washington had its own idea about what it was going to war for, and human rights leaders found themselves perilously close to propagating the nightmare that was being used to rationalize the War on Terror. Their most cherished concern—protecting the innocent—was being ideologically packaged in a way that was difficult to challenge. The notion of a "terrorist pathology" offered both Washington and human rights leaders a potent brew of the diseased, the barbaric, the uncivilized, the *not like us*—those, in short, at war with human rights. But as James Baldwin once warned, "it is a terrible, an inexorable law that one cannot deny the humanity of another without diminishing one's own."[47]

Yet, whatever the propaganda issues, who in the end is not outraged by the supreme injustice of killing innocents? What does it matter if Washington or any other power manipulates aspects of such an obvious crime to its own ends? It's still a crime. Examples like the following are simply too awful to justify in any way: "it was an outrage, an obscenity. The severed hand on the metal door, the swamp of blood and mud across the road, the human brains inside a garage, the incinerated, skeletal remains of an Iraqi mother and her three small children in their still-smoldering car . . . by my estimate, more than 20 Iraqi civilians."

As it happens, however, that is a description of the collateral damage caused by two missiles from an American jet—an unfortunate lapse from President Bush's promise to "protect innocent lives in every possible way."[48] It is an example of the proportionality that makes "us" different from "them" because our *intention* was not to kill these civilians, even if, as a Palestinian journalist has remarked, this is "*deliberate killing*—killing deliberately by mistake."[49] The killing is premeditated "in the literal sense that it is clearly foreseen and contemplated beforehand, with the repeated claim that those killed are the very minimum to be expected . . . commensurate with protecting our troops and achieving our military objectives."[50] This is the law; this is morality; this is the fine distinction that makes us different from them. Or as one scholar has translated the concept into the legalese of our time, "incidental civilian casualities from proportionate military operations are a tolerated cost of war, but deliberately killing noncombatants—even in reprisal—is unlawful."[51]

If the public responded as emotionally to high-altitude bombings or attacks by unmanned drones as it does to suicide bombings, human rights advocates would be putting forth their arguments in a different emotional and perhaps even moral context. In the wake of the My Lai massacre during the Vietnam War, antiwar activists raised the question of why deliberately killing unresisting women and children one by one generated more public revulsion than the numerically far more lethal use of bombing, napalm, strafing, and chemical defoliants from what was often an invisible distance. Individualizing (rather than generalizing) acts of terror may render them truly horrifying and personally mobilizing, but whether it captures the deeper truth is harder to say.

Propagandistically, of course, simplicity is essential to the operations of power and was absolutely central to Bush's War on Terror. But it is this very simplicity that has often made American human rights

organizations both victims of and unwilling accomplices to the ideological onslaught of their fiercely determined government. The blurring
of human rights rhetoric with Washington's strategic communications
policies undermined any effective human rights response. It was insufficient to criticize the Bush administration for failing to address the
pathology of terrorism without bringing an equally sharp focus to the
pathology of power. It was too easy to write off the other as hostile to
rights while assuming that those in power could simply embrace human
rights—if they only chose to. In the end, American human rights leaders espoused a variant of Washington's war of ideas—the notion of terrorism as a system of beliefs, attitudes, and feelings that allowed us to
lump all "extremist" acts together—even as they mobilized people
against the "War" on Terror.

AVOIDING THE USE OF "TERRORISM"

The use of the term "terrorism" is not uncontested in the human rights
world. Amnesty International has explained that it steers clear of the
word—it is "simply not an acceptable term of use given that there is no
internationally agreed definition of what the term means"; it "has not
been subject to the rigors of jurisprudence nor is there a broadly
accepted definition under which we may systematically evaluate governments' application of the terms and the actions they seek to justify
under protection of its rubric." The issue is "not merely semantic." The
problem is that the label tends to be applied only to individuals and
nonstate groups, while the fight against "terrorism" has been used by
states to "cloak actions that would otherwise be exposed as illegiti-
mate."[52] When, the organization demands, "was it ever agreed that the
state cannot be said to have committed acts of terrorism?"[53]

Those who argue that terrorism includes state terrorism have consistency and the weight of evidence on their side.[54] According to Edward
Peck, deputy director of Reagan's White House Task Force on Terrorism:

> In 1985, they asked us . . . to come up with a definition of terrorism
> that could be used throughout the government. We produced about

six, and in each and every case, they were rejected, because careful reading would indicate that our own country had been involved in some of those activities. . . . One of the terms, "international terrorism," means "activities that," I quote, "appear to be intended to affect the conduct of a government by mass destruction, assassination or kidnapping." [. . .] Yes, well, certainly, you can think of a number of countries that have been involved in such activities. Ours is one of them. Israel is another.[55]

But no leading human rights organization has ever charged Washington with state terrorism. Amnesty's refusal to enter this minefield by avoiding the word altogether is a pragmatic response to the inability of human rights organizations to cope with issues of state terrorism by Western powers but a principled stance as well: for one must apply it to both sides or to neither.[56] Amnesty chooses neither. Human Rights Watch continues to choose one, arguing that the U.S. government's "single overriding goal since September 11 has been to defeat terrorism." Yet to speak thus is to acquiesce to Washington's loaded definitions.[57] Washington deftly defines "terrorism" so as never to include its own actions; U.S. state terrorism is, by its definition, an oxymoron.

Media organizations have faced the same set of problems. The BBC's guidelines for its reporters state that their "credibility is undermined by the careless use of words which carry emotional or value judgments" and, further, that there is "no agreed or universal consensus on what constitutes a terrorist or a terrorist attack." The word "terrorist" itself can be "a barrier rather than an aid to understanding," since it is "a difficult and emotive subject with significant overtones" that is "regarded through a political prism." Loaded words "can imply judgments where there is no clear consensus about the legitimacy of military political groups." "Terrorist," in brief, implies an assessment of "the merits of the different perpetrators' causes, the acts of the different Governments against the perpetrators, or even the value of civilian lives further from home. We must be careful not to give the impression that we have come to some kind of implicit—and unwarranted—value judgment."[58]

Other words "can be used with precision to convey the awful consequences without needing to resort to labels," the BBC guidelines continue. Thus "'bomb attack' conveys more information more quickly than 'terrorist attack;' similarly 'suicide bomber,' 'bomber,' 'assassin,' 'gun man' help fill in the picture." As an example, the BBC offers its Northern Ireland correspondent report in the wake of the Omaha bombing in 1998:

> There should have been a carnival here, instead there was carnage. Saturday afternoon shoppers here because it was safe, crowded together away from a bomb scare. Instead the bomb was in their midst.
>
>   It killed three generations of one family . . . a 65 year old grandmother, her pregnant 30 year old daughter and her 18 month old daughter. A litany of the dead, . . . of the slaughtered innocents.

"It is worth asking yourself," concludes the BBC, "what the use of the word 'terrorist' would have added to that simple but powerful statement of what had happened."[59]

Reuters agrees. "As part of a policy to avoid the use of emotive words," the global news service has explained, "we do not use terms like 'terrorist' and 'freedom fighter' unless they are in a direct quote or are otherwise attributable to a third party. We do not characterize the subjects of news stories but instead report their actions, identity and background so that readers can make their own decisions based on the facts."[60]

"LEGITIMATE GRIEVANCES"

"We actually misnamed the War on Terror," President Bush told an audience of journalists. "It ought to be the struggle against ideological extremists who do not believe in free societies who happen to use terror as a weapon to try to shake the conscience of the free world."[61] The joke drew laughter.

But why should terror shake the conscience of the Free World? There's the rub. For beneath the ugliness of terrorism smolders ugliness of another kind: the harshness of the political and economic structures that Washington is well aware sustain and "breed" it. The issue for national security managers is more complex than terrorism; it is "extremism" of all kinds, often rooted in what they term legitimate grievances. Its causes are not simply fanaticism and the pathology of the fanatical mind but rather despair, opportunism, radicalism, the revenge of the weak against the plundering wealthy. Internal national security assessments employ a language far franker than the one the American media uses—a language that often acknowledges oppression, radicalism, resistance, the downtrodden, inequalities, opposition to U.S. military presence, and so on. To effectively wage propaganda warfare requires an understanding of resistance groups, exploitation, the appeal of martyrdom, the weakness of moderate forces. "Terrorism" is good propaganda but a weak analytical tool.

Administration leaders occasionally considered moving beyond the term, as when Donald Rumsfeld and other Defense Department officials spoke of a "war on radical extremism."[62] Bush himself resisted the shift but not the policy focus on "extremism of all kinds." Within the national security establishment, distinctions were drawn among those considered extremists of one sort or another, but for public consumption "terrorists" provided an accordion label—and human rights advocates often picked it up. Revolution became "insurrectionary terrorism"; attempts to overthrow colonial regimes, "liberation terrorism"; the focus on a single cause, "loner" or "issue terrorism"; efforts of a religious or ethnic group to gain independence for a subordinate part of a state, "separatist terrorism"; efforts aimed at driving out an occupying force, "occupation terrorism"; efforts aimed at humiliating a global power, "global terrorism."[63]

Presidential statements usually employ a sanitized vocabulary that explains unrest in terms of "underlying conditions"—poverty, corruption, religious conflict, and ethnic strife all create "opportunities" for terrorism.[64] National security analyses are much more candid. "New classes of haves and have nots" confront each other across a desperate chasm of wealth and power. For the first time in human history, "a majority of the world's population will live in cities," where the have-nots are already seeking "distributive justice, equality, and social harmony." The era of rural-based guerrilla warfare may be coming to an end, but huge cities portend acute problems of governance, highly disparate incomes, fierce ethnic and religious conflicts aggravated by periods of economic crisis. Change will no longer be linear but "logarithmic," building up, slowing down, and then bursting forth unexpectedly—much like terrorism.[65]

For the national security managers, the fight against terrorism justified intervention in other nations as no other ethos had since the fiercest days of anticommunism. The kind of preemptive strikes undertaken covertly throughout the Cold War now could be made openly. Deterrence was useless against terrorists—"When they're willing to commit suicide to further their agenda, what do they value that we can place at risk?"[66] asked the chairman of the Joint Chiefs of Staff. The challenge was acute: "a weak power can overcome a strong nation's designs."[67] Throw in weapons of mass destruction and "you have a case where relatively weak actors may have access to lethal power that rivals what the strongest nations have."[68]

Washington's response to this "new era" was to call for an ad hoc "coalition of the willing" on various issues.[69] The War on Terror required a "grand global realignment," with the United States leading a world in which the "great powers see themselves as falling on the same side of a profound divide between the forces of chaos and order."[70] National Security Advisor Condoleezza Rice declared that the War on Terror opened the way to a more "fluid and complicated set of alignments than anything we have seen since the formation of the Atlantic alliance in 1949."[71] In this new era, the United States was "unique" in its capacity to "build partnerships," to "lead the fight," to "adapt old alliances" while "bringing in new partners," and "aiding failing states."[72] For the first time since the seventeenth century the great powers could compete in peace instead of continually preparing for war—as long as they accepted the premise of U.S. centrality. While "frankly speaking of dissuading any potential adversary from challenging American military power" might seem "impolitic," Rice said, "surely such clarity is a virtue here."[73]

Terrorism was thus inextricably intertwined with U.S. primacy—

indeed, for some Washington analysts one explained the other. To be the world's center, they noted, was almost inevitably to be the focal point for widespread unease and popular resistance and thus to become the target of angry "extremists" of all sorts. Numerous populations were "excluded from the benefits" of the global economy; a billion people were malnourished; local autocrats rigged politics to their own ends; the "daily lot may be hunger, disease, displacement." As the young grew "increasingly dissatisfied," many had come to believe that "radical solutions are the last remaining choice." Large areas of the world were becoming "hard to govern lawless zones"—veritable "no-man's-lands" where "extremist movements find breathing space to grow and soft havens are created."[74] Compounding the problem, "terrorists" were using the media and the Internet in highly effective ways: the pain and injustice of the "oppressed" were becoming more and more visible on television and the web all over the world. At one time attacks on Palestinians had been widely but not pervasively reported. Now, as one former CIA official noted, Israeli actions were being replayed on television every hour.[75]

Washington knew very well that the "enemy" could not be reduced to either the pathological individuals nor the cultist groups that were convenient for public diplomacy. As the political scientist Robert Pape argues in his controversial study *Dying to Win: The Strategic Logic of Suicide Terrorism*, most "suicide terrorists" are local "patriots" responding to collective injustice—above all the humiliation of foreign occupation, particularly one in which the occupier appeared to be imposing an alien religion or value system.[76] Much intelligence work concurs. As Zbigniew Brzezinski pointed out, "missing from much of the public debate is discussion of the simple fact that lurking behind every terrorist act is a specific political antecedent."[77] But those antecedents were best left to debates among the professionals.

Human rights groups are well aware, of course, of the fury U.S. policies elicit in many parts of the world. But along with their mantra of taking no stand on war or the occupation in Iraq or military operations in Afghanistan or the territorial issues in the Palestine–Israel question, they have a tendency to suggest that a more open political process would diminish the violence—"Terrorism will succumb only where peaceful political change is a realistic option,"[78] and so on. Meanwhile, the CIA and other national security groups are quite capable of recognizing the legitimate grievances and the grounds for bitterness and "hatred" in various societies. Accounts of Hezbollah recognize its appeal to the "poor and downtrodden" (it is "the first party to oppose deprivation," "the champion of the peasants and the farmers, the laborers and the poor, the oppressed and the deprived, the workers and the homeless")[79] without questioning policies directed either against it or against other groups born out of "legitimate grievances." The national security establishment seeks to understand those grievances with some accuracy—so as to enable Washington to ride roughshod over them if necessary.

CHANGING THE ISLAMIC WORLD

American human rights reports on the Middle East follow the same pattern as human rights reports about every other area of the globe: praise for Washington's principles followed by criticism of its operational polices. To cite one example, in 2006 Human Rights Watch lauded President Bush for engaging Arab countries "on a range of human rights issues, something no past U.S. administration has done,"[80] for deploring "sixty years of Western nations excusing and accommodating the lack of freedom" in the Arab world, and for calling on the United States to commit itself to a new "forward strategy of freedom."[81] Washington's pressure had "helped create more space for some dissidents and genuinely independent political and civic organization."[82] The report then chastised Washington for inconsistency; as usual, Washington had failed to carry through on hopeful possibilities. Having spoken of democracy, it had still supported countless autocrats in places like Saudi Arabia, "a veritable wasteland when it comes to respect for fundamental human rights."[83]

As the war in Iraq raged on, U.S. human rights reporting became more forceful: the "promotion of democracy" had become tarnished by its association with "regime change through military force." The disconnect between Washington's rhetoric and its policies was stirring up deep suspicions of democracy promotion, weakening reformers and democracy advocates everywhere—"Hollow oratory only corrodes perceptions of U.S. credibility in pursuit of its principles."[84] And yet as often as not human rights reports on the Middle East read remarkably like Washington's own strategic communications documents. Their expla nations, their vocabulary, their vision of networks and civil society, their conviction that without external pressure the human rights situation would deteriorate, their very depiction of global processes all echo Washington's.

If human rights groups pointed to declining American credibility in the area of human rights, some twenty government task forces were even more alarmed. According to a typical report, Washington had "no credibility" left; its power to persuade was in a state of crisis, because American policies were seen "by the overwhelming majority of Muslims as a threat to the survival of Islam itself."[85] What we were calling terrorism was to Muslims a "renewal of the Muslim world," not simply a "religious revival."[86] Moreover, "Muslims do not hate our freedoms, they hate our policies." Support for Israel, the occupation of Iraq, and war in Afghanistan all evoked "legacies of Western colonial attitudes." Arabs held the United States responsible for propping up the "tyrannies of Egypt, Saudi Arabia, Pakistan, Jordan, and the Gulf states," creating for it a "strategically awkward—and potentially dangerous—situation."[87]

What Washington and human rights groups saw as a commitment to "universal values" Muslims saw as a war against their faith. They were nothing like the oppressed Eastern Europeans who had turned to Washington during the Cold War; they wanted liberation from the "apostate tyranny that the U.S. so determinedly promotes and defends."[88] They wanted freedom from *us*. Washington's task was to fashion the "war of ideas" so as to sustain policies that it had little intention of changing—a conundrum that inevitably led to contradictory tactical maneuvering and the usual charges of "misperception."

Washington was also far more blunt about what it means to handle the "processes of change." "Imagine a large map of the world," said the chairman of the National Intelligence Council. "Let's say we stick a pin in every country that had a low per capita income. And another for a high rate of infant mortality. Another for a sizable 'youth bulge' . . . And another pin to mark an absence of political freedoms and participatory government." What have you got at the end of this exercise? "A large number of vulnerable states—many in the Muslim world."[89]

As one task force commented, "the United States is not seeking to contain a threatening state/empire, but rather to convert a broad movement within Islamic civilization to accept the value structure of Western modernity—an agenda hidden within the official rubric of a 'War on Terrorism.'"[90] Democratization, in short, was a code word for support of "secular moderates linked to us—an admittedly scarce breed in the Arab world." According to a Council of Foreign Relations study, to "reduce the possibility that the Islamist movement will overwhelm more open Middle Eastern political systems, Washington should promote constitutional arrangements that would restrain the 'tyranny of the majority' to trample the rights of minorities." This was a shrewd reservation: in the name of those minorities, Washington could safeguard against any political system unfriendly to its reforms.[91] By and large, American human rights leaders have been sympathetic to this argument. "If you go from zero to a hundred in two seconds, you may well be worse off," noted Kenneth Roth of Human Rights Watch. "If you try to democratize all at once, without taking any of the preliminary steps needed to allow genuine civil society and the rule of law to emerge, then the mere holding of elections might well make you worse off and allow extremists into office."[92]

Though human rights groups rarely talk about class and social forces in the Islamic world, national security managers certainly do. Secular business people and middle-class professionals are the "strongholds of opposition to extremism . . . the first building blocks . . . that could be the basis of a democratic cadre and an indigenous force for nonviolent change."[93] Policies thus should focus on reaching, sustaining, and building local Muslim "networks" (the precursor to "civil society"), and promoting local NGOs in order to "extend our reach into the core of the societies and help us to find allies who share our passion for wider participation in society and the economy with special concern for the inclusion of youth and women."[94] "Radical Islamists" and "radical and dogmatic interpretations of Islam" may be few, but they hold the advantage largely because they have "developed extensive networks spanning the Muslim world and sometimes reaching beyond it, to Muslim communities in North America and Europe."[95] Moderates simply "do not have the resources to create these networks themselves; they may require an external catalyst." Washington thus looks to Muslims outside the Arab world, particularly in Indonesia, Turkey, and Europe, to promote a moderate, secular alternative. Their familiarity with Western societies, their exposure to liberal democratic values and the wealth of the West, and their success in maintaining their Muslim identity in a pluralistic society are all to be drawn upon. Once again "civil society" provides prophylaxis from "extremists," "radical" ways, and "violence."[96]

Washington, in short, sought "the development of a new class that could change the political and social balance in these countries" by fashioning an individualist ethos into a culturally seductive package. The focus was not on the nation or the civilization or the faith but, rather, on "personal control, choice, and change, personal mobility, meritocracy, individual rights (and particular women's rights)."[97]

Zeroing in on their likely constituents, Washington identified the "so-called secularists of the Muslim world: Business people, scientists, non-religious educators, politicians, public administrators, musicians, artists, poets, writers, journalists, actors, and their audiences and admirers"[98] as the most "moveable" targets. Among these the "priority targets" were liberal secular Muslim academics and intellectuals, who tended to gravitate to universities and research centers, as well as young moderate religious scholars uncomfortable in the mosque. Women's groups engaged in gender equality campaigns were another natural constituency. Finally, moderate journalists and writers needed help with broadcasting their work back into their own countries and, via the web, throughout the Islamic world. All these moderates had "political values congruent to the universal values underlying all modern liberal societies,"[99] but again empowering them as a class might "require an external catalyst."[100] As elsewhere, they needed money, organizing, ideas—and a pan-Islamic context to counter the radicals' advantage in organization, religious funding, and the centrality of the mosque in the local community."[101] They also needed "conceptual systems to guide and navigate" them toward American ways of thinking[102]—a far cry from the free flow of ideas Washington supposedly defended. Attention, not information, was key. In the words of a Defense Department task force, "What's around information is critical. Reputations count. Brands are important. Fifty years ago political struggles were about the ability to control and transmit scarce information. Today, political struggles are about the creation and destruction of credibility."[103]

Once again, local leaders could be quietly supported, invited to conferences, praised in the media, given awards and academic appointments, their reputations nourished. If they were abused, they could be spotlighted as human rights fighters; their plight movingly told, their families taken care of. In all these domains Washington appreciated the contributions of human rights—its workers, its honors, its support for NGOs fit with its own agenda well enough.

Washington launched a wide-ranging attack on radical Islamic credibility, seeking to create an "international database of partners (individuals, groups, organizations, institutions, parties) whose work is to be watched and coordinated."[104] To determine if a group was truly "moderate," a "reasonably complete picture of its worldview" was necessary.[105] Had it ever condoned violence? If it supported democracy, did it do so "in terms of individual rights?" Did it protect freedom of religion and uphold the right to change religions, the separation of church and state? "Does it support internationally recognized human rights?" Did it challenge Shari'a by advocating "non-shari'a options for those who prefer civil-law matters to be adjudicated under a secular legal system?" Did it support or receive any funding from "radical groups?"

At the same time, a frontal assault on radical Islam posed the risks that Washington might be seen as "anti-Islamic" even by some of its closest Middle Eastern allies. The approach to Shari'a is a case in point. As the European Court on Human Rights concluded in 2003, "Shari'a is incompatible with the fundamental principles of democracy"; it "clearly diverges from conventional values, particularly with regard to its criminal law and criminal procedures, its rules on the legal status of women and the way it intervenes in all spheres of private and public life in accordance with religious precepts."[106] But the Department of State preferred a more nuanced approach, quietly leaving to human rights workers less diplomatic attacks on Shari'a. Some human rights organizations called for encouraging feminists and a new generation of Islamic scholars to find alternatives within Shari'a, deepen their Islamic legal expertise, create stronger links with other women in the region, and rely less on criticism based on shaming, a highly counterproductive way of censuring religious conduct. But many more human rights professionals, having interviewed hundreds of individuals who had been flogged, accused of blasphemy, denied freedom of speech, punished for being gay, or condemned to stoning as adulterers, see little hope for protection of rights under Shari'a and a nonsecular state. As one Human Rights Watch commentary encapsulated the problem, "when religion is merged with the state, human rights suffer."[107]

Washington agrees, but prefers to speak just of women's rights, which provide the perfect wedge issue for challenging radical Islam and transforming Muslim societies. As Laura Bush herself said in a 2001 radio address, "The brutal oppression of women is a central goal of the terrorists. . . . Only the terrorists and the Taliban forbid education to women. Only the terrorists and the Taliban threaten to pull out women's fingernails for wearing nail polish. The plight of women and children in Afghanistan is a matter of deliberate human cruelty, carried out by those who seek to intimidate and control."[108] Human rights leaders heartily concurred.

But do arguments like this offer much perspective? Are there progressive voices in the Arab world other than the ones that so closely echo Washington and the leaders of the human rights community? Apparently there are, for recent polls suggest the opposite of what Western leaders like to think. They show little support for American and European interference in the internal affairs of Arab states; the respondents appear to want freedom and democracy without our support. Not surprisingly, "radicals" don't expect the United States to allow local populations to fashion their own political futures without direct American influence; more surprisingly, perhaps, a large number of "moderates" agree with them. Most notably, it is the politically radicalized Arabs who most strongly favor moving toward democracy, free speech, and elections; moderates tend to focus on education and gradual improvement.[109]

Polling further indicates that Middle Eastern conceptions of women's rights may be less clear-cut than human rights reports and Washington's public statements suggest. Arab women do not see Islam as inimical to their getting the vote or driving privileges, or to democracy or education. They see a place for Shari'a as a part (but not the whole) of the law. They see Islamic tradition as diverse and do not link it with genital mutilation. (The practice is almost unseen in Egypt.) "While expressing a positive perception of women's legal status in the West and asserting that this should be the case," very few women believe that "developing Western values will help their progress"; they also express unease with the "disrespect" men show women in the West, polls report.[110]

What Arab women say they least admire about their society is not all that different from what Arab men say—lack of unity, political and economic corruption, extremism, and dependence on outside power. They speak of human rights as part of a greater struggle against poverty, political repression, war, and the Western policies that reinforce them.[111] In an age of information flow and an increasingly literate Arab world sensitive to historic injustices, there is little possibility that the Middle East will be isolated or that alternative roles for women will remain undiscovered. Where human rights reports speak of inconsistency in Washington's policy, many Arabs see a long-term consistency; where they speak of hypocrisy, Arabs see a long-term strategy. The reports separate out problems rather than placing them in the broader social contexts that must be fundamentally changed in order to solve them. They promote the idea that Washington's primary aim is democratization rather than acknowledging that it pursues its own interests. While the polling results in the Middle East suggest that the two currents of human rights are very much interwoven in popular responses, human rights groups still go along with Washington as it turns them against each other in its ongoing "war of ideas."

AFGHANISTAN

If human rights organizations take no stand on war itself, the invasion of Afghanistan shows how they can nevertheless end up rationalizing one. They may refuse to consider the issue of aggression while tacitly supporting counterinsurgency strategies—in the name of international law, the laws of war, and NATO's "responsibilities."[112] In Afghanistan, they echoed Washington and NATO's rhetoric of "nation building" as though this aim truly underlay the policies. They constantly talk about the limits and dangers of state power, yet their response to the war in Afghanistan revealed their belief in the capacity—and the right—of foreign states to manage, guide, shape, and channel the most intricate affairs of other countries. The alternative, they argued, was the return of the Taliban and ever more "breeding grounds" for terrorists. Indeed, by 2002 Afghanistan had become "the primary focus of anti-terrorism efforts" for Human Rights Watch.[113]

Following the usual pattern, the optimistic appraisals soon gave way to dire warnings by national security professionals. The "security situation" was "deteriorating." Once again U.S. "credibility" was on the line; a "major defeat for the U.S. war on terrorism"[114] would "make it far more difficult to obtain international support in dealing with similar crises in the future," a 2003 Council on Foreign Relations study warned.[115] Human rights groups offered a parallel rhetoric: "The people of Afghanistan are teetering on the edge of the abyss again,"[116] but with "U.S. leadership and support," they could "still hope to live in peace and security," though the "window of opportunity is closing fast."[117] Once again a shortsighted Washington was betraying its true interests by taking the easy way—relying on local warlords and downplaying human rights concerns, thus slowing "the pace of progress."[118]

The task of the human rights community, argued Kenneth Roth, was to "convince the public that the situation is intolerable and ultimately, to mobilize public pressure on the Bush administration and its European allies to take the security steps that are needed to deliver on the promise of greater peace and security for the Afghan people." Human Rights Watch accepted Washington's claim that the United

States and NATO really were committed to creating "a new Afghanistan," that they would bring "a lawful, rights respecting government to
that troubled country." Since there could be "no reconstruction without
security" and "no security without reconstruction," they endorsed the
"integration of military and economic reconstruction efforts" that could
showcase the efficient way the "international community" dealt with
"post-conflict situations."[119]

The Pentagon's Defense Science Board copiously analyzed the lessons
of the "stabilization and reconstruction efforts" under way in Afghanistan (and Iraq) "to ensure stability, democracy, human rights, and a
productive economy."[120] Similarly, human rights leaders commended a
government that, even more than Ngo Dien Diem's in Vietnam, owed its
power to foreign allies. In another eerie parallel to the nation building
strategies that led to Vietnam's devastation, they embraced abstract
can-do social science models, speaking about "effective governance,"
"paving the way for reconstruction," "institution-building," promoting
"rights." They applauded their own detailed research as a "major contribution to public understanding of the situation on the ground"—as
though pointing to rights abuses offered any understanding of local
histories, cultures, or conflicts.[121]

Long ago, Afghanistan animated British colonial nightmares of falling dominoes. There is still a whiff of this fearfulness in human rights
ways of thinking. If the "community of nations" failed in Afghanistan,
all those "dedicated to the machinery of global order" would suffer a
defeat.[122] NATO, "whose own credibility is on the line," had to demonstrate that "Afghan warlords, while they have thousands of armed men
at their command, can hardly stand up to a serious western military
force, as amply demonstrated by the much-vaunted Taliban's rapid dissolution in the face of sustained force." For NATO, Human Rights
Watch warned, "failure would mean losing a raison d'être in a world
without a Soviet threat. . . . Failure in Afghanistan would be a signal of
the global community's impotence and insincerity in transforming
failed states."[123] With critics like these, the Defense Department hardly
needed advocates.

Some humanitarian groups were appalled by such attitudes. "Let's

keep the issue of competence in mind," a Doctors Without Borders official told an interviewer. "Humanitarian actors know how to provide aid,
but they are not diplomats or military strategists. We are not the best
suited to arbitrate among various political and military solutions."[124] But
he was in a minority. While the human rights abuses in Afghanistan
(brutal shortsighted counterinsurgency methods; civilian casualties
from air strikes; support for bloodthirsty warlords; revolting prison conditions and the torture of prisoners) were all well documented in reports,
nowhere did the issue of a foreign occupation appear front and center.
"There is no evidence suggesting that coalition or NATO forces have
intentionally directed attacks against civilians,"[125] Human Rights Watch
reported mildly—as though intentionality were the issue, as though the
problem were one of misjudgment and proportionality.

The reports tend to depict an Afghan population thankful for the
ousting of the Taliban and instinctively drawn to international human
rights groups and local NGOs, a people only asking for the United
States to live up to its promises with more assistance. They rarely cite
Afghans opposed to the American attacks, like RAWA, a progressive
women's group that insisted the Taliban should be overthrown by
Afghanis because there was "not one example in history where a foreign
force can bring freedom to another nation."[126] They do not quote Malalai Joya, a member of the Afghan parliament who argued that "as long
as these troops are in Afghanistan, the worse the war will be." Eight
years ago, she recounted, "the U.S. and its allies invaded Afghanistan
under the banner of women's rights," but now it's simply "hell in most
of the provinces. Killing a woman is as easy as killing a horse." The
occupying forces, she declared, must leave: "My people are caught now
between two powerful enemies, and they are being crushed. From the
sky, the bombs of the occupation forces are falling, killing civilians.
And on the ground, there is the Taliban, and also these warlords. So we
have three kinds of enemies. But the withdrawal of one enemy—these
U.S. occupation forces whose government sends them for war, and that
also supports the corrupt mafia system of Hamid Karzai with more
money and guys—will make it much easier to fight the enemies that are
left."[127] Such views are far removed from Amnesty's tepid complaint

that "the international community and the Afghan government have not met their pledge to provide the Afghan people, particularly women and girls, with better security, more responsive governance, and sustainable economic development."[128]

That U.S. backing may fuel support for fundamentalists and the warlords is hardly a view unknown to U.S. clandestine warriors. As one former CIA senior manager for covert operations in Afghanistan warned, "the Soviet Union tried to denigrate the Afghan mujahadeen by calling them bandits. This did not help the Russian cause. Americans are confronting a foe that is playing down and dirty—but remarkably effectively—on his own turf. Yes, there are criminals and foreign terrorists among them, but the Pentagon seems to understand little about the identity of its enemy beyond that." He added, "There were two stark lessons in the history of the 20th century: no nation that launched a war against another sovereign nation ever won. And every nationalist-based insurgency against a foreign occupation ultimately succeeded."[129]

Human rights leaders often appear baffled by suggestions that a foreign occupation is under way, that the regime in Kabul might be seen as foreign dominated, that resistance to foreigners has any public credibility except in fanatical fundamentalist minds, that some Afghans working with the "international community" are viewed as collaborators, and so on. They seem taken aback that a growing number of Afghans who detest the Taliban are so angered by the operations of NATO and the behavior of its troops that they are willing to take up arms against the quasi-occupation. Their reports continue to recycle much the same arguments: that insurgents disguised as civilians were carrying out "perfidious" attacks in violation of the law; that the "excessive deaths" attributed to the U.S. air campaign were not just the fault of Washington, that "the Taliban and al-Qaeda bore major responsibility for civilian harm during the air war" because in some cases they "used the civilian population to shield themselves from attack, a practice prohibited by international humanitarian law."[130]

The list of innocent civilians on whom attacks would constitute war crimes was long. No civilians who sided with the occupying power could be targeted. Afghanis who worked for foreign armed forces and government personnel (drivers, cooks, translators) were protected, as were Afghanis holding government posts or seeking to join the police or armed forces, workers in international NGOs, journalists, professionals, women, non-Afghan nationals—the entire civilian infrastructure of the occupation was off limits by law. (The contrast with the language the Reagan administration used to denounce Russian civilian advisors as part of an occupying force is worth noting.) Attacks on these groups fed the apocalyptic tone of the Bush administration's depiction of a Taliban fostering the "type of ideology and society the extremists want to impose on others throughout the world."[131] More and more, Afghanistan appeared as a "totalitarian nightmare," in George W. Bush's words— "a land where women were imprisoned in their homes, men were beaten for missing prayer meetings, girls could not go to school, and children were forbidden the smallest pleasures like flying kites."[132]

Under the Obama administration, human rights leaders continued to call for investigations into bombings of civilians, urged the promotion of women's rights, demanded that the United States break off ties with corrupt warlords, and reported on violence and fraud in elections. The Bush administration had articulated "many bold aspirations," Human Rights Watch wrote to President Obama in March 2009. "Scaling back" its ambitions for Afghan democracy now with an eye to more "achievable aims"[133] would be a terrible mistake. As usual the organization took "no position on the efficacy of an increase in US and NATO troops to fight the Taliban and other insurgents"—but then it took no stand against it, either.[134] Amnesty's views were much the same.[135]

Many of Washington's own analysts did not see the Taliban as anything approaching another Khmer Rouge. It is not that human rights leaders need to be geopoliticians—quite the opposite. But when they become proponents of an either/or range of options, they can end up propagating a kind of crackpot geopolitics, as the sociologist C. Wright Mills once called such simplifying thinking: either NATO-led forces pull off the reconstruction of the country or the Taliban in all its terror returns to power.

Comparing Washington's situation with the Soviets', a former CIA senior manager for clandestine operations in Afghanistan warned:

We paid a great price for demonizing the Taliban. We saw them as evil because they didn't let women work, but that's largely irrelevant in Afghanistan. They provided nationwide law and order for the first time in 25 years; we destroyed that and haven't replaced it. They're remembered in Afghanistan for their harsh, theocratic rule, but remembered more for the security they provided. In the end, we'll lose and leave.[136]

IRAQ

Unlike the war in Afghanistan, the one in Iraq led to a full-scale occupation—and a startling extension of human rights language and law into American counterinsurgency operations. In the West, the legality of the occupation proved far less controversial than the legality of the war had been. Human rights groups embraced the occupation as another step toward protecting the rights of civilians and noncombatants. While the UN did not at first sanction the occupation, in May 2003 the Security Council did so—insisting only that the belligerent force fully acknowledge its obligations as an occupying power.[137]

For human rights leaders, the occupation proved highly useful for elaborating upon the relationship between human rights and the laws of war—a process that implicitly legitimized the occupation itself, even if the "excesses" and violations of the occupiers came in for criticism. In the legal world of occupations, aggression and its outcomes are separated. As a classic 1940 work on international law lays out the situation: "The belligerent occupier even if he is the aggressor is entitled to exact from the civilian population the obedience due by it to the occupant under the rules of international law. It is not easy to understand how otherwise the population could expect to be treated in accordance with International Law. This is but one example of the necessity of maintaining the operation of rules of war regardless of the illegality of the war."[138] The legality of the war thus makes no difference: there are responsibilities the occupying power must assume—ensuring security and public order; the availability of food and adequate medical care; protecting the population "from violence by third parties, such as newly formed armed groups or forces of the former regime."[139]

In Iraq the law governing occupation has been a major human rights focus—but what does such a view of Iraq provide? "Duties" and "rights" say a great deal about the occupiers but little about the occupied. From a legal perspective, the violence in Iraq does not arise, fundamentally, from opposition to occupation but from the operational failures of the occupiers. Human rights leaders could have spoken bluntly of the laws *and* the injustice of occupation; they could have linked aggressive war *with* the perils of foreign domination and challenged the methods of the insurgents. To do so would have lent their copious reports a far more evenhanded moral tone. What emerges instead is an Iraq through the prism of law—a catalog of crimes, of procedures violated, of rules not properly adhered to. Once again, Washington is not "living up" to its obligations, is sacrificing its "credibility" with a "short-term" and "near-sighted strategy." Once again it is downplaying rights, making them "secondary to the dictates of military and counterinsurgency operations."[140]

The occupation's human rights failures have been extensively documented. There was the failure to "communicate effectively with the local population on security issues, and to deploy sufficient numbers of international police or constabulary (gendarme) forces, and of having relied on combat troops for policing duties without appropriate training."[141] There was the failure to set up enough courts and jails—the basics of a criminal justice system; "to protect invaluable historic cultural inheritances; to "call up the reserves" when military police might have been made available to patrol vigorously and end the "security vacuum."[142] Basic health services were allowed to deteriorate. The occupation authorities refused even to follow up on human rights reports on stockpiles of unsecured arms; Human Rights Watch "provided British and US forces with GPS coordinates in Baghdad and Basra," but to no avail. The United States thus failed to "neutralize the threat of such conventional weapons." In short, "security was not merely desirable," Human Rights Watch complained, "but reflected the legal obligation of the occupying power under international humanitarian law to restore and maintain order."[143]

Washington thus needed to do more, do better, and go further to protect the welfare of the local population. These reports betray the underlying conviction that following occupation law is what leads to successful occupations, that the law actually can and should offer a "road map." In this view it is not occupation of Iraq that has engendered human rights problems but the way the occupation has been carried out. Similarly, the failure to provide "stability" does not require rethinking of the fundamentals of occupation itself.

Benchmarks for withdrawal were notably absent in human rights reports, even after formal sovereignty was returned to Iraqi authorities on June 30, 2004. "Basic decency" suggested "that some duties are still owed the people of Iraq—and that a cut-and-run strategy would be wrong," Human Rights Watch argued. "Iraq's long-term welfare will depend on the US and British governments accepting that even de-occupying powers have certain long-term obligations to the people of the country they invaded. The stakes are too high to give those duties short shift."[144]

The "fight against terror" could succeed only if human rights laws were strictly adhered to, Human Rights Watch warned. Critical as its reports are of the counterinsurgency programs, the tactics were blamed, not the principle. As one Human Rights Watch leader testified to a congressional committee, "Listen to General David Petraeus, who recently told his troops in Iraq: 'This fight depends on securing the population, which must understand that we—not our enemies—occupy the moral high ground.' "[145]

The human rights reports acknowledge the polls showing that American troops were viewed not as liberators or peacekeepers but as a bitterly unwelcome occupying force. They include comments reflecting a growing popular anger toward the occupiers for excessive use of force on demonstrators, the killing of civilians, and the exemption of U.S. soldiers from trial in Iraqi courts. Such opposition reflects a "patriotic response to foreign dominance," Amnesty reported in 2005. The "gross violations of international human rights and humanitarian law" have "incensed" the Iraqi population. "We prefer to live under the terror of one of our own," Amnesty quotes a woman who had opposed Saddam Hussein, "than under the humiliation of foreign occupation."[146]

But in occupation law none of this *fundamentally* matters.[147] None of it challenges the legality of the occupation per se. Human rights leaders could have developed markers that defined the occupation as illegal when the occupiers violated too many of the agreed-upon norms and obligations. Lessons learned from the history of colonial domination might have been helpful in this regard. But there was no willingness to raise such questions; the human rights community would not tread where Washington had not already placed a green light. It would not put itself on a collision course with Washington by casting the United States as an unjust occupying authority.

Instead, it repeatedly urged the United States to "take all feasible precautions to minimize civilian causalities in the current air and ground offensive." In writing to Secretary of Defense Rumsfeld, Human Rights Watch brought up "possible wrongful or unlawful use of force by US soldiers in Iraq" and a pattern of "alleged illegal deaths that merit investigation."[148] Much was "alleged," very little stated as fact. The refusal of the U.S. military to keep statistics on civilian casualties suggested to Human Rights Watch that these were "not a paramount concern"[149]—an odd note given that the organization itself does "not attempt to quantify civilian deaths in Iraq."[150] Washington, of course, was quite prepared to argue endlessly over a host of issues—the ways U.S. troops fought in Falluja, whether they used "automatic weapons fire in an indiscriminate and excessive manner," proportionality, the bombing of residential areas, how to wage human rights–based counterinsurgency warfare. It much preferred these arguments to challenges to the basic legality of the occupation itself.

Human rights groups also provided meticulous reports on Abu Ghraib and other outrages. They described the climate that led to the abuses, the policies behind them, and their connection to other policies, such as rendition. But criminal as such acts were, and despite the possibility that American forces had used "excessive and indiscriminate force, tortured detainees and helped thousands of Iraqis without due process," Human Rights Watch argued that such behavior "does not justify attacks by insurgent groups that have deliberately targeted and killed civilians."[151] It did not matter whether these attacks could be interpreted as a war to drive out foreign occupiers ("the ends do not justify these means"), or whether they represented the response of the weak to a military superpower, or whether the U.S. occupation itself was illegal: "None of these justifications are defensible under international law." Civilians who side with or work for an occupying power cannot be targeted; to do so is "a cruel and unjustifiable breach of the most basic principles of humanity."[152]

As in Afghanistan, human rights groups insisted on holding to this line. Suicide attacks may well have been mainly directed at Iraqi police stations, the individuals within considered traitors or collaborators for working with the "foreign occupiers," but despite their security role these individuals were "civilian security forces" and thus "unlawful targets." Organizations and individuals funded or paid by the United States—women's rights groups, journalists, U.S. government aid workers—were likewise protected. Amnesty was aware of the powerful Iraqi opposition to the occupation; its reports quote the claims of insurgent leaders that U.S. withdrawal would end the resistance. Its reports underlined the diverse attitudes of different groups—Al-Qaeda's supporters carried out brutal beheadings and bombings while other insurgents condemned such brutal acts yet still insisted on the right to use violence to fight the occupiers. But just as Amnesty took no position on the war, it took no position on the "legitimacy of armed resistance against foreign or Iraqi troops."[153] Yet the two are hardly equivalent. As James Baldwin wrote:

> It is true that two wrongs don't make a right, as we love to point out to the people we have wronged. But one wrong doesn't make a right, either. People who have been wronged will attempt to right the wrong; they would not be people if they didn't. They can rarely afford to be scrupulous about the means they will use. They will use such means as come to hand. Neither, in the main, will they distinguish one oppressor from another, nor see through to the root principle of their oppression.[154]

If Amnesty's position—not to mention that of Human Rights Watch— had been that the occupation was criminal and foreign domination wrong, while violent resistance against it using the weapons of the weak was also criminal, it would have showed the occupation of Iraq in quite different light. It would have begun to embrace the abiding concerns of both of the currents, often conflicting, from which rights emerged in the first place. Alas, the human rights reports offer a very different perspective. In the politics of human rights that surround the occupation, there is simply no pervading sense of justice in the demands that the Americans leave. Violence is understood to be fueled by the excesses of the occupation, not by the fact of the occupation itself.

One of the outcomes of Nuremberg was the idea that war is "an evil thing" and aggressive war "the supreme international crime differing only from other war crimes in that it contains within itself the accumulated evil of the whole." Aggressive war is supreme because the "lesser crimes"—crimes against "laws and customs of war," against what we now speak of as "humanitarian laws"—follow from it. As one Nuremberg prosecutor observed: "Modern war, no matter how chivalrous, involves so much misery that to punish deviations from the conventions without punishing the instigators of an aggressive war seems like a mocking exercise in gentlemanly futility."[155]

THE ISRAELI OCCUPATION

Human Rights Watch's 2002 report "Erased in a Moment," which chronicles Israel's suffering from suicide bombers, counts the bombings "among the worst crimes that can be committed."[156] Their systematic nature "sets them apart from other abuses committed in times of conflict," since their target "is everyday life." They are "particularly terrifying in the sense that there is no possible shelter."[157] They are, in other words, obviously immoral and illegal—crimes against humanity. And their "great resonance with Palestinian public opinion"[158] is all the more reason to denounce the "martyrdom syndrome"; the pathologies that support these criminal acts must be rooted out. The Palestinian Authority may not be directly responsible for them, but it becomes morally accountable when it fails to denounce them and the culture of martyrdom that sustains them; the officials who praise such attacks as "the highest form of national struggle" are complicit in the crimes.[159] So the argument goes.

Human rights organizations give short shrift to the rationales offered for suicide bombings—that as part of a war for liberation from Israel's continuing occupation they are exempt from international humanitarian law; that attacking Israeli settlers is not targeting civilians; that as the attacks are carried out in retaliation for Israeli violations of humanitarian law they are a form of self-defense. The organizations counter that Israeli settlers retain their civilian status (as do reserve and off-duty soldiers). That they may be armed is irrelevant, according to Amnesty; so is the circumstance that Palestinians accused of attacks against the settlers "in some cases are assassinated by the forces," while settlers "who have assaulted Palestinians and destroyed their property are almost never prosecuted."[160]

"We don't have F-16s, Apache helicopters, and missiles," Palestinians further argue. "They are attacking us with weapons against which we can't defend ourselves. And now we have a weapon they can't defend themselves against. . . . We believe this weapon creates a kind of balance." While this issue comes up again and again in violent conflicts, to make exceptions, in the words of Amnesty, "would virtually swallow the rules of international humanitarian law, since most wars are between forces of unequal means. The prohibition against intentional attacks against civilians is absolute."[161]

Human rights reports tend to offer the clear-cut criminality of the suicide bombers on the one side and a parsed, legalistic sorting out of Israeli actions on the other. The label "terrorist" is applied by Human Rights Watch only to Palestinian acts. (Neither Amnesty nor Human Rights Watch has ever accused Israel of state terrorism.) "Indiscriminate attacks," that is, those that would be "expected to cause incidental loss of civilian life, injury to civilians, damage to civilian objects, or a combination thereof, which would be excessive in relation to the concrete and direct military advantage anticipated,"[162] are outlawed. In contrast to Nuremberg, however, the illegalities of occupation are set aside. Israeli excesses merely underline the need for Israeli governmental investigation and analysis. Were the civilians adjacent to the military installations hit by accident? Was everything feasible done to verify that the targets were not civilians or civilian objects? Did the attack seek to spare the population as far as possible?

It is difficult (though not impossible) to find compelling depictions of individual Palestinian pain in these reports. On the whole, accounts of Palestinian suffering tend to be on the dry side: houses demolished, deaths of individuals unable to get to a hospital, the wall, the road-blocks, Israeli checkpoints. Why the difference in tone? Because suicide bombing is morally worse than illegal occupation? The reports don't explicitly say so, but their tone implies it.

Human rights groups understandably do not wish to become involved in comparing atrocities. But whatever balance they strive for is completely lacking in the American media, Congress, White House statements, and a plethora of semiofficial groups whose near-apoplectic response to the Palestinian suicide bombers could not be further from their measured reaction to the systematic abuse of Palestinians by Israelis. The Palestinian suicide bombers "are so blinded by their narcissistic rage that they have lost sight of the basic truth that civilization is built on: the sacredness of every human life," Thomas Friedman writes in a typical *New York Times* op-ed column. This "madness," born "not out of desperation" against the occupation but out of "strategic choice" and a "feeling of empowerment," is a terrifying new weapon of the weak—and must be defeated or the power of the Western world itself will be at risk.[163]

Elsewhere, Israel's forty-year-long occupation casts a very different shadow. The suicide bombings evoke anger—anger at the bombings themselves but also at the conditions that have provoked them. Witness the 2008 report of the Special UN Rapporteur on the Situation in Palestine and the Other Occupied Arab Territories: the suicide attacks "must be condemned and have been condemned," but they must also be understood as the "painful but inevitable consequences of colonialism, apartheid, or occupation." History, it said, is "replete with examples of military occupation that have been resisted by violence—acts of terror," citing resistance by European countries to the Nazi occupation and by the South West Africa People's Organization (SWAPO) to South Africa's occupation of Namibia. "Acts of terror against military occupation must be seen in historical context." Indeed, the occupation is what distinguishes the case of Palestine from other human rights situations. Not only are specific Israeli actions often illegal; the occupation itself is arguably "unlawful as a result of the numerous violations of international law that have occurred during it."[164]

No such remarks are to be found in human rights reports, and their absence highlights the divide between the two currents of rights in striking form. Human rights groups prefer to speak of occupation law and of violations under that law, writing as though it were a codified, clear, and accepted body of statutes. It is not. The challenge to the "moral narrative of our time" is stark. If human rights organizations encouraged the development of an awareness that decried the military occupation of Palestine as intensely as the deeds of suicide bombers, they might offer a more compelling understanding of one of the world's most challenging injustices. Such an approach would shift the focus from attacks on innocent civilians to the lethal chaos that occupation can bring to innocents.[165] It could offer insight into the staggering obstacles that Palestinian efforts at nonviolent mobilization have met from Israeli repression over the decades—efforts that recede into the background of human rights reports.[166] None of this diminishes the horror on either side. As Robert Fisk writes:

> What did that eyeless, dead Israeli child ever do to the Palestinians? Could not the Palestinian bomber, in his last moments on earth, recognize this child as his daughter, his baby sister, his youngest cousin? Alas, no. He was too far down the road to his own death, too buried in his own people's tragedy. His was not an act of "mindless terror," the words Israeli spokesmen use as they try to deceive both the world and their own people. He was the logical product of a people who have been crushed, dispossessed, cheated, tortured, and killed in terrible numbers. The pressure cooker of the West Bank was his sauna. And he passed through the door.[167]

In assessing its coverage of the occupation in 2006, the BBC noted its "failure to convey adequately the disparity in the Israeli and Palestinian experience, reflecting the fact that one side is in control and the other lives under occupation."[168] The Israeli government rejects all such formulations, of course; "disputed territories," not "occupation," is its term. Israeli leaders set forth various legal and political arguments, often backed by Washington. ("We simply do not support the description of the territories occupied by Israel in the 1967 War as occupied Palestinian territory," Madeleine Albright stated in March 1994).[169] The Israeli government is highly attuned to the implications of "occupation"; accepting the term would make Israel a foreign occupier, delegitimizing its claim to the land and legitimizing Palestinian resistance. It speaks instead of its security needs, necessitated by terror—a stance largely unquestioned in official Washington. Supporters of Israel's policies now increasingly argue that the dispute is not about land or occupation at all, but rather about the growing radicalism of the Muslim world and its refusal to countenance a Jewish state in its midst. The more than 450,000 settlers on the West Bank and the constantly increasing number of settlements, the confiscation of land, the roadblocks and border closings, the preference given to Israeli products over locally owned ones within the occupied areas—these are all diversions from the real conflict, they say, and those who focus on them are engaging not only in anti-Israel propaganda but also in a kind of anti-Semitism.

Human rights groups strongly disagree with such views. They insist that it is indeed an occupation and demand that Israel abide by the laws governing occupations. The building of the wall, the illegal settlements, the treatment of Palestinians are the subject of numerous detailed reports.[170] According to Amnesty, Israeli abuses include

> unlawful killings; torture and ill-treatment; arbitrary detention; unfair trials; collective punishments such as punitive closures of areas and destruction of homes; extensive and wanton destruction of property; deportations; and discriminatory treatment as compared to Israeli settlers. Most of these violations are grave breaches of the Fourth Geneva Convention and are therefore war crimes. Many have also been committed in a widespread and systematic manner, and in pursuit of government

policy; such violations meet the definitions of crimes against humanity under international law.[171]

But Amnesty and Human Rights Watch stop short of questioning the legality of the occupation itself. Not so Jimmy Carter, who has called the occupation "one of the greatest human rights crimes on earth."[172] Words matter, as the furious response to the title of Carter's *Palestine: Peace Not Apartheid* demonstrates. "Apartheid" carries emotional, moral, and legal implications. Like slavery and colonialism, it is an inherently unjust, exploitative *system* and as such may compel its victims to rebel against tyranny. The expropriation of Palestinian land and the economic incentives the Israeli government provides the settlers are fundamental issues that plausibly deprive Israel of the legitimacy of an occupying authority and put the occupation in violation of human rights. "The pre-eminent obstacle to peace," Carter wrote, "is Israel's colonization of Palestine."[173] Colonization serves the interests of the occupiers at the expense of the interests of the occupied, thus breaching the foundation of the occupying power's legitimacy.

Just as Amnesty in the 1980s never explicitly condemned the system of apartheid per se,[174] only the injustices within it, so today it criticizes the illegal acts of Israel but not the legality of the occupation itself. Still, the difference here between Human Rights Watch and Amnesty is notable. Human Rights Watch refers to illegal settlements and occupation. Amnesty goes further, referring to a *military* occupation and to the settlements as a "colonization project"[175]—an inhumane policy under which Palestinians are classified as "aliens" and the destruction of Palestinian homes "is inextricably linked with Israeli policy to control and colonize areas of the West bank." This policy has "been conceived, stimulated, and implemented by the Government of Israel; colonization has not been a spontaneous popular movement taking place in the face of governmental resistance or indifference."[176] The construction of the "colonies" has depended "not just on finding land that is physically suitable, but on alienating it from the Palestinians, defending it against Palestinian use, and ensuring through such process as registration and leasing that Palestinians are disqualified from having any future benefit from that land."[177]

Yet despite such words, Amnesty pulls back from labeling the occupation itself illegal. Perhaps in the end the reasons are not all that surprising, for colonization, governing colonies, and treating a resident population as aliens tap directly into the right of resistance and the second current of human rights. The 1960 UN General Assembly Declaration on the Granting of Independence to Colonial Countries and Peoples holds that resistance "to forcible denial of self-determination" is legitimate and entails a right to receive support from outside actors. The General Assembly has specifically supported the Palestinian struggle under this declaration, recognizing "the legitimacy of the struggle of peoples against colonial and alien domination or foreign occupation."[178] Human rights groups, however, tend to find anathema views that link aggression to occupations, foreign domination to loss of independence— and the claimed right of various kinds of resistance to achieve self-determination, including armed struggle. But then what does protecting the rights of noncombatants really mean in an occupied land? When does proportionality in the methods used to ensure "order" give way to outright oppression? These may be hard issues to sort out, but they are not terribly different from the ones that Western peace movements confronted in the twentieth century during the struggles for decolonialization and independence.

Most recently, the UN's 2009 Goldstone Report on the Gaza conflict reiterated the Palestinian right to self-determination and the duty of all states "to promote its realization."[179] The report used proportionality as a tool to dissect the military policies of Israel and the Palestinian response. Israel's violations included "intentional attacks against civilians, the failure to protect Palestinians from violence by Israeli settlers and private individuals, policies of arbitrary detention," and more. Hamas, too, was deemed guilty of war crimes for directing some eight thousand rockets and mortars against southern Israel since 2001; but the report found no evidence either that it had used human shields or that it had hidden its forces in civilian areas as it responded to Israeli military operations. But then the report went beyond issues of proportionality to challenge the very nature of Israel's occupation of Gaza and the West Bank. Israel had "violated specific obligations it has as an Occupying Power"; Palestinians in Gaza have been deprived of "their means of sustenance, employment, housing and water," as well as "their freedom of movement and their right to leave and enter their own country."[180] The policy of blockade that preceded the military operations against Gaza amounted to "collective punishment intentionally inflicted by the Government of Israel" and was thus a crime against humanity.[181] Such accusations point to the occupation's eventually being classified as aggression—a line that human rights groups once again prefer not to cross.

Even the World Court has raised the issue of occupation as aggression, if only indirectly. In 1977 it found that South Africa's continued infringement of the rights and well-being of the inhabitants of Namibia was a conquest in disguise and thus justified the General Assembly's termination of the mandate—a decision that made South Africa an illegal occupier. The refusal of an occupying power to transfer control might thus constitute a form of aggression.[182]

In the final analysis, both Human Rights Watch and Amnesty remain focused on the laws of war and the protection of the innocent and of noncombatants. But this concentration avoids the all too obvious. Occupation can be regarded as an issue of law (with acts of resistance using the weapons of the weak categorized as war crimes). Or occupation can be regarded as an issue of foreign domination (and of aggression, crimes against peace, and self-determination). Or it can be regarded as an issue of both simultaneously, becoming in the process a paradigmatic instance of the contradictions between the two currents of rights, with a case to be made that the present-day fixation on the first current has lost sight of the injustices highlighted by the second.

THE WEAPONS OF THE WEAK

In the age of terrorism, human rights groups often speak as though they had resolved the key issues raised by crimes committed during uprisings against grave injustices. The state can fight back, of course, and proportionality is their analytic tool of choice to evaluate its actions. But how to assess the insurgents? As the twenty-first century began, they had come up with few satisfactory answers, and for good reason. Human rights reports offer little advice about either how to fight against brutal regimes or how to deal with "democratic regimes" under which decades of protest have led to few or no improvements for tens of millions of people.

The Maoists in Nepal and the Naxalites in India exemplify these tenacious issues. In Nepal, human rights reports denounced both the repressive Nepalese government and a violent Maoist insurgency movement. The Maoists had "murdered numerous local officials and alleged opponents to their causes, and engaged in widespread torture, intimidation, and extortion of people living in areas under their control,"[183] charged a typical Asia Watch report from 2005. When the Maoists agreed to participate in national elections, and then won, with the Maoist leader becoming prime minister, Asia Watch demanded "a comprehensive National Accountability Plan of Action" to try insurgent leaders (as well as former government ones). But how much understanding could such a plan actually offer? The issue is complex, involving as it does questions beyond whether such accountability promotes or hinders "national reconciliation." How to assess radical upheavals that coerce some of the poor into joining, even as others join willingly in violent mass struggles against those who have long oppressed them? Human rights reports paint a picture of innocent civilians "caught in a deadly tug-of-war between an armed Maoist movement on one side, and government security forces on the other."[184] True enough up to a point, and if human rights were simply about protecting "noncombatants" or formal procedural rights amid extremes of wealth and power, judgment would be easier. But there are equally compelling injustices to be considered when the poor starve or lack work or medicine or education—and are driven to violence when other means fail.

The Indian writer and activist Arundhati Roy confronted these issues in a 2007 interview dealing with the Naxalitie Maoist insurgency in India,[185] a group the U.S. State Department classifies as terrorists[186] and whose abuses have been lengthily documented by human rights organizations.[187] "I have no doubt," she wrote, "that the Maoists can be agents of terror and coercion too. I have no doubt they have committed unspeakable atrocities. I have no doubt that they cannot lay claim to undisputed support from local people—but who can? Still, no guerrilla army can survive without local support . . . and the support for Maoists is growing, not diminishing." But what is the proper response when "non-violent movements have knocked on the door of every democratic institution in this country for decades, and have been spurned and humiliated?" When people take up arms, she warned, there is "going to be all kinds of violence—revolutionary, lumpen, and outright criminal." Moral and legal accountability is not the same for the government and the insurgents: "The government is responsible for the monstrous situations it creates." And there is a systemic issue now manifest in the existence of a growing middle class reared on a diet of "radical consumerism and aggressive greed." We are witnessing "the most successful secessionist struggle ever waged in independent India—the secession of the middle and upper classes from the rest of the country. It's a vertical secession, not a lateral one. They're fighting for the right to merge with the world's elite somewhere out there in the stratosphere."[188] Washington's strategic communications specialists might blanch at Roy's tone, but aspects of her analysis are really not all that different from theirs.

Roy's view, it can be objected, is sociologically suspect and radical. Yet human rights reports are hardly sociologically or politically neutral either. They blur together violence and resistance of assorted kinds, leaving the impression of an unholy orgy of mayhem and the death of innocents. Some rights advocates do acknowledge the grievances that inflame the Naxalites—but the first current remains sacrosanct. In disagreeing with this outlook, Roy reiterates the limits of the present vision of human rights. "How can the rebels be the flip side of the State? Would anybody say that those who fought against apartheid—however brutal their methods—were the flip side of the State? How about those who fought the French in Algeria? Or those who fought the Nazis? Or those who fought colonial regimes? Or those who are fighting the US occupation of Iraq? Are they the flip side of the State?" Human rights leaders essentially respond, "Yes," at least as to the methods of the insurgents. The issue is much the same with terrorism—the killing of innocents and noncombatants. But doesn't this perspective, Roy asks, lead to a "condemnation game" that "makes politicians of us all and leaches the real politics out of everything"? Where those in need are "exhausted by these interminable 'democratic processes' only to be eventually humiliated, what are they supposed to do?" There are few answers in the human rights tool kit—just calls for more democratization, more human rights, more rule of law, more of everything that has long been encoded in the language of Washington and other powers as they proceed to label criminal so many of the methods insurgent groups have chosen throughout history.

"During the Algerian war," Sartre wrote, "I always refused to make a parallel between the terrorist use of bombs, the only weapon available to the Algerians, and the actions and extortions of a rich army of half a million, which occupied the entire country. It is the same in Vietnam."[189] Sartre is widely condemned in human rights writings today, especially for his defense of violence in his preface to Franz Fanon's *The Wretched of the Earth*. But that preface is by no means a glorification of violence. Sartre had few illusions about the terrible costs incurred when the dispossessed fight back; his challenge to the current human rights vision is to ask whether simply invoking laws against such varied kinds of resistance provides either understanding or justice. U.S. human rights organizations, however, have long since labeled the weapons of the weak criminal and acts of terror and left it at that—a stance heartily approved in Washington.

TORTURE

Even as American human rights organizations endorsed the struggle against terrorism, they vehemently denounced Washington's new policies on torture as "an affront to fundamental values of the human rights movement."[190] The problem was not "the aberrant misconduct of a few low level interrogators," Human Rights Watch concluded; the "use of torture and other mistreatment was a matter of policy dictated at the top" of the U.S. government.[191] After two decades of laying stress on the United States' rights-based traditions, it now found the United States to have "the only government in the world to claim openly as a matter of policy the power to use cruel, inhuman, or degrading punishment," not to mention running a veritable "gulag of off-shore detention centers."[192] Guantánamo, Amnesty echoed, was the "gulag of our time."[193] If Washington's policies and circumlocutions on torture stood, if accountability failed, if the "ultimate human corruption" was publicly practiced by the United States, Amnesty warned, then "we are witnessing the orchestrated destruction by the United States of the very basis, the fragile scaffolding, upon which international human rights have been built, painstakingly, bit by bit, since the end of World War."[194] The whole idea of "promoting democracy and human rights is so associated with the United States," Human Rights Watch concluded, that its "fall from grace has emboldened authoritarian governments to challenge the idea as never before. As the United States loses its moral leadership, the vacuum is filled by forces profoundly hostile to the cause of human rights."[195]

Along with torture went rendition, the spiriting of suspects into judicial black holes around the globe. "Under the [George W. Bush] administration's theory," charged Human Rights Watch, "it can, on its own say-so, without any judicial review, seize anyone anyplace in the world and hold him until the end of the 'global war against terrorism,' which may never come."[196] The organization's Washington advocacy director testified to the U.S. Senate Committee on Foreign Relations in July 2007:

> Imagine if the intelligence service of the United Kingdom suspected a lawful U.S. resident of sending money to the IRA in Northern Ireland, or the secret police in China or Burma accused an American of supporting rebels in their country, and on that basis, kidnapped that American off the streets of Washington or Indianapolis, bundled him on a plane, and held him for years in a secret facility, hidden even from the International Committee for the Red Cross.[197]

Human Rights Watch was appalled by what it called Washington's hypocrisy. On the one hand, Secretary of Defense Donald Rumsfeld was approving a raft of harsh new interrogation techniques that fit most definitions of torture[198]—"The use of stress positions (like standing) for a maximum of four hours"; isolation of up to thirty days; placing a hood on detainees "during transportation and questioning"; "Deprivation of light and auditory stimuli"; "Removal of all comfort items (including religious items)"; "Forced grooming (shaving of facial hair, etc.)"; "Removal of clothing"; "Using detainees' individual phobias (such as fear of dogs) to induce stress."[199] On the other hand, the Department of State in its annual human rights reports was denouncing other governments for employing many of the very same practices:

> Burma (forced squatting or other uncomfortable positions for long periods of time), Egypt (stripping and blindfolding of prisoners), Eritrea (tying of hands and feet for extended periods), Iran (sleep deprivation and suspension for long periods in contorted positions), Jordan (sleep deprivation and solitary confinement), Pakistan (prolonged isolation and denial of food or sleep), Saudi Arabia (sleep deprivation), Tunisia (food and sleep deprivation), and Turkey (prolonged standing, isolation).[200]

Yet while Human Rights Watch at times brands the leaders of other nations war criminals, it maintained an eerie silence about President Bush; "command responsibility" for American abuses apparently stopped with his subordinates. "Secretary Rumsfeld should be investigated for war crimes and torture by US troops in Afghanistan, Iraq, and Guantanamo," the organization declared, charging him with having created the conditions for the commitment of "war crimes and torture by sidelining and disparaging the Geneva Accords" and for the concealment of detainees from the ICRC. Similar charges, it argued, should be brought against CIA Director George Tenet and several generals, including Ricardo Sanchez and Geoffrey Miller.[201] It also supported efforts to have the German courts assume jurisdiction for prosecuting these alleged crimes,[202] since the United States itself was "not pursuing accountability for those most responsible."[203]

"We wrote a letter to President Bush," said the special counsel for

Human Rights Watch in a 2005 interview: "You are now on notice that the U.S. government is sending people to be tortured. You now have a legal responsibility to do something about it, or you could be prosecuted for torture. And nothing was done. The program continued."[204] Yet the president himself was never charged as a war criminal; there was never the kind of detailed investigation into his responsibility that human rights groups had undertaken in regards to various other leaders.[205] Why this timidity toward the man who called himself the "decider"?[206]

And beyond that—why torture? Why Guantánamo? Why the tearing asunder of the Geneva Accords? All this is wrong, American human rights leaders argued: criminal, foolish—and ineffective. It makes a mockery of the "human rights weapon" in the fight against terrorism and destroys Washington's credibility at its core. "How did this happen?" demanded the former dean of Yale Law School, now legal advisor to the Obama administration's Department of State. "How did the world get turned so totally upside down? How did we move from a policy of zero tolerance toward torture to a policy of zero accountability?"[207] Within the U.S. human rights narrative, few explanations are offered.

But Amnesty International's response has been different. Unlike Human Rights Watch, after 9/11 it challenged the basic leitmotif of the American human rights movement. "The common refrain about 'un-American' conduct or conduct inconsistent with 'American values,'" the organization argued in a 2006 analysis, "ignores why the US is no more immune than other powers from torture and human rights abuses."[208] And further: "Many people may consider that the USA's conduct over the past five years is the response of a unique administration to a unique event. It is not that simple. This administration's policies did not spring from nowhere."[209] Torture, in other words, is hardly un-American.

The policies and attitudes at United States–run secret prisons, Abu Ghraib, and Guantánamo, Amnesty argued, were not recent innovations. In country after country, it was typically the United States that had taught the local police and military the techniques of suppressing insurgencies and challenges to pro-American elites. Amnesty cited its earlier reports on the large numbers of detainees interrogated in South Vietnamese detention centers where there had been evidence of "extensive use of torture and murder of suspects."[210] It reviewed the anti-subversion training courses held in Panama for the Latin American military personnel who went on to torture in the 1980s; decades of CIA manuals advocating "torture, extortion, kidnapping, and execution"; the presence of American personnel at torture sessions in various Latin American countries whose methods prefigured the ones later utilized in Abu Ghraib and Guantánamo.[211] American human rights organizations have detailed many of these abuses as well, but unlike Amnesty, they have usually avoided putting the pieces together in a coherent historical narrative. That pattern has a lengthy history. As long ago as the Spanish American War, Senator George Frisbie Hoar complained that critics of the U.S. government "are counting up to the American people their mistakes in the past. They say: 'You have treated the Indians badly; you have treated the negroes badly. You made a great blunder and mistake in annexing Hawaii.'" The best way forward was to avoid all such comment: "take the case by itself, say nothing about the past and make a vigorous opposition."[212]

Amnesty did not stop with foreign policy; it underlined *systemic* aspects of American institutions conducive to Bush's War on Terror. A contempt for the other had been evolving for some time in the treatment of American prisoners. Why, Amnesty asked, had the United States become such a strikingly punitive nation, with a prison population that had quadrupled in size since 1980? The UN Committee Against Torture had criticized the use of remote-controlled electro-shock stun belts, restraint chairs, and "excessively harsh" conditions in super-maximum security prisons. In the "War on Terror such excessive use of restraints became routine;[213] indeed, Camp Five at Guantánamo Bay appeared to be "modeled on the super-max prisons on the US mainland. Detainees are held in solitary confinement for up to 24 hours a day in concrete cells and are under 24-hour video surveillance."[214] Nor was it coincidental that corrections officials from such institutions were among those accused of torture at Abu Ghraib.[215]

Amnesty described an escalating use of surveillance and punishment throughout American society during the 1990s. "The USA is engaged in a cruel, brutalizing, unreliable, unnecessary and hugely expensive activity for no measurable gain," the organization warned in denouncing the death penalty, itself a symptom of the nation's pervasive "culture of violence."[216] Bill Clinton, a moderate Democrat, had supported the death penalty as governor of Arkansas; under the harsh antidrug and antiterrorist laws of his presidency, legal rights of representation were eviscerated.[217] In October 1998 Amnesty launched its Rights for All Americans campaign to protest "deliberate and wanton police brutality"[218] and the ill treatment of the vulnerable—people of color, the mentally ill, gays, the homeless, the poor. Amnesty's reports found that the reformist impulse of the 1930s and the 1960s had given way to an atmosphere of uneasiness and fear, a precursor of the post-9/11 division between "them and us."[219]

All this is suggestive of a different tone and style of analysis than is to be found in Human Rights Watch's more legalistic reports.[220] Amnesty often zeros in on the way torture feeds on "discrimination and fear," drawing on an image of the frightening "other" in American life. Torture is "not a crime only against a body, it's also a crime against the imagination," one report quotes the UN Committee Against Torture. They go on to cite the writer Ariel Dorfman: "Torture presupposes, it requires, it craves the abrogation of our capacity to imagine someone else's suffering. . . . It demands this of the torturer, placing the victim outside and beyond any form of compassion or empathy, but also demands of everyone else the same distancing, the same numbness."[221] Such a chilling lack of empathy, Amnesty warned, was spreading in large ways and small:

> Souvenir T-shirts, available for soldiers to purchase in the Navy Exchange shopping mall in Guantánamo perpetuate a view of "war on terror" detainees as less than human. One depicts a rat in a turban, orange jumpsuit and shackles, with the words Guantanamo Bay: Taliban Lodge around it. Another depicts six shackled rats in orange jumpsuits, surrounded by the caption Al Qaeda six-pack—Guantanamo Bay, Cuba, Home of the sand rat.[222]

And what, Amnesty asks are we to make of a media milieu in the United States that countenances a former U.S. marine, working as a military analyst for Fox News, describing how he tortured a Viet Cong prisoner "by attaching electrodes to his genitals and threatening electrocution." "Worked like a charm," he said, suggesting that similar torture be used on Al-Qaeda suspects.[223]

European governments, for all their public complaints, were complicit in U.S. actions as well, Amnesty charged. They took no action "despite overwhelming evidence of complicity" in renditions, in sending suspects to countries known to torture, in abductions of their own citizens and secret detentions. They did not speak out in the "face of blatant illegality."[224] Washington was hardly alone in refusing to investigate itself.

Amnesty's assessments ultimately had little effect. The torture debate in the American press and the American human rights community was both intensely real and a red herring—real because Washington's policies represented a frontal assault on everything rights activists had fought for from the beginning; yet a red herring because the practices that had been exposed were merely a small part of a vast national security machine that had been rebuilt since Vietnam. Though the Abu Ghraib revelations might have caused the U.S. government some embarrassment, they did not keep it from proclaiming its commitment to aiding the victims of torture throughout the world with its Victims of Torture Fund (VTF) in 2005. The supporting documents envisioned "a world free of torture where survivors, their families, and communities receive the support they need to quell their suffering and rekindle their connection to everyday life." Working with NGOs, the VTF would provide "direct services to torture-directed survivors, their families and communities; train individuals to treat and help restore the functioning of those affected by torture, and increase the level of knowledge and understanding about the effectiveness of treatment and rehabilitation methods." The American government, President Bush stated, would see to the torture victim's protection, counseling, and, where necessary and possible, relocation in the United States: "We stand with the victims to seek their healing and recovery, and urge all nations to join us in these

efforts to restore the dignity of every person affected by torture."[225] No
further comment seems necessary.

THE FUTURE OF HUMAN RIGHTS

Law has always had an intricate and sometimes a contentious relationship with the power of the state; it is both an embodiment of and a constraint on that power. But, while central to democratic life, the rule of
law is neither the source of a nation's moral character nor the inspiration for its struggles for social justice. Rather, it often reflects the outcome of those struggles. The legalizing of human rights language thus
risks coming at a cost, finding itself swept into the machinations of
states and detached all too quickly from the popular struggles and
moral commitments needed to continually nourish justice. That cost is
nowhere more evident than in the institution of the International
Criminal Court, itself the culmination of a long drive to create new
norms of international behavior,[226] but whose goal has already been
tarnished by the very accusation human rights groups have long leveled
against Washington—hypocrisy.

The human rights movement has raised a mountain of legislation to
prevent crimes against humanity, but it is almost always the weak leaders, not the strong, who face charges. Thousands of dossiers have been
produced describing in meticulous detail the death squads and torture
and extrajudicial executions carried out by brutal regimes and pathological dictators around the world. When people with black or yellow or
brown skin, with Islamic or Communist or nationalist credentials murder their prisoners or bomb their villagers, they are condemned—often
quite selectively, to be sure—by the "civilized" world. And they *should*
be condemned. But the American leaders who ordered the free fire
zones in Vietnam and the Phoenix program, or directed the Contras
against the Sandinistas, or were complicit in Saddam Hussein's gas
warfare against the Kurds (and then the Iranians),[227] or set up and
operated Guantánamo are not taken to court. They face no trials. On
any human rights website you will find a growing number of prominent

leaders indicted for war crimes and crimes against humanity. Few are American or Western European or Israeli.

Human rights will have little future as a process of justice unless the leaders of democratic societies are also charged with crimes. Guantánamo and the torture scandals led to calls by human rights groups for charges to be leveled against Donald Rumsfeld, George Tenet, and others, but not against George W. Bush. The Obama administration has shown little enthusiasm for following up.[228] No courts have acted against high-level Americans. Measures that, had they been undertaken by a weaker country, would almost certainly have been judged criminal, have been greeted with criticism but little else.

Torture, Abu Ghraib, and Guantánamo constituted what Reed Brody of Human Rights Watch has called a "moment of truth in the human rights movement."[229] The results are not promising. If nothing is done once the crimes are exposed, if the leaders are left untouched, then "in generations to come," Brody has warned, "anytime human rights defenders call for the redress of abuses, Abu Ghraib is going to be cited as a justification, pretext or excuse."[230] Human rights will be weakened if Washington's criminal activity remains unchallenged, whether or not it ends up in the courts. Human rights can only be strengthened by a clear moral voice that demands of Americans what it finds easy to demand of others.

Human rights groups argue that they cannot address all crimes, that their resources are limited. They do what they can; justice is selective. Yet when justice is consistently inconsistent rather than merely inadequate, other issues arise. Justice that unceasingly fails to confront the powerful is not only selective, it has become a weapon of the powerful. Immunity for the prominent is a deeply corrupt basis for an international criminal court, and it points to one of the major challenges confronting the human rights movement.

Human rights organizations repeatedly opt for legalistic language that has marked the treaties, conventions, and covenants that states have negotiated among themselves for several decades. Current international rights norms consist of "complex and constraining rules targeted at the heart of domestic legal systems" and lay out detailed requirements in judicial language.[231] But while much that is admirable—and more that simply sounds so—has come from the effort to codify rights and some semblance of law internationally, the parsings of lawyers, the blending of academic and legal styles of argumentation present their own problems. The often noted bifurcation of uplifting covenants and legal progress on the one hand and gruesome atrocity stories on the other are not unconnected; they are part of the dynamic that impels the ongoing legalizing of rights. But this is a very limited and parched approach—and a bleak one.

Strikingly absent from the evolving legal system are the concerns of the peace movement: aggression, war, and occupation. In the wars in Afghanistan and Iraq the firm refusal of most human rights leaders to take a stand on these issues was painfully evident: "First, on most military matters, we are neutral, because we see our principal job as monitoring the way a war is fought, and to do that effectively you can't be seen as for or against a war. Human Rights Watch would have been much less effective in trying to shape the Pentagon's approach in Iraq if we were viewed as confirmed opponents of the war."[232]

This is a long way from Nuremberg. It is a long way from understanding Senator Fulbright's warning that aggressive and preemptive wars would "surely destroy freedom, because one simply cannot engage in barbarous action without becoming a barbarian, because one cannot defend human values by calculated and unprovoked violence without doing mortal damage to the values one is trying to defend."[233] And it is a long way from questioning how a "rights-based nation" can democratically commit aggression—and who is responsible when it does. Congress approved the war in Iraq and continues to fund it. That makes it legal under American law. But it does not make it legal under international law. It does not make it less aggressive for being democratically determined. And it doesn't make it just.

These issues have sometimes been masked by rationalizations based on "humanitarian interventionism."[234] But Iraq was not such a case; nor was Vietnam—the two bookends to the chapters written in the United States on human rights so far. The notion of human rights as a regulation and legalization of occupation, counterinsurgency, and war is of course anathema to the ideals of the peace movement, but it has hampered the human rights movement as well. Leaders spoke of democratization but never quite found the wherewithal to call for national referendums by Iraqis and Afghanis on the American presence. They were unable to envision ways that insurgents, dissidents, and radicals could fight back that were not violations of the laws of war. They lived in a world where cluster bombs could be outlawed but not nuclear weapons. They raised alarms but never called for pulling back American power, instead viewing "rights-based" American involvement not as a problem but, in fact, as a possible solution.

That human rights groups sought to regulate and limit violence without fundamentally challenging it, that rights became a way of rationalizing occupation, counterinsurgency, and the reconstruction of failed states says a great deal about the blind alley down which the human rights movement has gone. It has engendered a plethora of regulations and laws, but states still shape those regulations to their own ends—always in the name of the innocent, of the noncombatant. There is perhaps too much innocence here and too little combativeness. This is not just a matter of hypocrisy, or of pragmatism, but of a flawed compromise with the power of a small number of great states and the realpolitik that human rights organizations were founded to challenge.

Today in the United States human rights leaders lament the depredations of the Bush years and the egregious failures of the Obama administration to deal with the nation's dwindling credibility and its loss of moral vision, even as they applaud its rhetoric of democratization. They prefer to see a credibility gap that can be bridged, the temporary consequence of a lawless administration that a new president can repudiate. But excesses repudiated, then ignored, then forgotten are lessons not learned. Repudiation is excellent. Forgetting is not.

Yet credibility gaps and hypocrisy are issues of modest import when set amid the much larger, indeed epochal changes now under way. More than a half millennium of Western centrality is now convulsively coming to an end, and although this seismic shift has barely registered in either Obama's Washington or the human rights community, other, powerful nations and people are rising, bringing with them varied traditions, priorities, and pressing concerns that will be compatible with certain kinds of rights—and not with others.

In this new era, the two currents of rights will inevitably be buffeted and challenged; demands for equality and alternative ways to organize societies will raise tumultuous and wide-ranging challenges to the established orders. Human rights groups would do well to stand apart from all states, drawing out of diverse traditions whatever can illuminate rights and address the painful conflicts among different kinds of rights in a world of inequality and injustice. All too often, though, the traditions of protest, of mobilization, of contradictory demands for rights outside the West are hardly acknowledged by human rights leaders. Ignoring the rights of the second current will not help defend those of the first much longer.

As human rights leaders cast a forlorn look at the world of recent years, the Churchillian adage that democracy is a bad system but everything else is worse comes to mind. After all the torture, the wars, the constantly updated methods of counterinsurgency, the endlessly parsed proportionality of death, after Vietnam and Iraq and so many interventions, subventions, and varied forms of overt and covert action—after all these moral failures, it seems that still, in their eyes, only America can lead the world (with a little help, perhaps, from Europe). Russia and China "must be convinced that the route to influence and respect is not through callousness and thuggery, but through responsible global citizenship,"[235] Human Rights Watch has stated. It's clear who is to do the convincing—who is the responsible citizen, and who the thugs. American human rights organizations have never quite been able to stand *against* American preeminence. They have never really tried to, because they believe American power is more trustworthy and that it can be restrained by appeals to its better instincts and controlled by law. Then it can once again do more, lead others, assume the responsibility to protect, become ever more deeply involved—more, further, *better*.

This is an updated formulation of the pious old hope that enormous state power can be controlled through invocations to its better nature. But states, as John Adams reminded us, don't have great souls; they don't have better natures. The state is a cruel monster, Charles De Gaulle warned—a rule that admits of no exceptionalism. Defending Washington's rights-based—and self-interested—strategies, rather than welcoming a greater diversity of power among nations and peoples who in multiple, often contradictory ways will oppose some rights and favor others, will be no great boon for human rights. As we move toward the decline of an America-centered world, remaining open to a far more diverse world of contending rights largely buried and ignored at the origin of American globalism is not a hope to be lightly dismissed.

NOTES

The following abbreviations are used in the notes.

APP   The American Presidency Project database at the University of
          California, Santa Barbara
CIA/FOIA Official side for CIA materials under the Freedom of Information
          Act
DDRS   Declassified Documents Reference System database (Gale)
DNSA   Digital National Security Archive database
DOS   Department of State
FRUS   U.S. Department of State, *Foreign Relations of the United States*
          (Washington, D.C.: Government Printing Office)
HRW   Human Rights Watch
HRWWS   Human Rights Watch website
NED   National Endowment for Democracy
NIE   National Intelligence Estimate
NSC   National Security Council
PSB   Psychological Strategy Board
USIA   United States Information Agency
WNC   World News Connection database

Throughout quoted documents spelling is kept as it appears in the original; explanatory interpolations are provided only if essential to clarify meaning. Government documents almost always capitalize the word "communist" or "communism," and this is done in the text as well. However, "President" is almost always capitalized in United States Congressional and government documents, but not in the text. Documents cited from a database often use its description of the entry so as to provide easier access, though minor corrections in punctuation and capitalization are sometimes done to improve readability.

INTRODUCTION

1. Bertrand de Jouvenel, *On Power: The Nature and History of Its Growth* (Boston: Beacon Press, 1948), 238.
2. William F. Schulz, *In Our Own Best Interest: How Defending Human Rights Benefits Us All* (Boston: Beacon Press, 2001).
3. Aryeh Neier, "With Friends Like This," *International Herald Tribune*, June 24, 2005.
4. Harold D. Lasswell, *Propaganda Technique in the World War* (New York: Peter Smith, 1927), 222.
5. B. Rajagopal, *International Law from Below: Development, Social Movements and Third World Resistance* (Cambridge: Cambridge University Press, 2003), 187.
6. Upendra Baxi, *The Future of Human Rights* (New York: Oxford University Press, 2002).

CHAPTER 1: WASHINGTON'S WORLD BEFORE THE RISE OF HUMAN RIGHTS

1. Such descriptions abound in the literature about the Cold War as well as the popular media. For representative examples, see David J. Rothkopf, *Running the World: An Inside Story of the National Security Council and the Architects of American Power* (New York: PublicAffairs, 2006); Peter W. Rodman, *Presidential Command: Power, Leadership, and the Making of Foreign Policy from Richard Nixon to George W. Bush* (New York: Knopf, 2009); Walter Isaacson, *The Wise Men: Six Friends and the World They Made* (New York: Simon & Schuster, 1986); and Henry A. Kissinger, *Diplomacy* (New York: Simon & Schuster, 1994). For the classic self-portrait of the wise men, see Dean Acheson, *Present at the Creation: My Years in the State Department* (New York: Norton, 1969).
2. Rothkopf, *Running the World*.
3. Edward Gibbon, *Decline and Fall of the Roman Empire*, vol. 1 (New York: Modern Library, 1962), 1.
4. George Kennan, discussions with author, 1987–1988.
5. Harry Truman, "Remarks at a Meeting of an Orientation Course Conducted by the CIA," November 21, 1952, APP.

6. Dulles papers, Box 90, Princeton University.

7. Robert Divine, *Second Chance: The Triumph of Internationalism in America in World War II* (New York: Atheneum, 1967).

8. The phrase is from Sir Robert Seeley, *The Expansion of England: Two Courses of Lectures* (London: Macmillan, 1891), 8.

9. Harry Truman, *Year of Decisions*, vol. 1 (New York: Doubleday, 1955), 97.

10. Quoted by Michael Sherry, *In the Shadow of War: The United States Since the 1930s* (New Haven: Yale University Press, 1995), 131.

11. Solarium B, "Report on a Proposed Policy to Draw an Imaginary Line Around the Present Limits of the Soviet Bloc," July 16, 1953, 86–87, DDRS.

12. W. R. Kintner, CIA, "Examination of Value, Content and Means for U.S. to Wage Effective Ideological Warfare Against World-wide Communist Apparatus," June 4, 1952, DDRS (hereafter "Ideological Warfare").

13. George F. Kennan, *Measures Short of War: The George F. Kennan Lectures at the National War College, 1946–47* (Washington, D.C.: National Defense University Press, 1991), 302.

14. "A firm, well-developed ideology," "an over-all strategic concept," a "global psychological strategy," a "fighting faith," a "grand strategy," a "counter-ideology," a "persuasive totality of policy," a "global way of thinking," "a vigorous effective ideological program at home and abroad to vanquish communism"—such phrases permeate national security documents throughout the Cold War, and in updated variants ever since.

15. Kintner, CIA, "Ideological Warfare," June 4, 1952, DDRS.

16. PSB, "Preliminary Estimate of Effectiveness of U.S. Psychological Warfare Strategy," May 7, 1952, DDRS.

17. U.S. Department of State, "Suggestions for Improving the Position of the U.S. in the Face of the Communist Challenge," n.d. (Eisenhower years), 20.

18. George Kennan, *Measures Short of War*, 302.

19. George Kennan, Report by the Policy Planning Staff, "Review of Current Trends in U. S. Foreign Policy," February 24, 1948, FRUS, vol. 1, part II, 525.

20. Gandhi to Roosevelt, July 1, 1942, http://www.gandhimanibhavan.org/gandhicomesalive/comesalive_letter26.htm.

21. This according to Charles Allen; further materials on the Lodge Project to use human rights as an instrument of propaganda warfare against the Soviets are found in Rowland M. Brucken, "A Most Uncertain Crusade," (Ph.D. diss., Ohio State University, 1999), 379. Also see "Exploitation of Soviet, Satellite, and Chinese Communist Psychological Vulnerabilities Before and During the 8th UN General Assembly," May 28, 1953, and PSB, "'Human Rights' Project: Suggested Topics for Intelligence Development," May 19, 1953, DDRS.

22. See Dulles, "United States Policy Regarding Draft International Covenants on Human Rights," February 19, 1953, FRUS, 1952–1954, vol. 3, 1555.

23. Senator J. William Fulbright, discussions and interview with author, 1988.

24. NSC 68, 1950, http://www.mtholyoke.edu/acad/intrel/nsc-68/nsc68-1.htm.

25. Edmond Taylor, Assistant Director, Office for Plans and Policies, "Philosophy of Psychological Strategy" (lecture given at the National War College, February 12, 1952), DDRS.

26. For an extended discussion of visionary globalism see James Peck, *Washington's China* (Amherst: University of Massachusetts Press, 2006).

27. H. W. Brands, *The Devil We Knew: Americans and the Cold War* (New York: Oxford University Press, 1982), 33.

28. John Lewis Gaddis, *Strategies of Containment: A Critical Appraisal of Postwar American National Security Policy* (New York: Oxford University Press, 1982), 107.

29. Walt Rostow, Basic National Security Policy, S/P Draft, March 26, 1962, 176, DDRS.

30. NSC 7, DDRS.

31. Kintner, CIA, "Ideological Warfare," June 4, 1952, DDRS.

32. James Forrestal, *The Forrestal Diaries*, ed. Walter Millis and E. S. Duffield (New York: Viking Press, 1951), 128.

33. NSC 17, George C. Marshall, Secretary of Defense, to James S. Lay Jr.; Att. to Encl, June 28, 1948. J. Patrick Coyne report. NSC report, 11, DDRS.

34. Clark Clifford, "Union of Soviet Socialist Republics and Information Statement," May 15, 1946, 34, DDRS.

35. C. D. Jackson Papers, Princeton University, Minutes of Princeton meeting, May 10, 1952, 14.

36. Henry Kissinger, *White House Years* (Boston: Little, Brown, 1979), 129.

37. NSC 17, George A. Morgan sends PSB director copy of his paper "Philosophy of the World Struggle," April 10, 1952, 3, DDRS.

38. NSC 17, George C. Marshall, Secretary of Defense, to James S. Lay Jr.; Att. to Encl: Same subject Souers, Executive Secretary to the National Security Council, June 28, 1948. Encl: J. Patrick Coyne report, DDRS.

39. The Senate Committee on Foreign Relations, *Hearings on Psychological Aspects of Foreign Policy*, June 5, 19, and 20, 1969, 37.

40. Senator J. William Fulbright, discussions with author.

41. Edward P. Lilly, *Development of American Psychological Operations 1945–1950*, December 19, 1951, 8, DDRS.

42. C. D. Jackson, Jackson to Maryland State Teachers Association, October 31, 1947, C. D. Jackson papers, Box 102, file 2. Cited by John Allen Stern,

"Propaganda in the Employ of Democracy, Fighting the Cold War with Words" (Ph.D. diss., SUNY Stony Brook, 2002), 5.

43. Dr. Barghoorn, Schedule of priorities for psychological warfare outlined, October 22, 1951, DDRS.

44. William Benton, *Department of State Bulletin*, April 18, 1948, 518.

45. PSB Director Raymond Allen (lecture given at the Psychological Warfare Seminar, August 15, 1952), 14, DDRS.

46. Department of State, NSC 20/1, *The Position of the United States with Respect to Providing Military Assistance, A Report to the NSC*, August 18, 1948.

47. Zbigniew Brzezinski, *Power and Principle: Memoirs of the National Security Advisor, 1977–1981* (New York: Farrar, Straus and Giroux, 1983), 43.

48. George Kennan, *Measures Short of War*, 280–281.

49. Ibid., 237.

50. Harry S. Truman, *Off the Record: The Private Papers of Harry S. Truman*, ed. Robert H. Ferrell (New York: Harper & Row, 1980), 44–45.

51. Clark M. Clifford, Special Counsel to the President, *American Relations with the Soviet Union, Report to the President*, September 24, 1946, DDRS.

52. NSC 7, "The Position of the United States with Respect to Soviet-Directed Communism," March 30, 1948.

53. PSB, "Evaluation of the Psychological Impact of United States Foreign Economic Policies and Programs in France," February 9, 1953, DDRS.

54. John Foster Dulles in George Ball Papers, Princeton University, Box 153.

55. Dean Acheson, Oral interview, Truman archives database, Truman Presidential Library.

56. NSC 5412, "National Security Council Directive on Covert Operations" [10/12/51] March 15, 1954, http://www.ratical.org/ratville/JFK/USO/appC.html.

57. NSC 68, http://www.mtholyoke.edu/acad/intrel/coldwar.htm.

58. Department of State, "Analysis of U.S. Foreign Policy Based on Intelligence Estimates with Regard to U.S. 'Cold War' Efforts, Including Covert Operations Abroad," no. 3143, DDRS.

59. PSB, "Evaluation of the Psychological Impact of U.S. Foreign Economic Policies and Programs in France," February 9, 1953, 30–40, DDRS.

60. Solarium A, 106, DDRS.

61. Department of State, Memo on principal points made by Secretary of State John Foster Dulles in regard to Communist penetration throughout the world and proposals for a course of action to be taken by the Free World, May 8, 1953, 1, DDRS.

62. Department of State, "The Concept of Europe," May 8, 1951, DDRS.

63. CIA Report to the Psychological Strategy Board, January–June 1953, 3, http://www.foia.cia.gov/browse_docs.asp.

64. Charles Beard, *The Idea of National Interest: An Analytic Study in American Foreign Policy* (New York: Macmillan, 1934), 131.

65. Lilly, *Development of American Psychological Operations 1945–1951*, December 19, 1951, 3, DDRS.

66. Ibid.

67. NSC 68.

68. Max Weber, *Economy and Society* (Berkeley: University of California Press, 1978).

69. The Soviets simply "appropriate, degrade, and bastardize the words which are the hard-earned and world-accepted currency of free men." William Benton, *Department of State Bulletin* 18, April 18, 1948, 518.

70. As Daniel Rodgers concludes in his *Contested Truths: Keywords in American Politics Since Independence* (Cambridge, Mass.: Harvard University Press, 1998), this "rhetoric of freedom" was always "big and vague," drawing its "primary power not from its specificity but its all-pervasiveness" and "its ability to bind together the confusions and discordances of American life with a single, powerfully flexible noun" that stood as the opposite of twentieth-century totalitarianism, 215–16.

71. Zbigniew Brzezinski, "U.S. Foreign Policy, The Search for Focus," *Foreign Affairs* (July 1973): 708.

72. Quoted by Richard J. Barnet, *Roots of War: The Men and Institutions Behind U.S. Foreign Policy* (Baltimore: Penguin Books, 1972), 141.

73. Ibid.

74. Robert Griffith, "The Selling of America: The Advertising Council and American Politics," *Business History Review* 57 (Autumn 1983): 388–412.

75. Ibid., 390.

76. Phrase is common in the 1920s to capture the homogenizing, advertising, mass production of consumer goods and the emerging mass media. See James Truslow Adams, *Our Business Civilization; Some Aspects of American Culture* (New York: Albert and Charles Boni, 1929).

77. Quoted in Justin W. Q. Hart, "Empire of Ideas: Mass Communications and Transformation of U.S. Foreign Relations, 1936–1952" (Ph.D. diss., Rutgers, 2003), 82, 135, 137, 155–164.

78. Archibald MacLeish, Information Service Committee, Entry 401–403, Box 94, RG 353, National Archives (College Park, Md.). Also cited in Justin W. Q. Hart, "Empire of Ideas."

79. Daniel Boorstin, *The Image: A Guide to Pseudo-Events in America* (New York: Vintage Books, 1992), 241.

80. Numerous factors led to such an intensely ideological vision of freedom: the Americanization programs, a virtual cutoff of immigration after World War I, and workplace changes that weakened American's local, regional, and ethnic enclaves; the spread of mass culture and consumerism; the growing fear of Nazism and Communism; and labor leaders who sought to invoke freedom to justify their efforts to join the "consensus." But none of these factors proved sufficient to challenge the emerging anti-Communist ethos of freedom.

81. Gunnar Myrdal, *An American Dilemma: The Negro Problem and Modern Democracy* (New York: Harper & Row, 1962), 9.

82. James Truslow Adams, *The Epic of America* (Boston: Little, Brown, 1931).

83. In early 1952, the State Department sent out some 150 questionnaires to overseas American posts, requesting recipients to evaluate the impact of "key words in American and Free World Propaganda." No single term emerged as particularly helpful, though "communist imperialism" and "slavery" were favorites with American diplomats. "Independence," "national culture," and "sovereignty" were also popular. "Western civilization," on the other hand, was not considered highly effective; nor was "capitalism," "democratic unity," or "world friendship." Non-Americans tended, rather unattractively, to link "individualism" and "capitalism" in a way that made it difficult for Washington to espouse them as the ideological answer to "communism" and calls for radical change. See Edward W. Barrett, *Truth Is Our Weapon* (New York: Funk & Wagnalls, 1953), 146–148. Also "Key Words in American and Free World Propaganda," RG 306, National Archives (College Park, Md.), 133.

84. Barrett, *Truth Is Our Weapon*, 263.

85. As John Foster Dulles put it, "Laborers in the ideological struggle have long recognized that the Free World suffered from one handicap: the lack of a dynamic appeal that would fire men's imaginations with a zeal and fervor approaching that of Communists. I have never found any simple formula. Freedom is not a first rank goal for fanatics in such movements. Those seeking to escape themselves usually want equality and fraternity far more than liberty." John Foster Dulles, "Freedom and Its Purposes," Speech, National Council of Churches, Denver, Colorado, Dulles papers, Box 62, Princeton University.

86. Department of Defense, "Study on Ideological Strategy," June 9, 1954, DDRS.

87. George C. Marshall, Department of State, "China Round Table," October 6, 1949, 32, DDRS.

88. George Kennan, Department of State, "China Round Table" October 6, 1949, 32, DDRS.

89. Department of Defense, "Study on Ideological Strategy," June 9, 1954, DDRS.

90. William Barrett, *Truth Is Our Weapon* (New York: Funk & Wagnalls, 1953), 139.

91. Solarium A, 108, DDRS.

92. Psychological Strategy Board, "Evaluation of the Psychological Impact of U.S. Foreign Economic Policies and Programs in France," February 9, 1953, 34, DDRS.

93. Department of Defense, "Study on Ideological Strategy," June 9, 1954, 4, DDRS.

94. Ibid.

95. Ibid.

96. Robert J. McMahon, *The Cold War on the Periphery: The United States, India, and Pakistan* (New York: Columbia University Press, 1994), 41.

97. William Barrett quoted in Michael L. Krenn, *Fall-Out Shelters for the Human Spirit: American Art and the Cold War* (Chapel Hill: University of North Carolina Press, 2005), 88.

98. DOS, "Report on the Image of the U.S. in Other Countries and the Development of a Thoughtful Foreign Relations Program," Eisenhower administration, n.d., DDRS.

99. Ibid.

100. Department of Defense, "Study on Ideological Strategy," June 9, 1954, DDRS.

101. Ibid.

102. Ibid.

103. George Allen, "Report on the Image of the U.S. in Other Countries."

104. Ambassador Kenneth Young, *Diplomacy and Power in Washington-Peking Dealings: 1953–1967* (Chicago: University of Chicago Press, 1967), 28.

105. How modernization came to permeate the development of modern Chinese studies in the United States is analyzed in James Peck, "The Roots of Rhetoric," in *America's Asia* (New York: Pantheon, 1971) and "Revolution Versus Modernization and Revisionism," in *China's Uninterrupted Revolution: From 1940 to the Present*, ed. Victor Nee and James Peck (New York: Pantheon, 1975).

106. Arthur Schlesinger Jr., *A Thousand Days: John F. Kennedy in the White House* (Boston: Houghton Mifflin, 1965), 542.

107. W. W. Rostow to Robert Cutler, August 16, 1954, XVIII, no. 2, March–April 1992, DDRS.

108. Lyndon B. Johnson, "Briefing by the Vice President to the House Committee on Foreign Affairs," March 1, 1961, 4, DDRS.

109. Walt Rostow, Policy NSC Memo, March 1962, 21, DDRS.

110. Ibid.

111. Ibid., 85.

112. Walt Rostow, quoted by Gerald M. Meier and Dudley Seers, eds., *The Pioneers in Development* (New York: Oxford University Press, 1984), 240.

113. Department of State, *Report of Long-Range Study on Communist China's Military and Political Factors Prepared by a Special State-Defense Study Group,* June 1, 1966, V-33, V-35, DDRS.

114. U.S. Information Agency, "USIA procedures to carry out Operation Coordinating Board plan for a 'U.S. Doctrinal Program,'" n.d. (Truman administration), DDRS.

115. Department of State, "Report on a Six-Month Trip around the World to Study U.S. Propaganda Overseas," June 17, 1955, 5, DDRS.

116. Ibid.

117. Ibid.

118. Kintner, CIA, "Ideological Warfare," June 4, 1952, 12, DDRS.

119. Solarium A, NSC Report, July 16, 1953, DDRS.

120. Department of State, "Some Thoughts About American Propaganda," n.d., 7, DDRS.

121. "People's Capitalism," *New York Times*, February 15, 1956, 30; "Eisenhower Visits Capitalism Show," *New York Times*, February 14, 1956; and "U.S. Exhibit Ready to Vie with Reds," *New York Times*, August 19, 1956, 32.

122. "The Indian Image of the United States, A Preliminary View: Part II: The American Way of Life," RG 306, National Archives.

123. Carl Kaysen, *Report of the President's Task Force on Foreign Economic Policy,* November 25, 1964, A-27, DDRS.

124. Arthur Schlesinger Jr., *Report to the President on Latin American Mission,* February 12–March 3, 1961, White House, April 29, 1961, DDRS.

125. "Conclusions and Recommendations of the President's Committee on Information Activities Abroad," chapter 1, December 1960, DDRS.

126. Department of State, "Memo on the Situation in Underdeveloped Countries Where Communist-Inspired Guerrilla Warfare Exists," November 20, 1961, 20, DDRS.

127. Walt Rostow, "Redraft of Cross's Draft Paper on Communist Guerrilla Type Violence," August 15, 1961, 2, DDRS.

128. George F. Kennan, *Measures Short of War,* 106–107.

129. Seymour Hersh, *The Price of Power: Kissinger in the Nixon White House* (New York: Summit Books, 1983), 265.

130. Audrey R. Kahin and George Kahin quoting Ambassador Cumming in

Subversion as Foreign Policy: The Secret Eisenhower and Dulles Debacles in Indonesia (New York: New Press, 1995), 75.

131. Ibid., 10.
132. President's Committee on Information Activities Abroad, "Conclusions and Recommendations," White House, December 1, 1960, 2, DDRS.
133. USIA, "United States Doctrinal Program," January 15, 1954, 15, DDRS.
134. Department of State, "The Concept of Neutralism, Neutralism in Asia and Africa Detailed," n.d. (Eisenhower administration).
135. Robert McMahon, *The Cold War on the Periphery: The United States, India, and Pakistan* (New York: Columbia University Press, 1994), 224.
136. Arthur Schlesinger Jr., quoting the Colombian historian German Arciniegas, in his *Report to the President on Latin American Mission,* February 12–March 3, 1961, White House, April 29, 1961, DDRS.
137. Mao Zedong, *On Diplomacy* (Beijing: Foreign Languages Press, 1998), 173.
138. Frederick Douglass, *My Bondage and My Freedom* (New York: Miller, Orton, 1857), 281.
139. William Edward Hartpole Lecky, *History of European Morals from Augustus to Charlemagne* (New York: George Braziller, 1955), 338.
140. J. M. Coetzee, *Waiting for the Barbarians* (New York: Penguin, 1982), 133.
141. *A Study of USIA Operating Assumptions*, vol. 3, December 1954, Box 7, TC19-20, RG 306, Office of Research, Special Reports.
142. Department of State, "Suggestions for Improving the Position of the United States in the Face of the Communist Challenge," n.d. (Eisenhower administration), 1, DDRS.

CHAPTER 2: THE CARTER YEARS: AMERICAN FOREIGN POLICY FINDS A SOUL

1. Jimmy Carter, Universal Declaration of Human Rights Remarks at a White House Meeting Commemorating the 30th Anniversary of the Declaration's Signing, Dec. 6, 1978, American Presidency Project (hereafter APP), http://www.presidency.ucsb.edu/index_docs.php.
2. Jimmy Carter, Inaugural address, January 20, 1977, APP. John Quincy Adams and John F. Kennedy each mentioned the term once in their inaugural addresses.
3. Billy Graham to President Carter, April 9, 1977, April 1, 1977—April 30, 1977 folder, Box HU-1, WHFC, Jimmy Carter Library, as quoted in Edward Bailey Hodgman, "Détente and the Dissidents: Human Rights in U.S.–Soviet Relations, 1968–1980" (Ph.D. diss., University of Rochester, 2003), 270.

4. Jimmy Carter, Interview with a group of news directors, July 15, 1977, APP.

5. Jimmy Carter, Presidential News Conference, March 24, 1977, APP, and Commencement address, Notre Dame University, May 22, 1977, APP.

6. Anthony Lake to the Secretary of State (Vance), "The Human Rights Policy: An Interim Assessment," January 20, 1978, 11, 5, DDRS.

7. Henry Kissinger, "Continuity and Change in American Foreign Policy, *Society* 15, no. 1 (November–December 1977): 97–103.

8. Quoted in Joshua Muravchik, *The Uncertain Crusade: Jimmy Carter and the Dilemmas of Human Rights Policies* (New York: Hamilton Press, 1986), 3.

9. Jimmy Carter, *Don Richardson Conversations with Carter* (Boulder, Colo.: Lynne Rienner Publishers, 1998), 252–253.

10. CIA, "World Trends and Contingencies Affecting US Interests," June 6, 1968, 1, http://www.foia.cia.gov/browse_docs.asp (hereafter FOIA).

11. Memorandum from Robert Osgood to NSC, "An Overview of the World Situation," May 21, 1969, DDRS.

12. Zbigniew Brzezinski, *NSC Weekly Report* no. 37, November 18, 1977, DDRS.

13. See Zbigniew Brzezinski, *Between Two Ages: America's Role in the Technetronic Era* (New York: Viking Press, 1971), for an early statement of this view and *Out of Control: Global Turmoil on the Eve of the Twenty-First Century* (New York: Scribner's, 1993), 92, for his later summing up of America as the center of such a globalizing process.

14. Anne E. Geyer and Robert Y. Shapiro, "A Report: Human Rights," *Public Opinion Quarterly* 52, no. 3 (Autumn 1988).

15. Daniel Patrick Moynihan, "The Politics of Human Rights," *Commentary* 64 (August 1977): 22.

16. J. William Fulbright, *The Arrogance of Power* (New York: Random House, 1967).

17. Interview with J. William Fulbright. Also see J. William Fulbright, *The Price of Empire* (New York: Pantheon, 1989), 87, 148, and J. William Fulbright, "The War and Its Effects: The Military-Industrial-Academic Complex," in Herbert Schiller, *Super-State: Readings in the Military Industrial Complex* (Urbana: University of Illinois Press, 1970).

18. J. William Fulbright, *The Price of Empire*, 137.

19. Ibid., 13.

20. Martin Luther King Jr., *Where Do We Go from Here: Chaos or Community?* (Boston: Beacon Press, 1968), 186.

21. Martin Luther King Jr., quoted by Jacquelyn Down Hall, "The Long Civil Rights Movement and the Political Uses of the Past," *Journal of American History* (March 2005): 1233.

22. Counterintelligence Research Project, CI Special Report, Student Non-Violent Coordinating Committee, October 10, 1967, 2, DDRS.

23. Susan Sontag, *Trip to Hanoi* (New York: Farrar, Straus and Giroux, 1968), 87.

24. Samuel P. Huntington, "Transnational Organizations in World Politics," *World Politics* 25, no. 3 (April 1973): 344.

25. Calvin Colton, *History and Character of American Revivals of Religion* (London: Frederick Westley and A. H. Davis, 1832), 58.

26. Zbigniew Brzezinski, *Between Two Ages*, 305–306.

27. Ibid.

28. Ibid., 305, 306.

29. Ibid., 278.

30. Alfred Jenkins, "Mainland Developments Demand a Clearer U.S. Policy," August 3, 1966, DDRS.

31. Zbigniew Brzezinski, *Between Two Ages*, 33. The trilateral Commission reports from the 1970s provide particularly detailed explorations of this emerging "global perspective." In particular, see Richard N. Cooper, Trilateral Commission Task Force Report, *Toward a Renovated International System*, January 1977.

32. Address by the Secretary of State (Muskie) at the University of Wisconsin, October 21, 1980, in *American Foreign Policy Basic Documents, 1977–1980* (Washington, D.C.: Department of State, 1983), 445.

33. Richard J. Barnet, "Global Reach," *New Yorker*, December 9, 1974, 58.

34. CIA, "Implications of Economic Nationalism in the Poor Countries," June 29, 1971, http://www.faqs.org/cia/docs/58/0000251186/IMPLICA TIONS-OF-ECONOMIC-NATIONALISM-IN-THE-POOR-COUN TRIES*.html.

35. Ludmilla Alekseeva quoted in Hodgman, "Détente and the Dissidents," 96.

36. Andrei Sakharov, *My Country and the World* (New York: Random House, 1975), 39.

37. Edward Bailey Hodgman, "Détente and the Dissidents," 128.

38. "Jews Are Forbidden to Leave the Country," *New York Times*, April 2, 1969, 26.

39. Jackson quoted in Edward Bailey Hodgman, "Détente and the Dissidents," 170.

40. Sam Gibbons quoted in ibid., 178–179.

41. Nixon conversation with Arthur Burns, quoted in ibid., 158.

42. J. William Fulbright to author; also see Fulbright's *The Price of Empire*, 31.

43. House of Representatives, *Human Rights in the World Community: A Call for U.S. Leadership*, report by the Subcommittee on International Organizations and Movements, March 27, 1974, 10.

44. "US Urged to Act on Human Rights," *New York Times,* March 28, 1974, 17.

45. Foreign Assistance Act of 1973, Public Law 87–195, sec. 32. Quoted in David P. Forsythe, *Human Rights and U.S. Foreign Policy: Congress Reconsidered* (Gainesville: University of Florida Press, 1988), 8.

46. House Committee on International Relations, *The Status of Human Rights and Its Relationship to U.S. Economic Assistance Programs*, report by Subcommittee on International Organizations, 141.

47. Discussion of Human Rights and Development, H461-49, November 8, 1975.

48. Bernard Gwertzman, "U.S. Blocks Rights Data on Nations Getting Arms; U.S. Won't Give Rights Data to Congress," *New York Times*, November 19, 1975, 1.

49. Hugh Arnold, "Henry Kissinger and Human Rights," *Universal Human Rights* 2, no. 4 (October–December 1980): 57–71.

50. House of Representatives, *Human Rights in the World Community*, 10.

51. Kathleen Teltsch, "Moynihan Calls on U.S. to 'Start Raising Hell' in the U.N.," *New York Times*, February 26, 1975, 3.

52. House Committee on Foreign Affairs, *Hearings on Human Rights in Chile, Subcommittee on Inter-American Affairs*, 1974, 21.

53. Quoted by Greg Grandin, *Empire's Workshop: Latin America, the United States, and the Rise of the New Imperialism* (New York: Metropolitan Books, 2006), 60.

54. Senator Frank Church, "Covert Action: Swampland of American Foreign Policy," speech at Pacem in Terris IV conference, December 4, 1975.

55. Senate Committee on Foreign Relations, *Covert Action in Chile 1963–1973; Report of the Select Committee to Study Governmental Operations with Respect to Intelligence Activities*, 94th Cong., 1st sess., http://foia.state .gov/Reports/ChurchReport.asp.

56. U.S. Ambassador Edward Korry, quoted in Peter Kornbluh, "Chile and the United States: Declassified Documents Relating to the Military Coup," September 11, 1973, National Archives Electronic Briefing Book no. 8, http://www.gwu.edu/~nsarchiv/NSAEBB/NSAEBB8/nsaebb8i.htm.

57. Frank Church, "Covert Action."

58. Ibid., 7.

59. Warren Christopher, "Human Rights: An Important Concern of U.S. Foreign Policy, Testifying Before the Subcommittee on Foreign Assistance of the U.S. Senate, Committee on Foreign Relations," March 7, 1977. Department of State Bulletin, March 28, 1977, 290.

60. Remarks by the president before the United Nations, October 5, 1977, in *American Foreign Policy Basic Documents, 1977–1980*, 417.

61. William Lloyd Garrison, "The Lessons of Independence Day," July 4, 1842, in *American Patriotism: Speeches, Letters, and Other Papers Which Illustrate the Foundation*, ed. Selim Hobart Peabody (New York: John B. Alden, 1886), 477.

62. David S. Reynolds, *John Brown: Abolitionist* (New York: Knopf, 2005), 270.

63. Ibid., quoting John Brown (all capitals in original), 218.

64. Ibid., 444.

65. Ibid., 5.

66. William Jennings Bryan, *The Commoner Condensed* (New York: Abby Press, 1902).

67. George Sewall Boutwell, *The Crisis of the Republic* (Boston: Dana Estes, 1900), 196.

68. Woodrow Wilson, April 15, 1917, *President Wilson's State Papers and Addresses*, Introduction by Albert Shaw (New York: George H. Doran, 1917), 387.

69. Ibid.

70. Theodore Roosevelt, French Academy address, April 1910.

71. Charles Lindbergh, *Why Is Your Country at War and What Happens to You After the War* (Washington, D.C.: National Capital Press, 1917), 132.

72. Richard. F. Pettigrew, *Imperial Washington: The Story of American Life from 1870–1920* (Chicago: Charles H. Kerr, 1922), 196.

73. Emma Florence Langdon, *The Cripple Creek Strike, 1903–1904* (Denver: Great Western Publishing, 1904), 245.

74. William Allen White, *The Old Order Changeth: A View of American Democracy* (New York: Macmillan, 1910), 94.

75. Simone Weil, "Human Personality," in *An Anthology*, ed. Sian Miles (New York: Grove Press, 2000), 62.

76. Ibid., 60–61.

77. Ibid., 61. An enormous literature has developed on "rights talk," the law, and the relationship between rights and human needs. In particular, see Mary Ann Glendon, *Rights Talk: The Impoverishment of Political Discourse* (New York: Free Press, 1993).

78. Weil, "Human Personality."

79. Eric Foner, *The Story of American Freedom* (New York: W. W. Norton, 1998), 286.

80. Ibid.

81. Ibid.

82. Zbigniew Brzezinski, *Power and Principle: Memoirs of the National Security Manager, 1977–1981* (New York: Farrar, Straus and Giroux, 1983), 123.

83. Zbigniew Brzezinski, *The New Dimensions of Human Rights: Fourteenth*

Annual Morgenthau Memorial Lecture on Ethics and Foreign Policy, 1995, http://www.cceia.org/resources/publications/morgenthau/269.html.

84. CIA, intelligence memorandum, World Trends and Developments, February 1977, 9, FOIA.

85. Ibid.

86. CIA, "Implications of Economic Nationalism in the Poor Countries," June 29, 1971, FOIA.

87. Zbigniew Brzezinski, "U.S. Foreign Policy: The Search for Focus," *Foreign Affairs* (July 1973): 717.

88. Zbigniew Brzezinski to Jimmy Carter, "Weekly National Security Report No. 9," April 16, 1977, DDRS.

89. Ibid.

90. "Presidential Review Memorandum/NSC-28: Human Rights," 76–77, DDRS.

91. Robert Gates, *From the Shadows: The Ultimate Insider's Story of Five Presidents and How They Won the Cold War* (New York. Simon & Schuster, 1996), 95.

92. "Euro-communism and CIA," 16; "Prospects for Eastern Europe," June 10, 1977; CIA, "Soviet Policy at the Crossroads," July 8, 1977, 3; CIA, "Soviet View of the Dissident Problem Since Helsinki, May 1, 1977, 15, FOIA. Also see Gates, *From the Shadows,* 88.

93. CIA, "Soviet Policy at the Crossroads."

94. Ibid., 6.

95. Ibid.

96. CIA, "Soviet View of the Dissident Problem Since Helsinki."

97. Robert Gates, *From the Shadows,* 88.

98. Richard Holbrooke, House Committee on Foreign Affairs, *Reconciling Human Rights and U.S. Security Interests in Asia*, report by Subcommittee on Asian and Pacific Affairs, August 10, 1982, 9.

99. See National Security Archive, "Carter Confronts the Revolution," *Nicaragua: The Making of U.S. Policy, 1978–1990,* http://www.gwu.edu/~nsarchiv/nsa/publications/nicaragua/nicaragua.html.

100. Vance to Carter, n.d., cited by Bruce J. Schulman and Julian E. Zelizer, *Rightward Bound: Making America Conservative in the 1970s* (Cambridge, Mass.: Harvard University Press, 2008), 257.

101. Viron Vaky, Senate Foreign Relations Committee, executive sess., quoted in National Security Archive, *Nicaragua: The Making of U.S. Policy, 1978–1990.*

102. Lawrence Pezzullo and Ralph Pezzullo, *At the Fall of Somoza* (Pittsburgh: Pittsburgh University Press, 1993), 71.

103. John A. Soares Jr., "Strategy, Ideology, and Human Rights," *Journal of Cold War Studies* 8, no. 4 (Fall 2006): 69.

104. Robert Gates, *From the Shadows,* 151.

105. A draft letter from Carter to Pope John Paul II bluntly expressed his general attitude and concerns. "Elements of the extreme left" were using "violence and terrorism designed to destroy the existing order and replace it with a Marxist one which promises to be equally repressive and totalitarian. They are aided and abetted in these efforts by Cuban interventionism." Quoted by John A. Soares Jr., "Strategy, Ideology, and Human Rights," 66.

106. Robert Gates, *From the Shadows,* 153.

107. Jimmy Carter, toasts of the President and the Shah at a state dinner, December 31, 1977, APP.

108. Jimmy Carter, Remarks at the American Federation of Labor and Congress of Industrial Organizations 13th Constitutional Convention, November 15, 1979, APP.

109. Jimmy Carter, News conference, February 12, 1979, APP.

110. Jimmy Carter, "National Governors' Association Toasts at a White House Dinner Honoring Governors Attending the Association's Winter Session," February 27, 1979, APP.

111. Jimmy Carter interview with Barbara Walters, ABC-TV, December 14, 1978, APP.

112. Jimmy Carter interview with Bill Moyers, PBS, November 13, 1978, APP.

113. White House Statement, "American Hostages in Iran," November 19, 1979.

114. Anthony Lake to Cyrus Vance, "Assessment of U.S. Human Rights Policy One Year After Its Inception," January 30, 1978, DDRS.

115. Warren Christopher, "The Diplomacy of Human Rights: The First Year," American Bar Association speech, February 13, 1978, in *American Foreign Policy Basic Documents, 1977–1980* (Washington, D.C.: Department of State, 1983), 422.

116. The same argument is made in Peter L. Berger, "To Insure Reliable Human-Rights Information," *New York Times,* June 4, 1977, 15.

117. These quotes are from two versions of Zbigniew Brzezinski's proposal for a human rights foundation. See Zbigniew Brzezinski to Jimmy Carter, "Human Rights Foundation," January 24, 1978, draft, and February 7, 1978, draft, DDRS.

118. Jimmy Carter and Zbigniew Brzezinski discuss creation of a human rights foundation, December 3, 1977, DDRS.

119. Zbigniew Brzezinski to Jimmy Carter, "Human Rights Foundation," January 24, 1978, draft, and February 7, 1978, draft, DDRS.

120. Ibid.

121. Ibid.

122. Memorandum from Smith to Fallows, at 2, in: Folder 5/22/77-Notre

Dame Speech [2], Box 6 5/17/77-California Trip (UAW) [3] through 5/23/77-Signing Ceremony-Drought & Tax Cut Legislation, Collection Speechwriter's Office-Chron File, Carter Library, quoted by Hauke Hartmann, "U.S. Human Rights Policy Under Carter and Reagan," *Human Rights Quarterly* 23, no. 2 (2001): 402–430.

123. Zbigniew Brzezinski, "Weekly National Security Report, no. 9," April 16, 1977, DDRS.

124. Jeri Laber, *The Courage of Strangers: Coming of Age with the Human Rights Movement* (New York: PublicAffairs, 2002), 97–98. Also "Panel in New York to Monitor Human Rights in US," *New York Times*, February 25, 1979, 3.

125. Though long-standing human rights groups predate the 1970s, such as the quasi-official Freedom House (1941) and the International League for Human Rights (1942), and UN and European commissions also had been founded, the growth of the leading human rights organizations in the United States comes only in the mid- to late-1970s with such pathbreaking groups as the Lawyer's Committee for Human Rights (1975). For background to the kinds of human rights materials first engendered in the UN and various European organizations, see Thomas Reynold, "Highest Aspirations of Barbarous Acts," *Law Library Journal* 71 (February 1978).

126. Jeri Laber, *The Courage of Strangers*. Also, University of Massachusetts "Kennedy Library Forum: Human Rights—Then and Now," September 23, 2002, http://www.cs.umb.edu/~rwhealan/jfk/forum_laber.html, accessed December 13, 2006.

127. Ibid.

128. Quoted by Kirsten Sellars, *The Rise and Rise of Human Rights* (Thrupp, UK: Sutton, 2002), 148.

129. On U.S. government and CIA involvement in the Institute for the Study of the USSR, see "United States Government Support of Covert Action Directed at the Soviet Union," Memorandum for the 303 Committee, December 9, 1969, http://www.fas.org/irp/cia/product/frus1969.pdf. The Institute's task was to produce "research papers and publications targeted at the developing countries in Africa, Middle East, and the Far East."

130. Alexander Solzhenitsyn, "A World Split Apart" (commencement speech, Harvard University, Cambridge, Mass., June 8, 1978), http://www.americanrhetoric.com/speeches/alexandersolzhenitsynharvard.htm

131. Reuel Marc Gerecht, " 'Hearts and Minds' in Iraq: As History Shows, Ideas Matter More Than Who Pays to Promote Them," *Washington Post*, January 10, 2006, A15.

132. Ibid.

133. Testimony of Wilson Ferreira-Aldunate, *Human Rights in Uruguay and Paraguay*, House Committee on International Relations, Subcommittee on International Relations, June 17, 1976, 28.

134. Particularly valuable are Kirsten Sellars's *The Rise and Rise of Human Rights* (Thrupp, UK: Sutton, 2002); Jonathan Power, *Against Oblivion: Amnesty International's Fight for Human Rights* (Glasgow: Fontana, 1981); Stephen Hopgood, *Keepers of the Flame: Understanding Amnesty International* (Ithaca, N.Y.: Cornell University Press, 2006); Kirsten Sellars, "Human Rights and the Colonies: Deceit, Deception, and Discovery," *The Round Table* 93, no. 377 (October 2004): 709–724.

135. Tom Buchanan, "Amnesty International in Crisis, 1966–67," *Twentieth Century British History* 15, no. 3 (2004): 267–289.

136. Tom Buchanan quoting Eric Baker, "'The Truth Will Set You Free': The Making of Amnesty International," *Journal of Contemporary History* 37, no. 4 (2002): 579.

137. Ibid.

138. Ibid., 584.

139. Cosmas Desmond, *Persecution East and West: Human Rights, Political Prisoners and Amnesty* (New York: Penguin, 1983), 80.

140. Editorial, *New York Times*, December 14, 1978, A30.

141. Edy Kaufman, "Prisoners of Conscience: The Shaping of a New Human Rights Concept," *Human Rights Quarterly* 13, no. 3 (August 1991): 339–367.

142. Cosmas Desmond, quoting Nelson Mandela, *Persecution East and West*, 48.

143. Tom Buchanan, "'The Truth Will Set You Free,'" 585.

144. Ibid.

145. Guenter Lewy, quoting James E. Bristol, director of the AFSC Program on Non-violence, in *Peace and Revolution: The Moral Crisis of American Pacifism* (Grand Rapids, Mich.: William E. Eerdman, 1988), 48–49.

146. Quoted in Guenter Lewy, *Peace and Revolution*, 101.

147. "Jimmy Carter, Human Rights, Cambodia," *Diplomatic History*, 258. Also see Edward S. Herman, "Pol Pot and Kissinger on War Criminality and Impunity," *Third World Traveler*, http://www.thirdworldtraveler. com/Kissinger/PolPotKissinger_Herman.html. Some officials did try to change U.S. policy, recommending that "we urgently reappraise the promises of US policy toward Hanoi . . . to persuade Hanoi to open up the doors to saving the Khmer people. . . . We should squarely face the necessity of openly approving the eradication of the Pol Pot regime, which is utterly anathema on human rights and basic moral grounds. There can be no political, strategic, or other excuse for equivocation by

the US government on this score . . . any more than when Tanzania invaded and ousted the Idi Amin regime (or we invaded to end Nazism)." Lincoln P. Bloomfield, NSC memo to Zbigniew Brzezinski and Henry Owen, "Kampuchean Relief: Drastic New Approaches," December 3, 1979, DDRS. Next to this recommendation is handwritten the response: "Boo!"

148. J. William Fulbright, *The Price of Empire*, 127.
149. Carter, American Society of Newspaper Editors remarks, April 10, 1980, APP.
150. Jeri Laber, "Afghanistan's Other War," *New York Review of Books*, December 18, 1986, 20.
151. J. William Fulbright, *The Price of Empire*, 10.
152. James Baldwin, *No Name in the Street* (New York: Dell, 1973), 149.

CHAPTER 3: THE REAGAN ADMINISTRATION: DEMOCRATIZATION AND PROXY WARS

1. Secretary Haig's news conference, January 28, 1981, in *Department of State Bulletin* 81, no. 2047 (February 1981).
2. Elliott Abrams, House Committee on Foreign Affairs, *Review of U.S. Human Rights Policy: Hearings Before the Subcommittee on Human Rights and International Organizations*, 98th Cong., 1st sess., March 3, June 28, and September 21, 1983, H381–31, 1984.
3. Ibid., 2.
4. David K. Shipler, "Missionaries for Democracy: U.S. Aid for Global Pluralism" captures this missionary ethos in the National Endowment for Democracy, *New York Times*, June 1, 1986.
5. George Schultz, *Turmoil and Triumph: My Years As Secretary of State* (New York: Scribner's, 1993), 591.
6. Michael McClintock, *The American Connection* (London: Zed Books, 1985), 16, quoting Frank R. Barnett, "A Proposal for Political Warfare," *Military Review* (March 1961): 3.
7. "Insurgency and Instability in Central America," CIA estimate, April 9, 1981, 1, FOIA.
8. CIA, "Soviet Support for International Terrorism and Revolutionary Violence," May 29, 1981, Special National Intelligence Estimate, November 2, 1981, 3, FOIA.
9. Ibid., 15.
10. Ronald Reagan, "Remarks on Signing the Human Rights Day, Bill of Rights Day, and Human Rights Week Proclamation," December 10, 1986, http://www.reagan.utexas.edu/archives/speeches/1986/121086a.htm.

11. U.S. National Security Strategy, April 1982, 2, DDRS.
12. CIA Intelligence Assessment, "Soviet Elite Concerns About Popular Discontent and Official Corruption," December 1, 1982, 1, FOIA.
13. Robert Gates, *From the Shadows: The Ultimate Insider's Story of Five Presidents and How They Won the Cold War* (New York: Simon & Schuster, 1996), 188.
14. CIA, "Gorbachev and the Problems of Western Radio Broadcasting into the USSR," November 1, 1987, 15, FOIA.
15. Ibid., 27. The phrase is from a Soviet publication, *Literaturnaya Gazeta*, that the CIA was monitoring.
16. Herbert E. Meyer (Vice Chair, National Intelligence Council) to CIA Director, "What Should We Do About the Russians?" June 28, 1984, 2, FOIA.
17. Ibid., 7.
18. Robert Gates quoting Reagan, *From the Shadows*, 194.
19. Herbert E. Meyer, Vice Chair, NIC, to Deputy Director CIA, "Why Is the World So Dangerous?" November 30, 1983, FOIA.
20. Abrams interview, January 14, 1994, in Michael Hausenfleck, "The Reagan Doctrine: A Conceptual Analysis of the Democracy Imperative in U.S. Foreign Policy, 1981–1988" (Ph.D. diss., Brandeis University, 1995), 183.
21. Ronald Reagan, "Address Before a Joint Session of Congress on the State of the Union," February 6, 1985, APP.
22. For further discussion see Michael McClintock, *Instruments of Statecraft: U.S. Guerilla Warfare, Counter-Insurgency, and Counter-Terrorism, 1940–1990* (New York: Pantheon Books, 1992).
23. John Singlaub to William Casey, July 28, 1986, in National Security Archive, quoted in Lucy J. Mathiak, "American Jihad: The Reagan Doctrine as Policy and Practice" (Ph. D. diss., University of Wisconsin, 2000), 12.
24. Walter Raymond's Deposition, Memo from Walter Raymond to William Clark, *Report of the Congressional Committees Investigating the Iran-Contra Affair*, 100th Cong., 1st sess., 1987, Appendix B, vol. 22, 190–196.
25. Ibid.
26. "Exporting Democracy," *Washington Post*, June 28, 1983, A14.
27. "Why Not Aid Friends Openly?" *New York Times*, March 23, 1982, A26.
28. Ronald Reagan, "Speech to British Parliament," June 8, 1982, http://www.historyplace.com/speeches/reagan-parliament.htm.
29. Ibid.
30. National Security Decision Directive 75, "Management of Public Diplomacy Relative to National Security," January 14, 1983, http://www.fas.org/irp/offdocs/nsdd/nsdd-075.htm.

31. Ronald Reagan, "Speech to British Parliament," June 8, 1982, http://www
    .historyplace.com/speeches/reagan-parliament.htm.

32. NSC, "Fundamental Policy Issues Associated with U.S. International Infor-
    mation Programs," 17–18, DDRS.

33. Aryeh Neier, *Taking Liberties* (New York: PublicAffairs, 2003), xxxi.

34. The "project democracy" group included CIA director William Casey,
    White House speechwriter Anthony Dolan, USIA deputy director W.
    Scott Thomson, and Heritage Foundation director Edwin Feulner. The
    other group, which drafted Reagan's Westminster speech, included Mark
    Palmer (deputy undersecretary to Lawrence Eagleburger and a former
    speechwriter of Henry Kissinger), Walter Raymond (senior staff officer in
    the Operations Directorate at the CIA and soon to oversee democratization
    efforts at the NSC), Michael Samuels (international vice president of the
    U.S. Chamber of Commerce), and William Brock III (Republican National
    committee chair and later U.S. trade representative). Elizabeth Cohn,
    "Idealpolitik in U.S. Foreign Policy: The Reagan Administration and the
    U.S. Promotion of Democracy" (Ph. D. diss., American University, 1995),
    160–161.

35. Lucy J. Mathiak, "American Jihad: The Reagan Doctrine as Policy and
    Practice," 27.

36. Quoted from Carnes Lord, who served in the Reagan years as the national
    security advisor to the vice president and as the director of international
    information and communications policy on the National Security Coun-
    cil Staff at the White House. See Lord's "In Defense of Public Diplomacy,"
    Commentary 77, no. 4 (April 1984): 42.

37. National Endowment for Democracy, "Annual Report," 1986, 3. To closely
    interweave government and private, covert and overt, see National Secu-
    rity Council, "International Political Information Activity," DDRS, which
    explores steps for the establishment of an effective interagency process to
    manage foreign public diplomacy.

38. David K. Shipler, "Missionaries for Democracy," 16.

39. Paul Bremer to William P. Clark, "Strategy for Building Democracy in
    Communist and Non-Communist Countries," April 13, 1982, 2, DDRS.

40. William Colby, "Political Action—in the Open," *Washington Post*, March 14,
    1982, D8.

41. David K. Shipler, "Missionaries for Democracy," 16.

42. Aryeh Neier, *Taking Liberties*, 159.

43. Ibid.

44. GAO/NSAID-94–83, 1994, 10. For just how much continuity existed
    from the Clinton to the Bush years (and the centrality of human rights

language), see USAID, "At Freedom's Frontiers: A Democracy and Governance Strategic Framework," December 2005, PD-ACF-999.

45. Aryeh Neier, *Taking Liberties*, 193, 188, 169.
46. Aryeh Neier, "Human Rights in the Reagan Era: Acceptance in Principle," *The Annals* 506 (November 1989): 40.
47. Ibid.
48. William F. Schulz, *In Our Own Best Interest: How Defending Human Rights Benefits Us All* (Boston: Beacon Press, 2001), 9.
49. Stephen Hopgood, *Keepers of the Flame: Understanding Amnesty International* (Ithaca, N.Y.: Cornell University Press, 2006), 211.
50. Aryeh Neier, "Human Rights in the Reagan Era," 38.
51. Aryeh Neier, "How Not to Promote Democracy and Human Rights," University of Connecticut, 2006, 6, http://humanrights.uconn.edu/documents/papers/DemocracyHumanRightsANeier.pdf.
52. Holly Burkhalter, "The Reagan Administration's Human Rights Record (1988)," http://www.thirdworldtraveler.
53. Ibid.
54. Ibid.
55. Aryeh Neier, "Human Rights in the Reagan Era," 31.
56. Neier, *Taking Liberties*, 156.
57. Jeri Laber and Alice H. Henkin, op-ed, "In Turkey: a Gain for Rights," *New York Times*, December 25, 1985, 17.
58. Elliott Abrams, letter, *New York Times*, August 10, 1984, A25.
59. *New York Times*, August 16, 1984, A22.
60. Ronald Reagan, "Remarks on Signing the Human Rights Day, Bill of Rights Day, and Human Rights Week Proclamation," December 10, 1986, APP.
61. Cynthia Brown, *With Friends Like These* (New York: Pantheon, 1985).
62. Ibid., 133.
63. Richard Holbrooke, *Foreign Assistance Legislation for FY84-FY85 (Part 5): Economic and Security Assistance in Asia and the Pacific*, CIS-NO: 84-H381–19. Source: House Committee on Foreign Affairs, February 25, l983.
64. Aryeh Neier, *Taking Liberties*, 193.
65. Ibid., 191.
66. Cynthia J. Arnson, "Congress and Central America: The Search for Consensus" (Ph. D. diss., Johns Hopkins University, 1988), 573.
67. Senate Committee on Foreign Relations, *Hearings on Certification Concerning Military Aid to El Salvador*, February 8 and March 11, 1982, 97th Cong., 2nd sess., 18.
68. Robert Gates, *From the Shadows*, 314 and 302.

69. Elliott Abrams, "Intervention in Latin America: Cuba Sí, Yanqui No?" *The National Interest* (Summer 1986).

70. "We Support Military Assistance to the Nicaraguans Fighting for Democracy," *New York Times*, March 16, 1986, 217.

71. Cynthia Brown, *With Friends Like These*, 162.

72. Ibid., 119.

73. The commission included Elie Abel (USA); Hubert Beuve-Méry (France); Elebe Ma Ekonzo (Zaire); Gabriel García Márquez (Colombia); Sergey Losev (Soviet Union); Mochtar Lubis (Indonesia); Mustapha Masmoudi (Tunisia); Michio Nagai (Japan); Fred Isaac Akporuaro Omu (Nigeria); Bogdan Osolnik (Yugoslavia); Gamal El Oteifi (Egypt); Johannes Pieter Pronk (Netherlands); Juan Somavía (Chile); Boobli George Verghese (India); Betty Zimmerman (Canada).

74. National Security Council, "The Fundamental Policy Issues Associated with U.S. International Information Programs and Activities in the Context of the U.S. National Security Policy," 5 (n.d., Reagan administration), DDRS.

75. The MacBride Report, *Many Voices, One World: Towards a New More Just and More Efficient World Information and Communication Order* (London: Kegan Paul, 1980), 90, 254 (hereafter MacBride 1). Also http://unes doc.unesco.org/images/0004/000400/040066eb.pdf.

76. The MacBride Report, *Many Voices, One World: Towards a New More Just and More Efficient World Information and Communication Order*, abridged version (New York: UNESCO, 1980), 45 (hereafter MacBride 2).

77. MacBride 1, 59, 160.

78. MacBride 1, 145, 79.

79. MacBride 1, 144.

80. NSC, "The Fundamental Policy Issues Associated with U.S. International Information Programs and Activities in the Context of the U.S. National Security Policy," 6, DDRS.

81. MacBride 1, 136. Bold in original.

82. The Group of 77, a bloc of more than one hundred developing countries, had come with a detailed description of a "New World Information Order." After strenuous negotiations, the sections that were most offensive to the West were removed. These included "the right of peoples . . . to comprehensive and true information," "the right of each nation" to inform the world about its affairs, and "the right of each nation to protect its cultural and social identity against the false or distorted information which may cause harm."

83. Bernard Nossiter, "U.N. Report on Press Is Causing Concern," *New York Times*, January 8, 1981, A11. Also "The Debate Sharpens on a New World

Information Order," *New York Times*, February 15, 1981, E3, and Herbert I. Schiller, "Breaking the West's Media Monopoly," *The Nation*, September 21, 1985.

84. *New York Times*, May 10, 1979, A11.

85. Elliott Abrams testimony, House Committee on Foreign Affairs, *Review of U.S. Participation in UNESCO: Hearings and Markup Before the Subcommittee on International Operations, and on Human Rights and International Organizations*, 97th Cong., 1st sess., on H. Res. 142, March 10, 1982, 82.

86. MacBride 1, 146.

87. Aryeh Neier, *Taking Liberties*, 167, 194.

88. For a detailed, yet typical approach to NLF "terror," see Ariah Project, "A Study of the Use of Terror by the Viet Cong, Prepared by Military Assistance Command, Special Operations Group (MAC/SOG) Headquarters 5th Special Forces Group (ABN) Nha Trang R.V.N. for United States Missions in VI," May 1966, http://www.vietnam.ttu.edu/star/images/044/0440416006.pdf.

89. Amnesty International, *Guatemala: The Human Rights Record* (London: Amnesty International Publications, 1987), 96.

90. The phrase is Jeane Kirkpatrick's.

91. Elliott Abrams, "El Salvador: Are We Asking the Right Questions," *New York Times*, July 29, 1982, A23.

92. Jeane J. Kirkpatrick, "Establishing a Viable Human Rights Policy," Kenyon College's Human Rights Conference, April 4, 1981, 327. Also see Jeane Kirkpatrick, "The Myth of Moral Equivalence," January 1986, from Imprimis, in *Congressional Record*. As Kirkpatrick concluded: "It is necessary only to look at the sober discussion of human rights in such places as the Amnesty International Reports or the Helsinki Watch discussions to see that those organizations and most of the people who discuss the subject today are using skewed vocabulary which guarantees the outcome of the investigation by definition. The 'newspeak' of human rights morally invalidates the governments by definition and morally exculpates the guerrillas by definition," http://www.thirdworldtraveler.com/Human%20Rights%20Documents/Kirkpatrick_HRPolicy.html.

93. Jeane Kirkpatrick, "Legitimacy and Force," *Human Rights in El Salvador*, Address to the Third Committee of the 36th UN General Assembly, December 1, 1981, 118.

94. Jeane Kirkpatrick, "The Myth of Moral Equivalence," address before the Royal Institute for International Affairs, London, April 9, 1984, in her *Legitimacy and Force* (New Brunswick, N.J.: Transaction Books, 1987), 66.

95. National Security Archives, "U.S. Policy in Guatemala," Document 12. Of

course, this was the conventional understanding in various military debates then and ever since. "The brutal reality of insurgent and counter-insurgent warfare is that there is no such thing as a 'clean' war, either on the ground or in the air . . . the government is bound to bomb rebel areas and inflict civilian casualities even if no decisive effect is likely to occur. The government forces cannot allow the rebels to hold sanctuaries within the country where they can rest, rearm, recruit, and stage operations unmolested." James S. Corum, *Airpower Journal* 12, no. 2 (Summer 1998).

96. David Kennedy, *On War and Law* (Princeton, N.J.: Princeton University Press, 2006), 167.

97. Ibid., 45.

98. Americas Watch and American Civil Liberties Union, *Report on Human Rights in El Salvador* (New York: Vintage Books, 1982), x.

99. Cynthia Brown, *With Friends Like These* (New York: Pantheon, 1985), 136.

100. Americas Watch Report, *A Year of Reckoning: El Salvador a Decade After the Assassination of Archbishop Romero* (New York: Americas Watch Committee, 1990).

101. Marvin E. Gettleman, Patrick Lacefield, Louis Menashe, David Mermelstein, and Ronald Radosh, *El Salvador: Central America in the New Cold War* (New York: Grove, 1981), 196.

102. Americas Watch and American Civil Liberties Union, *Report on Human Rights in El Salvador*, x.

103. Michael McClintock, *Instruments of Statecraft: U.S. Guerilla Warfare, Counterinsurgency, and Counterterrorism, 1940–1990*, chapter 13, "The Carter Years," http://www.statecraft.org/chapter13.html#16.

104. Senate Committee on Foreign Relations, House Committee on Foreign Affairs, Legislation on Foreign Relations Through 1986, *Current Legislation and Related Executive Orders*, vol. 1 (Washington: GPO, 1987), Section 502B(b), 137.

105. The Lawyers Committee for International Human Rights, Americas Watch, *El Salvador's Other Victims: The War on the Displaced*, April 1984; Americas Watch and American Civil Liberties Union, *Report on Human Rights in El Salvador*.

106. Michael McClintock, *The American Connection*, vol. 1, *State Terror and Popular Resistance in El Salvador* (London: Zed Books, 1985), 307.

107. Ibid., 305, 307.

108. Quoting Aryeh Neier in Noam Chomsky, *Turning the Tide* (Boston: South End Press, 1985), 26.

109. Interview with Ambassador John Negroponte, [n.d.], http://www.ww4report.com/negropontedeathsquad.

110. Thomas Powers, "A Lethal Big Brother Fighting a Remnant of the Cold War, the CIA Kept Killers on the Payroll," *Los Angeles Times*, April 9, 1995, 1. Also Kate Doyle, "Death Squad Diary," *Harper's Magazine*, June 1999, 50, and Judy Mann, "A Tale of Unspeakable Evil in Honduras," *Washington Post*, June 8, 1988, B3. Susanne Jonas, "Indecent Liaisons: The U.S. and Guatemala's Army," *Christian Science Monitor*, April 17, 1995, 19. Jefferson Morley, "Death from a Distance: Washington's Role in El Salvador's Death Squads," *Washington Post*, March 28, 1993, C1.

111. Benjamin Schwartz, "Dirty Hands," *The Atlantic*, December 1988, http://www.theatlantic.com/issues/98dec/salv2.htm.

112. Michael McClintock's *Instruments of Statecraft* provides an excellent analysis of U.S. counterinsurgency manuals, http://www.statecraft.org/chapter13.html#16.

113. Congressman Stephen Solarz, quoted in Benjamin Schwartz, "Dirty Hands," 110.

114. Cynthia Brown, *With Friends Like These*, 139, 140.

115. Benjamin Schwartz, "Dirty Hands," 109.

116. Ronald Reagan, quoted in House Committee on Foreign Affairs, *The Situation in El Salvador: Hearings Before the Subcommittees on Human Rights and International Organizations and on Western Hemisphere Affairs*, 98th Cong., 2nd sess., January 26, 1984.

117. Judy Mann, "A Tale of Unspeakable Evil in Honduras," B3.

118. "The Truth About Guatemala," *Boston Globe*, April 7, 1995, 21. Also see Democracy Now, "Is the US Organizing Salvador-Style Death Squads in Iraq?" January 10, 2005. Also "Reagan Was Behind One of the Most Intensive Campaigns of Mass Murder in Recent History," June 8, 2004, http:www.democracynow.org/2004/6/8/journalist_allan_nairn_Reagan_was_behind.

119. Noam Chomsky, *Deterring Democracy* (New York: Hill and Wang, 1992), 389.

120. Michael McClintock, "Watching the Neighbors: Low-Intensity Conflict in Central America," chapter 17, http://www.statecraft.org/chapter17.html.

121. Michael McClintock, *An Un-American War of War*, chapter 18, http://www.statecraft.org/chapter18.html.

122. See Alfred McCoy's superb study, *A Question of Torture: CIA Interrogation From the Cold War to the War on Terror* (New York: Henry Holt, 2006).

123. Aryeh Neier, "Salvador Rights: Some Gains," *New York Times*, July 20, 1983, A19.

124. Elliott Abrams, letter, *New York Times*, February 22, 1986, 22.

125. Ibid.

126. *Psychological Operations in Guerrilla Warfare: The CIA's Nicaragua Manual*, with essays by Joanne Omang and Aryeh Neier (New York: Vintage Books, 1985), 57.

127. Ibid., 112.

128. Michael McClintock quoting *Congressional Report*, chapter 18, "An Un-American Way of War," http://www.statecraft.org/chapter18 (accessed February 16, 2007).

129. Americas Watch, *Human Rights in Nicaragua: Reagan Rhetoric and Reality* (New York: Americas Watch, 1985), 16.

130. Ibid., 2.

131. Americas Watch, *Violations of the War by Both Sides, in Nicaragua, 1981–1985* (New York: Americas Watch Committee, March 1985), 1.

132. Amnesty International at House Committee on Foreign Affairs, *The Central American Counterterrorism Act of 1985 Hearings*, 99th Cong., 1st sess., October 24, 1985 and November 19, 1985.

133. Aryeh Neier, "The US and the Contras," *New York Review of Books* 3, no. 6 (April 10, 1986).

134. Cynthia Brown, *With Friends Like These*, 159.

135. Aryeh Neier, *Taking Liberties*, 217.

136. Aryeh Neier, "The US and the Contras."

137. Ibid.

138. International Court of Justice, Military and Paramilitary Activities In and Against Nicaragua (*Nicaragua v. United States of America*), http://www.icj-cij.org/docket/index.php?sum=367&code=nus&p1=3&p2=3&case=70&k=66&p3=5.

139. Ibid.

140. Ibid.

141. Ibid., para. 134.

142. Ibid., para. 266.

143. CIA, "Chile: Prospects for a Democratic Transition," August 1, 1987, FOIA.

144. Washington's worries that Pinochet was polarizing Chile to the benefit of the left is evident in numerous NSC/CIA reports. See NSC, "Background Paper on Chile." Topics include: U.S.–Chilean relations; human rights issues; Communist influence in Chile; terrorism; democratic transition issues; economic conditions, DDRS.

145. Barbara Gamarekian, "How the U.S. Political Pros Get Out the Vote in Chile," *New York Times*, November 18, 1988, B6. Also Shirley Christian, "Group Is Channeling U.S. Funds to Parties Opposing Pinochet," *New York Times*, January 15, 1988, A1.

146. Aryeh Neier, "Human Rights in the Reagan Era," *The Annals* 506 (November 1989): 33–34.

147. The issue of credibility and funding was occasionally raised about the Human Rights Commission of Nicaragua (Comisión de Derechos Humanos de Nicaragua—CPDH) accepting money from the U.S. government. The Lawyers Committee for Human Rights critique, "Review of the U.S. Department of State's Country Reports on Human Rights Practices for 1989," noted that CPDH's "acceptance of funds from the U.S. government at a time when the U.S. is intent on overthrowing the Nicaraguan government seriously jeopardizes CPDH's claim to independence," 127.

148. The CIA acknowledged responsibility for some 726 articles and broadcasts in Latin America slanted against Allende in just the six-week period before the election in 1970. Staff report, "Covert Action in Chile 1963–1973," in Senate Select Committee to Study Governmental Operations with Respect to Intelligence Activities, *Covert Action: Book 7*, 94th Cong., 2nd sess., 1976, 25.

149. Amnesty International, *Annual Report 1975–1976* (London: Amnesty International), 54.

150. Aryeh Neier, "The US and the Contras."

151. "The Sandinista Road to Stalinism," *New York Times*, July 10, 1986, A22.

152. "Nicaragua Bares the Nightstick," *New York Times*, October 18, 1985, A30.

153. Envio team, "The Politics of Human Rights Reporting in Nicaragua," *Revista Envoi*, no. 60 (June 1986), http://www.envio.org.ni/articulo/3506.

154. Americas Watch, *Fitful Peace: Human Rights and Reconciliation in Nicaragua Under the Chamorro Government* (New York: Americas Watch, 1991), 2.

155. Some human rights scholars were uneasy about such views. In Nicaragua most of the business- and land-owning classes had once reached accommodations with Somoza and there was little reason to believe they would not seek and obtain U.S. support for destroying the Sandinistas and "block egalitarian reform." Tom J. Farer, "Looking at Nicaragua: The Problematique of Impartiality in Human Rights Inquiries," *Human Rights Quarterly* 10 (1988): 141–156.

156. William J. Casey, quoted by Bob Woodward, *Veil* (New York: Simon & Schuster, 1987), 281.

157. Casey quoted in Digital National Security Archive, "Nicaragua: The Making of U.S. Policy, 1978–1990."

158. The campaign of public diplomacy was massive, yet quite typical in its operations and underlying ideological assertions. Public Diplomacy Office Review, "The Human Costs of Communism: The Nicaraguan

Experience in Historical Perspective" is a representative example, a lengthy argument pointing to a plethora of like-minded work supported by the government.

159. Aryeh Neier, "The Contra Contradiction," *New York Review of Books* 34, no. 6 (April 9, 1987).

160. Aryeh Neier, "Human Rights in the Reagan Era," 38.

161. Aryeh Neier, "A Matter of Principle, *The Nation*, April 21, 1991, 520–522.

CHAPTER 4: HUMAN RIGHTS AND CHINA

1. Robert Dole, *Congressional Record*, June 6, 1989, p. 10873.

2. George Mitchell, *Congressional Record*, June 6, 1989, p. 10872.

3. Roberta Cohen, "People's Republic of China: The Human Rights Exception," *Human Rights Quarterly* 9, no. 4 (November 1967).

4. Ronald Reagan, quoted in James Mann, *About Face: A History of America's Curious Relationship with China from Nixon to Clinton* (New York: Knopf, 1999), 146–147.

5. Roberta Cohen, "People's Republic of China," 451.

6. Ibid., 467.

7. Ibid., 466.

8. Roberta Cohen quoting Congressman Edward J. Derwinski, 468.

9. Aryeh Neier, *Taking Liberties* (New York: PublicAffairs, 2003), p. 160.

10. For a detailed account of Washington's global strategizing about China from 1945 to 1968 see James Peck, *Washington's China* (Amherst: University of Massachusetts Press, 2006).

11. Ibid.

12. Ibid.

13. Ibid., chapter 8.

14. Richard Nixon, "Asia After Vietnam," *Foreign Affairs* (October 1967).

15. Carl Kaysen, "Report of the President's Task Force on Foreign Economic Policy," November 25, 1964, A-27, DDRS.

16. "Summary Minutes of Meeting of the Interdepartmental Committee of Under Secretaries on Foreign Economic Policy," January 10, 1962, FRUS, 1961–1963, 9: 664.

17. Carl Kaysen, "Report of the President's Task Force on Foreign Economic Policy," November 25, 1964, T-22, DDRS.

18. William Bundy and Anthony Solomon to Rusk, "A New Approach to Our Trade and Transaction Controls Against Communist China—ACTION MEMORANDUM," forwarded to Rostow by James C. Thomson Jr., August 4, 1966, p. 2 [LBJ ASIA 4-0983].

19. CIA, "Economic Benefits to Communist China of a Removal of U.S. Trade Controls," June 1966, 84a, FOIA.

20. "Communist China: Long-Range Study on Economic Trends and Prospects in Communist China" by the Special State-Defense Study Group, June 1966, vol. 1, 218, DDRS.

21. Patrick E. Tyler, "U.S. Strategy for Insuring No Rivals Develop," *New York Times*, March 8, 1992, A1.

22. George Bush and Brent Scowcroft, *A World Transformed* (New York: Knopf, 1998), 42.

23. Ibid., 63.

24. Paul Wolfowitz, "Statesmanship in the New Century," in *Present Dangers: Crisis and Opportunity in American Foreign and Defense Policy*, ed. Robert Kagan and William Kristol (San Francisco: Encounter Books, 2000), 316–317. Also Patrick E. Tyler, "U.S. Strategy for Insuring No Rivals Develop."

25. Douglas Paal, NSC official, quoted in James Mann, "Fear of China's Collapse Is Greatly Exaggerated," *Los Angeles Times*, March 24, 1999, http://articles.latimes.com/1999/mar/24/news/mn-20477.

26. Zbigniew Brzezinski, *Out of Control: Global Turmoil on the Eve of the 21st Century* (New York: Scribner's, 1993), 196–199.

27. Samuel Berger, "Building a New Consensus on China," Speech to the Council on Foreign Relations, June 6, 1997, http://www.mtholyoke.edu/acad/intrel/bergchin.htm.

28. Zbigniew Brzezinski, *Out of Control*, 199.

29. Paul Bracken, *Fire in the East: The Rise of Asian Military Power and the Second Nuclear Age* (New York: Harper Perennial, 2000).

30. David Shambaugh in *Chinese Foreign Policy: Theory and Practice*, ed. David Shambaugh and Thomas W. Robinson (New York: Oxford University Press, 1994), 211.

31. Congressional Research Service, *China's Foreign Policy and 'Soft Power' in South America, Asia, and Africa*, Study prepared for the Senate Committee on Foreign Relations, (April 2008), 2.

32. Senate Finance Committee, "Trade with China and Its Implications for U.S. Foreign Policy," March 23, 2000. Testimony by Robert Kagan.

33. Ibid. Testimony by Richard Perle.

34. Human Rights Watch, "World Report 1990," Introduction, http:www.hrw.org (hereafter HRWWS).

35. Human Rights Watch, "World Report 1989," Introduction, HRWWS.

36. Human Rights Watch, "World Report 1992," 2, HRWWS.

37. Human Rights Watch, "Annual Report 1991," HRWWS.

38. Ibid.

39. Human Rights Watch, "Asia Watch Overview," 1990, http://www.hrw.org/
   legacy/reports/1990/WR90/ASIA.BOU-04.htm#P353_85049. Eagleburger's
   quote is cited by Human Rights Watch.

40. George Bush and Brent Scowcroft, *The World Transformed*, 7.

41. The president's news conference, June 5, 1989, in the *Weekly Compilation
   of Presidential Documents* (Washington: GPO, 1989), vol. 25, no. 3 (June 12,
   1989), 839–843.

42. A sampling of the *Congressional Record* from June 6, 1989 to June 12, 1989
   provides hundreds of such invocations of the American Dream, the Chinese tyrants standing against the tide of democracy, and the ways the
   Chinese were fighting for "our ideals."

43. Senator Conrad in the *Congressional Record* 146, no. 111 (September 19,
   2000): S 8667.

44. Senator Durbin in ibid.

45. Senator Hatch in ibid.

46. Senator Roth, *Congressional Record* 146, no. 106 (September 12, 2000): S 8375.

47. Senator Dodd, *Congressional Record* 146, no. 107 (September 13, 2000): S
   8445.

48. Senator Jesse Helms, ibid.

49. Senator Paul Wellstone, *Congressional Record* (September 12, 2000).

50. Human Rights Watch, "Annual Report," 1998, Introduction, xxiii, HRWWS.

51. Human Rights Watch, "Report 1993," Introduction, http://www.hrw.org/
   legacy/worldreport/Intro97.htm#P1_0.

52. Money from the overseas Chinese community continued to pour into
   China even after 1989. For an overview of these trends, see Guotu Zhuang,
   "Trends of Overseas Chinese Business: Network in East Asia As Mirrored
   from Overseas Chinese Investment in Mainland China Since 1978," *Ritsu-
   meikan International Affairs* 4 (2006): 1–23.

53. David C. Gompert, *Right Makes Might: Freedom and Power in the Information Age* (Washington, D.C.: Institute for National Defense, 1998), 24.

54. Human Rights Watch, "Annual Report, 1989," HRWWS.

55. Senator Domenici, *Congressional Record* 146, no. 107 (September 13,
   2000): S 8445.

56. William F. Schulz, *In Our Own Best Interest: How Defending Human
   Rights Benefits Us All* (Boston: Beacon Press, 2001), 103.

57. Harry Wu, "Permanent Normalized Trade Relations with the People's
   Republic of China," *Hearing Before the Committee on Commerce, Science,
   and Transportation*, 106th Cong., 2nd sess., April 11, 2000.

58. Senator Patrick Moynihan, *Congressional Record* 146, no. 106 (September
   12, 2000).

59. Mike Jendrzejczyk, quoted in Steven Teles, "Public Opinion and Interest Groups in the Making of US–China Policy," *The Domestic Sources of US–China Policy*, ed. Robert Ross (Armonk, N.Y.: M. E. Sharpe, 1998).

60. William Schulz, *In Our Own Best Interest*, 65.

61. Ibid., 79–82.

62. As an example of this increasingly prominent tendency, see Lisa Misol, "Human Rights Watch Report," 2006, 41ff, http://www.cfr.org/publica tion/9667/human_rights_watch.html.

63. Minky Worden, Human Rights Watch, "Sleep Well: Nine 'Right' Things to Remember When Investing in Asia," September 19, 2005, HRWWS, http://hrw.org/english/doc/2005/09/13/china11732_txt.htm (accessed January 31, 2006).

64. Aryeh Neier, *Taking Liberties*, 284.

65. July 2002 report to Congress of the U.S.–China Security Review Commission, 42, http://www.uscc.gov/researchpapers/2000_2003/reports/anrp02.htm.

66. Tom Porteous, London director, Human Rights Watch, "Miliband's Moment of Truth," *Guardian Unlimited*, February 24, 2008.

67. The Tibetan Policy Act was part of the Foreign Relations Authorization Act for Fiscal Years 2002 and 2003 (HR 1646).

68. Szu Cheng, "US's New Approach to Hong Kong Politics," *Bauhinia Magazine*, June 2006, and Zach Coleman, "Democracy by Stealth," *The Standard* (Hong Kong), September 4, 2004.

69. Jonathan Spence, *To Change China: Western Advisers in China, 1620–1960* (New York: Penguin Books, 1980), 291, 290.

70. Ibid., 290.

71. Department of State, East Asia and Pacific, *Supporting Human Rights and Democracy: The U.S. Record 2004–2005*, http://www.state.gov/g/drl/rls/shrd/2004/43109.htm.

72. Human Rights in China website, http://china.hrw.org/timeline/2005/dev astating_blows/acknowledgements.

73. Human Rights in China, "Funding the Rule of Law and Civil Society," 2003, no. 3, www.hrichina.org/public/PDFs/CRF.3.2003/funding3.2003.pdf.

74. USAID Budget Justification, 2003, Office of Democracy and Governance, www.usaid.gov/pubs/cbj2003/cent_prog/dcha/dg.html. Also USAID quoted in Human Rights in China, "Funding the Rule of Law and Civil Society."

75. Ibid., 25.

76. Yue Jianyong, "The United States and China in the Age of Globalization," *Chinese Political Science*, July 27, 2003, http://www.uscc.gov/research papers/2004/04_05_12editedusandchinaglobalization.htm.

77. Ru Guangrong, "The Negative Impact of the Internet and Its Solutions,"

The Chinese Defense Science and Technology Information Monthly 121, no. 5 (1998).

78. Aryeh Neier, Human Rights Watch World Report 1989, Introduction, 2, http://www.hrw.org/legacy/reports/1989/WR89/Introduc.htm#TopOf Page.

79. Robin Munro, Asia Watch, *Human Rights in China After Martial Law: Punishment Season* (New York: Human Rights Watch, 1990), 72.

80. Ibid., 72–73, 75.

81. Norris Smith, "Communications Within and with China," in Raymond D. Gastil, *Freedom in the World: Political Rights and Civil Liberties, 1983–1984* (Santa Barbara, Calif.: Greenwood Press, 1984), 292–293.

82. Ibid., 293.

83. Catharin E. Dalpino, *Deferring Democracy* (Washington, D.C.: Brookings Institution Press, 2000). See particularly chapter 4: "Radicals and Radios: The U.S. Response to Authoritarian Regimes."

84. Ibid.

85. NSA, "The USSR and China at the Summit: Common Goals, Enduring Differences, Bureau of Intelligence and Research, DDRS.

86. Bureau of Intelligence Research Report, July 25, 1990, DDRS.

87. Ibid.

88. Ibid.

89. Other funded journals included *The Chinese Intellectual*, *Press Freedom Guardian*, and *The New Era*. There was also funding for numerous institutes: the China Strategic Institute for publications on constitutional reform in China, the Princeton Initiative set up as a center for exiled dissident Chinese intellectuals, the Foundation for China to work for Taiwan's democratic development. The list is a lengthy one. Other grants went for publication of articles and work about Tibet: the Tibet Fund, the International Campaign for Tibet, the Tibet Multimedia Center, the Tibetan Young Buddhist Association, the Political Defiance Committee. Not all these publications have survived; others have emerged. The NED, set amid an overlapping world of foundations and organizations, has been tied to a remarkable number of them.

90. Human Rights Watch states that Human Rights in China is a separate organization, separately incorporated, funded, and staffed. Historically, Human Rights Watch had initially given space to Human Rights in China, Teodor Stan, "Where Are We on Human Rights in China?" An interview with Robert L. Bernstein, *Bard Politik: The Bard Journal of Global Affairs*, vol. 3 (Spring 2003), 22. Reports also have been coauthored. See Human Rights in China/Human Rights Watch/Asia, "China: Whose Security?

State Security in China's New Criminal Code," April 1997, vol. 9, no. 4, http:www.hrw.org/reports/1997/china5.

91. These NED figures, along with a detailed quantitative analysis, are in Eric T. Hale, "A Quantitative and Qualitative Evaluation of the National Endowment of Democracy, 1990–1999" (Ph.D. diss., Louisana State University, 2001), 173–184.

92. Edgar Snow, *Journey to the Beginning* (New York: Vintage, 1972) and *Edgar Snow's China: A Personal Account of the Chinese Revolution*, ed. Lois Wheeler Snow (New York: Random House, 1981).

93. James Lilley, "U.S. Consideration of Permanent Normal Trade Relations with China," *Hearing of the Senate Finance Committee on U.S. Trade with China*, March 23, 2000, 70.

94. Human Rights Watch, "World Report," 2003, China, 97, http://www.hrw .org/legacy/wr2k3/asia4.html.

95. Human Rights Watch, "Nipped in the Bud: Suppression of the China Democracy Party," September 1, 2000, http://www.unhcr.org/refworld/ docid/3ae6a8730.html.

96. Messages from Chairman Wanjun Xie of the Chinese Democracy Party, December 28, 2007, http://www.cdpweb.org/english/.

97. Human Rights Watch, "World Report," 2006, China and Tibet, HRW WS.

98. *Ta Kung Pao* editorial says Human Rights Watch report "repugnant to HK people," September 10, 2004.

99. Spence, *To Change China*, 291–292.

100. T. Kumar, advocacy director for Asia, Amnesty USA, House Committee on International Relations, "Human Rights in China," January 20, 1999.

101. Roberta Cohen, "People's Republic of China," 541.

102. Bill Clinton, "Why I'm Going to China," *Newsweek*, June 1998, http://www .washingtonpost.com/wp-srv/newsweek/why.htm.

103. Ibid.

104. Sharon K. Hom, executive director, Human Rights in China, Carnegie Endowment for International Peace, "Reframing China Policy, U.S. Engagement and Human Rights in China," March 5, 2007, http://www .carnegieendowment.org/files/Hom_paper.pdf.

105. Catharin Dalpino, House Subcommittee on Internal Operations and Human Rights, March 7, 2001, http://www.brook.edu/printmme.ebs?page=/ pagedefs/9333cca490edff3a7a61f2980a14165.xml.

106. Thomas J. Christensen, "China's Role in the World: Is China a Responsible Stakeholder?" U.S.–China Economic and Security Review Commission, August 3, 2006, http://www.nbr.org/publications/asia_policy/AP4/AP4 %20Garrison.pdf.

107. Roberta Cohen, "People's Republic of China," 536.

108. Sharon Horn, "Reframing China Policy."

109. Thomas J. Christensen, "China's Role in the World."

110. Richard Hofstadter, *Anti-Intellectualism in American Life* (New York: Vintage, 1966) and Louis J. Hartz, *The Liberal Tradition in America: An Interpretation of American Political Thought Since the Revolution* (New York: Harcourt, Brace, Jovanovich, 1955) suggest the wide-ranging concerns with America's lack of intellectual sophistication and "maturity."

111. Thomas Friedman, "Deal with China Urged by Bentsen; Treasury Chief Is Conciliatory Toward Beijing on Rights," *New York Times*, March 20, 1994, 20.

112. Jack Belden, *China Shakes the World* (New York: Harper, 1949), 467.

113. Ibid., 498–499.

114. Roberta Cohen, "People's Republic of China, 467.

115. Human Rights Watch, "World Report 2007," 12, HRW WS.

116. Amnesty International, *The 1994 World Report on Human Rights Around the World*, India (London: Hunter House, 1994), 157.

117. Human Rights Watch, *World Report 2006*, China (New York: Human Rights Watch and Seven Stories Press, 2006), 244.

118. Human Rights Watch, "Annual Report, 2009," India, http://www.hrw .org/en/node/79327.

119. Department of State, *India: Country Reports on Human Rights Practices*, March 4, 2002, http://www.state.gov/g/drl/rls/hrrpt/2001/sa/8230.htm.

120. Department of State, *China: Country Reports on Human Rights Practices*, March 6, 2007, http://www.state.gov/g/drl/rls/hrrpt/2006/78771.htm.

121. Department of State, *India: Country Reports on Human Rights Practices*, 2003, http://www.state.gov/g/drl/rls/hrrpt/2003/27947.htm.

122. John Kenneth Knaus, *Orphans of the Cold War: America and the Tibetan Struggle for Survival* (New York: PublicAffairs, 1999).

123. Human Rights Watch, "China-India: Letter to Indian Prime Minister About Upcoming Visit of Chinese President, November 16, 2006, www .hrw.org/ . . . /china-india-letter-indian-prime-minister-about-upcoming-visit-chinese-president.

124. Ibid.

125. Ambassador Sha Zukang, quoted in Hong Kong Wen Wei Po, "Interviews PRC Ambassador on Defeat of US-China Human Rights Resolution," April 17, 2004.

126. WWP interviews PRC ambassador on defeat of US's China Human Rights Resolution, Hong Kong Wen Wei Po in Chinese, April 17, 2004, World News Connection database (henceforth WNC).

127. Yue Jianyong, "The United States and China in the Age of Globalization," *Chinese Political Science* (July 27, 2003), http://www.uscc.gov/research papers/2004/04_05_12editedusandchinaglobalization.htm.

128. Ibid.

129. "Huanqiu Journal Carries Signed Article Criticizing US Human Rights Diplomacy," April 12, 2004, WNC.

130. Zhang Binsen, "China Should Abandon the Foreign Policy of 'taoguang yanghui' ['Bide Our Time, Build Our Capacities'], http://www.uscc.gov/researchpapers/2004/04_03_18taoguangyanghui.htm.

131. Cheng Gang and Xie Xiang, "Results of Public Opinion Poll on Chinese People's Attitudes Towards U.S.," *Renmin Wang*, March 7, 2005.

132. Gao Fuqui, "The Real Purpose of the American March in Central Asia," *Liaowang*, May 10, 2002, WNC.

133. As Yu Sui argues in "Rice's Trip Highlights Central Asia Hot Spots," Liaowang, October 22, 2005, WNC, aid is provided to the local opposition and dressed up in human rights language. Ideological warfare is undertaken using NGOs to act as political vanguards and external funding to assist the process. Local rulers and critics of the United States are "vilified" as corrupt and repressive, creating "de jure" grounds for the opposition to seize power.

134. Yu Sui, "Rice's Trip Highlights Central Asia Hot Spots," *Liaowang*, October 22, 2005, WNC.

135. Xu Jian, "Four Main Trends in Changes in the Asia-Pacific Situation," *Liaowang*, October 24, 2005, WNC.

136. George Kennan, *American Diplomacy* (Chicago: University of Chicago Press, 1952), 82ff.

137. Dong Yunhu, "An Extremely Hypocritical Human Rights Report— Commenting on 'Supporting Human Rights and Democracy: The US Record 2003–2004,'" Xinhua Domestic Service, May 21, 1004, WNC.

138. Information Office of the State Council of the People's Republic of China, "The Human Rights Record of the United States in 2003," http://english.peopledaily.com.cn/200503/03/eng20050303_175406.html.

139. Xinhua, Full text of "Human Rights Record of US in 2007," http://english.cri.cn/3126/2008/03/13/1321@333402.htm.

140. "A criticism of the views of Bourgeois International Law on the question of population," quoted in *The Chinese Human Rights Reader*, 242. And Shu Yun, "Who Are the True Defenders of Human Rights?" *People's Daily*, July 7, 1989. See also Xinhua, "Human Rights Record of US," WNC.

141. Aryeh Neier quoting Human Rights Watch, in Aryeh Neier, "Asia's Unacceptable Double Standard," *Foreign Policy* (Fall 1993): 45.

142. Human Rights Watch, *World Report, 2001* (New York: Human Rights Watch, 2000), xix, HRWWS.

143. China Society for Human Rights Studies, "China: Human Rights in Name, Swaying Power in Reality," *1997 Human Rights Report of the US State Department*, March 2, 1998, WNC.

144. Zhao Qizheng, director-general of the State Council Information Office (SCIO), "Different Views Between China and the West on Human Rights," November 24, 2003, http://au.china-embassy.org/eng/xw/t45640.htm.

145. Ni Lexiong, "The Sino-U.S. Relation and Its Structural Clash," *The Global Time* (huanqiu), http://www.uscc.gov/researchpapers/2004/04_03_18rela tionstructuralclash.htm.

146. J. William Fulbright, *The Price of Empire* (New York: Pantheon, 1989), 33.

147. China Society for Human Rights Studies, "China: Human Rights in Name, Swaying Power in Reality."

148. "No Foreign or Indigenous Dogmatism—China Should Have Its Own Definition of 'Democracy,'" *Ta Kung Pao*, September 11, 2002. An awareness of the unreasonable and unfair world order doesn't mean China can't use it for its own ends. "Although unreasonable and unfair by nature, [it does] present certain easy 'benefits' and 'advantages,' including providing the 'benefit of an easy ride' for China. We should not repel and reject everything outright." Wang Yizhou, "Multi-polarity Does Not Equal an Anti-US Position," *The Global Times*, Beijing, Summer 1999, WNC.

149. *Wen Wei Po* interviews PRC ambassador on defeat of US's China Human Rights Resolution, in Chinese, April 17, 2004, WNC.

150. Zhao Qizheng, director-general of the State Council Information Office, "Different Views Between China and the West on Human Rights," November 24, 2003, http://au.china-embassy.org/eng/xw/t45640.htm.

151. *Wen Wei Po* editorial on "US Voted Off UN Human Rights Commission," May 5, 2001, WNC.

152. Human Rights reports of the US, 2006, p. 8.

153. Lawyers Committee for Human Rights, *Critique: Review of the U.S. Department of State's Country Reports on Human Rights Practices for 1995* (Charlottesville: University of Virginia Press, 1996), 27.

154. Xinhua, "US Human Rights," in English, March 1, 1999, WNC.

155. Ibid.

156. Xinhua, "China, United States: US Human Rights Record Attacked," March 4, 1997, WNC.

157. Henry Steele Commager, *Commanger on Tocqueville* (Columbia: University of Missouri Press, 1993), 96.

158. Dong Yunhu, Xinhua, "Inclusion of Human Rights in the Constitution," March 14, 2004, WNC.

159. Ibid.

160. Dong Yunhu, Xinhua, "PRC Official Urges Respecting 'Different Modes' of Human Rights Development," November 22, 2006, WNC.

161. Liu Nanlai, "Developing Countries and Human Rights, *Renquann de pubianxing he techusing*," in *The Chinese Human Rights Reader: Documents and Commentary 1900–2000*, ed. Stephne C. Angle and Marina Svensson (Armonk, N.Y.: M. E. Sharpe, 2001), 398–399.

CHAPTER 5: POST-REAGAN: HUMANITARIANISM
AMID THE RUINS

1. Strobe Talbott, *The Russian Hand: A Memoir of Presidential Diplomacy* (New York: Random House, 2002), 134.

2. Anthony Lake, "From Containment to Enlargement," September 21, 1993, http://www.mtholyoke.edu/acad/intrel/lakedoc.html.

3. USAID, "Foreign Aid in the National Interest: Promoting Freedom, Security, and Opportunity," 1, www.usaid.gov/ . . . /Full_Report–Foreign _Aid_in_the_National_Interest.pdf.

4. Ibid.

5. Anthony Lake, *Six Nightmares: Real Threats in a Dangerous World and How America Can Meet Them* (Boston: Little, Brown, 2000), xv.

6. Amnesty International, *1994 Report on Human Rights Around the World* (Alameda, Calif.: Hunter House, 1994), 13.

7. Rand Corporation Report, *U.S. and Russian Policymaking with Respect to the Use of* Force, eds. Jeremy R. Azrael and Emil A. Payin, Introduction, 1996, http://www.rand.org/pubs/conf_proceedings/CF129/CF-129.intro duction.html.

8. Zbigniew Brzezinski, *Out of Control: Global Turmoil on the Eve of the Twenty-First Century* (New York: Scribner's, 1993), 183.

9. Ibid., 115.

10. Zbigniew Brzezinski, "Hostility to America Has Never Been So Great," *New Perspectives Quarterly* (Summer 2004): 7.

11. John C. Gannon, NIC chairman: "The CIA in the New World Order," February 1, 2000, https://www.cia.gov/news-information/speeches-testi mony/2000/dci_speech_020200smithson.html.

12. Ibid., 71. "Despite the potential benefits of globalization and technological change," concludes a World Bank evaluation, "world poverty has increased and growth prospects have dimmed for developing countries

during the 1980s and 1990s." Nagy Hanna, *1999 Annual Review of Development Effectiveness* (ARDE), *OED* Working Paper Series, no. 11, Summer 2000. Also, CIA, "Global Trend 2015," 31.

13. John C. Gannon, "The CIA in the New World Order."

14. Ibid. and Zbigniew Brzezinski, *Out of Control*, 191.

15. John C. Gannon, "The CIA in the New World Order."

16. NIC, "Global Trends, 2020," 33.

17. Ibid., 29.

18. Samantha Power, "Force Full," *New Republic*, March 3, 2003, 28.

19. National Intelligence Council, "Mapping the Global Future," report of the National Intelligence Council's 2020 Project, December 2004, 104.

20. See Department of State, "Description of the Coordinator for Reconstruction and Stabilization," http://www.state,gov/s/crs/c12936.htm.

21. "The Failed States Index," *Foreign Policy* (July/August 2005): "About 2 billion people live in countries that are in danger of collapse. In the first annual Failed States Index, FOREIGN POLICY and the Fund for Peace rank the countries about to go over the brink," http://www.ncpa.org/sub/dpd/index.php?Article_ID=1934.

22. State Failure Task Force, "Phase II Findings," July 31, 1998, ix, www.wilson center.org/events/docs/Phase2.pdf.

23. Samuel Berger and Brent Scowcroft, *In the Wake of War: Improving U.S. Post-Conflict Capabilities* (New York: Council on Foreign Relations, 2005), www.cfr.org/publication/8438/in_the_wake_of_war.html.

24. USAID, "Strategic Framework for Africa," February 24, 2006, 7, http://pdf .usaid.gov/pdf_docs/PDACG573.pdf.

25. CIA analyses also point to the increased pressure "on behalf of humanitarian responses" from "the dominance of the democratic states," heightened public awareness, the shifts with the ending of the Cold War, and growing NGO pressures." CIA, "Global Humanitarian Emergencies: Trends and Projections, 1999–2000, August 1, 1999. CIA website (accessed June 3, 2007).

26. Reed Brody, "Right Side Up: Reflections on the Last Twenty-Five Years of the Human Rights Movement," *Human Rights Watch World Report, 2004*, http://www.hrw.org/legacy/wr2k4/17.htm.

27. Ibid.

28. Quoted in "Preventative Diplomacy: Revitalizing A.I.D. and Foreign Assistance for the Post-Cold War Era," *The New USAID Background Package*, July 1994, 26.

29. Reed Brody, "Right Side Up."

30. Ibid.

31. Irene Khan, *The Unheard Truth* (New York: W. W. Norton, 2009), 118.

32. Reed Brody, "Right Side Up."

33. Irene Khan, *The Unheard Truth*, 119.

34. Ibid., 113.

35. Jack Donnelley, quoted in David Chandler, *From Kosovo to Kabul: Human Rights and International Intervention* (London: Pluto Press, 2002), 5.

36. Micheline R. Ishay, *The History of Human Rights: From Ancient Times to the Globalization Era* (Berkeley: University of California Press, 2004), 2.

37. Lynne H. Henderson, "The Wrongs of Victim's Rights," *Stanford Law Review* 37, no. 4 (April 1985): 948.

38. Michael Ignatieff, *The Warriors Honor: War and the Modern Conscience* (New York: Henry Holt, 1998), 23.

39. Wendy Brown, "The Most We Can Hope For: Human Rights and the Politics of Fatalism," *South Atlantic Quarterly* 103, no. 2/3 (2004): 453.

40. Reed Brody, "Right Side Up."

41. USAID, "Foreign Aid in the National Interest."

42. USAID, "Mitigating and Managing Conflict," http://www.usaid.gov/fani/overview/overview_mitigatingconflict.htm.

43. USAID, "Mitigating and Managing Conflict," 109.

44. USAID, "Field Presence and Agency Reorganization: A Bibliography 1975–Present," October 21, 2001, pdf.dec.org/pdf_docs/PNACN399.pdf.

45. USAID Global Development Alliance, "Predecessor Inventory Activity, 1990–Present," October 1, 2001, pdf.usaid.gov/pdf_docs/PNACN852.pdf.

46. USAID, *Providing Humanitarian Aid*, Chapter 5, 120, http://www.usaid.gov/fani/Chapter_5–Foreign_Aid_in_the_National_Interest.pdf.

47. USAID, *Providing Humanitarian Aid*, Chapter 5, 121.

48. David Chandler, "The Road to Military Humanitarianism," *Human Rights Quarterly* 23, no. 3 (2001).

49. USAID, *Providing Humanitarian Aid*, Chapter 5, 118.

50. Benenson quoted in Stephen Hopgood, *Keepers of the Flame: Understanding Amnesty International* (Ithaca, N.Y.: Cornell University Press, 2006), 24.

51. USAID, *Providing Humanitarian Aid*, Chapter 5.

52. Ibid.

53. For a notable exception, see Holly Burkhalter, "Transcript of Seminar Three," Bard College, December 16, 1999, http://hrp.bard.edu/resource_pdfs/hhrs.burkhalter.pdf.

54. Human Rights Watch, *Human Rights World Report*, Introduction, 2000.

55. Rony Brauman and Joelle Tanguy, "The Médecins Sans Frontières Experience," quoted in Kimberly Salomé Greenberg, "Médecins Sans Frontières," *Concord Review* 13, no. 2 (2002): 58.

56. "MSF Principles and Identity: The Challenge Ahead," *International Activity Report 2005*, www.doctorswithoutborders.org/publications/ar/report_print.cfm.

57. Jean-Herve Bradol, "Challenges to Humanitarian Action: The Impact of Political and Military Responses to International Crises," March 31, 2004, www.msf.org/msfinternational/invoke.cfm?component=article&objectid=12A05194-12B4-4403 . . . method–full_html-61k.

58. Jean-Herve Bradol, "In the Shadow of Just Wars," March 31, 2004.

59. Nicolas de Torrenté, MSF-United States, "Not So Benign: When Lofty Political Goals Have Bad Humanitarian Consequences," 2003, www.doctorswithoutborders.org/publications/ar/report_print.cfm?id=3296.

60. "MSF Principles and Identity: The Challenge Ahead," *International Activity Report 2005*, www.doctorswithoutborders.org/publications/ar/report_print.cfm.

61. Ibid.

62. Fabrice Weissman, "Humanitarian Action and Military Intervention: Temptations and Possibilities," *Disasters* 28, no. 2 (2004): 210.

63. Ibid., 208, 211.

64. Nicolas de Torrenté, "Not so Benign," www.doctorswithoutborders.org/publications/ar/report_print.cfm?id=3296.

65. Jean-Herve Bradol, "In Support of Competition-Based Access to Medicines," *Le Monde*, February 28, 2007.

66. Nomination of Warren M. Christopher to be Secretary of State, Senate Committee on Foreign Relations, January 13, 1993, p.24.

67. Morton Halperin, October 1994, quoted by Ralph McGehee, http://www.serendipity.li/cia/ciabase/ciabase_report_1.htm.

68. Council on Foreign Relations, *Threats to Democracy: Prevention and Response*, TaskForce Report (Madeleine K. Albright, chair), November 2002, 16–17, http://www.cfr.org/publication/5180/threats_to_democracy.html.

69. USAID, "Democracy and Governance," November 1991, http://www.usaid.gov/policy/ads/200/demgov/demogov.pdf and *After the Transition: Problems of Newly Democratizing Countries*, ed. Tracy L. Brandt (Washington, D.C.: National Academy Press, 1992).

70. *After the Transition*, ed. Tracey L. Brandt, 5.

71. Jonah Gindin, *In the Name of Democracy: Towards a Global Political Intervention Monitor*, http://inthenameofdemocracy.org/?q=node/3 (accessed February 7, 2005).

72. Department of State, *Country Reports on Human Rights Practices for 1999* (Washington, D.C.: GPO, 1999).

73. Human Rights Watch, "World Report 1995," xiv.

74. "Women in Development: AID's Experience 1973–1985," Program Evaluation Report vol. 1, no. 18, http://www.eric.ed.gov:80/ERICDocs/data/eric docs2sql/content_storage_01/0000019b/80/13/a2/27.pdf.

75. Human Rights Watch, "World Report 1994," xii.

76. USAID, "Program and Operations Assessment Report," no. 29, "Linking Democracy and Development: An Idea for the Times," June 2001. Also USAID, "Democracy and Governance: A Conceptual Framework," November 1998.

77. Human Rights Watch, "Annual Report 1994," Introduction (New York: Human Rights Watch, 1993), xvii.

78. Human Rights Watch, "World Report 1992," 29.

79. USAID, "Foreign Aid in the National Interest: Promoting Freedom, Security, and Opportunity," 7.

80. USAID, "Program and Operations Assessment Report," no. 12, February 1996, http://usaidgov/pubs/usaid_eval/ascil/pnabs534.txt.

81. USAID, "Democracy and Governance," November 1991, http://www.usaid .gov/policy/ads/200/demgov/demogov.pdf and *After the Transition: Problems of Newly Democratizing Countries*, ed. Tracy L. Brandt (Washington, D.C.: National Academy Press 1992). Also USAID, "Democracy and Governance," 15.

82. Department of State, *Country Reports on Human Rights Practices for 1999* (Washington, D.C.: GPO, 1999).

83. Ibid.

84. USAID, "Program and Operations Assessment Report," no. 12, February 1996, http://usaidgov/pubs/usaid_eval/ascil/pnabs534.txt.

85. Ibid., www.usaid.gov/pubs/usaid_eval/html_docs/enews81.htm

86. USAID, "Evaluations News," vol. 8, no. 1, 1996, 5 of 16, and USAID, "Program and Operations Assessment Report," no. 12, February 1996, 35 of 38. USAID, "Policy Implementation: What USAID Has Learned," January 2001, http://www.usaid.gov/our_work/democracy_and_governance/publi cations/pdfs/pnach306.pdf.

87. USAID, "Policy Implementation: What USAID Has Learned," January 2001.

88. Ibid., 15.

89. USAID, "Foreign Aid in the National Interest," 48.

90. USAID, "Promoting Democratic Governance," 51, http://www.usaid.gov/ fani/Chapter_1–Foreign_Aid_in_the_National_Interest.pdf.

91. USAID, Operations Assessment, no. 12, 34 of 38.

92. USAID, "Summary of Mechanisms for PVO-NGO," December 13, 2004, 5.
93. USAID, "Program and Operations Assessment Report," no. 12, February 1996.
94. USIAD, "Participation Forum," no. 18, April 25, 1996. Topic: Engaging Civil Society and Governments on the Greater Horn of Africa.
95. Department of State, Bureau of Democracy, Human Rights, and Labor, "Guiding Principles on Non-governmental Organizations," December 14, 2006, http://www.state.gov/g/drl/rls/shrd/2006/82643.htm.
96. USAID, Center for Democracy and Governance, "Role of Media in Democracy," June 1999, 1.
97. Ibid., 18.
98. Appendix B, Assessment Tools, in USAID, "The Role of Media in Democracy: A Strategic Approach," June 1999.
99. USAID, "Role of Media in Democracy," 1.
100. Ibid., 18.
101. Ibid.
102. Ibid. 7.
103. David Kennedy, *Dark Sides of Virtue: Reassessing International Humanitarianism* (Princeton, N.J.: Princeton University Press, 2004), 155.
104. Ibid., 106.
105. Ibid., 159–160.
106. William F. Schulz, *In Our Own Best Interest*, 81.
107. Human Rights Watch, "World Report 2001," Introduction, xvi.
108. Lisa Misol, "Private Companies and the Public Interest: Why Corporations Should Welcome Global Human Rights Rules," 2006, 41, 45, HRW WS. Also see Human Rights Watch, "World Report 1996," xxii.
109. Human Rights Watch, "World Report 1996," xxiii.
110. Lisa Misol, "Private Companies and the Public Interest," 51.
111. William F. Schulz, *In Our Own Best Interest*, 66.
112. Department of State, *Country Reports on Human Rights Practices for 1999* (Washington, D.C.: GPO, 1999).
113. David Lewis, "Interview with Michael Edwards on the Future of NGOs," Fall 1998, www.globalpolicy.org/ngos/intro/general/1998/edwards.htm.
114. Quoted in Julia E. Seidler, *Exporting Democracy Without Citizens: Goals and Practices of American Agencies Providing Journalism Assistance Programs in the Ukraine* (Ph.D. diss., University of Iowa, 2001), 156.
115. Soros quoted in Julia E. Seidler, *Exporting Democracy Without Citizens*, 156.

116. Connie Bruck, "The World According to Soros," *New Yorker*, January 23, 1995, 70.

117. Ibid., 57.

118. Michael Dobbs, "U.S. Advice Guided Milosevic Opposition Political Consultants Helped Yugoslav Opposition Topple Authoritarian Leader," *Washington Post*, December 11, 2000, A1.

119. Ibid.

120. For a participant view, see Sarah E. Mendelson, "When Democracy Promotion Works," *International Trade* 26, no. 2 (Summer 2004), http://hir.harvard.edu/index.php?page=article&id=1277.

121. Matt Kelley, "U.S. Money Has Helped Opposition in Ukraine," *San Diego Union-Tribune*, December 11, 2004, http://www.signonsandiego.com/uniontrib/20041211/news_1n11usaid.html.

122. USAID, "Rising Democracy: Grassroots Revolutions," September 2005, http://www.usaid.gov/our_work/democracy_and_governance/publications/pdfs/democracy_rising.pdf.

123. Ibid.

124. USAID, "Policy Implementation, What USAID Has Learned," January 2001, 4, http://www.usaid.gov/our_work/democracy_and_governance/publications/pdfs/pnach306.pdf.

125. Ibid.

126. Human Rights Watch, "World Report 2006," Introduction, 7.

127. Human Rights Watch Briefing Paper, "Managing Civil Society: Are NGO's Next," November 22, 2005, www.hrw.org/backgrounder/eca/russia1105.

128. Anthony Lake, *Six Nightmares: Real Threats in a Dangerous World and How America Can Meet Them* (Boston: Little Brown, 2000), 219.

129. David Rieff, *At the Point of a Gun: Democratic Dreams and Armed Intervention* (New York: Simon & Schuster, 2005), 116.

130. Human Rights Watch, "World Report 1998," Africa, 10.

131. Mahmood Mamdani, "Amnesty or Impunity? A Preliminary Critique of the Report of the Truth and Reconciliation Commission of South Africa (TRC)," *Diacritics* 32, no. 3–4 (2002): 33–59. See Mbeki's response for the ANC response, "Statement on the Report of the TRC Joint Sitting of the Houses of Parliament," February 15, 1999, http://www.anc.org.za/ancocs/history/mbeki/1999/tm0225.html, and Human Rights Watch's response urging Mbeki to "accept that the ANC had committed grave human rights abuses and that the justness of the ANC's cause could not serve to justify these abuses." "Decision to Deny ANC Leaders Amnesty Applauded," March 4, 1999, http://hrw.org/english/docs/1999/03/04/safric832_txt.htm.

132. Mahmood Mamdani, "Amnesty or Impunity?" 33–59. Also see Mbeki's response for the ANC response, "Statement on the Report of the TRC Joint Sitting of the Houses of Parliament," February 15, 1999, http://www.anc.org.za/ancocs/history/mbeki/1999/tm0225.html.

133. Morton E. Winston, "Assessing the Effectiveness of International Human Rights NGO's," in *NGOs and Human Rights: Promise and Performance*, ed. Claude E. Welch (Philadelphia: University of Pennsylvania Press, 2001), 33.

134. Aryeh Neier, *Taking Liberties* (New York: PublicAffairs, 2003), 335.

135. The following acts, when committed willfully and if they cause death or serious injury to body and health constitute grave breaches: making the civilian population or individual civilians the object of attack; launching an indiscriminate attack affecting the civilian population or civilian objects in the knowledge that such attack will cause excessive loss of life, injury to civilians, or damage to civilian objects, launching an attack against works or installations containing dangerous forces in the knowledge that such an attack will cause excessive loss of life, injury to civilians, or damage to civilian objects; making nondefended localities and demilitarized zones the object of attack; making a person the object of an attack in the knowledge that he is *hors de combat*, and depriving a person protected by the conventions or by Protocol 1 of the rights of a fair and regular trial. *Truth and Reconciliation Commission of South Africa Report*, sect. 5, chap. 3, "Holding the ANC Accountable," 651.

136. Jeremy Cronin, "Tutu's Report Tells the Truth, But Not the Whole Truth," *Sunday Independent*, November 1998, http://hrp.bard.edu/resources.

137. Ibid.

138. USAID, "Project grant agreement between the Republic of Rwanda and the United States of America for Democratic Initiative and Governance Project (DIG)," September 18, 1992. USAID Rwanda study, "Democratic Initiative and Governance," Project identification and document outline, April 1992, USAID website Rwanda file, no. 681; USAID Aid Mission to Rwanda, "Country Program Strategic Plan for Rwanda: Demographic, Political, and Economic Transition to the 21st Century," May 1992; USAID Bureau for Africa, "US Agency for International Development, Africa region: Compendium—Assessment of Program Impact Reports for Fiscal Year 1991," June 1992; USAID, "Project Grant Agreement Between the Republic of Rwanda and the United States of America for Democratic Initiative and Governance Project (DIG)," September 1992.

139. For example, Gerard Prunier, *The Rwanda Crisis: History of a Genocide* (New York: Columbia University Press, 1995); Gerard Prunier, *Africa's*

World War: Congo, the Rwandan Genocide, and the Making of a Conti-nental Catastrophe (New York; Oxford University Press, 2009); Mahmood Mamdani, *When Victims Become Killers: Colonialism, Nativism, and the Genocide in Rwanda* (Princeton, N.J.: Princeton University Press, 2002).

140. Gerard Prunier, *Africa's World War.*

141. As various observers have noted, the divide between Hutus and Tutsis was not nearly so sharply drawn; many Hutus who had worked with Tutsis were killed as well. See Mahmood Mamdani, *When Victims Become Killers: Colonialism, Nativism, and the Genocide in Rwanda.* In the 1990s the word "genocide" was applied only to the Hutus and not to the actions of the RPF's invading force from Uganda. In August 2010, however, a 600-page UN report raised the question of whether "crimes against humanity, war crimes, or even genocide" had been committed by the U.S.-backed Kagame regime against fleeing Rwandans and Congolese Hutus. See Chris McGreal, "Leaked UN Report Accuses Rwanda of Possible Genocide in Congo," *The Guardian*, August 26, 2010, 1, and Howard W. French, "U.N. Report on Congo Killings Questions Genocide Account," *New York Times*, August 28, 2010, A1.

142. USAID Rwanda study, ii. Also, USAID, "Project Grant Agreement Between the Republic of Rwanda and the United States of America."

143. USAID Mission to Rwanda, "Democratic Initiatives and Governance," September 18, 1992, i.

144. Ibid.

145. Ibid, ii. Also USAID, "Project Grant Agreement Between the Republic of Rwanda and the United States of America."

146. The panel was chaired by Sir Ketumile Masire (former president of Botswana), with Amadou Toumani Toure (former head of state of Mali) serving as vice chair. The other members of the panel were P. N. Bhagwati (former chief justice of the supreme court of India); Hocine Djoudi (former Algerian ambassador to France); Ellen Johnson-Sirleaf (former Liberian government minister); Stephen Lewis (former ambassador and permanent representative of Canada to the UN); and Lisbet Palme (Chairperson of the Swedish Committee for UNICEF, Expert on the UN Committee on the Rights of the Child).

147. Organization of Africa Unity, *Rwanda: The Preventable Genocide*, 4.21, www.africa-union.org/Official_documents/ . . . /Report_rowanda_genocide.pdf.

148. USAID, "Project Grant Agreement Between the Republic of Rwanda and the United States of America," 4.

149. Ibid., 11.

150. Ibid., 6.

151. Human Rights Watch, "World Report 1994," Africa, http://www.hrw .org/reports/1994/WR94/Africa.htm#PO-O (accessed June 18, 2007).

152. Alison Liebhafsky Des Forges, *Leave None to Tell the Story: Genocide in Rwanda, 1999*, p. 47, http://www.hrw.org/legacy/reports/1999/rwanda/.

153. Gerard Prunier, *Africa's World War: Congo, the Rwandan Genocide, and the Making of a Continental Catastrophe* (New York: Oxford, 2009), xxxvi.

154. Organization of Africa Unity, *Rwanda: The Preventable Genocide*, 4.22.

155. Ibid., 5.21.

156. Ibid., 10.4.

157. Ibid., 7.29.

158. Bill Sutherland, *Guns and Gandhi in Africa: Pan-African Insights on Nonviolence, Armed Struggle and Liberation* (Trenton, N.J.: Africa World Press, 2000), 74.

159. Alex De Waal, "Human Rights Organizations and the Political Imagination: How the West and Africa Have Diverged," *Journal of Human Rights* 2, no. 4 (December 2003); 484.

160. Ibid.

161. Issa G. Shivji, "Contradictory Developments in the Teaching and Practice of Human Rights Laws in Tanzania," *Journal of African Law* 35, no. 1–2 (1991): 116–127.

162. Thomas Carothers, "Civil Society," http://www.strom.clemson.edu/becker/ prtm320/Carothers.html.

163. Some CIA reports suggest the agency was well aware that the Tutsi invasion from Uganda would weaken the regime of President Habyarimana, lead to rising ethnic tensions as his power weakened, and likely result in "large-scale reprisals against Tutsis." Walter Barrows, NIO for Africa, http://www.foia.cia.gov to Deputy Director, CIA (accessed June 28, 2007).

164. Samantha Power, *A Problem from Hell: America and the Age of Genocide* (New York: Harper Perennial, 2007).

165. Samantha Powers, testimony, "Rwanda's Genocide Looking Back," *Hearing Before the Subcommittee on Africa*, April 22, 2004, 108th Cong., 2nd sess., 27.

166. Samantha Power, *A Problem from Hell*, 364.

167. Organization of Africa Unity, *Rwanda: The Preventable Genocide*, 5.8.

168. Ibid., 11.9.

169. Ibid., 12.22.

170. Ibid., 12.23.

171. Ibid., 12.28.

172. Stephen Kinzer, "France's Role in the Rwandan genocide," *Boston Globe*, August 14, 2008.

173. Quoting Mitterand in Republique Du Rwanda, *Commission Nationale Independante Chargée de Rassembler les Preuves Montrant l'Implication de l'Etat Français Dans le Genocide Perpetre au Rwanda en 1994,* November 15, 2007, 30.

174. Ibid., 32, 30. Then again, the accusations of a French judicial magistrate against President Kagame and key leaders of the RPF for their involvement in the assassination of President Habyarimana, the immediate spark for the genocide, aren't likely to go too far either. No ICC is likely to wade into these waters.

175. Prunier, *Africa's World War*, 19.

176. As Mamdani writes, various factors were in play: the failure of cease-fire discussions, "a reckless internal opposition," a "naïve RDF," and the donor community that "force-fed Rwanda a reform agenda out of a textbook without regard to the situation on the ground and secure in the knowledge that they would not have to suffer the consequences of their actions," an immunity that "bred a reckless irresponsibility." Mahmood Mamdani, *When Victims Become Killers,* 203, 214.

177. Prunier, *Africa's World War*, 15–16.

178. Prunier, *Africa's World War*, 20.

179. Mahmood Mamdani, "The Politics of Naming: Genocide, Civil War, Insurgency," *London Review of Books*, March 8, 2007, http://www.lrb.co.uk/v29/n05/mamd01_.html. Also, Mike Hume, *London Times*, April 7, 2004: "Paul Kagame, the Rwandan President, has accused France of helping to prepare the genocide by supporting the Hutu-dominated regime. Rather less is said about American and British support for the other side in Rwanda's civil war—Kagame's Tutsi-led Rwandan Popular Front. The RPF was based in and backed by neighbouring Uganda, the main Anglo-American proxy in the region. Rwandan rebels in the Ugandan military received training from the British. Kagame attended a US army and staff college in Kansas."

180. At least this offers a plausible explanation for the RPF opposing it.

181. Afterward the military/intelligence links with Kagame were quite public and close. See Lynne Duke, "U.S. Faces Surprise, Dilemma in Africa," *Washington Post*, July 14, 1998, A1. Also Gerard Prunier, *Africa's World War.*

182. Tom Malinowski, House Committee on International Relations, *United States Support of Human Rights and Democracy Hearing Before the Sub-*

committee on International Terrorism, Nonproliferation, and Human rights, 108th Cong., 2nd sess., July 7, 2004, http://commdocs.house.gov/committees/intlrel/hfa94707.000/hfa94707_0f.htm.

183. See David Kennedy, *Dark Sides of Virtue*, 169–198.

184. Edward S. Herman and David Peterson, "The Dismantling of Yugoslavia: A Study of Inhumanitarian Intervention (and a Western Liberal-Left Intellectual and Moral Collapse)," *Monthly Review* (October 2007).

185. Human Rights Watch, "World Report 1989," Yugoslavia, http://www.hrw.org/legacy/reports/1989/WR89/Yugoslav.htm#TopOfPage.

186. Human Rights Watch, "Yugoslavia: Human Rights Developments, 1992," 6, http://www.hrw.org/reports/1992/WE92/HSW-08.htm#P995_282970 (accessed June 8, 2007).

187. Ibid., 1.

188. Jeri Laber and Kenneth Anderson, *New York Times*, November 10, 1990, 23, an editorial noted as an op-ed by Helsinki Watch in Human Rights Watch, "World Report 1989," Yugoslavia, 1990, http://www.hrw.org/reports/1990/WR90/HELSINKI.BOU-05.htm#P714_157941 (accessed June 8, 2007).

189. Robert Hayden, "Don't Turn Yugoslavia into Europe's Lebanon," letter, *New York Times*, December 3, 1990, A18.

190. Warren Zimmerman, "The Last Ambassador: A Memoir of the Collapse of Yugoslavia," *Foreign Affairs* (March/April 1995): 13.

191. Richard Holbrooke, "America: A European Power," *Foreign Affairs* (March/April 1995).

192. Aryeh Neier, "The Attack on Human Rights," *New York Review of Books*, November 2, 2006, http://www.nybooks.com/articles/19500.

193. Alex de Waal, "Reflections on the Difficulties of Defining Darfur's Crisis as Genocide," *Harvard Human Rights Journal* 20:25–33.

194. Kenneth Burke, *A Grammar of Motives* (Berkeley: University of California Press, 1969).

195. Norman G. Finkelstein, *The Holocaust Industry: Reflections on the Exploitation of Jewish Suffering* (London: Verso, 2000), 12.

196. Alan E. Steinweis, "The Auschwitz Analogy: Holocaust Memory and American Debates over Intervention in Bosnia and Kosovo in the 1990s," *Holocaust and Genocide Studies* 19, no. 2 (2005): 276–451.

197. International Court of Justice, Judgment, February 26, 2007, Application of the Convention on the Prevention and Punishment of the Crime of Genocide (*Bosnia and Herzegovina v. Serbia and Montenegro*), 131, 71, 25, 72, 124, http://www.icj-cij.org/docket/files/91/13685.pdf.

198. Ibid.
199. Helsinki Watch, *War Crimes in Bosnia–Herzegovina*, vol. 2 (New York: Helsinki Watch, 1993), 2.
200. The much-invoked CIA report, *Sanitized Bosnia: Serb Ethnic Cleansing*, January 5, 1995, FOIA, was among the strongest arguments for the primacy of Serb responsibility for ethnic cleansing in Bosnia. The report begins quoting Human Rights Watch reports, and concludes that some 90 percent of the displacement had been carried out by Serb forces. The word "genocide" was not used. The public attention to the leaked (and possibly written to be leaked) memo was notable for its not being compared to others that questioned its figures.
201. Aryeh Neier, *War Crimes: Brutality, Genocide, Terror, and the Struggle for Justice* (New York: Times Books, 1998), 186.
202. Ibid., 202.
203. Congressman James Moran, *Genocide in Bosnia–Herzeghovina, A Hearing Before the Commission on Security and Cooperation in Europe*, Washington, D.C. April 4, 1995, http://www.fas.org/irp/congress/1995_hr/genoci deinbosnia.html.
204. Congressman Christopher Smith, ibid.
205. Quoted by David Binder and Walter R. Roberts, "The Only Good Serb Is a . . ." *Mediterranean Quarterly* (Summer 1998): 34.
206. Harold D. Lasswell, *Propaganda Technique in the World War* (New York: Peter Smith, 1927).
207. J. C. H. Blom et al., *Srebrenica: Reconstruction, Background, Consequences and Analyses of the Fall of a Safe Area*, NIOD Report, published on behalf of the Dutch government, April 10, 2002, http://srebrenica.bright side.nl/srebrenica.
208. Ibid., "Epilogue," point 1.
209. Ibid., point 11 text.
210. Ibid.
211. Human Rights Watch, "World Report 1994," Bosnia–Herzeghovina, http://www.unhcr.org/refworld/type,ANNUALREPORT,HRW,BIH ,467fca8ab,0.html.
212. Irene Kahn, *The Unheard Truth*, 82.
213. *Human Rights Dialogue* 2, no. 5 (Winter 2001): 21.
214. See Neier, *Taking Liberties*, 351–353.
215. For example, Human Rights Watch, "Prosecute Now!" (August 1993).
216. Kenneth Roth, "The Case for Universal Jurisdiction," *Foreign Affairs* (September 10, 2001).

217. Kirsten Sellars, *The Rise and Rise of Human Rights* (Thrupp, UK: Sutton, 2002), 179.

218. David J. Scheffer, "International Judicial Intervention," *Foreign Policy*, no. 102 (Spring 1996): 51.

219. Michael Mandel, *How America Gets Away with Murder: Illegal Wars, Collateral Damage and Crimes Against Humanity* (London: Pluto Press, 2004); Edward Herman, "The Politics of the Srebrenica Massacre," *Z Magazine*, July 7, 2005, http://www.zcommunications.org/the-politics-of-the-srebrenica-massacre-by-edward-herman.

220. "Amnesty International Accuses NATO of Illegal Bombing Raid," *Baltimore Sun*, June 8, 2000, http://articles.baltimoresun.com/2000-06-08/news/0006080149_1_nato-civilian-casualties-amnesty-international/2.

221. Eric A. Heinze, "The Rhetoric of Genocide in U.S. Foreign Policy: Rwanda and Darfur Compared," *Political Science Quarterly* 122, no. 3 (2007): 359–383.

222. Richard Holbrook quoted in Deborah Murphy, "Narrating Darfur: Darfur in the U.S. Press," in *War and Peace in Darfur*, ed. Alex de Waal (Cambridge, Mass.: Global Equity Initiative, 2007), 319.

223. The response to Darfur also marks the culmination of a decade of increasing evangelical involvement in human rights. For this aspect of the story, see Allen D. Hertzke, *Freeing God's Children: The Unlikely Alliance for Global Human Rights* (Lanham, Md.: Rowman and Littlefield, 2004).

224. Kenneth Roth, "Justice for Tyrant," *Washington Post*, November 26, 1998, A31.

225. When the U.S. Holocaust Memorial Museum, the official U.S. government memorial to the Holocaust, declared a genocide emergency for Darfur in 2004, their website offered a pathbreaking user-friendly way to understand the ongoing atrocities:

> "Now you can witness the destruction in Darfur via Google Earth. Zoom down and see what a burned village looks like from above, the vast tent cities of people displaced from their homes, and photographs on the ground of refugees struggling to survive. Read eyewitness testimony of atrocities in attacked villages. Visualize what genocide looks like today in Darfur. Learn more about the layers." Ushmm + Google Earth, "Genocide Emergency: Darfur, http://www.ushmm.org/google earth, (accessed June 16, 2007). Darfur was the museum's first major effort in its web-based "Genocide Prevention Mapping Initiative," a massive collaborative project between the museum and Google to build

an interactive "global crisis map" to share and understand information quickly, to "see the situation" of genocides when they are developing. Of course, there are no such mapping sites on U.S.-funded government institutions about Iraq—such as the U.S. Institute of Peace website. Ushmm + Google Earth, "Genocide Emergency: Darfur," http://www. ushmm.org/googleearth (accessed June 16, 2007).

226. Mahmood Mamdani, "The Politics of Naming: Genocide, Civil War, Insurgency," *London Review of Books*, March 8, 2007, http://www.lrb.co. uk/v29/n05/mamd01_.html. Also, see Mahmood Mamdani, *Saviors and Survivors: Darfur, Politics, and the War on Terror* (New York: Doubleday Religion, 2010).

227. Colin Powell, Senate Foreign Relations Committee, *The Crisis in Darfur*, September 9, 2004, http://geneva.usmission.gov/press2004/0910Crisisin Darfur.htm. Also see Eric A. Heinze, "The Rhetoric of Genocide in U.S. Foreign Policy: Rwanda and Darfur Compared," *Political Science Quarterly* 122, no. 3 (2007): 359–383.

228. MSF Challenges U.S. Darfur Genocide Claim, October 4, 2004, quoted from "US 'Hyping' Darfur Genocide Fears," *The Observer* (London), October 2004, 3.

229. Associated Press, "Obama: Don't Stay in Iraq over Genocide," July 20, 2007, http://www.msnbc.msn.com/id/19862711/.

230. "Genocide is the most serious of international crimes: this proposition is undisputed." It is the "crime of crimes," stated the International Criminal Tribunal for Rwanda (ICTR). See Richard May and Marieke Wierda, "Is There a Hierarchy of Crimes in International Law," in *Man's Inhumanity to Man*, ed. Antonio Cassese and Lal Chand Vohrah (The Hague: Martinus Nijhoff, 2003), 513.

231. Human Rights Watch, "War Crimes in Bosnia–Herzegovina," vol. 2, 2.

232. Michael Mandel, *How America Gets Away with Murder*, 6.

233. Aryeh Neier, letter, *New York Review of Books*, November 2, 2006, vol. 53, no. 17.

234. Kenneth Roth quoted by Aryeh Neier, ibid.

235. Quoted by Noam Chomsky, "War on Terror," Amnesty International Annual Lecture Hosted by Trinity College, January 18, 2006, http://www .chomsky.info/talks/20060118.pdf.

236. Ronald Reagan, Speech to B'nai B'rith, September 6, 1984, http://www .jewishvirtuallibrary.org/jsource/US-Israel/RR9_6_84.html.

237. *Foreign Aid in the National Interest*, chap. 5, "Looking Ahead," http:// www.usaid.gov/fani/ch05/lookingahead03.htm.

238. National Security Strategy, March 2006, http://georgewbush-whitehouse.archives.gov/nsc/nss/2006/.

239. Congressman Steny Hoyer, quoted in Mark Ivor Satin, *Radical Middle: The Politics We Now Need* (New York: Basic Books, 2004), 153.

240. Kenneth Roth and Ruth Wedgwood, "Is America's Withdrawal from the New International Criminal Court Justified?" *World Link* 15, no. 4 (July/August 2002).

CHAPTER 6: TERRORISM AND THE PATHOLOGY
OF AMERICAN POWER

1. Associated Press, The President's News Conference with Prime Minister Junichiro Koizumi of Japan, Tokyo, Japan, February 18, 2002.

2. See Frank Bruni, "Bush and His Presidency Are Transformed," *New York Times*, September, 22, 2001, B2.

3. http://georgewbush-whitehouse.archives.gov/news/releases/2005/08/20050813.html

4. George W. Bush, "Global War on Terror: National Strategy for Combating Terrorism," *Vital Speeches* 72, no. 24 (September 15, 2006).

5. Remarks by the President at the United States Air Force Academy Graduation Ceremony, United States Air Force Academy, June 2, 2004, APP.

6. Ibid.

7. George W. Bush, Address to the Joint Session of Congress, September 20, 2001, in "National Strategy for Combating Terrorism 2003," 29.

8. National Security Council, "Strengthen Alliances to Defeat Global Terrorism and Work to Prevent Attacks Against Us and Our Friends," http://georgewbush-whitehouse.archives.gov/nsc/nss/2006/sectionIII.html

9. Department of State, "National Strategy for Combating Terrorism," February 2003, www.state.gov/documents/organization/60172.pdf.

10. Remarks by the President at the United States Air Force Academy Graduation Ceremony, United States Air Force Academy, June 2, 2004, APP.

11. Harry S. Truman, special message to the Congress on Greece and Turkey: "The Truman Doctrine," March 12, 1947, APP.

12. Dwight D. Eisenhower, Address at the Columbia University National Bicentennial Dinner, New York City, May 31, 1954, APP.

13. Lyndon B. Johnson, Remarks in Atlantic City at the Convention of the American Association of School Administrators, February 16, 1966, APP.

14. Ronald Reagan, Remarks following discussions with Prime Minister Shimon Peres of Israel, October 17, 1985, APP.

15. Peter J. Katzenstein, "Same War, Different Views: Germany, Japan, and Counterterrorism," *International Organization* 57, no. 4 (Autumn 2003): 734.

16. Kuala Lumpur Declaration on International Terrorism, April 1–2, 2002, http://www.oic-oci.org/english/conf/fm/11_extraordinary/declaration.htm.

17. Benjamin Netanyahu, Preface in *International Terrorism: Challenge and Response*, ed. Benjamin Netanyahu (New Brunswick, N.J.: Transaction, 1981), 1.

18. Kofi Annan, UN radio, March 11, 2005.

19. http://georgewbush-whitehouse.archives.gov/nsc/nss/2002/nss3.html.

20. National Strategy for Combating Terrorism, February 2003, www.state.gov/documents/organization/60172.pdf.

21. Paul Hoffman, "Human Rights and Terrorism," *Human Rights Quarterly* 26, no. 4 (2004).

22. Kenneth Roth, "Human Rights and the Campaign Against Terrorism," Carnegie Council, March 14, 2002, interview with Joanne J. Meyers, http://www.cceia.org/resources/transcripts/109.html.

23. Human Rights Watch, "World Report 2005," 6.

24. Human Rights Watch, "World Report 2006," 2.

25. Human Rights Watch, "World Report 2003," xxxii.

26. Kenneth Roth, "Constitutional Democracy Colloquium," *Dissent*, no. 43 (Fall 2004): 14.

27. President Bush Graduation Speech at West Point, June 1, 2002, APP.

28. Paul Johnson, "The Seven Deadly Sins of Terrorism," in *International Terrorism*, ed. Benjamin Netanyahu (New Brunswick, N.J.: Transaction, 1981), 15.

29. Lord Chalfont, "Opening Remarks: Terrorism and the Gulag," in ibid., 328.

30. Benzion Netanyahu, "Introduction," in ibid., 5.

31. Ibid.

32. William P. Barr, Senate Committee on the Judiciary, "Targeting Innocent Civilians," November 28, 2001.

33. Human Rights Watch, *Cluster Munitions and the Proportionality Test*, Memorandum to Delegates of the Convention on Conventional Weapons, April 7, 2008, Human Rights Watch website (hereafter HRWWS).

34. Michael Mandel, *How America Gets Away with Murder* (London: Pluto Press, 2004).

35. Major General George J. Keegan, Jr., "The Myth and the Reality of the PLO," in *International Terrorism,* ed. Benjamin Netanyahu (New Brunswick, N.J.: Transaction, 1981), 340.

36. Benzion Netanyahu, "Opening Session: The Face of Terrorism," in ibid., 5.

37. Benjamin Netanyahu, *Terrorism: How the West Can Win* (New York: Farrar, Straus and Giroux, 1986), 5, 36.

38. Paul Johnson, "The Seven Deadly Sins of Terrorism," 12.

39. Kenneth Roth, "Misplaced Priorities: Human Rights and the Campaign Against Terrorism," *Harvard International Review* (Fall 2002).

40. Kenneth Roth, *Philanthropy News Digest*, Foundation Service (June 16, 2003), http://foundationcenter.org/pnd/newsmakers/nwsmkr.jhtml?id=36500031.

41. Kenneth Roth, "Walk the Freedom Talk, Mr. Bush," *The Globe and Mail*, November 26, 2003, A21.

42. Kenneth Roth, "A Dangerous Security," *World Link* 15, no. 1 (January–February 2002): 43.

43. Human Rights Watch, "World Report 2003," xxv.

44. Ambassador Henry A. Crumpton, Coordinator for Counterterrorism, testimony, Senate Foreign Relations Committee, June 13, 2006, p. 26.

45. Senator John Danforth, "Terrorism versus Democracy," *International Terrorism: Challenge and Response* (New Brunswick, N.J.: Transaction, 1981), 117.

46. Ibid.

47. James Baldwin, *The Price of the Ticket* (New York: Macmillan, 1985), 213.

48. Robert Fisk quoted in Michael Mandel, *How America Gets Away with Murder*, 47.

49. Mandel, *How America Gets Away with Murder*, 51.

50. Ibid.

51. Ben Saul, "Two Justifications of Terrorism: A Moral Legal Response," *Foreign Policy in Focus*, January 10, 2006, http://www.fpif.org/pdf/papers/0601justifications.pdf.

52. Kate Gilmore, Amnesty International, "'The War Against Terrorism': A Human Rights Perspective," http://asiapacific.amnesty.org/pages/ec_briefings_fora_terror.

53. Ibid.

54. See Noam Chomsky, *Failed States: The Abuse of Power and the Assault on Democracy* (New York: Metropolitan Books, 2006); Noam Chomsky, *Rogue States* (Boston: South End Press, 2000); and Noam Chomsky, "The United States Is a Leading Terrorist State," interview with David Barsamian, *Monthly Review* 53, no. 6 (November 2001).

55. Edward Peck, *Democracy Now*, July 28, 2006, http://www.democracynow.org/2006/7/28/national_exclusive_hezbollah_leader_hassan_nasrallah.

56. For example, Noam Chomsky, "International Terrorism: Image and Reality," in *Western State Terrorism*, ed. Alexander George (London: Routledge, 1991).

57. Kenneth Roth, "A Dangerous Security," *World Link* 15, no. 1 (January–February 2002).

58. BBC Editorial Guidelines, "Terrorism, Use of Language When Reporting," http://www.bbc.co.uk/guidelines/editorialguidelines/advice/terrorism language/ourapproach.shtml.

59. Ibid.

60. Norman Solomon quoting Reuters, "Media Spin Revolves Around the Word 'Terrorist,'" October 5, 2001, http://www.commondreams.org/views01/1005-02.htm.

61. George W. Bush, "Remarks to the UNITY: Journalists of Color Convention," August 6, 2004, http://www.presidency.ucsb.edu/ws/index.php?pid =63453&st=We+actually+misnamed+the+war+on+terror&st1=. See also Dana Milbank, "Reprising a War with Words," *Washington Post*, August 17, 2004, A13, www.washingtonpost.com/wp-dyn/articles/A6375-2004Aug16 .html.

62. Such debates continued throughout the Bush administration. See Mike Nizza, "Thoughts on Tweaking the 'War on Terror' Message," *New York Times*, May 29, 2008. "Words matter," a Homeland Security memo argued in calling for a shift in language. "The terminology the [U.S. government] uses should convey the magnitude of the threat we face, but also avoid inflating the religious bases and glamorous appeal of the extremists' ideology." Perhaps, then, instead of speaking of a "war on terror," use "a global struggle for security and progress"—an admittedly less mobilizing phrase. CNN, "Agency Urges Caution with Terrorist Language," May 30, 2008, http://www.cnn.com/2008/US/05/30/terrorist.terms/index.html.

63. Michael Ignatieff, *The Lesser Evil: Political Ethics in an Age of Terror* (Princeton, N.J.: Princeton University Press, 2005), 83.

64. CIA, "National Strategy for Combating Terrorism, February 2003, p. 6, https://www.cia.gov/news-information/cia-the-war-on terrorism/Counter_ Terrorism_Strategy.pdf.

65. Robert L. Hutchings, Chairman, National Intelligence Council, "Terrorism and Economic Security," International Security Management Association, Scottsdale, Arizona, January 14, 2004, http://www.dni.gov/nic/ speeches_terror_and_econ_sec.html.

66. General Richard Meyers, Chairman, Joint Chiefs of Staff, "The U.S. Military: A Global View of Peace and Security in the 21st Century," *U.S. For-*

eign Policy Agenda 7 (December 2002): 14, http://www.ciaonet.org/olj/fpa/fpa_dec02_myers.pdf.

67. Ibid., 15.

68. Ibid.

69. Robert L. Hutchings, Chair, NIC, "The World After Iraq," April 8, 2003, www.nti.org/e_research/official_docs/cia/cia040803.pdf.

70. Dr. Condoleezza Rice, "A Balance of Power That Favors Freedom," October 1, 2002, http://www.manhattan-institute.org/html/wl2002.htm.

71. Robert L. Hutchings, NIC, "The World After Iraq," April 8, 2003, http://www.nti.org/e_research/official_docs/cia/cia040803.pdf.

72. George W. Bush, Address to the Joint Session of Congress, September 20, 2001, in "National Strategy for Combating Terrorism," February 2003, p. 2, www.state.gov/documents/organization/60172.pdf.

73. Dr. Condoleezza Rice, "A Balance of Power That Favors Freedom."

74. Robert L. Hutchings, Chairman, National Intelligence Council, "Terrorism and Economic Security."

75. Jerrold M. Post, former CIA official, exemplifies such analyses. See *The Mind of the Terrorist: The Psychology of Terrorism from the IRA to Al-Qaeda* (New York: Palgrave Macmillan, 2007).

76. Robert A. Pape, *Dying to Win: The Strategic Logic of Suicide Terrorism* (New York: Random House, 2005), 23.

77. Zbigniew Brzezinski, "Confronting Anti-American Grievances," *New York Times*, September 1, 2002, C9.

78. Kenneth Roth, "Walk the Freedom Talk, Mr. Bush," *Globe and Mail* (Toronto), November 26, 2003, A21.

79. Jerrold M. Post, *The Mind of the Terrorist*, 163, 166.

80. Human Rights Watch, "World Report 2006," 8.

81. Kenneth Roth, "Darfur and Abu Ghraib," *Human Rights World Report*, (2005): 11.

82. Human Rights Watch, "World Report 2006," 8.

83. Human Rights Watch Backgrounder, "Human Rights in Saudi Arabia: A Deafening Silence," December 2001, p. 2.

84. Joseph T. Siegle and Morton H. Halperin, "Bush's Rhetoric Battles with His Policies, *International Herald Tribune*, February 8, 2005, http://www.soros.org/initiatives/washington/articles_publications/articles/halperin_20050209.

85. Department of Defense, *Report of the Defense Science Board Task Force on Strategic Communications*, September 2004, pp. 43, 35, http://www.acq.osd.mil/dsb/reports/2004-09-Strategic_Communication.pdf.

86. Ibid., 43.

87. Ibid.

88. Ibid., 36.

89. Robert L. Hutchings, National Intelligence Council, "The Sources of Terrorist Conduct," March 19, 2004, http://www.dni.gov/nic/speeches_terror_and_econ_sec.html.

90. Ibid., 36.

91. Council on Foreign Relations, *In Support of Arab Democracy: How and Why*, 2005, http://www.cfr.org/content/publications/ . . . /Arab_Democracy_TF.pdf.

92. Kenneth Roth, *Philanthropy News Digest* (June 16, 2003): 11, http://foundationcenter.org/pnd/newsmakers/nwsmkr.jhtml?id=36500031.

93. Advisory Group on Public Diplomacy for the Arab and Muslim World, "Changing Minds, Winning Peace: A New Strategic Direction of U.S. Public Diplomacy in the Arab and Muslim World," 53–54, http://www.state.gov/documents/organization/24936.pdf.

94. Ibid., 53.

95. Angel Rabasa, Cerryl Nenard, Lowell H. Schwartz, Peter Sickle, *Building Moderate Muslim Networks* (Santa Monica, Calif.: RAND, 2007), iii.

96. Ibid., 51.

97. Department of Defense, *Report of the Defense Science Board Task Force on Strategic Communications*, September 2004, 56.

98. Ibid., 52.

99. Angel Rabasa et al., *Building Moderate Muslim Networks*, 3, http://www.rand.org/pubs/monographs/2007/RAND_MG574.pdf.

100. Ibid., xii.

101. Ibid., xx.

102. Department of Defense, *Report of the Defense Science Board Task Force*, September 2004, 53

103. Ibid., 20. This is the argument also made by Joseph S. Nye Jr., "The Information Revolution and American Soft Power," *Asia-Pacific Review* 9, no. 1 (2002): 69.

104. Angel Rabasa et al., "Building Moderate Muslim Networks," xxi.

105. Ibid., 69.

106. European Court of Human Rights, *Case of Refah Partisis (the Welfare Party) and others v. Turkey*, February 13, 2003. Also Naz K. Modirzadeh, "Taking Islamic Law Seriously: INGOs and the Battle for Muslim Hearts and Minds," *Harvard Journal of Human Rights* 19 (Spring 2006).

107. Kathleen Peratis, "Turn to Sharia to Promote Human Rights in Muslim Countries," September 29, 2006, http://www.forward.com/articles/4794/.

Also see Jean-Paul Marthoz and Joseph Saunders, "Religion and the Human Rights Movement," Human Rights Watch, "World Report 2005," HRWWS.

108. Laura Bush, Radio Address, November 17, 2001, APP. Also see Carol A. Staible, "Unveiling Imperialism: Media, Gender, and the War on Afghanistan," *Media, Culture, and Society* 27, no. 5 (2005): 765.

109. John L. Esposito and Dalia Mogahcd, *Who Speaks for Islam: What a Billion Muslims Really Think* (New York: Gallup Press, 2007), 80.

110. Ibid., 107.

111. As Olivier Roy notes, "Isolating the issue of women's rights, as if women were also some sort of specific and separate group (it is difficult to speak in terms of minority here), is also a problem: how is one to address the 'Islamist' women? The point is not that we need to 'know better' in order to avoid mistakes; it is that we should not use concepts and models that may create more problems than solutions." Roy, "The Predicament of 'Civil Society' in Central Asia and the 'Greater Middle East,'"*International Affairs*, no. 5 (2005): 1011.

112. Iain Levin, Human Rights Watch, "NGOs in a Changing World Order: Dilemmas and Challenges," ICVA Conference, Geneva, February 14–15, 2003, http://www.icva.ch/doc00000934.html.

113. Human Rights Watch, "World Report 2003."

114. Council on Foreign Relations, "Afghanistan: Are We Losing the Peace?" June 2003, http://www.cfr.org/content/publications/attachments/Afghanistan_TF.pdf.

115. Ibid.

116. Sam Zarifi, Human Rights Watch, September 27, 2006, http://www.rferl.org/content/article/1143726.html.

117. Human Rights Watch, press release, "Afghanistan: Bush, Karzai, Musharraf Must Act Now to Stop Militant Abuses," September 26, 2006, http://www.hrw.org/en/node/90282/section/7.

118. Sam Zarifi, "Losing the Peace in Afghanistan," in Human Rights Watch, "World Report 2004," 1, http://hrw.org/wr2k4/5.htm#_Toc58744954.

119. Kenneth Roth, *Philanthropy News Digest* (June 16, 2003), http://foundationcenter.org/pnd/newsmakers/nwsmkr.jhtml?id=36500031.

120. Department of Defense, *Transition to and from Hostilities*, December 2004, iii, http://www.acq.osd.mil/dsb/reports/2004-12-DSB_SS_Report_Final.pdf.

121. Kenneth Roth, *Philanthropy News Digest*, http://foundationcenter.org/pnd/newsmakers/nwsmkr.jhtml?id=36500031, p. 8.

122. Sam Zarifi, "Losing the Peace in Afghanistan," 2–3.

123. Ibid., 3, 12.

124. MSF, Interview with Jean-Herve Bradol, "Humanitarian Action and Political Action—Don't Confuse the Two," May 22, 2007, http://www.doc torswithoutborders.org/publications/article.cfm?id=2054&cat=ideas -opinions.

125. Human Rights Watch, "The Human Cost: The Consequences of Insurgent Attacks in Afghanistan," 2007, http://www/hrw.org/reports/2007/ afghanistan0407/1a.htm.

126. Marian Rawi, "Betrayal," *Third World Traveler*, January–February 2004, http://www.thirdworldtraveler.com/Women/Betrayal_Afghan_Women .html.

127. Malalai Joya, "No Nation Can Liberate Another," November 3, 2009, http://socialistworker.org/2009/11/03/no-nation-can-liberate-another. Also Malalai Joya, *A Woman Among Warlords: The Extraordinary Story of an Afghan Who Dared to Raise Her Voice* (New York: Scribner's, 2009).

128. Amnesty International, *Afghanistan: No More Empty Promises in Paris*, June 11, 2008, ASA 11/007/2008.

129. "Iraqi Insurgents Take a Page from the Afghan 'Freedom Fighters,'" *New York Times*, November 9, 2003, WK7.

130. Human Rights Watch, "World Report 2003," Afghanistan, https://199.173 .149.140/wr2k3/asia1.html.

131. Strategic Communication and Public Diplomacy Policy Coordinating Committee, *U.S. National Strategy for Public Diplomacy and Strategic Communication*, December 14, 2006, 21, http://uscpublicdiplomacy.org/ pdfs/stratcommo_plan_070531.pdf.

132. George W. Bush, "Global War on Terror: National Strategy for Combating Terrorism," *Vital Speeches* 72, no. 24 (September 15, 2006): 3.

133. *Human Rights Watch Letter to President Barack Obama on Afghanistan*, March 26, 2009, http://www.hrw.org/en/news/2009/03/26/human-rights -watch-letter-president-barack-obama-afghanistan.

134. Ibid.

135. Amnesty International, "NATO Afghanistan Summit: Crucial Moment for Human Rights," April 3, 2009, http://www.amnesty.org.uk/news_ details.asp?NewsID=18143.

136. Michael Scheuer, "Six Questions for Michael Scheuer on National Security," *Harper's Magazine*, August 23, 2006, http://www.harpers.org/ archive/2006/08/sb-seven-michaelscheuer-1156277744.

137. Legal specialists argue that U.S. conduct was governed principally by the Geneva Conventions and the Hague Regulations. See Mary Ellen O'Connell, "The Occupation of Iraq: What International Law Requires

Now," Jurist Legal Intelligence Forum, April 17, 2003, http://jurist.law
.pitt.edu/forum/forumnew107.php#3.

138. L. F. L. Oppenheim, *International Law*, 1940, p. 218, cited by Ben Clarke,
"The Rules of Permissible Use of Force by Resistors in Occupied Iraq,"
November 5, 2004, http://www.islamonline.net/english/In_Depth/Iraq_
Aftermath/2004/05/article_05.shtml.

139. Human Rights Watch, "The War in Iraq and International Humanitarian Law: Frequently Asked Questions on Occupation," May 16, 2003,
http://www.hrw.org/legacy/campaigns/iraq/ihlfaqoccupation.htm.

140. Joe Stork and Fred Abrahams, "Sidelined: Human Rights in Postwar
Iraq," Human Rights World Watch, "World Report 2004," http://www
.hrw.org/legacy/wr2k4/6.htm (accessed October 10, 2009).

141. Ibid.

142. Kenneth Roth, *Philanthropy News Digest*.

143. Human Rights Watch, "Iraq: Coalition Ignored Warnings on Weapons
Stocks," October 29, 2004, http://hrw.org/english/docs/2004/10/29/Iraq
9575_txt.htm.

144. Kenneth Roth, "The Right Exit: What Are the Responsibilities of an Occupying Power in Its Withdrawal," March 15, 2004, http://hrw.org/English/
docs/2004/03/15/iraq11517_txt.htm (accessed December 7, 2007).

145. Testimony of Tom Malinowski, Senate Committee on Foreign Relations,
*Extraordinary Rendition, Extraordinary Detention, and Treatment of
Detainees: Restoring Our Moral Credibility and Strengthening Our Diplomatic Standing*, July 26, 2007, http://hrw.org/english/docs/2007/07/
06usint16514_txt.htm (accessed October 11, 2007).

146. Amnesty International, "Iraq, in Cold Blood: Abuses by Armed Groups,"
July 24, 2005, http://www.amnesty.org/en/library/info/MDE14/009/2005
(accessed December 8, 2007).

147. Human Rights Watch, "The War in Iraq and International Humanitarian Law: Frequently Asked Questions," April 7, 2003, http://www/hrw
.org/campaign/iraq/ihfaq.htm.

148. "US Pentagon Should Probe Civilian Deaths," letter to Donald Rumsfeld,
June 17, 2004.

149. Human Rights Watch, "Off Target: The Conduct of the War and Civilian
Casualties in Iraq," December 2003, http://www.hrw.org/reports/2003/
usa1203/3/htm#_Toc57442226.

150. Ibid.

151. Human Rights Watch, "Iraq: Insurgent Groups Responsible for War
Crimes: Report Challenges Justifications for Attacks on Civilians," October 3, 2005, http://hrw.org/english/docs/2005/1-/03/iraq11804_txt.htm.

152. Human Rights Watch, "Iraq: Insurgent Groups Responsible for War Crimes."

153. Amnesty International, "Iraq, In Cold Blood: Abuses by Armed Groups," July 24, 2005, http://www.amnesty.org/en/library/info/MDE14/009/2005.

154. James Baldwin, "Negroes Are Anti-Semitic Because They're Anti-White," *New York Times*, April 9, 1967.

155. Quoted by Michael Mandel, *How America Gets Away with Murder*, 47.

156. Human Rights Watch, "Erased in a Moment: Suicide Bombing Attacks Against Israeli Civilians," October 2002, http://www.hrw.org/legacy/reports/2002/isrl-pa/.

157. Ibid., 17.

158. Ibid., 53.

159. Ibid., 17, 37, 3.

160. Amnesty International, "Enduring Occupation: Palestinians Under Siege in the West Bank," June 2007, 4, http://static.amnesty.org/resources/Israel_Report0706.

161. Ibid., 57.

162. Human Rights Watch, "Israel, the Occupied West Bank and Gaza Strip, and Palestinian Authority Territories," May 2002, http://www.hrw.org/legacy/reports/2002/israel3/ (accessed March 15, 2009).

163. Thomas Friedman, "Suicidal Lies," *New York Times*, March 31, 2002.

164. John Duggard, "Human Rights Situation in Palestine and the Other Occupied Arab Territories," UN Human Rights Council, 7th sess., http://www.scribd.com/doc/4430320/Human-Rights-Situation-in-Palestine-and-Other-Occupied-Arab-Territories (accessed January 21, 2008).

165. It might also explore the techniques to destroy nonviolent resistance to the occupation and the "overall violence with which Israeli forces met this nonviolent resistance." See "Faces of Hope, Palestinian Nonviolent Resistance to Occupation Since 1967," AFSC Middle East Resources Series, Fall 2005, http://www.afsc.org/israel-palestine/ht/a/GetDocumentAction/i/44960.

166. Human rights reports offer descriptions of Israeli violations of occupation and humanitarian law in the ways they repress both nonviolent and violent Palestinian resistance. Occasionally, Amnesty leaders have criticized the presumption that the Palestinian struggle is mainly violent, pointing to a history of nonviolent resistance that goes back decades. (See Edith Garwood, Amnesty USA, "Public Remarks Ignore Palestinian Nonviolence Movement's Roots," January 29, 2010, Amnesty USA website.) But little sense of collective struggle emerges in these documents or how it might be waged. For an example of some of the early nonviolent efforts, see Noam Chomsky, "Scenes from the Uprising," *Z Magazine*,

July 1988. For regular reporting on Palestinian nonviolent resistance efforts, see *The Palestine Monitor*, http://palestinemonitor.org/spip/.

167. Robert Fisk, *The Great War for Civilization: The Conflict in the Middle East* (New York: Vintage, 2007), 480.

168. Report of the Independent Panel for the BBC Governors on Impartiality of BBC Coverage on the Israeli-Palestinian Conflict, April 2006, 7, http://www.bbcgovernorsarchive.co.uk/docs/reviews/israelipalestiniangover nors_statement.pdf.

169. Madeleine Albright, UN Security Council Official Records, 3351st meeting, March 18, 1994, UN Doc. S/PV.335 (1994), 12.

170. Human Rights Watch, "Israel's 'Separation Barrier' in the Occupied West Bank: Human Rights and International Humanitarian Law Consequences," a briefing paper, February 2004, http://hrw.org/english/docs/2004/02/20isrlpa7581_txt.htm.

171. Amnesty International, "Israel and the Occupied Territories," 5. Also, Human Rights Watch, "Torture and Ill Treatment: Israel's Interrogation of Palestinians from the Occupied Territories," 1994.

172. Jimmy Carter, *Palestine: Peace Not Apartheid* (New York: Simon & Schuster, 2007), 216.

173. "Colonialization of Palestine Precludes Peace," March 13, 2006, http://www.cartercenter.org/news/documents/doc2320.html.

174. Morton E. Winston, "Assessing the Effectiveness of International Human Rights NGOs," in *NGOs and Human Rights: Promise and Performance*, ed. Claude E. Welch (Philadelphia: University of Pennsylvania Press, 2001), 33.

175. Amnesty International, "Israel and the Occupied Territories: Demolition and Dispossession: The Destruction of Palestinian Homes Amnesty," September 17, 2001, 14, http://www.amnesty.no/web.nsf/pages/28C795B 26ABAEFACC1256ACA003BBA96.

176. Ibid., 13.

177. Ibid.

178. Amnesty International, "Without Distinction—Attacks on Civilians by Palestinian Armed Groups," July 10, 2002, 4, http://www.amnesty.org/en/library/info/MDE02/003/2002.

179. Human Rights Council, *Human Rights in Palestine and Other Occupied Arab Territories: Report of the United Nations Fact-Finding Mission on the Gaza Conflict*, September 15, 2009, para. 269.

180. Ibid., para. 75.

181. Ibid., para. 1675.

182. Orna Ben-Naftali, Aeyal M. Gross, and Keren Michaeli, "Illegal Occupation:

Framing the Occupied Palestinian Territory," *Berkeley Journal of International Law* 23 (2005).

183. Saman Zarifi, Research Director of Asia Watch, *Human Rights Situation in Nepal, Testimony Before the Senate Foreign Relations Committee*, May 17, 2005. Also Human Rights Watch, "Nepal: Years of Terror, Then Broken Promises," October 15, 2009, http://www.hrw.org/en/news/ . . . / nepal-years-terror-then-broken-promises.

184. For example, Human Rights Watch, "'Being Neutral is Our Biggest Crime:' Government, Vigilante, and Naxalite Abuses in India's Chhattisgarh State," July 2008, 5, http://www.hrw.org/en/node/62132/section/6.

185. Arundathi Roy interview, "It's Outright War and Both Sides Are Choosing Their Weapons," March 27, 2007, http://naxalnaxalitemaoist.wordpress.com/category/arundhati-roy/.

186. Department of State, *Annual Report to Congress on Terrorism*, 2008, http://www.state.gov/documents/organization/45323.pdf.

187. For example, Human Rights Watch, "Being Neutral is Our Biggest Crime."

188. Arundathi Roy, ibid. For a thoughtful elaboration of these issues see Arundathi Roy, *Field Notes on Democracy: Listening to Grasshoppers* (Chicago: Haymarket Books, 2009).

189. Ian Birchall, "Sartre and Terror," *Sartre Studies International* 11, nos. 1, 2 (2005), 257–258.

190. Human Rights Watch, "World Report 2006," 2.

191. Human Rights Watch, "World Report 2007."

192. Kenneth Roth, "Getting Away with Torture," *Global Governance: A Review of Multilateralism and International Organizations* 11, no. 3 (July 2005): 389.

193. Irene Khan, Amnesty International, Foreword, "Annual Report 2005," http://www.amnesty.org/en/library/info/POL10/014/2005.

194. William Schulz, Remarks at Welcoming Plenary, 2003, Amnesty USA website.

195. Testimony of Tom Malinowski, Senate Committee on Foreign Relations, "Extraordinary Rendition, Extraordinary Detention, and Treatment of Detainees: Restoring Our Moral Credibility and Strengthening Our Diplomatic Standing," July 26, 2007, http://hrw.org/english/docs/2007/07/06usint16514_txt.htm.

196. Human Rights Watch, "World Report 2006," 12.

197. Testimony of Tom Malinowski, "Extraordinary Rendition," http://hrw.org/english/docs/2007/07/06usint16514_txt.htm (accessed October 11, 2007).

198. Human Rights Watch, "Getting Away with Torture? Command Responsibility for the U.S. Abuse of Detainees, April 2005, http://www.hrw.org/reports/2005/us0405/6.htm#_ftnref111.

199. Ibid.

200. See Human Rights Watch, "U.S. State Department Criticism of 'Stress and Duress' Interrogation Around the World," April 2003.

201. Human Rights Watch, "Getting Away with Torture?" http://www.hrw.org/reports/2005/us0405/6.htm#_ftnref111. See also Human Rights Watch, "U.S. State Department Criticism of 'Stress and Duress' Interrogation."

202. Human Rights Watch, "Getting Away with Torture?" 9.

203. Ibid., 82.

204. Amy Goodman, *Democracy Now*, April 25, 2005, http://www.democracynow.org.

205. "You call for a special prosecutor to investigate George Tenet, former director of the CIA, and Donald Rumsfeld, Defense Secretary," Amy Goodman asked Reed Brody. "Why do you stop there? Why don't you move up the chain of command from Cheney to Bush?" To which the answer: "Well, let's see what happens. . . . I think a special prosecutor could ultimately also look at the culpability of the President." Amy Goodman, *Democracy Now*, April 25, 2006. Discussion with Reed Brody, Special Counsel, Human Rights Watch, http://www.democracynow.org/print.pl?sid=05/04/25/1342206 (accessed October 6, 2007).

206. Amnesty USA executive director William Schultz called "on foreign governments to uphold their obligations under international law by investigating all senior U.S. officials involved in the torture scandal." The list included such officials as Donald Rumsfeld, but on Bush the phrasing is parsed: "we would be remiss if we ignored President George W. Bush's role in the scandal." Cheney is not mentioned. "Annual Report," May 25, 2005, http://www.amnestyusa.org/annualreport/statement.html.

207. Harold Hongju Koh, "Can the President Be Torturer in Chief?" May 2006, https://secure.acslaw.org/files/Microsoft%20Word%20-%202_Koh.pdf.

208. Amnesty International, "United States of America: Five Years on the 'Dark Side': A Look Back at 'War on Terror' Detentions," December 13, 2006, AI index: AMR51/195/2006.

209. Ibid., 2.

210. Amnesty International, "United States of America, Human Dignity Denied, Torture and Accountability in the 'War on Terror,'" 39/142.

211. Ibid.

212. Robert L. Breisner, *Twelve Against Empire: The Anti-Imperialists, 1898–1990* (Chicago: University of Chicago Press, 1968), 154.

213. Amnesty International, "United States of America, Human Dignity Denied," 316.

214. Ibid.

215. Ibid.

216. Amnesty International, "USA: Flouting World Trends, Violating International Standards," March 1, 2001.

217. AI Index: AMR 51/166/99, October 13, 1999.

218. Amnesty International, "United States of America: Race, Rights and Police Brutality."

219. Amnesty International, "United States of America, Human Dignity Denied."

220. Human Rights Watch launched their own reports on police and prison conditions in the United States, expanding into a number of issues such as women's rights. Yet unlike Amnesty, they tend to set these problems in a less historical and cultural setting.

221. Amnesty International, "United States of America, Human Dignity Denied."

222. Amnesty International, "United States of America: Human Dignity Denied," http://www.amnesty.org/en/library/info/AMR51/145/2004.

223. Ibid.

224. Amnesty USA, "Europe Silent on Renditions," October 2007, http://www .amnestyusa.org/document.php?id=ENGNWS210092007&lang=e. Also see "Europe in 'State of Denial' over role in US rendition and secret detention," June 26, 2008, http://www.ammado.com/nonprofit/843/arti cles/2291.

225. USAID, "Victims of Torture Fund: Portfolio Synopsis 2005–2006," http:// pdf.usaid.gov/pdf_docs/pdach032.pdf.

226. Human Rights Watch, "World Report 2008": "Human rights are a system of law; treaties and jurisprudence, provision and precedent. . . . its construction seems one of the major works of the twentieth century. . . . Only slowly did human rights principles harden into law, and assume the expectation that they would protect, not just critique . . . to codify what was known; to set out a common understanding developed over three decades," http://hrw.org/wr2k8/yogyakarta/index/htm. For a critique of the belief that such legalization constitutes a restraint, and more generally, on the failure of human rights law to make a difference where it is most needed, see Emile M. Hafner-Burton and Kiyoteru Tsutsui, "Preventing Human Rights Abuse," *Journal of Peace Research* 44 (July 2007): 407–425.

227. Joost R. Hiltermann, A *Poisonous Affair: America, Iraq, and the Gassing of Halabja* (Cambridge: Cambridge University Press, 2007).

228. "The little action taken by the new administration on accountability for past human rights violations has cemented the impunity nurtured in the past, for at least some of the perpetrators. Further change is urgently needed," said Amnesty International in "Mixed Messages, Counter terror and Human Rights—President Obama's first 100 Days," http://www .amnesty.org/en/library/asset/AMR51/043/2009/en/b5ea3f7f-1955-40c0-b5bb-108492f902f3/amr510432009en.pdf. Human Rights Watch said much the same in its "Report Card on President Obama's First 100 Days," April 24, 2009.

229. Human Rights Watch, "Q&A: Reed Brody on the Road to Abu Ghraib," July 8, 2004, http://www.hrw.org/en/news/2004/07/07/qa-reed-brody-road-abu-ghraib.

230. Ibid.

231. Laurence R. Helfer, "Over Legalizing Human Rights: International Relations Theory and the Commonwealth Caribbean Backlash Against Human Rights Regimes," *Columbia Law Review* 102, no. 7 (November 2002).

232. Kenneth Roth, *Philanthropy News Digest*, http://foundationcenter.org/pnd/newsmakers/nwsmkr.jhtml?id=36500031.

233. J. William Fulbright, *The Arrogance of Power* (New York: Random House, 1967), 154.

234. Neither Human Rights Watch nor Amnesty International saw the invasion of Iraq as a "humanitarian" undertaking. See Kenneth Roth, "War in Iraq: Not a Humanitarian Intervention," in Human Rights Watch, "World Report 2004," HRWWS.

235. Human Rights Watch, "World Report 2007," Introduction, HRWWS.

ACKNOWLEDGMENTS

My boundless thanks to my extraordinary editor and publisher, Sara Bershtel, whose great commitment, intellectual gifts, and unstinting support have enriched every page of this book. From our earliest discussions, her intuitive sense of what this work could be and her acute, spirited questioning proved invaluable. Craig Seligman was a pleasure to work with as well; to both his editorial skills and his remarkable intellectual talents, this book owes a great deal. Jonathan Cobb read an early version of the manuscript; his astute analysis of its arguments and themes proved very helpful. Tom Engelhardt has been a stalwart and constantly stimulating intellectual companion throughout the many years of writing this book. My ongoing discussions with Laurie Sheck have been and continue to be one of the great pleasures of my life. Without her incisive probing and angles of thought this book would not be what it is. Finally, to Burtin and Phyllis Sheck, whose loving support has been a constant in my life for over thirty years, I offer my most heartfelt thanks.

INDEX

abolitionism, 59, 173
Abrams, Elliott, 85–86, 92, 103, 108, 111, 118
Abu Ghraib, 166, 167, 234, 261, 276, 277, 279, 281
Acheson, Dean, 11, 12, 13, 23, 24
Adams, James Truslow, 30
advertising, 28, 29, 88, 106, 198, 223
Afghanistan, 92, 93, 166, 253–58
    human rights, 253–58
    Soviet invasion of, 67, 83–84, 86, 90, 91, 123, 256, 257
    U.S. invasion of, 167, 231, 245, 247, 253–58, 275, 282, 283
AFL-CIO, 72, 76, 96
Africa, 17, 71, 187, 206–17. *See also specific countries*
African-Americans, 17, 172, 205–6
African Development Foundation, 55, 193
African National Congress (ANC), 79, 207–8
aggression vs. genocide, 225–29
AIDS, 172
Albright, Madeleine, 193, 267
Algeria, 272, 273
Allen, George, 35
Allende, Salvador, 55–58, 126

al Qaeda, 235, 256, 262, 278, 279
American Friends Service Committee (AFSC), 81–82
Americas Watch, 100–102, 104, 109, 112, 115, 118–19, 121–24, 126–27
Amin, Idi, 190
Amnesty International, 3, 7, 69, 72, 73, 77–81, 100, 102, 109, 115, 118, 119–24, 126, 127, 132, 158, 160, 161, 177, 185–86, 190, 200, 207, 218, 220, 224, 232, 240–41, 255, 257, 260, 262, 264, 267, 268, 269, 270, 274, 276–79
    founding of, 77–79
    Rights for All Americans campaign, 278
Amnesty International USA, 2, 77, 98, 145, 146, 154, 156, 200
Andropov, Yuri, 91
Angola, 47, 88, 92, 93, 209
Annan, Kofi, 233
anti-Americanism, 42, 94, 104, 155, 179
anticommunism, 3, 8, 18–41, 46–48, 87
    early Cold War, 18–41, 48–49, 89, 133–35
    of Helsinki Watch, 74–75
    Reagan era, 85–129

anti-Semitism, 76, 267
apartheid, 7, 55, 79–80, 81, 168,
    206–7, 268, 272
Arab-Israeli conflict, 54, 220, 232,
    236, 245, 263–70
Argentina, 66, 92, 99, 100
Asia Foundation, 149
Asian-American Free Labor Institute
    (AAFLI), 152
Asia Watch, 131, 32, 271
assassination attempts, 87, 128
Augustus Caesar, 12, 13, 14

Baker, Eric, 78
Baker, James, 204
Baldwin, James, 84, 238, 262
Bangladesh, 55, 190
Barnet, Richard J., 52
Barrett, Edward, 30
Battalion 3–16, 119
Bay of Pigs, 87
BBC, 241–42, 266
Beard, Charles and Mary, *Rise of
    American Civilization*, 26, 27
Belden, Jack, *China Shakes the World*,
    158–59
Benenson, Peter, 77–80, 190
Berger, Samuel, 182
Bernstein, Robert, 73, 74, 148
Berrigan, Daniel, 7, 49, 80
Berrigan, Philip, 7, 49, 80
Biden, Joseph, 222
bin Laden, Osama, 237
Boland Amendment, 123
Bolívar, Simón, 175
Boorstin, Daniel, 29
Bosnia, 214, 215, 219, 220–25
    genocide, 220–25
Boutwell, George Sewall, 60
Brazil, 55, 66
Bremer, Paul, 96
Brezhnev, Leonid, 90, 91
Brody, Reed, 281
Brooks, Van Wyck, 30

Brown, John, 59–60, 205
Bryan, William Jennings, 60
Brzezinski, Zbigniew, 22, 44, 47, 51,
    62–65, 68–71, 91, 97, 104, 109,
    139, 178, 179, 204, 245
Bundy, McGeorge, 73
Bundy, William, 136
Burke, Kenneth, 220
Burma, 274, 275
Bush, George H. W., 126, 137
    human rights policy, 137–48, 157,
        164, 218, 220
Bush, George W., 165, 196, 230
    human rights policy, 226, 230–80,
        281, 283
    response to 9/11, 231, 235, 236
    War on Terror, 230–63, 273–80
business, 28–29, 40, 249
    global marketplace, 51–52, 134–36,
        143–47, 200
    See also corporations; economy

Cambodia, 46, 81–84, 90, 92, 158,
    190
Camus, Albert, *The Rebel*, 186, 187
capitalism, 12, 22, 25–29, 37, 39–40,
    43, 60–61, 91, 140
    global, 19, 25–26, 31, 37, 39,
        143–47
Carothers, Thomas, 214
Carrington, Lord, 219
Carter, Jimmy, 44, 45, 143, 228, 230,
    268
    human rights policy, 45–84, 85,
        87, 91, 97, 131
    Palestine: Peace Not Apartheid, 268
Casey, William, 86, 90–92, 96, 128
Central Intelligence Agency (CIA),
    2, 14, 26, 48, 52, 53, 57, 63–65,
    68, 75, 76, 86, 100, 153, 162, 179,
    180, 181–82, 256
    Reagan era, 89–93, 96, 103–4,
        114–29
certification, failure of, 113–21

Cheney, Dick, 118
children, 142, 184, 194, 251
    as civilian casualties, 232–40
Chile, 3, 41, 47, 55–58, 99, 100,
    125–26, 129
    Allende government, 55–58, 126
    Pinochet government, 65–66, 100,
        125–26
China, 2, 128, 130–76, 274, 284
    Communism, 31, 130–76
    Cultural Revolution, 131, 158, 174
    dissidents, 145, 151–55
    economy, 131, 132–37, 143–47,
        158, 164, 168–71
    end of Cold War and, 137–40
    Great Leap Forward, 158
    human rights, 130–76
    India vs., 160 62
    industrialization, 36
    judging, 155–57
    MFN status, 143–45
    NGOs and, 148–51
    Nixon and, 131, 135, 136
    Opium Wars, 8, 166
    post-Tiananmen, 140–48
    Revolution, 7, 31, 132, 134, 157–60
    Soviet Union and, 133–36
    Tiananmen crisis, 130–32, 137,
        138, 140, 142, 150, 151, 158
    views of the United States, 162–74
China Alliance for Democracy, 152
Chinese Democratic Party (CDP),
    154
Chomsky, Noam, 49
Christianity, 43, 61, 142
Christopher, Warren, 58, 69, 193
Church Committee, 57–58, 126
civilian casualties, 232–40, 256,
    260–62, 271
civil rights, 4, 5, 6, 17, 18, 29, 43–44,
    73, 127, 168–69, 185, 205
    movement, 43–44, 61, 205–6
civil society, 195–99, 212, 213–14,
    247, 249

Clark, William, 96
Clifford, Clark, 23
Clinton, Bill, 138, 153, 165, 177, 231
    human rights policy, 145, 156, 164,
        177–84, 193–96, 202, 230–31,
        278
CNN, 130
Cold War, 3, 4, 5, 7, 11, 46–47, 49, 76,
    78–79, 85, 87, 128, 132, 150–51,
    161, 182, 183, 189, 213, 216, 217,
    227, 235, 237, 244, 247
    early, 11–44, 48–49, 89, 133–35
    end of, 130, 137–40, 177, 183, 213,
        217, 220
    Reagan era, 85–129
    U.S. ideology for, 18–29, 43
colonialism, 6, 7, 8, 11, 17, 22, 34, 39,
    83, 124, 169, 175, 184, 210, 247,
    268, 269
    decline of, 11, 15, 32
color revolutions, 165, 201–6
communications, 106–108
    global, 106–108
    mass, 354, 50,51, 63, 107
    technology, 35, 40, 51, 107, 142
Communism, 7–8, 47, 79, 90, 128,
    182, 189, 210, 231, 280
    Chinese, 31, 130–76
    early Cold War years, 11–44,
        48–49, 89, 133–35
    Soviet, 18–41, 62, 90
Congo, 215, 217, 226
Congress, U.S., 2, 5, 19, 24, 50, 55–58,
    95, 111, 113, 120, 206, 222, 265,
    282
    China debate, 130–31, 141–47
    El Salvador and, 101–3, 117
    human rights legislation, 54–57,
        69–70, 101
Constitution, U.S., 173
consumerism, 32–33, 50, 60–64,
    106–7, 272
Contras, 86, 88, 100, 120–29,
    236, 280

corporations, 15, 30, 40, 60–61, 107, 141
　China and, 141, 143–47
　multinational, 51–52, 63, 105, 125, 146–47, 201
　responsibility, and "rule of law," 199–201
Costa Rica, 111
Council on Foreign Relations, 154, 193, 248, 253
counterinsurgency operations, 88, 92–93, 113–29
　failure of certification and, 113–21
　in Iraq, 258–63
covert operations, 24–25, 67, 256
　in Nicaragua, 121–29
　Reagan era, 88, 92–93, 96, 113–29
Croatia, 202, 223, 224
Cronin, Jeremy, 208–9
Cuba, 23, 36, 67, 89, 99, 103, 122, 126, 128, 205, 227
Czechoslovakia, 75, 204

Dalai Lama, 132, 147, 162
Darfur, 220, 225–27
death squads, 116, 117–21
Declaration of Independence, 175
decolonization, 7, 11, 15, 32, 269
Defense Department, 14, 31, 34, 114, 243, 250, 254
De Gaulle, Charles, 23, 285
democracy, 4, 5, 34, 40, 87, 152, 173, 193, 194, 203, 205
Democracy Corps, 193
Democratic Initiative and Governance Project, 211
Democratic Party, 46, 96, 117, 143
democratization, 16, 85–129, 139, 144, 147, 173, 178, 184, 185, 193, 206, 209, 220, 233, 273, 283
　African, 206–217
　George W. Bush era, 230, 238, 246–48
　Clinton era, 193–95, 201–4

color revolutions, 201–6
　co-optation of, 125–29
　human rights battles and, 97–105
　ideology and organization of, 93–97
　MacBride Commission and, 105–9
　as political warfare, 89–93
　Reagan era, 85–129, 141, 185
Deng Xiaoping, 138, 174
Deng Yinghao, 153
Depression, 12, 152, 28, 29, 39
Derian, Patricia, 66, 67
desegregation, 44
de Waal, Alex, 213
Doctors Without Borders, 191–92, 220, 226, 255
Dodd, Christopher, 142
Dole, Robert, 130
Domenici, Pete, 145
Dorfman, Ariel, 278
Douglass, Frederick, 43, 172
Duarte, José Napoleón, 102–3
Du Bois, W. E. B., 17, 59, 205
Dulles, John Foster, 14, 18, 23, 25, 41, 134–35
Durbin, Dick, 142

Eagleburger, Lawrence, 140
Eastern Europe, 13, 64, 65, 75, 76, 92, 131, 137, 150, 217–25, 247
　color revolutions, 201–6
　post-Cold War, 201–6, 217–25
　See also specific countries
East Germany, 65, 137
economy, 6, 26–29, 36, 37, 43, 175, 185, 194–95, 248
　Carter era, 63
　China and, 131, 132–37, 143–47, 158, 164, 168–71
　Depression, 15, 28
　global, 6, 34, 51–52, 106–8, 132–37, 143–47, 200
　Reagan era, 94–95, 105–9
　warfare, 87, 91, 128, 134–36, 143, 144, 217

education, 6, 39, 64, 185
Egypt, 247, 252, 275
Eisenhower, Dwight, 17, 18, 21, 35, 36, 39, 41, 42, 133–35, 231
El Salvador, 7, 67, 88, 100, 101–3, 111, 115–18, 121, 127
　human rights abuses, 101–3, 111–18, 123
　1979 coup, 115
embargoes, 87, 128, 134–36, 143, 144
Ethiopia, 88, 92
ethnic cleansing, 220–25
Europe, 6, 25–26, 64–65, 159, 210, 249
　capitalism, 25–26, 39, 40
　decline of colonialism, 32
　end of Cold War, 137
　See also specific countries
European Court on Human Rights, 250
European Union, 193, 204, 217–18, 220
expansionism, 14, 90, 169
extremism, 242–46, 249–52, 267

famine, 172, 189
Fanon, Franz, The Wretched of the Earth, 273
Fascell, Dante, 96
female infanticide, 142
Fisk, Robert, 266
FLMN, 112, 118
Ford Foundation, 73, 97, 149, 154, 201
Foreign Affairs, 135, 154
Forrestal, James, 15, 20
France, 16, 137, 175, 205, 272
　Rwanda and, 215–16
Fraser, Donald, 55, 56, 77
freedom, 4, 6, 27–30, 62, 174, 178
Freedom House, 73, 100, 198, 202
free press, 108, 185, 194, 197–98
Free World, 4, 17, 27, 36, 47, 59, 88, 242

Friedman, Thomas, 265
Fulbright, J. William, 18, 21, 45, 48–49, 83, 84, 170, 282
Fund for Free Expression, 131

Gandhi, Mohandas, 7, 17, 79, 175, 205
Garrison, William Lloyd, 59
Garvey, Marcus, 205
Gates, Robert, 64, 67, 103
gay rights, 5, 44, 185
Gaza, 269–70
Geneva Accords, 275, 276
Geneva Conference (1954), 134
Geneva Conventions, 224, 267
genocide, 220–25
　aggression vs., 225–29
　Bosnia, 220–25
　Darfur, 220, 225–27
　debate, 220–25
　Rwanda, 209–17
Georgia, 202, 203
Germany, 26, 136, 210, 211
　Nazi, 1, 12, 21, 208, 222, 227, 265, 272
　postwar, 11, 12
　reunification, 137
　World War I, 26, 60
Gibbon, Edward, The Decline and Fall of the Roman Empire, 12
Gibbons, Sam, 54
globalism, 12, 132, 140, 141, 165, 220, 285
　anticommunism and, 18–26
　Carter era, 50–53
　early Cold War, 11–14, 133–35
　economy, 6, 34, 51–52, 106–8, 132–37, 143–47, 200
　post-Cold War, 177–229
　terrorism, 243
　visionary, 13–14, 37
Goldberg, Arthur, 72–73
Goldstone Report, 269
Gorbachev, Mikhail, 137, 218

Gray, Gordon, 21
Great Britain, 8, 133, 137, 205
  capitalism, 39
  colonialism, 17, 254
  industrial revolution, 34
  intelligence, 75
  postwar, 11, 16, 17
Great Society, 62
Greeks, 61, 231
Guantánamo, 2, 166, 234, 274–78,
  280, 281
Guatemala, 3, 47, 88, 100, 110, 117,
  118, 123, 127, 128, 227
guerrilla warfare, 87, 110–12, 115–17,
  120–21, 244, 271–73
gulags, 142, 143
Gulf War (1991), 138, 153, 166

Habyarimana, Juvenal, 210
Hague, 235
Haig, Alexander, 85
Haiti, 175, 214
Halperin, Morton, 193
Hamas, 269
Harriman, Averell, 11
Hatch, Orrin, 142
health care, 39, 171, 172, 173, 191–92,
  199, 259
Helms, Jesse, 143
Helms, Richard, 57
Helsinki Accords, 72, 75
Helsinki Watch, 72, 73–77, 84, 96–97,
  99–100, 218
Henderson, Loy W., 33
Hezbollah, 246
Himalayan Foundation, 149
Hitler, Adolf, 20, 83, 227
Hoar, George Frisbie, 277
Ho Chi Minh, 40
Holbrooke, Richard, 66, 82, 101, 104,
  220
Hollywood, 33, 165
Holocaust, 6, 83, 221, 222
Honduras, 88, 111, 117, 118, 119, 127

Hong Kong, 134, 147–48, 152, 153
Hoover, Herbert, 15
Howe, Julia Ward, 59–60
humanitarianism, 177–229, 234, 238
  civil society and, 195–99, 212,
    213–14, 247, 249
  color revolutions and, 201–6
  as a fighting faith, 183–86
  intervention and, 187–92, 282
  militant, 220–25
  post-Cold War, 177–229
  rights as a system of power, 193–95
human rights, 1–9
  George H. W. Bush policy, 137–48,
    157, 164, 218, 220
  George W. Bush policy, 226, 23–80,
    281, 283
  Carter policy, 45–84, 85, 87, 91, 97,
    131
  in China, 130–76
  Clinton policy, 145, 146, 164,
    177–84, 193–96, 202, 230–31,
    278
  creation of independent groups,
    69–72
  early Cold War years, 18–41,
    48–49, 133–35
  future of, 280–85
  international regime, 69–72
  Kennedy-Johnson years, 36, 39, 62,
    87, 109, 135–36
  new ideological warfare, 62–68
  Nixon policy, 54–58, 65, 109, 131,
    135, 136, 141
  Obama policy, 257, 281, 283
  post-Cold War, 177–229
  Reagan policy, 85–129, 131, 141, 185
  terminology, 17
  terrorism and, 230–85
  U.S. hypocrisy and, 48, 56–58,
    82–84, 98, 118–20, 162–74, 182,
    229, 274–75, 280, 283
  See also specific countries, groups,
    and organizations

Human Rights in China (HRIC), 148, 152

Human Rights Watch, 2, 72, 73–77, 95, 132, 140–41, 143, 145, 148, 150, 152–54, 158, 160–62, 163, 168, 184, 185–86, 190–91, 194–95, 204, 217, 218, 220, 222–24, 227, 237, 241, 246, 251, 253, 254, 255, 257, 259, 260–64, 268, 270, 282, 284
    torture and, 273–78

Huntington, Samuel, 50, 104

Hussein, Saddam, 220, 260, 280

Hutus, 188, 210, 215

idealism, 1–3, 45, 58
    Carter era, 45–47, 62, 143

Ignatieff, Michael, 186

imperialism, 22, 33, 35, 91, 175, 179

India, 17, 33, 35, 36, 40, 133, 160–62, 166, 172, 190, 205
    China vs., 160–62
    human rights, 160–62, 271–73
    Naxalite Maoist insurgency, 271–73

Indonesia, 41, 66, 168, 249

industrialization, 22, 34, 36

Initiative Group for Human Rights, 53

Inter-American Development Bank, 55

Inter-American Foundation, 193

International Court of Justice, 124–25, 225

International Criminal Court, 280

International Helsinki Federation for Human Rights, 97

internationalism, 17, 26

International Monetary Fund (IMF), 11, 36, 105, 181, 201, 210, 214, 217

International Red Cross (IRC), 188–89, 274, 275

Internet, 142, 145, 149, 150, 163, 245

interventionism, 189–92, 233
    Clinton era, 180–84
    humanitarianism and, 187–92, 282

Iran, 66, 67–68, 275
    1979 hostage crisis, 68
    Revolution, 7, 67–68, 90

Iran-Contra scandal, 88

Iraq, 167, 225, 227, 258–63
    Kurds, 220, 280
    terrorism, 258–63
    War, 165, 167, 225, 226, 231, 239, 245–47, 258–63, 275, 282, 283

Islam, 20, 232, 246–52, 280
    law, 250–52
    radical, 249–52, 267

isolationism, 27, 93, 178

Israel, 56, 92, 142, 205, 227
    Arab conflict, 54, 220, 232, 236, 245, 263–70
    settlements, 263–70
    Six-Day War, 54, 220, 267
    terrorism and, 263–70

Jackson, C. D., 21

Jackson, Henry "Scoop," 54–55, 68, 139, 236

Jackson, Robert, 227

Jackson-Vanik Amendment, 54

Japan, 11, 36, 133, 135, 138, 139
    economy, 133, 136
    postwar, 11, 12

Javits, Jacob, 54

Jefferson, Thomas, 175

Jenkins, Al, 51

Jews, 53, 54, 64, 208, 267
    emigration, 54–55, 142
    Holocaust and, 6, 83, 221, 222
    Soviet, 53–55, 76

Jiang Jieshi, 134

Jim Crow laws, 17, 44

John Paul II, Pope, 65, 91

Johnson, Lyndon B., 36, 62, 87, 109, 135, 231

Jordan, 247, 275

Joya, Malalai, 255

Kagame, Paul, 215, 216
Kagan, Robert, 139
Karzai, Hamid, 255
Kashmir, 161–62
Kemal, Mustafa, 175
Kennan, George, 13, 16, 17, 22, 31, 39, 40, 166
Kennedy, John F., 36, 39, 87, 109, 136, 230
KGB, 53, 75
Khan, Genghis, 14, 25
Khmer Rouge, 82–83, 190, 257
King, Martin Luther, Jr., 6, 7, 49, 79, 206
Kirkpatrick, Jeane, 100, 111
Kirkpatrick, Lane, 96
Kissinger, Henry, 20, 41, 46, 56, 57, 65, 68, 96, 140, 204
Kosovo, 167, 190, 191, 220–25
Kurds, 220, 280
Kyrgyzstan, 202

Laber, Jeri, 74–75
Lake, Anthony, 46, 69, 177, 204, 214
Langdon, Emma Florence, 60
Laos, 46
Lasswell, Harold, *Propaganda Technique in the World War*, 2
law, 5, 7, 8, 17, 29, 37, 60, 99, 112, 124–25, 166, 167, 173, 175, 188, 192, 258–60, 280, 282, 283
  international humanitarian, 258–60, 264
  rule of, 194, 199–201, 213
  Shari'a, 250–52
Lawyer's Committee for Human Rights, 115, 118, 172
League of Nations, 14–15
le Carré, John, 134, 153
Lecky, William, 43
Lenin, Vladimir, 36, 83
Leuchtenburg, William, 28
Levy, Howard, 80

Lewis, Sinclair, 30
Lilley, James, 153
Lincoln, Abraham, 59
Lindbergh, Charles, 60
linkage, 65
Liu Zhongli, 157
Locke, John, 175
Lodge, Henry Cabot, Jr., 17
London, 3, 69, 73, 190
Louis XIV, King of France, 14
L'Ouverture, Toussaint, 175
Lovett, Robert, 11
Luce, Henry, 15
Lu Hsun, 153
Lukashenko, Alexander, 203

MacBride, Seán, 80, 106
MacBride Commission report, 105–9, 149
MacLeish, Archibald, 29
Malcolm X, 205
Mamdani, Mahmood, 207, 216, 226
Mandela, Nelson, 7, 79–80, 213
Maoists, 271–73
Mao Zedong, 43, 51, 158
Marshall, George, 31
Marshall Plan, 11, 32
Marx, Karl, 36, 39, 168
Mbeki, Thabo, 207
McCarthy, Joseph, 24
McCloy, John, 11
McLuhan, Marshall, 50
McNamara, Robert, 136
media, 5, 27, 29, 50, 54, 58, 63, 75, 86, 90, 106–8, 126–27, 151–52, 154, 172, 197–99, 206, 214–15, 219, 230, 241–42, 245, 265, 279
  free press, 108, 185, 194, 197–98
  See also radio; *specific publications*; television
middle class, 39, 180, 272
Miles, Richard, 202
Miller, Geoffrey, 275
Mills, C. Wright, 257

Milošević, Slobodan, 199, 202, 223, 225
Mitchell, George, 130
Mitterand, François, 216
modernization, 35–41, 50
Mondale, Walter, 96, 120
Montaigne, Michel de, 230
Montt, Efraín Ríos, 100
Moran, James, 222
Moyers, Bill, 68
Moynihan, Daniel Patrick, 48, 56
multiculturalism, 5, 218
Mumford, Lewis, 30
Museveni, Yoweri, 215
Muskie, Edmund, 52
Muslims, 91, 188, 246–52
    Bosnian, 220–25
    radical, 249–52, 267
    secular, 249
    women, 249–52, 255
My Lai massacre, 239
Myrdal, Gunnar, *An American Dilemma*, 29–30

Namibia, 265, 270
Napoleon Bonaparte, 14
National Democratic Institute, 202
National Endowment for Democracy (NED), 86, 95–97, 125–26, 152, 154–55, 194, 202
nationalism, 42, 52, 82, 90, 158
National Security Council (NSC), 1, 14, 17, 93, 153, 181
    George H. W. Bush years, 137–38
    Carter years, 50–51
    Cold War ideology, 18–26, 43
    Reagan years, 93, 94, 106
national security establishment, 1, 176, 180, 243
    George H. W. Bush years, 137–48, 157
    George W. Bush years, 230–80, 281
    Carter years, 45–84, 85, 87, 91
    China and, 132–76

early Cold War years, 11–44, 48–49, 133–35
    failure of certification and, 113–21
    origins of, and anticommunism, 18–26
    post-Cold War, 177–229
    Reagan years, 85–129
    War on Terror, 230–63, 273–80
NATO, 25, 94, 99, 100, 137, 164, 190, 220, 225, 253–57
Naxalites, 271–73
Nazism, 1, 12, 21, 208, 222, 227, 265, 272
Negroponte, Nicholas, 116
Nehru, Jawaharlal, 33, 42
Neier, Aryeh, 2, 95, 97–98, 120, 123, 125, 129, 220, 227
Nepal, 271–73
New Deal, 15, 17, 28, 62
Newly Independent States (NIS), 201
New Yorker, 52
New York Times, 54, 76, 78, 93, 99, 104, 109, 120, 127, 219
Ngo Dien Diem, 254
Nicaragua, 66, 67, 68, 85, 86, 88, 89, 92, 100, 103–4, 111, 167, 199, 227, 236, 280
    covert operations in, 121–29
    human rights abuses, 103–4, 121–29
    revolution, 90, 103–4, 121–29
9/11, 231, 235, 236, 241, 276
Nixon, Richard M., 41, 54, 228, 230
    China and, 131, 135, 136
    human rights policy, 54–58, 65, 109, 131, 135, 136, 141
Nobel Peace Prize, 69, 76, 81, 191
noncombatants, 207, 232, 283
    rights of, 109–13, 116, 185, 207–8, 232–40, 258, 260–62
    terrorism and, 232–40, 258, 260–62, 271

nongovernmental organizations
(NGOs), 2, 70–73, 86, 114,
148–51, 184, 188–91, 194,
196–98, 200–201, 204, 205,
212–14, 248, 250, 255, 279
China and, 148–51
nonviolence, 8, 81
Northern Ireland, 242, 274
nuclear weapons, 4, 36, 133
Nuremberg, 81, 83, 227, 229, 263,
264, 282
Nyerere, Julius, 212–13

Obama, Barack, 9, 154, 226, 276
human rights policy, 257, 281, 283
oil, 165, 170
Olympics, 143, 152
Omaha bombing (1998), 242
OPEC, 105
Open Society Institute, 132
Operation Phoenix, 46, 47
Orange Revolution, 202, 204
Organization of African Unity, 211,
212, 215
Orlov, Yuri, 77

Pahlavi, Mohammad Reza, Shah of
Iran, 67–68, 90
Pakistan, 190, 247, 275
Palestine Liberation Organization
(PLO), 231–32, 236
Palestinian Authority, 263
Palestinian-Israeli conflict, 54, 220,
232, 236, 245, 263–70
Panama, 167, 227, 277
Pape, Robert, *Dying to Win: The
Strategic Logic of Suicide
Terrorism*, 245
Paraguay, 100
peace movements, 4, 6, 61
Peck, Edward, 240–41
Pentagon, 1, 114, 136, 153, 256, 282
People's Daily, 168
Perle, Richard, 54, 139

Petraeus, David, 260
Philippines, 47, 60, 77, 99
Pinochet, Augusto, 65–66, 100, 125–26
"Pledge of Resistance," 129
Poland, 65, 75, 91, 199
Pol Pot, 82, 158
popular culture, 33, 35, 165
Portugal, 77
poverty, 42, 171–72, 214, 243
Powell, Colin, 226
Powers, Samantha, *A Problem from
Hell*, 214, 217
prisoners of conscience, 79–80, 233
prisoners' rights, 44, 99, 142, 147,
152, 160, 166–67, 172, 185, 234
privatization, 94–95, 200, 218
"Project America," 28–29
Proxmire, William, 96
proxy warfare, 87, 121–25, 128,
216–17
Prunier, Gerard, 210, 212
Psychological Strategy Board (PSB),
17, 21, 26, 32, 34, 150
psychological warfare, 21, 26, 27, 119,
150
Putin, Vladimir, 204

racism, 17, 29–30, 43–44, 49, 168,
169, 172–73, 175
radio, 53, 65, 75, 76, 151, 152, 163
Radio Free Asia, 151, 152
Radio Free Europe, 53, 65, 75, 76
RAWA, 255
Reagan, Ronald, 72, 85, 228, 230–31,
240
democratization strategy, 85–129,
141, 185
human rights policy, 85–129, 131,
141, 185
Reagan Doctrine, 88, 92
refugees, 131, 168
religion, 29, 43, 61, 64, 147, 243
Islamic world and, 246–52
persecution, 142

Republican Party, 60, 96
revolution, 4, 7, 22, 33–34, 42, 89,
    104, 109, 159, 243
  color, 165, 201–6
  terminology, 34
  See also specific countries
Rice, Condoleezza, 244
Rieff, David, 206
rights (term), 61
Romans, 12, 13, 43, 61
Romero, Óscar, 113, 116
Roosevelt, Eleanor, 17, 175
Roosevelt, Franklin D., 15, 17
Roosevelt, Theodore, 60
Rostow, Walt, 36, 38, 51
Roth, Kenneth, 228, 234, 237, 248, 253
Roth, William, 142
Roy, Arundhati, 271–73
rule of law, 194, 199–201, 213
Rumsfeld, Donald, 243, 261, 274–75,
    281
Rusk, Dean, 136
Russia (post-Soviet Union), 165, 181,
    201, 202, 204, 284
Rwanda, 197, 209–17, 220
  genocide, 209–17
Rwandan Patriotic Front (RPF), 210,
    211, 215–17

"safe areas," 223–24
Sakharov, Andrei, 53, 54, 77, 80
Salisbury, Lord, 238
SALT, 55
samizdat, 53, 75, 76
Sanchez, Ricardo, 275
Sandinistas, 66–67, 121–29, 199, 280
Sandino, Augusto, 175
Sartre, Jean Paul, 273
Saudi Arabia, 92, 246, 247, 275
Scheffer, David, 225
Schlesinger, Arthur, Jr., 39
Schultz, George, 87, 93
Schulz, William, 98, 145, 146
Scowcroft, Brent, 182, 204

Sen, Amartya, 172
Senate, U.S., 14, 69, 274
  Nye Committee, 27
Serbia, 188, 202, 219, 220–25
Sharanksy, Natan, 77
Shari'a, 250–52
Sherwood, Robert, 29
Shevardnadze, Eduard, 202
Shivji, Issa, 213
Singlaub, John, 92
Six-Day War, 54, 220, 267
slavery, 8, 59, 168, 169, 172–74, 268
Smith, Christopher, 222
Snow, Edgar, 134, 153
Socialism, 38
Solarz, Stephen, 117
Solzhenitsyn, Alexander, 53, 75–77
  Gulag Archipelago, 54
Somalia, 214, 216
Somoza, Anastasio, 66–67
Sontag, Susan, 50
Soros, George, 194, 201–2, 205
South Africa, 7, 206–9, 265, 270
  apartheid, 7, 55, 79–80, 168, 206–7
South Korea, 23, 55, 66, 77, 99, 135
South West Africa People's
    Organization (SWAPO), 265
Soviet Union, 2, 131, 142, 158, 228
  Carter years and, 47, 49, 53–55, 62,
    64–65, 67, 75–77
  China and, 133–36
  collapse of, 177, 178
  Communism, 18–41, 62, 90
  dissidents, 53–55, 64–65, 75–77
  early Cold War years, 13, 16,
    18–41, 133–35
  human rights abuses, 72, 99, 143
  invasion of Afghanistan, 67, 83–84,
    86, 90, 91, 123, 256, 257
  Jews, 53–55, 76
  nuclear weapons, 133
  Reagan years and, 85, 88, 89–91,
    94, 99–100, 103, 123, 129
  See also Russia (post-Soviet Union)

Spanish American War, 277
Spence, Jonathan, *To Change China*, 148, 155–56
Srebrenica, 221, 223
Stalin, Joseph, 20, 34, 133, 158
State Department, 14, 16, 17, 44, 46, 55–56, 97, 101, 114, 131, 148, 153, 161, 181, 193, 196, 251, 271, 275
sterilization, forced, 142
Sudan, 175, 226
suffrage, 73
suicide terrorism, 231, 236, 239, 245, 262–66
Sununu, John, 204
Sweden, 205

Taft, Robert, 15
Taiwan, 92, 134, 135, 138, 139, 147, 152, 153
Talbott, Strobe, 202
Taliban, 251, 253–58
Tanzania, 190, 210
technology, 35, 40, 51, 107, 142, 144, 145
telecommunications, 142, 145
television, 32, 130, 163
Tenet, George, 275, 281
terrorism, 42, 109–10, 230–85
    Afghanistan and, 253–58
    Arab-Israeli conflict, 263–70
    civilian casualties, 232–40, 256, 260–62, 271
    human rights and, 230–85
    Iraq and, 258–63
    suicide, 231, 236, 239, 245, 262–66
    terminology, 240–42, 243
    torture and, 273–80
    War on Terror, 230–63, 273–80
think tanks, 1, 2, 72, 195, 199
Third World, 33, 34, 36, 38, 47, 51, 71, 78, 81, 88, 90, 94, 129, 159, 189
    decline of developmentalism, 185
    See also specific countries

Tiananmen crisis, 130–32, 137, 138, 140, 142, 150, 151, 158
Tibet, 132, 142, 147, 161–62
Timmerman, Jacobo, 77
torture, 2, 55, 78, 89, 99, 100–102, 160, 166, 167, 185, 207, 222, 255, 261, 273–80, 281
    Abu Ghraib, 166, 167, 234, 261, 276, 277, 279, 281
    Bush policy on, 234, 273–80, 281
    Guantánamo, 274–78
trade, 16, 54, 200
    China and, 134–36, 143–47
    embargoes, 87, 134–36, 143, 144
    unions, 99
Trade and Development Agency, 193
Trial of the Four, 53
tribal rights, 185
Truman, Harry, 14, 15, 18, 21, 22–23, 32, 36, 40, 150, 228, 230, 231
Tunisia, 275
Turkey, 99–100, 175, 249, 275
Tutsis, 188, 210, 215, 216, 220
Tutu, Desmond, 207, 208

Uganda, 190, 210, 215, 216
Ukraine, 201, 202, 203, 204
UNESCO, 106, 108
unilateralism, 166, 180
United Nations, 2, 7, 11, 36, 59, 63, 69, 71, 166, 214, 228–29, 269
    Bosnia and, 221–25
    China and, 133, 134, 164, 170
    Commission on Human Rights, 17, 56, 69, 71
    Committee Against Torture, 277, 278
    General Assembly, 63, 105, 221, 269
    High Commission for Human Rights, 69
    human rights covenants, 167–68, 175, 226, 228

Security Council, 138, 192, 224,
258
Truth Commission Report, 116
Universal Declaration on Human
Rights, 1, 4, 17, 45, 49, 79, 108,
185–86
United States, 1–9, 171
anticommunism, 18–41, 46–47,
48
Carter era, 45–84
China and, 130–76
Chinese views of, 162–74
consumerism, 32–33
early Cold War years, 11–44
human rights hypocrisy, 48, 56–58,
82–84, 98, 118–20, 162–74, 182,
229, 274–75, 280, 283
popular culture, 33, 35, 165
Reagan era, 85–129
War on Terror, 230–63, 273–80
See also national security
establishment
U.S. Agency for International
Development (USAID), 70, 149,
177, 188, 190, 196, 197, 202, 203,
209, 211, 228
U.S.-Hong Kong Policy Act, 147–48
U.S. Information Agency (USIA),
39–40, 44, 70
universalism, 176, 189
Uruguay, 55, 77, 100
Democracy and Governance
programs, 194, 210

Vaky, Viron, 66
Vance, Cyrus, 66, 68, 219
Velvet Revolution, 204
Victims of Torture Fund
(VTF), 279
Vietnam, 82–83, 115, 128, 227, 254,
277, 279
human rights abuses, 46, 82–83,
110

postwar, 104–5, 235
War, 3, 6, 36, 40, 44–47, 50, 68, 74,
75, 80–84, 90, 104, 110, 129, 190,
239, 280, 282
Voice of America, 75

War on Terror, 230–63, 273–80
Washington, George, 13–14, 59
Washington Post, 54, 76, 93
Watergate, 46
Weber, Max, 27, 200
Wedgwood, Ruth, 228
Weil, Simone, "Against Human
Rights," 61, 71
Wellstone, Paul, 143
West Bank, 266, 267, 268, 270
Willkie, Wendell, 15
Wilson, Woodrow, 14, 60
Wolfowitz, Paul, 137
women:
as civilian casualties, 232–40
genital mutilation, 252
Muslim, 249–52, 255
rights, 5, 29, 39, 44, 64, 73, 171,
185, 194
Woodward, Bob, 128
Woolsey, James, 202
World Bank, 11, 36, 181, 200, 201,
210, 214
World Court, 221, 227, 270
World War I, 12, 26, 60, 223
World War II, 6, 11–13, 16, 17, 28
WTO, 149
Wu, Harry, 145–46, 152

Young, Andrew, 63, 67
Yugoslavia, 41, 164, 199, 217–20, 222,
224
civil war, 217–20

Zhao Qizheng, 171
Zhou Enlai, 134, 153
Zimmerman, Warren, 219

ABOUT THE AUTHOR

JAMES PECK is the author of *Washington's China*. Founder of the
Culture and Civilization of China project at Yale University
Press and the China International Publishing Group in Beijing,
he has written for *The New York Times* and the *San Francisco
Chronicle*, among other publications. He lives in New York City.